FLAMENCO NATION

The Construction
of Spanish National Identity

Sandie Holguín

THE UNIVERSITY OF WISCONSIN PRESS

The University of Wisconsin Press
1930 Monroe Street, 3rd Floor
Madison, Wisconsin 53711-2059
uwpress.wisc.edu

Gray's Inn House, 127 Clerkenwell Road
London EC1R 5DB, United Kingdom
eurospanbookstore.com

Copyright © 2019
The Board of Regents of the University of Wisconsin System
All rights reserved. Except in the case of brief quotations embedded in critical articles and reviews, no part of this publication may be reproduced, stored in a retrieval system, transmitted in any format or by any means—digital, electronic, mechanical, photocopying, recording, or otherwise—or conveyed via the internet or a website without written permission of the University of Wisconsin Press. Rights inquiries should be directed to rights@uwpress.wisc.edu.

Printed in the United States of America

This book may be available in a digital edition.

Library of Congress Cataloging-in-Publication Data
Names: Holguín, Sandie Eleanor, author.
Title: Flamenco nation: the construction of Spanish national identity / Sandie Holguín.
Description: Madison, Wisconsin : The University of Wisconsin Press, [2019] | Includes bibliographical references and index.
Identifiers: LCCN 2018045773 | ISBN 9780299321802 (cloth: alk. paper)
Subjects: LCSH: Flamenco—Spain—History. | National characteristics, Spanish. | Nationalism—Spain—History—20th century. | Spain—Civilization.
Classification: LCC DP48 .H76 2019 | DDC 946/.07—dc23
LC record available at https://lccn.loc.gov/2018045773

Contents

List of Illustrations	vii
Acknowledgments	xi
Introduction	3

PART I SETTING THE STAGE

1.	Inventing an Ancient Past for a Modern Form, 1789–1875	27
2.	The Perils of Flamenco in Restoration Spain, 1875–1923	58

PART II FLAMENCO ON THE REGIONAL AND INTERNATIONAL STAGE

3.	Flamenco and Catalan Nationalism in Barcelona, 1900–1936	97
4.	The Marriage of Flamenco, Politics, and National Liberation, 1914–1936	122
5.	Spain on Display Abroad and at Home, 1867–1922	144

PART III FLAMENCO AND THE FRANCO REGIME

6.	Rebuilding the Fractured Nation, 1939–1953	177

7. Tourism and the Return of Flamenco, 1953–1975 204

Coda 241

Glossary 259
Notes 263
Bibliography 325
Index 351

Illustrations

Maps

Map 1. The flamenco heartland   2
Map 2. Seville from S. Teackle Wallis's perspective   5
Map 3. Madrid with locations of cafés cantantes, ca. 1845–1936   55
Map 4. Seville with locations of cafés cantantes, ca. 1845–1936   56
Map 5. Barcelona with locations of cafés cantantes in the Raval, ca. 1875–1936   100

Figures

Figure 1. Gustave Doré, *The Tobacco Factory in Seville*, ca. 1862–73   6
Figure 2. Gustave Doré, *A Dancing Academy, Seville*, ca. 1862–73   7
Figure 3. Gustave Doré, *Gipsies Dancing in a Court of Sevilla*, ca. 1862–73   31
Figure 4. Francisco Goya, *Majas on a Balcony*, ca. 1808–10   36

Figure 5. Antonio Rodríguez, *To the Palace: A Serious Petimetre*, 1808 — 37
Figure 6. Ortíz, The Michelin Man as a flamenco dancer, 1911 — 49
Figure 7. Ortíz, The Michelin Man with a stereotypical Andalusian woman, 1913 — 49
Figure 8. Interior of the Café del Burrero, ca. 1881 — 53
Figure 9. Tito, *La Bailaora*, 1914 — 85
Figure 10. Tito, *El Flamenco*, 1914 — 86
Figure 11. Tito, *La Gitana*, 1914 — 87
Figure 12. F. Bac, "Tout à l'Espagne," in *La caricature*, 1889 — 152
Figure 13. Drum, "Tout à l'Espagne," in *La caricature*, 1889 — 152
Figure 14. Drum, "Tout à l'Espagne," in *La caricature*, 1889 — 153
Figure 15. Poster of "The Gypsies of Granada," 1889 — 156
Figure 16. Photo of a woman thought to be Soledad, ca. 1889 — 157
Figure 17. Photo of Juana Vargas, "La Macarrona," dancing, 1935 — 172
Figure 18. Thomas Cook pamphlet for San Sebastian, 1936 — 209
Figure 19. Iberia Airlines advertisement, 1958 — 212
Figure 20. Iberia Airlines advertisement, 1968 — 213
Figure 21. Entrance to the Cortijo El Guajiro tablao, 1960s — 216
Figure 22. El Moro, Pepe Lucena, El Chocolate, El Negro, and Matilde Corral, ca. 1955–60 — 217
Figure 23. Thomas Cook brochure for summer holidays in the Iberian Peninsula, 1951 — 218
Figure 24. Iberia Airlines advertisement in a Thomas Cook brochure, 1952–53 — 218
Figure 25. Iberia Airlines advertisement in a Thomas Cook brochure, 1953 — 219
Figure 26. Iberia Airlines advertisement in a Thomas Cook brochure, 1954 — 220
Figure 27. Advertisement for San Sebastian in Thomas Cook's *Holidaymaking* magazine, 1957 — 223
Figure 28. Advertisement for San Sebastian in Thomas Cook's *Holidaymaking* magazine, 1959 — 223
Figure 29. Tourist map of Spain in Thomas Cook's *Holidaymaking* magazine, 1963 — 224
Figure 30. Advertisement for Corelli's shoes, 1965 — 235
Figure 31. Advertisement for Arnel fashions, 1965 — 236
Figure 32. Advertisement for Bates' bedspreads, 1965 — 237

Figure 33. Carmen Amaya, 1958 — **245**
Figure 34. A potato restaurant in Toledo, Spain, 2010 — **250**

Table

Table 3.1. Music periodicals devoted to *sardanas*, *orfeóns*, and
cants corals in Catalonia, 1900–1930 — **113**

Acknowledgments

The idea for this book began in a former monastery in Barcelona. My husband, toddler son, and an additional caretaker accompanied me there for a summer that proved to be the hottest on record. While they were all sweltering in the heat, I trotted down to libraries and archives. I had plans to write an urban history of late nineteenth-century Barcelona, but those plans fell apart. I panicked. But then we went to a flamenco show in a courtyard of that monastery. The guitarist began playing the notes to a song, and suddenly my mind raced with questions. I wondered why I was watching a flamenco show in Barcelona when I knew that flamenco originated in Andalusia. That question led me to other questions about national identity and, well, I now had a new idea for a book. Listening to flamenco guitar had quelled my earlier anxieties about not having a research topic. So, yes, it is true: music can soothe the savage breast.

People often talk about how lonely it is to write a book. I cannot argue with that. But sole authorship is a fallacy. Writing a book is also a collaborative process that requires the invisible work of so many people, and I would like to recognize them and the various institutions that made this work come to fruition.

Despite the wonders of the internet, historical research necessitates traveling to archives and libraries, and that requires money. For their financial support, I would like to thank the following institutions: the National Endowment for the Humanities for its NEH Fellowship; the Individual Research Grant from the Program for Cultural Cooperation between the Spanish Ministry of Education, Culture and Sports and United States Universities; the Ministerio de Ciencia e Inovación, Gobierno de España; the Oklahoma Humanities Council Research Grant; and the University of Oklahoma for the following grants: the Presidential International Travel Grant, Research Council Grants, and Faculty Enrichment Grants. My scholarship was also supported by an Arts & Humanities Faculty Fellowship from the Arts and Humanities Working Group through funding from the Office of the Vice President for Research (VPR) at the University of Oklahoma Norman campus. Finally, financial support for the illustrations and maps was provided by the Office of the Vice President for Research, University of Oklahoma.

In addition to financing, if one has children, one has to find childcare to create the time and space to do research and write. I could not have done any of this work without the amazing childcare skills of the people at Carol's House—namely, Carol Jacob, Dan Boone, and Noah Boone. Their day care was such an oasis for my children when they were young. Thanks also to Jill Sibray, who made that original trip to Barcelona with us.

Librarians and archivists can make or break one's research. Many thanks to the archivists and librarians of Acción Católica (Madrid); Archivo de la Comunidad de Madrid; Archivo General de la Administración (Alcalá de Henares); Archivo de Villa (Madrid); Archivo del Ministerio de Asuntos Exteriores (Madrid, archive now defunct and moved to AGA); Archivo Municipal de Sevilla (Seville); Archivo Nacional de la "Nueva Andadura," Real Academia de la Historia (Madrid); Arxiu Municipal de Barcelona; the Biblioteca de Catalunya (Barcelona); the Biblioteca Nacional de España (Madrid); the graphics department of the Bibliothèque Nationale de France (Paris); the Centro Andaluz de Documentación del Flamenco (Jerez de la Frontera); Filmoteca Española (Madrid); Centro de Documentación Turística de España, Instituto de Turismo de España (Madrid) ; the Newberry Library (Chicago); New York Public Library for the Performing Arts; Thomas Cook Archives, Peterborough, United Kingdom; the Special Collections of the University

Acknowledgments

of Chicago; the Special Collections of the University of Illinois, Chicago; and the University of Oklahoma library, especially the interlibrary loan division.

A special shout-out to Paul Smith at the Thomas Cook Archives, who let me wander the archives freely and who provided many of the images for this book. David Greenstein at the University of Illinois, Chicago, culled the Spanish Village collections from the 1933–34 Century of World Progress Exposition herd, and although I did not use many of those materials for this project, I will use them in the near future. Asunción Muñoz Montalvo at the Instituto de Turismo de España helped me navigate the labyrinthian process of Spanish copyright law. Librarians at the University of Oklahoma have aided me in my detective work: Jen Waller tried to help me figure out how to track down defunct companies in the United States. To Laurie "the Goddess" Scrivener, who is the first librarian I turn to here when I have a research conundrum to solve, I owe my most appreciative thanks. Her talents are great, and she deserves more appreciation than she gets. Finally, to my dear friend Andrew H. Lee at New York University, who has acted as my librarian-in-retainer, I want to express my deepest appreciation for sending everything flamenco my way and for tracking down people and sources that I have had difficulty finding.

The University of Oklahoma's Department of History has been very kind to me. I have had the generous financial and moral support from two department chairs: Robert Griswold and Jamie Hart. My colleagues, especially "Committee G," have provided much collegial support, especially in the form of food and wine. Throughout this project, and especially over the last couple of months, Christa Seedorf and Janie Adkins have streamlined difficult bureaucratic processes like the dreaded Concur website and helped me tame the wayward copy machine. I appreciate the fact that they have managed my craziness with good humor and grace. Thanks also to Gaby Báez and Kathleen Sheppard for their help with some of the early stages of this research.

The final production of this book could not have been done without the map-making skills of Todd Fagin and Bob Rundstrom, both at the University of Oklahoma, or the editorial skills of Raphael Kadushin, Sheila McMahon, Amber Rose, and Scott Mueller at the University of Wisconsin Press.

Colleagues, some of whom I have met and some of whom I have not, have been very generous with their time and expertise. Thanks to Chris Ealham for getting me started with a few early sources in Barcelona, and to William Washabaugh, who was unstinting with his time and knowledge from the inception of this project to its very end. I feel very fortunate that Javier Moreno Luzón and Xosé Manoel Núñez Seixas reached out to me early in my project to join their workshop on Nationalist Imaginaries and Spanish National Identity in the Twentieth Century. I met a group of scholars there that proved essential to my intellectual growth. Pau Medrano Bigas provided me with digitized copies of the Spanish Michelin Man after I sent him an inquiry about a source. Jorge Villaverde kindly shared his research with me on "Sunny Spain in London." My intellectual life has been sustained by the people who make up the Association for Spanish and Portuguese Historical Studies and the Southwestern Spanish History Symposium. They have listened to my conference papers and have provided good criticism of this project along the way. I would like to thank them all by name, but our field is so tiny that there would be nobody left to review this book if I named them. In Spain I have been lucky to call Ana Moreno Garrido my friend. She has aided me tremendously by finding sources, meeting archivists with me, teaching me about early Spanish tourism, and writing to bureaucratic entities for me.

A number of people have read various draft chapters of this book. Thanks to the two outside readers for the University of Wisconsin Press who gave the manuscript a close read and offered me various paths for revisions. Jennifer Davis, Katie Hickerson, Bruce Boggs, Tamara Zwick, William Washabaugh, and Bob Rundstrom read multiple chapters and were able to provide insights that came from working in different disciplines or from studying different regions of the world. Jennifer and Katie, especially, pushed me to deepen my analysis.

My friends have sustained me over the years with their counsel and love. They have borne witness to my joy and suffering, and I cannot express enough how much their friendship means to me, from the friends I met while in graduate school (and even before)—Kathleen Kennedy, Montserrat Miller, David Ortíz Jr., Deborah Ortíz, Louise Townsend, Tamara Zwick—to those I met after I moved to Oklahoma—David Chappell, Lupe Davidson, Jennifer Davis, Elyssa Faison, Jill Irvine, Misha Klein, Andrew H. Lee, Danyelle O'Hara, Garret Olberding, Amy Olberding, Corinne Pernet, Joshua Piker, Francesca Sawaya, Karin Schutjer, Melissa Stockdale, Jane Wickersham, and Fay Yarbrough.

And now my family. My mom, Eva Holguín, despite wanting to see her grandchildren more often over the last couple of years, respected my need for isolation so that I could finish writing. I know that was

Acknowledgments

difficult for her, and I hope to make up for our scarcity over the next few years. My brother and sister-in-law, Jerry and Carol Holguín, made it possible, however, for all of us to get together at their house and rely on their hospitality instead of mine for family reunions. I could not have asked for a better sibling and sister-in-law. My children, Erik and Miguel, have kept me grounded and have taught me so many lessons over the years about how to be a human being. They will never know the depth of my love, but I hope they feel at least some of it every day. Finally, my husband, Bob, deserves many accolades. Bob has been husband, father to our children, friend, critic, sounding board, conversation partner, travel companion, cartographer, research assistant, ranter, and a romantic and sensitive soul. We may not always see things in the same way, but I know that I have lived a better life by looking at the world through his eyes. I thank him for all of his support and work, and mostly for taking a chance on me.

There are two people who did not get to see this book come to fruition: Saulo Holguín, my father, who was so excited when I first told him about this book project, and Carolyn Boyd, my informal mentor and Spanish historian extraordinaire, who demonstrated that one could be both intellectually rigorous and kind, and both a scholar and a mother. It is in their memory that I dedicate this book.

Flamenco Nation

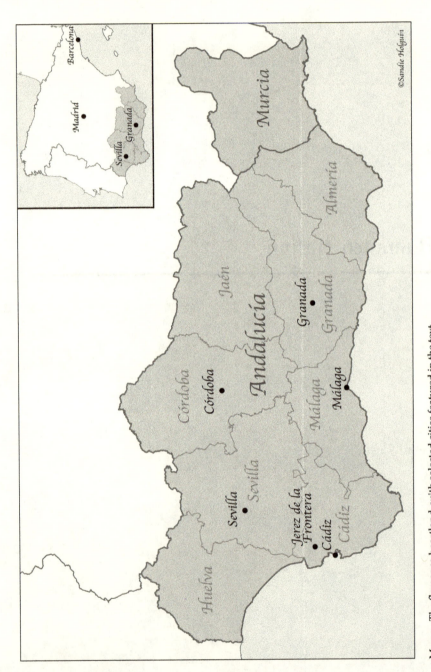

Map 1. The flamenco heartland, with selected cities featured in the text.
Mapmaker: Todd Fagin. Map designer: Robert Rundstrom.

Introduction

Flamenco doesn't have a history—it's a dance.
Spanish consulate worker to author, Houston, Texas, 2010

It is not always agreeable to the Spaniard to find that dancing is regarded by the foreigner as a peculiar and important Spanish institution. Even [Juan] Valera, with all his wide culture, could not escape this feeling; in a review of a book about Spain by an American author, entitled *The Land of the Castanet*—a book which he recognised as full of appreciation for Spain, Valera resented the title. It is, he says, as though a book about the United States should be called *The Land of Bacon*.
Havelock Ellis, *The Soul of Spain*, 1914

As European grain prices reached their zenith in the spring of 1847, protesters took to rioting. While touring Seville on May 7, the American S. Teackle Wallis found himself thrust into one of these melees. Reacting to a grain shortage, the city council passed an edict imposing price ceilings on bakers' goods. In response the bakers shuttered their stores, depriving the city of bread. A little after 9:30 a.m., throngs of people pushed toward the government-run tobacco factory, and soon enough, "crowds of men and women were rushing madly, with wild screams" through the streets leading to the town hall on the Plaza de San Francisco, a close distance away and within earshot of Mr. Wallis's hotel room, where he soon shuttered himself away. The people who had overrun the factory emptied it of its tobacco and its three to four thousand *cigarreras*, the working-class female laborers, and locked the guards inside the building. Loading their skirts with stones, the cigarreras led the angry procession back to the plaza. Threats against local politicians ensued, while soldiers fired shots and protestors lobbed whatever projectiles they could find. After a time, new detachments entered the city and the captain-general declared martial law. Hoping to address at least some of the populace's grievances, he sent troops to nearby Alcalá to bring back bread for the hungry. And so "when evening came, the revolution was at an end, and all mouths were stopped effectually, in more senses than one," Wallis remarked.[1]

Meanwhile, a couple of days later, while martial law was still in force and "theaters were, of course, forbidden," Wallis's guide from the hotel, Mr. Bailly, offered to take him to a dancing-master friend's place to attend a "private ballet." Wallis, Bailly, and an unidentified "young Englishman" took off at around half-past ten "in search of unlawful entertainment," and rambled through a dark passageway that led to a "a room with a tiled floor, where a few benches and some very smoky lamps gave token of preparation." There sat a couple of musicians. The audience consisted of "a few elderly dames, decent, though poor," and other spectators gathered in the passageway. Once the "gentlemen amateurs (aficionados) came in . . . their appearance was the signal for the castanets to sound, and the corps de ballet to show themselves. A black-eyed, gipsy-looking girl, one of the cigarreras of the riot, led the way." After providing a detailed description of her dress and body, Wallis concluded: "The silkiness of her hose was not much to speak of (if one must be candid), but her dancing implements were excellent to look upon, as such things nowadays go. In form and motion, altogether, she had but small resemblance to the fury, who, two days before, had shouted, 'Death to the jefe politico!' and had broken the heads of his defenders."[2]

Descriptions like the one above littered the travel narratives written by Europeans and North Americans who visited Spain in the mid to late nineteenth century. They often remarked on the seemingly chaotic

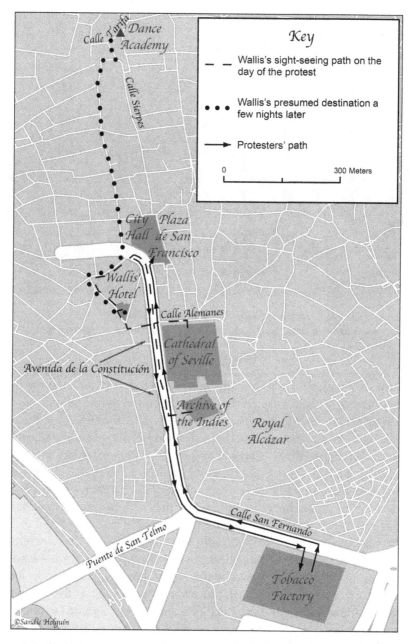

Map 2. Seville. An approximation of S. Teackle Wallis's walking path in Seville during the grain riot and the night he viewed a protoflamenco show as described in his travel narrative, *Glimpses of Spain*.

Mapmaker: Todd Fagin. Map designer: Robert Rundstrom.

Figure 1. *The Tobacco Factory in Seville*, by Gustave Doré, ca. 1862–73.
Source: Jean Charles Davillier, *Spain*, translated by J. Thomson (New York: Scribner, Welford and Armstrong, 1876).

nature of Spaniards in public life, and when these writers had the opportunity to witness private dances, they tended to be spellbound by the performances. Mostly male, they cast their critical gazes on the female dancers' appearance and their ability to titillate spectators through dance. What sets Wallis's account apart from those of many others is his clear astonishment at the dancer's capacity to be both a riot leader taking on a traditionally masculine role and a performer well aware of her ability to seduce her male audience with her "dancing implements."[3] This juxtaposition of harpy rioter and passionate dancer seemed inexplicable to an outsider like Wallis. But to many Spaniards, the cigarrera's dance, which appears to have been some prototype of a dance we now consider part of the flamenco genre, would have gone hand-in-hand with her participation in a riot. But whether perceived as the result of class or ethnic identities, both the dance and the riot signaled disregard for established law and order, a propensity for criminality, and a threat to all moral authority.[4] For although flamenco now garners respectability, symbolized by its position on UNESCO's Intangible Cultural Heritage of Humanity list, it was once considered a vulgar and pornographic spectacle best left to disappear from some hidden corner of the city. Indeed, many past critics considered flamenco a scourge of the

Figure 2. *A Dancing Academy, Seville*, by Gustave Doré, ca. 1862–73. This is an artistic rendition of the kind of performance that Wallis probably would have witnessed in 1847.
Source: Jean Charles Davillier, *Spain*, translated by J. Thomson (New York: Scribner, Welford and Armstrong, 1876).

Spanish nation, deploring it as an entertainment that lulled the masses into stupefaction and hampered Spain's progress toward modernity.

But ask people outside of Spain today what comes to mind when they hear the word "Spain," and they will usually answer something like "bullfights," "flamenco," and (more recently) "tapas." Flamenco has captured the imagination of foreigners and Spaniards alike since its commercial beginnings somewhere in the late eighteenth century, and the interest has not dissipated to date. In fact, statistics garnered from 2009 indicate that "the flamenco industry generated the equivalent [of] 0.07 percent of domestic GDP and 2.42 percent of the GDP of Spain's cultural industries."[5] Flamenco has such appeal for the tourist visiting Spain that businesses can get away with nonsensical names like Flamenco Cleaning Services, located in Playa Flamenca—an example of banal nationalism at its finest.[6]

So, how then did flamenco, castigated as a degenerate form of song and dance associated with both the Gypsies, a despised ethnic minority in Spain, and Andalusia, a region often derided as backward, become inexorably tied to Spain's national identity?[7] Why did flamenco persist as a symbol of the nation when so many elites within Spain worked feverishly for nearly a century to excise it from the country? These are the basic questions that this book tries to answer. Basic perhaps, but trying to answer them plunges us quickly into the complexity of Spanish culture and history, into the dynamic interplay among competing strains of nationalism, foreigners' perceptions of Spain, commercial interests, changing gender roles, ideas about race, urbanization, cosmopolitanism, and the growth of mass culture. My work seeks to understand flamenco and the culture and industry that grew around it over the course of approximately two hundred years and explain the multivalent meanings of flamenco both in and beyond Spain as a way to grasp the elaborate construction of modern Spanish national identity. I argue that national identity is not constructed solely by self-serving nationalist elites but instead relies on the popular classes and on a dynamic interplay between regional, national, and international forces. Sometimes the identity that adheres to a nation does not correspond with the identity that nationalist elites try to claim for themselves, as Spanish elites discovered. Over the course of the nineteenth century, flamenco became reified as one of two major expressions of Spanish national identity—the other one being bullfighting—via the cultural tropes that circulated among foreigners and Spaniards.

Still, it seems that flamenco has been written about ad infinitum. A limited search of the books dealing with flamenco in the WorldCat library database elicits close to five thousand entries, and over three hundred in this century alone. These works analyze the contents of the songs, valorize the performers of the past and present, provide sociological and anthropological analyses of the performers, search for the "authentic" origins of the art form, catalog references to flamenco in literature and art, provide musicological frameworks for understanding the musical forms, and more. Some even venture to understand the relationship between flamenco and national identity.[8] So why yet another book about flamenco? Because for something that looms as powerfully as flamenco in the Spanish imaginary, there is little written that situates the evolution of this performance within the larger Spanish and European historical, cultural, and political trends of the nineteenth and twentieth centuries.[9] Literary scholars,[10] musicologists,[11] sociologists,[12] anthropologists,[13] folklorists,[14] dance historians,[15] journalists/writers,[16] art historians,[17] and flamenco aficionados[18] have researched and written about flamenco, but most historians have ignored the topic, probably because the cultural turn came late to the study of Spanish history. Until fairly recently, Spanish historiography has focused primarily on political, economic, and social history—a consequence, most likely, of having to reckon with the collateral damage of a thirty-six-year dictatorship. Compared to uncovering once-censored material on the Spanish Civil War and Franco's dictatorship, flamenco may have been seen as trivial in comparison. And for historians within Spain itself, flamenco, along with the bullfight, was viewed as a national embarrassment, a stereotype fraught with too much historical weight.[19] Similarly, nationalism scholars have given only limited attention to the role that foreign nations have played in national identity construction.

As understood by Spanish elites from approximately 1850 to 1950, flamenco was like that relative you hide away from friends and neighbors for fear that they will judge you by your relations. These elites often rejected flamenco as a symbol of national identity because it was considered a product of mass culture and it often attracted seemingly unsavory types as both performers and spectators. Flamencomania (or *flamenquismo*), as critics deemed this phenomenon, represented Spain's political and spiritual decline; it showcased all of modernity's horrors: class- and race-mixing, blurred gender divisions, commercialized sexuality, secularization, cosmopolitanism, and the breakdown of hierarchies. In a word: degeneration.[20] But before the Spanish Civil War began in 1936, foreign tourists sought out flamenco entertainment in their visits to Spain precisely *because* of the performances' reputed unsavory nature. As I hope this book makes clear, they believed the *gitano* performers represented a kind of passionate "noble savage" oblivious to the passage of time in that bleak industrial era. When flamenco performances finally could be decontextualized from their sordid surroundings and turned into a kind of folkloric attraction for outsiders during the Franco regime (1939-75)—that is, when it could stimulate more tourism for Spain—only then could flamenco be officially recognized as a national symbol for the country.[21]

Flamenco and Caveats about Its Origins

Nobody really knows where the term "flamenco" came from. In fact, there are scholars like William Washabaugh who reject the idea that we can even define a flamenco style, "that anyone can say 'this' is flamenco, but 'that' is not. Just talking about it as an object is problematic."[22] He is right, of course. Getting at the genesis of artistic forms and then rigidly defining them, especially those forms that rely on sound and movement, is risky, given that both are ephemeral and not adequately explained through documentary evidence—this is especially true for flamenco dance, for which there was no formal teaching of the dances separate from other forms of Spanish dances until the early twentieth century, and guitar, which lacked any written notation until 1902.[23] And yet we all know that flamenco dancing differs from classical ballet, that flamenco song parts company with rock 'n' roll. So, for clarity's sake, let us say that flamenco performances normally include some combination of *cante* (song), *toque* (guitar playing), *baile* (dance), *palmas* (polyrhythmic hand-clapping), and *pitos* (finger snapping), and they incorporate the call and response known as *jaleo*, which the Junta de Andalucía defines as "'hell raising' and involves the hand clapping, foot stomping, and shouts of encouragement."[24] As I show in chapter 1, the staging of the performance became standardized in the nineteenth century, although the places where flamenco singing and dancing was performed varied. Flamenco occurred within theatrical productions, in taverns, in specially designed places known as *cafés cantantes*, and later, *tablaos*, and in bullrings, cabarets, nightclubs, and bars. Usually there was a platform or stage where the guitarists and the people who performed the palmas and pitos flanked the dancers in the center. The *cantaores* occupied different parts of the stage, depending on whether they were considered the star vehicle or whether their performance was subordinate to that of the dancer.[25] Although flamenco dance costumes vary widely today, in the past they were more uniform: long dresses with wide skirts, and headpieces with flowers attached for women (the long train known as the *bata de cola* most likely made its appearance at the beginning of the twentieth century),[26] for men, tight-fitting black pants and a shirt held together by a sash, often covered by a vest reminiscent of a bullfighter's jacket, and sometimes a wide-brimmed hat.

Theories for the origins of the term "flamenco" include: the comparison of Gypsy revelers to the wild Flemish (flamenco) soldiers that Charles I brought to Spain in the sixteenth century; a harking back to the days of al Andalus, when an Arabic word that sounded similar to flamenco, *felamengu*, meant itinerant or fugitive peasant and could therefore be linked somehow to the expulsion of religious minorities after 1492;[27] and, finally, a kind of Spanish Gypsy argot used as a form of ridicule.[28] The term "flamenco" itself did not appear in common parlance until the mid-nineteenth century.[29] But parsing the origins of this word does little to elucidate what the performances meant to spectators and critics. Nor, for that matter, can we determine its links to nationalism and other cultural-political matters. For my purposes, the debate is secondary, except when it is necessary to understand the views of historical actors who might have felt compelled to claim the word for their own nationalistic purposes.[30]

In contrast, the historiography of what one might call the origins of a flamenco style of performance is politically charged within Spain, reflecting one's political position taken on race, regionalism, and nationalism. For some scholars and flamenco aficionados, there was once a pure and thus authentic flamenco untainted by the ravages of commercialism developed in Spain by gitanos after their arrival in 1447. They kept their artistry a secret from the *payos* among whom they lived and performed their songs and dances among themselves, especially on special occasions like weddings.[31] Only in the nineteenth century, the argument continues, did the gitanos open up their secrets to the outside world via dance academies and cafés cantantes, thus adulterating a form of music that was once pure.[32] Others eschew the notion of a hermetically sealed musical tradition and place the birth and dissemination of flamenco in the nineteenth century, noting that the structural elements of modern industrialization and urbanization helped shape a new hybrid musical style that met the emotional, social, and political needs of a modern urban populace. These scholars do not deny that the stylistic influences on flamenco performances had historical roots in earlier time periods and among different groups of people; they just refuse the idea that commercialization tainted some ur-flamenco style.[33] Still others, like Mercedes Gómez-García Plata, take a hybrid approach, arguing that it was the commercial culture of the café cantante that saved whatever remained of the pure flamenco style that had emerged during the eighteenth century, whereas William Washabaugh avers that both of what I would term the "authentic school" and the "commercial school" have claims to truth but that neither school takes into account the institutional constraints that might have influenced both indigenous (grassroots) beginnings and commercial developments simultaneously.[34]

I concur with the most recent scholarship that claims that the modern era gave birth to flamenco.[35] The flamenco song and dance styles emerged as a result of cultural hybridity, combining stylistic elements found in Andalusian and gitano communities as well as some found outside of Spain.[36] In short, what today we call flamenco is a modern phenomenon consolidated in the mid-nineteenth century, with musical influences found in earlier eras. Flamenco, like the bullfight, blossomed in nineteenth-century Spain, as industrialization and urbanization began to transform the way people lived and interacted in urban areas.[37] It paralleled the rise of other forms of mass culture like music halls, *cafés concerts*, and cabarets (and later, jazz clubs, sporting events, vaudeville, and movies), which spectators could witness in Europe, the United States, and Latin America.[38]

More importantly, flamenco never developed in isolation, although the musical form was rooted both physically and symbolically in the southern regions of Andalusia and Murcia. By the time it became a fully fledged commercialized art form, it had diffused throughout all the major urban centers of Spain. Still, the variety of songs—*palos*—and dances speak to Spain's long history of migration, immigration, and the back-and-forth that emerged from the flow of numerous peoples. In fact, a subset of flamenco songs called *cantes de ida y vuelta* (songs of leaving and returning) was linked to Spanish migration to and from the Caribbean and the rest of Latin America. As one might distinguish between Mississippi Delta blues and Chicago blues, flamenco songs and dances are often tied to the region, city, or, in some cases, the neighborhood from which they emerged. Therefore, many of the names of these palos reflect either their location of origin or the place where they were popularized. For example, the *cante minero* is a palo specific to the mining regions of Murcia; the *fandangos de Huelva* are a flamencoized version of an eighteenth-century Andalusian dance; *la rumba catalana* emanates from a mid-twentieth-century mix of flamenco, Afro-Cuban *rumba*, and rock 'n' roll that emerged from the Catalan capital, Barcelona; and the *soleá de Triana* refers to Seville's gitano neighborhood of the same name.[39] Flamenco styles and performances also evolved in reaction to European cultural trends outside of Spain and the national rivalries that intensified at the end of the nineteenth century.

Thus flamenco—or the ways that people imagined it—became a highly charged subject around which centralizing nationalists, regional nationalists, foreigners, gitanos, and payos argued both literally and metaphorically about Spain and its place in the modern world. Foreigners, particularly nineteenth-century Romantic writers from Britain, France, and the United States, helped to shape flamenco as a symbol of Spanish national identity.[40] But this assertion does not address how flamenco and the cradle of its birth, Andalusia, came to be a primary representative of all the diverse regions of Spain. For example, the *jota*, a dance that was performed throughout many more regions of the country than flamenco, is seldom taken as a marker of Spanish national identity. Instead, it was flamenco that persevered and thrived to become the symbol of Spain, despite the many attempts over the last two centuries to eradicate it.

Nationalism and National Identity

Just as with flamenco, studies of nationalism and national identity have proliferated like so many mushrooms after a heavy rainfall. Ever since the publication of Benedict Anderson's *Imagined Communities* and Eric Hobsbawm's and Terrence Ranger's edited volume, *Invented Traditions*, and Ernest Gellner's *Nations and Nationalisms* (all, coincidentally, published in 1983), scholars have been trying to piece together this phenomenon we call nationalism and the even more elusive concept, national identity.[41] Much of the literature on nationalism has attempted to unearth the processes by which masses of people found themselves identifying with something called a nation—a term with seemingly infinite definitions—and the ways that various groups have worked toward transforming that inchoate nation into a nation-state replete with political, economic, and military power. Although there is still disagreement as to whether or not loyalty to a nation is an ancient or modern phenomenon, the scholarship has reached a consensus on the constructed nature of nationalism—that is, most scholars contend that there is no such thing as an unchanging, essential nation into which people can pour their loyalties, dreams, and desires.[42] As Alejandro Quiroga so adeptly observes: "Individuals are not born with fixed, immutable national features. . . . People are 'nationalised' as they incorporate the nation as part of their identity. Against a backdrop of complex historical developments, national identities are created, transmitted and transformed at different social levels. These procedures are complicated further by the simultaneous processes of identity formation that shape diverse loyalties, such as religious, class and regional allegiances."[43] Although much of the earlier literature on nationalism focused on top-down approaches to creating the nation by highlighting various elites' attempts to create administrative, infrastructural, and cultural avenues for nation and nation-state formation, newer scholarship on nationalism has begun to look at "nationalism from below" and the gendered assumptions that go into nationalization.[44] Add to this mixture the recent literature discussing the relationship between regionalism and nationalism, and one begins to realize that many components go into the making of this nationalism stew.[45] Like a stew, certain ingredients mix well with one another to create a successful dish, whether by contrast or complementarity. Include the wrong ingredient, and the dish fails to coalesce. Similarly, imposing or rejecting a particular national language, a national myth, or a racial category can enhance or shatter a nation's seemingly apparent unity. Whether we are dealing with the creation of a meal or a nation, we cannot analyze its success or failure without looking at the processes that went into its construction. And yet, sometimes by looking at the development of a seemingly complete process, we tend to be anachronistic and fail to see other possible outcomes. As Joep Leerssen warns, when "nationalism studies are conducted as a sort of archeology of the modern state," we tend "to filter 'failed nationalisms' from our view," taking the modern nation-state as some kind of teleological endpoint.[46]

In Spain's case, much of the literature on nationalism has proved problematic. While Spain had the trappings of a nation-state and the empire to go with it after 1492, it did not follow the nationalization trajectory of the so-called modern European states of the nineteenth century—France, Germany, and Great Britain. That is, the argument runs, while the Spanish state embraced liberal reforms, worked to centralize and secularize political, administrative, and legal power, and attempted to create the infrastructure to unify disparate parts of the nation through railway networks and schools, it failed. Instead, as a result of weak nationalization, regional nationalisms emerged in places like Catalonia and the Basque country to resist the claims of the centralizing state.[47] This failure narrative has dogged Spanish historiography in the post-Franco era, although flaws in this reading began to be apparent in the 1990s. On the one hand, recent works have challenged the idea that places like France and Germany represented the only way to nationalize properly. On the other hand, they argue that by looking at nationalism from a top-down, state-driven point of view, the Spanish nationalization project does indeed look weak, especially because the Spanish state did not have the economic resources or the political stability to fully fund the educational, technological, or even civic projects that theorists of nationalism deem necessary for creating a nation. But if one were to look at nationalization through other avenues such as civil society, the press, regionalism, the municipality, religious organizations, or popular culture—and in the case of flamenco, through the additional avenues of advertising and tourism—one can see that nationalization took various and competing forms in Spain over the course of the late nineteenth century and into the twentieth.[48] Difference does not equal failure.

National identity is an even more slippery term than nation or nationalism, but it is the expression I will be using most often in my discussions of flamenco. A nation may describe a group of people that has ties to a particular language, culture, territory, history, and political trajectory. But national identity is a type of conceptual shorthand, a way people think they can sum up the complexity of all the people living in a particular territory, usually a nation-state. National identity calls into being the cultural traits that appear to inhere in one's nation, but those traits can differ, depending on who is doing the defining and when. In this sense, national identity is closely related to and sometimes conflated with national stereotypes, with all of their intrinsic shortcomings. U.S. residents, for example, might understand baseball, rock 'n' roll, and apple pie as core symbols of their nation, whereas foreigners might envision the United States as the reckless land of the Wild West, and cowboys and Indians. North Americans might partially identify with these ideas and myths, but this symbolic shorthand would not come close to painting a portrait of how they perceive their relationship to the nation nor would it reveal how this identification might have changed over time. And just because one feels an affinity for some aspect of one's national identity, it does not mean that the identification is strong or consistent. As Beyen and Giderachter point out, "Not everyone who fanatically supports his or her national football team is also willing to die for the fatherland."[49]

Similarly, Spain's national identity has been defined over various points in its modern history as being tied to Inquisitors, beggars, bandits, bullfighters, Gypsies, and flamenco dancers. Usually foreigners imposed those identities onto the country, often by way of contrast with the more "progressive" nations of northern Europe or as a Romantic-era backhanded compliment, demonstrating how Spain had not fallen prey to the soul-sucking effects of industrialization, how it had remained "authentic."[50] Flamenco and its cultural progenitor, the Gypsy, have remained steadfast markers of national identity in Spain. But here's the rub: with very few exceptions, Spanish elites and social reformers never liked nor wanted this art form to represent themselves or their nation. They spent at least a century trying to cleanse what they perceived to be the flamenco stain from Spain. It proved much more difficult for them to eradicate than the Black Legend.[51] For foreigners, Andalusia became the synecdoche for Spain, and Andalusia meant castanets and bulls. But Spaniards involved in creating other variants of nationalism struggled against the weight of these stereotypes, sometimes accommodating them and sometimes not. One of the perspectives I take that makes this study of flamenco different from other works that explore processes of nationalization and national identity is that I consider foreigners' roles in interaction with Spanish elites and everyday people in creating such a seemingly fixed identity.

The powerful opposition to flamenco does not by any means imply that flamenco was unpopular in Spain. It *was* popular. And although it is nearly impossible to quantify how most people in Spain felt about flamenco or how they incorporated it as part of their sense of national identity, there are indirect measures that can inform our understanding. For example, the number of places where people could witness flamenco performances, venue sizes, attendance statistics, as well as the amount of publicity generated for flamenco, will be fleshed out throughout the book as evidence for its popularity.[52] From the 1850s until around 1914, flamenco (and bullfighting) dominated Spain's cultural topos. And that is precisely what bothered many elites during the height of flamencomania. Everyday Spaniards were not listening to them. Those who flocked to flamenco performances seemed to confirm what scholars of "nationalism from below" have theorized, that "ordinary people . . . construe a national identity out of elements that are not always scooped out to them by elites."[53] Although interest in flamenco flagged after the Great War, and part of the reason for its decline came from the emergence of other competing forms of mass culture like jazz and the cinema, flamenco never died as an art form. After a lull hastened by the Spanish Civil War and its aftermath, interest in flamenco grew in strength again after the 1950s and became inseparable from Spain's identity after the tourist boom of the 1960s. Indeed, the association of Andalusia and flamenco with Spain was so strong that in 1953 the film director Luis García Berlanga successfully built an entire film's comedic plot on the premise that a village in Castile had to mobilize all its resources to transform itself into an Andalusian village in order to persuade and charm U.S. secretary of state George Marshall into providing Spain with Marshall Plan money during his visit.[54]

Writing about Ephemeral Arts

Historians have generally been less willing than other scholars to tackle the relationship between music, history, and national identity, leaving it to ethnomusicologists, folklorists, or cultural studies scholars to capture the ephemeral arts that historians have difficulty lassoing.[55] Because musical performance and its embodiment through dance are fleeting experiences, they are not adequately explained through documents and archival evidence. Additionally, music, as geographers John Connell and Chris Gibson write, "is inherently mobile," and yet it is also linked with place.[56] How can historians capture and analyze something that moves both in waves (sound) and through the body (dance)? Sometimes it requires talking around the subject. That is not to say that historians have completely ignored musical performance and its relationship to history and politics. In fact, cultural historians have recently begun to fill this lacuna, finding in music another fruitful avenue for analyzing the ways that people have created meaning and understood the world around them.[57]

But again, how does one write about music and national identity? Obviously, national anthems often speak to the formation of a unique national identity. It is difficult to hear the Marseillaise and not think of the French Revolution and its role in shaping French identity. But to study the impact of nationalism on music—or music on nationalism—is methodologically fraught. Still, we can think historically about processes of nationalization through music (or the failure thereof). We know that in the nineteenth century, European musicologists and folklorists followed Johann Gottfried Herder's lead in trying to distill a nation's essence through its cultural production. Of the many nationalist enterprises Europeans fostered in that century, music topped the charts. It became, as Krisztina Lajosi remarks, "a political instrument to enhance national sentiments," and it became a fundamental part of nationalist discourses.[58]

How did one decide what kind of music was national and who had the authority to decide it? Some scholars like Benjamin Curtis and Carl Dahlhaus claim that a piece is national if a composer deems it so.[59] That is certainly an argument that works well for discussing Béla Bartók, Rimsky-Korsakov, or Manuel de Falla, all composers recognized as part of their respective national canons. When we think about national music, especially in the nineteenth century, we think of classical composers, musicians who played for aristocratic or bourgeois audiences and who melded putative ancient mythologies with folk music and transformed them into something new. In these cases, national music may have been performed in urban areas, but the fount of musical inspiration supposedly came from the countryside. Curtis posits even further that national music cannot exist without "a public that is nationalized," and therefore, "there must first be a project to construct that national public."[60] We know that in the Spanish case, there were many projects to construct a national public, but if we look at the process of nationalization as a top-down phenomenon, then there could not have been any kind of national Spanish music, especially since Spain, a theater-dominated society, lagged behind other European countries in establishing symphony orchestras.[61] And yet historians like Clinton Young have made a compelling argument for *zarzuela*'s (light opera) role in nationalizing the Spanish masses.[62] Similarly, I would argue, although many elites (excluding some of the aristocracy) disdained flamenco, it became a musical identity affixed to Spain through other forces separate from the usual top-down, state-centered constructions of national identity. Advertising, tourist practices, world's fairs, literature, painting, film, and simply the pleasures of mass entertainment worked bottom-up and horizontally in creating a national form of music.

The Elephants in the Room: Race and Gender

One cannot discuss flamenco without commenting on the racial category "Gypsy," and yet the language of race as it is often discussed in the literature of post-Holocaust Europe and among U.S. historians works poorly to uncover the uses to which "the Spanish Gypsy" was put. As Joshua Goode has convincingly demonstrated, Spanish conceptions of race in the nineteenth and early twentieth century differed significantly from those of the Germans, French, and other Europeans, despite having been the perpetrators of racial purity laws in the fifteenth century. Racial discourse, he contends, permeated fictional, journalistic, and scholarly literature between 1875 and 1936, and it "produced racial ideas focused on national unity, either emphasizing or deemphasizing regional differences (depending upon the outlook of the racial thinker) and also on the quelling of class unrest and dramatic political fractionalization."[63] Many people used the term "race" (*raza*) promiscuously: one could be part of the human race, the Andalusian race, the Basque race, the Spanish race, or the Gypsy race. But the term rarely conjured up notions of racial purity because, he elucidates, Spanish thinkers of all sorts, aided by discussions in medicine and anthropology, began to see racial fusion as the building block of the Spanish "race." Still, Spanish Gypsies were excluded from this concept of racial fusion because they supposedly led nomadic lives segregated away from "real" Spaniards. Their segregation from Spanish populations deemed more advanced explained their seemingly criminal natures, according to people like Spanish criminologist Rafael Salillas y Panzano, and thus became a rationale for their criminalization and demonization.[64]

In real life, gitanos faced the disdain that marks many despised ethnic minorities; they were deemed criminals, beggars, scam artists, and labeled as filthy animals. The prejudice was made tangible through segregation, poverty, and lack of opportunities. In the cultural imagination of Spain and Europe, however, the mythic "gypsy," as literary scholar Lou Charnon-Deutsch explains, "roughly corresponds to a Romantic construction that still abounds in contemporary culture. Anyone who exhibits rebellious tendencies can be classified a gypsy." Thus bohemian types like artists or musicians or fortune-tellers could be designated as gypsies, even if they did not seem to fit certain phenotypic or "racial" characteristics.[65] In trying to make readers understand the distinction between the real lives of Gypsies and the European fictionalization of Gypsy lives, Charnon-Deutsch employs the uppercase and lowercase letter *g* as helpful signposts. As opposed to Gypsies who lived as oppressed minorities in Spain, gypsies were constructed to be understood as a cultural category rather than a racial one, and this conversion to a cultural category elevated their status in the world of theater and music.[66] Although Charnon-Deutsch's classificatory scheme does help us to understand the popularity of flamenco and its gitano performers—in contrast to the unpopularity of gitanos as real people—in the end, this distinction between racial and cultural categories falls apart.[67]

Where Charnon-Deutsch hits the mark, however, is in understanding how Europeans and people in Spain appropriated cultural/racial constructions of gitanos for their own ideological purposes. The Gypsy and its conflation with Andalusia/Spain represented the exotic Other for Europeans.[68] Representing Spain as Gypsy meant that the dominant European powers could view Spain as backward while simultaneously feeling a Romantic nostalgia for a bygone life when things were simpler and people lived closer to nature. Various nongitanos within Spain could also construct the gitanos as an "internal Other" on which to place their hopes, fears, and desires. In this compelling adaptation of Edward Said's *Orientalism*, Charon-Deutsch contends that "Spanish culture" maintained this "dual relationship with the foundational narratives of Orientalism."[69] As we shall witness throughout this book, the association of exotic gitanos with flamenco also worked to link flamenco with a carefree backwardness at best and criminality at worst.

Gender—and to a lesser extent, sexuality—plays a significant role in our understanding of flamenco and national identity, so much so, that its pervasiveness, like oxygen, is rendered invisible. Gender operates as a system of power relations in the world, whether in the nation, religion, politics, the family, or the stage, and it is a system that by its very invisibility seems natural and unbound by time or place. For example, as Nira Yuval-Davis points out, women have been just as important as men in the construction of nations and nationalism, but in most accounts of these various nationalist projects, women have been written out of these grand narratives. In the process they have often been excluded from the rights of national citizenship.[70] But women have always "reproduce[d] nations, biologically, culturally, and symbolically," she argues, especially in their roles as bearers of children for the nation and as "border guards" who help enforce particular cultural codes of behavior.[71] Those codes, what we might call the performance of masculinity and femininity, are not enforced just by the priest, the politician, and the patriarch but also by the mother, the daughter, and the girlfriend. It is during times of crises, however, that these roles, which may have once seemed natural, are called into question. As John Tosh notes, "One of the characteristic features of national crisis is that it may bring about drastic change in the socially acceptable ways of being a man."[72] National crisis might also bring about such changes in the socially acceptable ways of being a woman, too, given that in a gendered system, masculinity and femininity are defined against one another.

And for much of the nineteenth and twentieth centuries, elites across the political spectrum perceived a Spain in crisis, weak and fissiparous, as witnessed by its defeat in the Spanish-American War (1898) and by the growth of nationalism in Catalonia and the Basque Country. These cultural anxieties began to be expressed as anxieties about gender and sexuality, as we shall discover most explicitly in chapters 2 and 3, and to a lesser degree in chapter 6. For critics living in Spain, flamenco performers, their performances, and their audiences were often marked as degenerate; thus, these critics explicitly linked the breakdown of gendered and racial categories to the decline of Spain as a whole.

Outside of Spain, flamenco, race and gender operated a bit differently. The Spanish Gypsy, probably the best-known icon linking Spain and flamenco in the cultural imaginary, was, and still is, usually coded female. In the popular imagination, however, flamenco not only expressed "Gypsyness" but also embodied the idea of the "eternal feminine" coined by Simone de Beauvoir.[73] Flamenco performers—singers, guitar players, and dancers—could be both male and female, but Europeans tended to gender the singers and guitar players as male and the dancers female, as witnessed in the numerous newspaper accounts, advertisements, and later, tourist brochures of the nineteenth and twentieth centuries.[74] Perhaps this gendering occurred because the majority of writers who witnessed protoflamenco and flamenco performances in the early nineteenth century were males, and they tended to focus on the way the dancers sexually aroused them. Men were allowed to occupy public and transgressive spaces, and they dominated the literary landscape. Most women were not permitted such license. Thus it makes sense that the narratives created about female flamenco dancers were drawn to suit these men's tastes.

By the turn of the nineteenth century, foreigners' linking of Spain with flamenco had the effect of feminizing and Orientalizing Spain's national identity just at the very moment when Spaniards were agonizing over their colonial losses. Outside of Spain and especially in France, people focused more on flamenco dance than on flamenco singing, and the dance was understood to be about female carnality and sexual satiety. Even when male dancers were included in foreign written accounts of flamenco, they were often described as feminine and compared to Middle Eastern belly dancers, thus contributing to the Orientalist narrative about Spain as mysterious, malleable, and backward. As foreigners implicitly gendered Spain as female and racialized it as Gypsy, they managed to convey to Spaniards that Spain was weak, but like a beautiful woman who needed their protection and affection, lovely to spend time with. Most Spanish elites reacted to this condescension with fury and tried to find ways to eliminate flamenco from Spain's culture in order to reassert Spain's place at the top of the hierarchy of nations. In times of greatest national crises—for example, during the breakdown of the Restoration or just after the Spanish Civil War—religious and political elites targeted flamenco for eradication, viewing it as the most visible example of carnality run amok and responsible for the breakdown of traditional gender roles within the family and society.

Flamenco: A Performance in Three Parts and Seven Acts

As one might notice, the relationship between Europe, Spain, and flamenco is much more complex than scholars have suggested. For many

Spanish elites, flamenco captured their feelings of shame about Spain's declining status as a great power in the modern era. Foreigners, however, devised and projected a national identity onto Spaniards that was firmly cemented in the premodern era. Flamenco was a large part of that projection. In many ways Europeans helped to transform the cultural meaning of flamenco for Spanish artists and intellectuals in much the same way that Europeans championed African American jazz and blues and opened the way for Americans to embrace the music of an oppressed ethnic minority in a poverty-stricken region of the United States. Analogous dynamics occurred in Brazil with the samba and in Argentina with the tango.[75] Thus one can begin to notice similarities between the way various industrializing and industrial nations negotiate (for better or worse) their national identities through avenues of mass culture.

This book synthesizes a great deal of interdisciplinary literature about flamenco while threading through my own arguments about how this art form became affixed to Spain's national identity. In addition to this introduction, it is divided into three parts and a coda: part I (chapters 1-2), part II (chapters 3-5), part III (chapters 6-7), and, finally, a coda. Chapter 1 works to introduce the novice to the basics of flamenco history. It traces the origins and diffusion of flamenco from the end of the eighteenth century to the beginning of the Restoration (1875), which many scholars view as the golden age of flamenco. I demonstrate how flamenco flourished in Andalusia, both as a consequence of the rise of a mass urban culture in Spain and as a response to increased foreign tourism. Chapter 2 explores the phenomenon of *antiflamenquismo* (the battle against flamenco) among three distinct elite groups, the Catholic Church and its conservative allies, left-leaning intellectuals and politicians, and leaders from revolutionary workers' movements. I explore how these various groups aimed their sights on the world of flamenco to critique Spain's political, economic, and cultural ills during the convulsive period of the Restoration (1875-1923). Chapters 3 and 4 lay out the emerging regional nationalisms and their champions' varied responses to flamenco. In the case of Catalonia, Catalan nationalists would fight against what they imagined to be the foreign values associated with flamenco and flamenquismo, and they worked to create alternative cultural paths for Catalans to follow. Andalusian nationalists' responses to flamenco varied, but in the end, the most consequential Andalusian nationalist was Blas Infante. In order to strengthen Andalusia and Spain simultaneously, he exalted the ideologies that he believed united Andalusian nationalism, federalism, and flamenco. Chapter 5 takes us away from Spain and to international exhibitions. Although mostly focused on Parisian World Expositions, this chapter also details how Spanish elites desired to have their nation represented and how that projected Spanish national identity failed to live up to their expectations on the world stage. Spain was again flamencoized via performances held in the various Spanish pavilions and in entertainment zones within the city. This chapter also demonstrates how flamenco's success fed into European avant-garde composers' notions of musical authenticity, creating a feedback loop among Spanish avant-garde artists who eventually tried to convince other Spaniards that flamenco was art. Chapters 6 and 7 grapple with the Franco regime's ambivalence about using flamenco as a principal marker of Spanish identity. Chapter 6 reveals that the Catholic Church and leaders of the Spanish Falange thoroughly discouraged flamenco and other forms of musical entertainment. Instead, the female contingent of the fascist Falange Party, the Sección Femenina, established folk singing and dancing groups as a way to counteract the dangers of flamenco and solidify a new kind of national identity after the civil war that was predicated on "unity in difference." Finally, chapter 7 looks at the way the Franco regime, in conjunction with a developing Spanish tourist industry, changed course again to promote flamenco as a foundational part of Spain's identity in order to bolster tourism to Spain. By changing the narrative about flamenco, the Franco regime was able to bring in millions of tourists and their money to help fund the economic boom of the 1960s. The coda brings us up to the present, when the dynamics between globalization and regional autonomy have once again transformed flamenco practices. What you will discover as you read the following pages is that a musical form that took shape with the help of a select group of tourists at the beginning of the nineteenth century became woven into the fabric of Spain's identity by the onslaught of people that arrived almost two hundred years later. This is one account of how flamenco became national.

Part I

SETTING THE STAGE

Historians like to discover the genesis of an idea or an event. In the case of flamenco, that is not possible, although many have tried. The best one can do is to offer an educated synopsis of the many elements that went into the alchemic mix that we now call flamenco. Therefore, these next two chapters provide the reader with an understanding of flamenco's place within the grand sweep of history and within the specific context of Spanish history during the Restoration (1875–1923).

Chapter 1 is for the reader who knows little about flamenco performances' beginnings. It synthesizes the scholarly literature to demonstrate how the components of today's typical flamenco performance really began to emerge at the end of the eighteenth century and became stylized in the nineteenth century. It also traces how the art form became associated with the lower orders of society. Finally, it illustrates how the interaction between foreigners and Spaniards, both as performers and as audiences, shaped this distinctly modern performance genre.

Chapter 2 drops us into the last half of the nineteenth century, when flamenco reached its apogee in terms of its appeal to a cross-class, male audience. Despite its popularity, flamenco's association with the Spanish lower classes and with the seamier aspects of urban life led many elites from across the political spectrum to condemn both flamenco performers and their audiences. To these elites, this flamencomania reflected all that was wrong with Spain, and in their critiques of this modern entertainment they proposed alternative solutions to return Spain to the pantheon of great European powers.

1

Inventing an Ancient Past for a Modern Form, 1789—1875

Contrariness gave birth to flamenco. And opposition sustained its life. As we witnessed in the anecdote that opened this book, flamenco blossomed among the seedy sections of Andalusian cities. Historically, its performers emerged from the marginalized people of urban areas like Seville, Granada, Jerez, Córdoba, and later, Madrid and Barcelona. Somewhere among the chaotic strife of the late eighteenth and early nineteenth centuries, a pivotal time in the reconfiguration of Spain's relations with other European powers, a new form of musical performance arose that cloaked itself in ancient garb and appealed to both Spanish chauvinists and foreign Romantics looking for something to ease the distress of a world marred by revolution and industrialization.

When scholars tell the story of flamenco's appearance in literary texts, they often begin with José Cadalso and the 1789 publication of his posthumous epistolary novel, *Cartas marruecas*. It is here that we first glimpse sketches of something akin to the flamenco performances that would elicit both ire and attraction. The work, like many that would dog Spanish literature and politics for almost two centuries, is both a portrait and a critique of a Spain in decline. In the section most pertinent to this discussion, Letter 7, the narrator tells his sorry experience of accompanying a young aristocrat to his estate in the countryside. During their journey, the aristocrat companion reveals himself to be ignorant of the world, his lands, and his responsibilities, feeling much more at ease in the company of idlers. When the men arrive at their destination, many people are already there, preparing for a hunting party the next day. Gitano revelers are also present, as is a great quantity of wine. The gitanos sing, dance, smoke, and play castanets, and the young aristocrat and his other noble friends join in the celebration (what in Spanish would be called a *juerga*). The narrator attempts to avoid this dissolute group by going to sleep, but the racket keeps him up all night. Describing this scene contemptuously, he warns his readers that as long as the leading lights of Spanish society continued to participate in such juergas, Spain would remain a backward nation. In place of such merrymaking, he exhorts, Spanish elites must educate themselves in the latest scientific trends to advance Spain's fortunes. And so, with Cadalso's work, the seed of flamenco germinated in the literature of disdain and decline, and many antiflamenco writers of the nineteenth and twentieth centuries would follow suit.[1]

Cadalso's work illustrates many of the problems critics associated with (and would continue to associate with) flamenco in the nineteenth and twentieth centuries. The juergas were raucous, the spectators and performers inebriated, libidinous, uncontrollable, and immoral. Aristocrats, those who were meant to serve as moral and intellectual exemplars to the rest of the population, lived as wastrels, mixing with the lowest of the lowest caste, gitanos, and felt no shame in doing so. Meanwhile, the Spanish kingdom was in disarray, with the French and British challenging Spain's hegemony on the imperial stage and employing the tools fashioned from the Scientific Revolution and Enlightenment to exert their economic political control over domestic and foreign populations. Did Spanish elites follow suit and reform their educational, legal, religious, economic, and political systems? No. They conjured up parties, drank excessively, shouted, and clapped to the polyrhythmic beats of the castanets. Or so thought liberal reformers like Cadalso.

But there is a flip side to Cadalso's story: those who participated in flamenco culture, whether as performers, spectators, or other sorts of cultural producers, appeared to relish their outsider status and refused to imbibe reformers' nostrums. They were unwilling to operate under foreign codes and would find ways to nurture a musical form that they deemed Spanish. This "Spanishness" would also be reinforced by foreign visitors (mostly British and French) who looked to Spain as an example of a country that continued to preserve a traditional way of life seemingly lost to other countries. As with all mythologies, these tales are exciting, but their veracity is secondary to the narrative lessons they were meant to impart.

Flamenco was anything but traditional. Although one could find traces of traditional folk songs and dances in the flamenco genre, the style grew out of urban soil. Flamenco may have felt ancient and timeless to some, but it developed out of a Spain and Europe that were contending with the forces of modernity. To situate readers in the nineteenth-century world from which flamenco arose, this chapter begins first with a brief history of the components that together would evolve into the flamenco form—toque, baile, and cante—and then continue to elucidate the historical processes that shaped Spain and Europe between the French Revolution and Spain's Restoration (1789-1875). Finally, it will show how these historical processes fostered dynamic interactions between Spaniards and foreigners in different urban settings, changing both the tenor of and reactions to flamenco performances.

A Brief History of Flamenco Toque, Baile, and Cante before the Nineteenth Century

With the exception of castanets, no instrument is more associated with Spain than the guitar, and yet it generally gets short shrift in the histories of flamenco, perhaps because for so many years people saw it as mere backdrop to the main show of cante or baile. But from its inception the Spanish guitar enjoyed great popularity.[2] Considered part of the lute family, the European guitar developed during the Renaissance, although it looked slightly different, containing four pairs of strings known as courses. During the Baroque period, Spaniards popularized (and perhaps invented) the five-course guitar. Although the French and Italians introduced single-string guitars in the late eighteenth century, Spaniards became the chief players of this instrument, and musicians viewed the guitar as Spanish. By the middle of the eighteenth century, the Spanish guitar, with its fan-bracing of the soundboard, six single strings, long neck, and open sound hole became the prototype for the classical and Andalusian (flamenco) guitars. In the early part of the nineteenth century, the guitar diverged enough from the lute so as to form a new kind of species of stringed instrument, but there was little difference between the concert guitar and the more informal Andalusian one. Among the nineteenth-century transformations were machine heads that replaced wooden pegs, fixed frets, an open sound hole, a higher bridge, and a narrower neck. The wood used in a flamenco guitar tended to be made from cypress, which was both lighter and less expensive than the traditional rosewood of classical guitars, making the flamenco guitar more accessible to commoners and allowing flamenco guitarists, who usually hold the instrument almost upright, to carry the weight of the guitar more easily.

Technical specifications aside, the guitar's dissemination and cultural appropriation are what interest us here. According to scholars who have looked at violin-maker guild archives, the guitar became the stringed instrument in highest demand during the sixteenth and seventeenth centuries, and by the end of the sixteenth century, it became Spain's most popular instrument by far. The Spanish guitar achieved fame in the late sixteenth century because of the manner in which people played it, strumming the strings rather than plucking them, as one might with a *vihuela* or lute, and functioning more as rhythmic background than as an instrument one might want to hear alone in its own right. This new style, *el estilo rasgueado*, or the "Spanish style" as non-Spaniards called it, took less skill to achieve than plucking out individual notes, which meant that anybody who could get his or her hands on a guitar could learn to play at a very basic level in a short time. Guitar playing spread quickly in Spain, so that by around 1640 "guitar strumming [took] over the streets, outdoor comedy shows, plazas, [and] markets, and [reached] to the royal palace."[3] It also became quickly integrated into the Spanish comedic theater, and literature of the seventeenth century abounds with examples of guitar strummers, who could be found most often in picaresque novels.

Soon the guitar and its rasguedo style became associated with the lower orders of society—with wanderers, gitanos, beggars, and, most specifically, barbers. A corpus of Spanish Golden Age literature portrayed barbers as layabouts, always more interested in singing and dancing than in doing their actual vocation, haircutting and minor surgery. In fact, the guitar became closely tied with barbers, at least in the social imaginary.[4] This characterization of the rasgueado style with things lowly occurred in the classical concert world as well. Even as classical musicians integrated the guitar into their concerts, they avoided playing in the Spanish style, linking it to "the 'strange' and lascivious Spanish dances where one would jump, strike feet, and play castanets."[5] Concert guitarists chose to pluck instead. By the seventeenth century, just as there began to be a separation of popular and

Inventing an Ancient Past for a Modern Form, 1789–1875   31

Figure 3. *Gipsies Dancing in a Court of Sevilla*, by Gustave Doré, ca. 1862–73.
Source: Jean Charles Davillier, *Spain*, translated by J. Thomson (New York: Scribner, Welford and Armstrong, 1876).

aristocratic culture in the theater, the same kind of split occurred with guitar playing: plucking guitars in the same manner as other stringed instruments—what we would now call the classical style of guitar—became limited to aristocratic musical culture, while a mix of strumming and plucking became affixed to popular culture, especially in Andalusia, where this form of guitar playing achieved its greatest height.[6] The other telling piece of evidence of a split between classical and popular guitar was musical notation. Classical guitar had to be taught and standardized for concert playing; therefore, professional musicians needed musical notation to read. The paucity of written musical notation for the rasgueado style of guitar speaks of a music that, like most folk music, was passed on from one member of a family to another, from one village to another—no writing was necessary. This oral transmission of the Spanish style, coupled with the relatively inexpensive materials needed to make the guitar, helps account for the lower orders' appropriation of this instrument and aids us in understanding how this popular guitar and, later, flamenco guitar, was disseminated.[7] Among Andalusians, the Andalusian/flamenco guitar became strongly associated with the resident gitanos, more so through the artistic renderings of Gustave Doré, who populated his work with gitano musicians, reinforcing the Romantic image of the Spanish/gitano as entertainer.

Cante, especially the form that would become known as *cante jondo* (deep song), has received the most attention from scholars and flamenco aficionados.[8] But cante came in many forms, adopting and adapting styles from a multitude of sources. When we speak of cante we are including not just the lyrics and meter of a song but also the melismatic style of singing. Foreign travel writers of the nineteenth and early twentieth centuries often characterized the singing as "monotonous," "plaintive," or as "high-pitched" cries, "low incantation[s]," "oriental monotony," and "wail[s]."[9] These cries, known as *jipíos*, punctuated the singers' performances as they tried to achieve a *voz afillá*—that is, a frayed and hoarse-sounding voice.[10] The *cante flamencos'* precursors were numerous, although not so easily verifiable, given that much of the music was passed down through oral traditions in earlier centuries. Still, scholars have identified a series of influences dating back to the Middle Ages and the expulsion period—namely, the religious music of Moriscos and Sephardic Jews in combination with the music of gitanos; the cries coming from wandering vendors hawking their wares, known as *pregones*; the calls that blind beggars bellowed to receive alms; and Catholic liturgical music. Additionally, the music and its verses were most likely generated by a fusion of Andalusian folk songs with those of gitanos and fugitive Moriscos who presumably lived in hiding in the gitano neighborhoods of Andalusian cities and towns after the expulsion.[11] The cantes that would become part of the flamenco oeuvre owed their survival to writers who, beginning in the eighteenth century, compiled and collated folk songs they perceived to be disappearing as a result of musical influences from abroad. Nineteenth-century Romanticism accelerated this process of collecting folk songs.

Like cante flamenco, *baile flamenco* also evolved under conditions made possible by the interaction of diverse people in continuous contact with one another. Despite the promotional material that travel writers and boosters from Cadiz propagated about the ancient origins of the dance, baile flamenco was not nearly so old.[12] Rather, the main sources for baile flamenco came from Andalusian, gitano, and African/Afro-Caribbean dance traditions—and, surprisingly for many, from other European professional dancers in the nineteenth century who performed their versions of Spanish dance on the stage. Some of the Andalusian influences came from the early *bailes de candil* (candle dances) that peasants danced among themselves in guesthouses and inns and that others danced during fiestas and in great entertainment halls. Other forms followed, like the *seguidillas, fandangos,* and *jácaras* from the sixteenth and seventeenth centuries, and by the eighteenth century these dances and the *bolero,* often dubbed by Spaniards and foreigners alike as "the national dance," began to be showcased in theaters as visual accompaniment to the smaller comedic set pieces known as *sainetes* and *entremeses.*[13]

Meanwhile, gitanos, as Roma people all over Europe had done, transplanted and transformed their musical traditions after entering Spain around 1425. Some made their living by traveling around Spain in musical troupes, often as families, performing their dances in streets and plazas, at religious and civic festivals—wherever they were permitted—accompanied by spirited voices, guitars, tambourines, palmas, and castanets. They also performed in more intimate circles, in the homes of distinguished and well-paying gentlemen (*señoritos*) who might want to have a rousing good time—in what became known as the juerga. Gitano dances (or other Spanish dances like the romances and seguidillas interpreted "in the gitano manner," which usually involved the rapid-fire foot-striking [*zapateado*]) also figured prominently on the Spanish stage, side by side with the Andalusian dances noted above. Sometimes, although not often, these dances were actually performed by gitanos. Scholars José Luis Navarro and Eulalia Pablo claim that some of these Gypsy-style dances, already present in the seventeenth century, were beginning the "first historical fusion: that of the [gitano] interpretive forms with the steps and movements of popular Spanish dances. They were initiating that which two centuries later would comprise the flamenco footwork."[14] Lastly, in terms of the early influences on baile flamenco, we have to contend with the slave trade. As Spaniards captured Africans, enslaved them, and brought them to ports like Seville, Africans brought their own song and dance cultures to bear on the lands on which they were forced to toil. Their religious dances, which Spaniards perceived as being too erotic for Christians because of the rhythmic movements below the waistline, toned down over the years and were incorporated into the Corpus Christi festivals and other religious dances that Andalusians and gitanos enacted. A similar sort of cultural interchange occurred when African slaves, forced to carry their songs and dances to places like Cuba, transformed the musical cultures there. Once rooted in the Caribbean, the music and dance then crossed back over the Atlantic to southern Spain via the americanos who returned to

Spain.[15] European dancers outside of Spain also contributed to the flamenco dance fusion, as we shall witness shortly.

Toque, cante, and baile flamenco all developed out of wider European and trans-Atlantic processes that were transforming the world in the shift from the early modern to the modern period.[16] These forms eventually coalesced into what would be called flamenco in the nineteenth century. They seemed to have the imprint of Spanish rural folk traditions, and thus could be viewed as authentically Spanish both by those Spaniards who believed that their land had been overrun by foreign ideas and by outside visitors who imagined they had discovered a land forgotten by time. But the art form itself was quintessentially modern, decidedly urban, and less Spanish than we might imagine.

Resisting the French (and Other Europeans) through Cultural Practices: The Nineteenth Century

Flamenco's triumph in the middle of the nineteenth century owes much of its success to the volatile forces of nationalism and nostalgia unleashed by the French Revolution and the rejection of Enlightenment ideals like cosmopolitanism. Although scholars now argue that there were multiple Enlightenments that varied from country to country and discipline to discipline, one could claim that however these Enlightenments played out in Europe, they all emphasized the primacy of reason, the formation of an orderly administration, and a belief in progress. These shared premises shaped a politics and culture of cosmopolitanism.[17] A work like Immanuel Kant's " Idea for a Universal History from a Cosmopolitan Point of View" (1784) represented the apex of this faith in cosmopolitanism.[18] It laid out the steps by which the world would evolve, bit by bit, into a series of enlightened states guided by the principles of reason and created by constitutions and just laws. Just a few short years later, the French Revolution shattered the idea for many that cosmopolitanism would rescue Europe from the tyrannies of absolutism and religion. Instead, it became discredited, and by the early nineteenth century, national distinctiveness replaced the cosmopolitan creed.[19]

The development of Spanish nationalism as a reaction against Enlightenment cosmopolitanism is a bit more complicated to untangle because of Spain's relationship to the French monarchy.[20] After the War of Spanish Succession (1701–14) the French Bourbon line succeeded the Hapsburg one, although the French monarchy itself had to renounce

Inventing an Ancient Past for a Modern Form, 1789–1875

any claims to rule over Spain. With the Bourbons now in place on the Spanish throne, and with the importation of many French advisors, French cultural and intellectual influence reigned in the Spanish court and intensified during the Bourbon reforms under Charles III (1759-88) and later under Napoleonic occupation (1808-14). Those who sought to implement these Enlightenment reforms, the *afrancesados* (also known as *ilustrados*), worked to restructure Spain and its empire's administrative apparatus to create a more rationalized bureaucracy and productive economy and to lessen the influence of the Catholic Church over the state. For the afrancesados, of whom our earlier interlocutor, Cadalso, was one, Spain was mired in a sea of backwardness, led by a hapless aristocracy who needed to be refashioned into real leaders. The country and its empire required substantial reforms in order to compete successfully with the other great powers, France and Britain. Not content solely with importing administrative practices, the afrancesados aped the dress and manners of the French aristocracy and bureaucratic classes, and they adopted their cultural preferences as well.[21]

But there was also resistance and discomfort with this French cultural hegemony, and it was expressed in many quarters, especially among the working classes and the aristocracy in Madrid, who demonstrated their dissatisfaction by adopting the persona and dress of the *majo* or *maja*. People familiar with Francisco Goya's paintings will have encountered them, Madrid's working-class men and women who dressed flamboyantly, the men sporting dark cloaks and large floppy hats that covered their faces, and the women, fancy headdresses and exposed lacy petticoats, suggesting a certain sexual freedom (see figure 4). These artisans, living cheek-by-jowl among the many royal courtiers and bureaucrats who hustled through the capital's center, dressed to establish their opposition to what they saw as the feminized afrancesado court culture represented by the stock character of the *petimetre* (see figure 5). The majos and majas, and the people who imitated them, expressed their politics and nationalism through dress. As folklorist Dorothy Noyes has remarked, "The *petimetre* and the *majo*, represent[ed] respectively the French and the indigenous, bourgeois and plebeian extremes of fashion."[22] Not only did the majos and majas repudiate foreign dress, they rejected the music and dances imported via France and Italy and assertively danced the Andalusian-inflected seguidillas, a dance form that would eventually become a staple of flamenco. For many, especially those who rejected the Bourbon reforms, the majos came to symbolize the voice of the true Spanish people, and by the

Figure 4. *Majas on a Balcony*, ca. 1808–10, attributed to Francisco Goya.
Source: https://www.wikiart.org/en/francisco-goya/majas-on-a-balcony.

1760s the Spanish nobility demonstrated their resistance to these changes by emulating the majo dress. The fashion for majismo trickled upward so steadily that by 1799 Goya was painting Queen María Luisa as a maja.[23] Not only did the nobility walk among the people "disguised" as majos, but they mixed with the commoners at bullfights and became patrons (and sometimes lovers) of both bullfighters and actresses (who also performed as majas on and off stage). The power of majismo did not go unnoticed, and some ilustrados like Jovellanos sought to loosen the grasp of majo culture by calling for reforms in the world of entertainment, especially in the theater.[24] Majismo became one of the first ways that Spanish aristocrats and the lower orders could ally together and perform a type of Spanish nationalism, and this alliance

Figure 5. *To the Palace: A Serious Petimetre*, by Antonio Rodríguez. Engraver: Josef Vázquez. Madrid, 1808. Courtesy of the Fundación Joaquín Díaz, funjdiaz.net.

of the "unreformable" aristocracy with the "unruly" classes formed a cultural kinship that resonated in the flamenco culture of the nineteenth century and up until the civil war.

After the French occupied Spain in 1808, those afrancesados who served in Joseph Napoleon's court were discredited and tarred with the brush of treason.[25] Meanwhile, Spain's popular resistance to the occupation fueled legends about guerrilla priests, fierce women, and fearless peasants who toppled the mighty power of the bloodthirsty and godless French. Notwithstanding British aid in France's defeat, the narrative of Spanish bravery in the face of France's overwhelming military strength helped create a popular nationalism among Spain's people that was reinforced by Romantics in post-Napoleonic Europe. The nationalism that grew in opposition to French cultural and military hegemony was further reinforced in the nineteenth century, when the ideology of cultural nationalism propagated by people like Johann Gottfried Herder disseminated throughout Europe, encouraging nationalists to seek out their nation's essential sources of genius, most of which were supposed to be found among the rural folk.

As one of the foundational theorists of cultural nationalism, Herder promoted the idea that each nation has a unique soul that can be illuminated through its language and music (which he viewed as closely linked together) and through other forms of culture, broadly speaking. Gather and classify these cultural forms, and one could uncover the essential and authentic spirit of a nation and its collective genius. While Herder wrote in praise of national uniqueness in the face of seemingly cosmopolitan overreach, his nationalism did not necessarily come from a place of antagonism; for example, German culture is *superior to* French culture. Rather, all nations equally had something powerful and authentically theirs to contribute to world civilization.[26] As the nineteenth century moved forward, however, attempts by various members of Europe's intelligentsia to define their respective national geniuses for projection onto the world's stage took a more competitive and hierarchical turn.

In Europe, budding nationalists began to assert their nationalism through the "cultivation of culture," which, to adopt this category of analysis from Joep Leerssen, reflects intellectuals' new fascination and "canonization" of vernacular culture to represent a nation in all its specificity. Hence, intellectuals began to interest themselves in folktales, songs, dances, and other creative activities of people in the rural hinterlands. They decontextualized these cultural practices and then "recontextualised and instrumentalised [them] for modern needs and values," and in the process they invested these forms of vernacular culture "with a fresh national symbolism and status."[27] Intellectuals in Spain followed this same trajectory, concentrating on cultivating what they took to be Spain's indigenous culture(s), especially as a backlash against the French, and to a lesser degree, the Italians, and while these emerging folklorists cast their net widely to capture cultures from all

Cante

In terms of cante, intellectuals' desire to repurpose folk music for Spanish national aspirations had already begun during the French occupation, even among some afrancesados themselves. One of the earliest examples of such a project came from the eighteenth-century writer and afrancesado Don Preciso, a guitarist and singer himself. His *Colección de las mejores coplas de seguidillas, tiranas, y polos que se han compuesto para cantar a la guitarra* (Collection of the best verses of seguidillas, tiranas, and polos composed for singing with guitar) preserved for future generations what have now become canonical forms of flamenco songs, although his compilation contained folk music from other regions as well. Despite working as a scribe for the Royal Court before and during Joseph Bonaparte's occupation of the throne, Don Preciso used his writing for patriotic purposes. He argued that Spaniards carried with them a song and dance tradition that could hold its own against that of any other nation. He railed against the importation of Italian and French opera and their detrimental effects on Spanish music, "which like a horrible storm that withers the laborer's ripened fruit, ended all of our music, not because Italian music was better . . . but because our musicians, always unimaginative and eternally ignorant, extolled opera and denigrated our music."[28] In language representative of both Romantic and Herderian nationalist ideas, he critiqued the slavish parroting of foreign musical forms and the "destruction of the Spanish spirit and character," lamenting the loss of musical skill and feeling among those precious few youths who still knew how to play and sing a seguidilla or a tirana.[29] He thus began the process of canonizing and standardizing what he perceived to be dying musical forms by publishing the lyrics and meter of regional music. But as Gerhard Steingress points out, these songs were not "anonymous popular songs" but rather songs written by artists—including Don Preciso himself—that seemed like those sung by the popular classes of Spain. In fact, Steingress emphasizes that these "national" songs had been influenced by neoclassical styles of verse.[30]

During much of the nineteenth century, other writers also contributed to the ever-growing collections of popular verse, seemingly because some people believed that foreign music and the effects of growing industrialization and urbanization were erasing the remnants of popular music emanating from rural Spain.³¹ These works began to develop into what would be known as the *costumbrista* genre: works that depicted regional manners, customs, and class behavior. The Andalusian Fernán Caballero wrote fiction that focused primarily on promoting the conservative values of rural Andalusia in works such as *Cuadros de costumbres populares andaluzas* (1852) (Sketches of popular Andalusian customs) and *Cuentos y poesía andaluces* (1859) (Andalusian stories and poetry).³² Emilio Lafuente Alcántara complained in the prologue of his work *Cancionero popular: Colección escogida de coplas y seguidillas* (1865) (Popular songbook: Selected collection of coplas and seguidillas) that numerous scholars had dissected and disseminated canonical works of Spanish literature and ancient Spanish songs, providing Spaniards with a deep understanding of their own history, and yet this knowledge did not aid contemporary Spaniards to understand themselves in the present day. He wanted the "rich treasure" of popular poetry that was "natural and spontaneous" to be studied more assiduously. For these songs reflect "the genuine manifestation of their most intimate feelings," and they "show us [these emotions] without artifice or dissimulation." And like European Romantics of his day, he believed that by conserving "for the future these songs," the reader/singer would understand the "uses, language, and emotions of our people." Even though he admitted that "all of the provinces of our country have their favorite songs," he concentrated on songs sung in Castilian, and then chose to focus mostly on songs from Andalusia and Aragon, adding to the notion that Andalusia was most representative of Spain.³³

Felipe Pedrell (1841–1942), a composer from Cataluña, did much to shape musical nationalism in Spain in the nineteenth century. Considered by many of his students to be the "father of Spanish musicology," he studied Continental European classical and folk music histories and then spent much of his lifetime researching Spanish musical traditions, including liturgical, classical, and folk traditions.³⁴ In such works as *Por nuestra música*, he lobbied for the creation of a national music that incorporated Spanish folk music—that is, "natural music"—into modern operatic and symphonic compositions, which he deemed "artificial music."³⁵ Concerned that Spanish composers created derivative music and would therefore never be taken seriously by international audiences and critics, he actively implored Spanish composers to draw on the rich and diverse traditions of Spanish folk music (read broadly) to breathe new life into stale compositions. He also wrote about flamenco, but only as one of the many regional musical forms in Spain's pantheon.³⁶

Pedrell's fame did little to solidify cante flamenco as *the* music of Spain; in fact, Pedrell tended to view Spanish music as a multiplicity of songs, a country of diverse regional music that together formed what we could call Spanish music. Instead, the person most known for gathering, collating, and publishing hundreds of songs that would be called by the more modern appellation "cante flamenco," was Antonio Machado y Álvarez, better known by his pen name, Demófilo, and father to the poets Antonio and Manuel Machado. Demófilo, one of the first people in Spain to call himself a folklorist and who eventually headed folklore studies at the Institución Libre de Enseñanza, echoed Herder's credo that folk songs (and dances) contained the expression of national identity and national genius.[37] In his youth, under the tutelage of his father, Antonio Machado y Núñez, Demófilo immersed himself in anthropological and folkloric studies and was one of the founding members of the Anthropological Society of Seville in 1871. Influenced by the establishment of a folklore society in London in 1878 and a friendship with the German linguist and folklorist Hugo Schuchardt, he became interested in establishing a similar folklore society in Spain in order to study Spanish folk tales, songs, and dances with intellectual rigor. In 1879 he began compiling folk songs from all around Spain, and in 1881 he created two folklore societies, El Folk-lore Español and El Folk-lore Andaluz. By 1882 he edited a journal linked to the Andalusian folkloric society, also named *El Folk-lore Andaluz*.

Despite his catholic interests, he made his greatest impact with his studies of cante flamenco. His fascination with these songs evinced itself already by 1871, when he wrote an article called "Cantes flamencos" in *Revista mensual*, and culminated in the publication of his *Colección de cantes flamencos* in 1881. Written after spending time with Schuchardt listening to cante in Seville's popular venues of the day, the cafés cantantes, Demófilo contributed information about cante that had not been present in the earlier books of verse discussed above. He wrote in the ethnographic spirit, interviewing the most acclaimed singers of his day who were performing cante flamenco and enshrining their songs and ideas in print. He gave a name to this new "poetic-musical genre," calling it "cante flamenco," and disassociated it from folk music, arguing it did not come from nor represent the Spanish people. Instead, it originally belonged to gitanos—who Demófilo obviously saw as a different "race" from Andalusians—but it had been "Andalusianized." Its movement away from taverns to professional (read: inauthentic) cafés cantantes was but a step toward its decline. He also classified the verse differently than others had in the past. Rather than looking at the verses' themes or meter, he classified them more by the type of musical style one would use to sing them. Finally, he attempted to write the verse in the dialect in which they were sung, thus hoping to emulate the sounds that people might hear during performances.[38] Mixed in with this desire to uncover the cante flamenco's roots was a quest for authenticity in the face of music's commercialization in the urban centers.[39] Despite the fact that the music he was writing about was not really some kind of ancient gitano music on its way to destruction because of the commercial café cantante he deplored, he took the flamenco songs he heard seriously and gave them an intellectual's imprimatur. Moreover, he situated this new genre in urban centers, thus arguing that cante flamenco had no relationship to the rural areas that produced folk music.

Baile

In contrast to the cantes, which were mostly collected and created within Spain as a nationalist reaction against foreign encroachment, the nineteenth-century dances that would evolve into baile flamenco depended on a dynamic relationship between insiders and outsiders, between foreign writers who came as tourists and the artists who tailored their performances to their audiences' expectations. There remains little doubt that baile flamenco was a hybrid of non-gitano Andalusian dances, and gitano, Continental European, Latin American, and, later, African American dances over the course of almost a century.[40] Still, flamenco was forged in the crucible of Andalusia.

Why Andalusia became the focus of this dynamic has probably more to do with the contingencies of history than anything else. In the earlier part of the century, foreigners visited Andalusia more than other parts of Spain for practical reasons—it saw less warfare than other parts of Spain. Southern Spain, especially the important port city of Cadiz, had been the site of a successful resistance to the French troops that had occupied the rest of the country during the Revolutionary Wars and had already received its fair share of international attention for resisting the French and for promoting constitutional monarchy. Andalusia again played an important role in fomenting the short-lived Revolution of 1820, but the 1823 French invasion to restore absolutism to Spain quashed these liberals' dreams and forced many of them into exile in France and England. Some of these refugee liberal intellectuals became cultural, commercial, and intellectual mediators between southern Spain and their lands of exile, all at the moment when Romanticism began to take hold on the European continent. These exiled intellectuals fed their counterparts in England and France images of "an idealized, distant, and orientalized Andalusia."[41] And so when things settled down in southern Spain, the well-heeled classes from abroad were primed to visit. Those who admired Andalusia did so because in many ways it seemed the antithesis of northern and western Europe. To them, Spain was a land stuck in time, devoid of the trappings of modern industrialized civilization, and their writings consistently reflected what they viewed through that Romantic prism.

While most Hispanophiles are familiar with the works of Theophile Gautier, Charles Davillier and Gustave Doré, Georges Bizet, and Prosper Mérimée in solidifying our Romantic notions of the passionate but fickle Gypsy dancer, they may not know that these stories were reinforced and solidified both by the hundreds of travel narratives that came out over the course of the century and by the way that "Spanish" dance was performed on other parts of the European continent. George Borrow and Richard Ford wrote the most famous of these travel narratives in English during the nineteenth century.[42] These works, among numerous others, colored both foreigners' perceptions of the flamenco world and, by extension, of Spain. By the late 1840s, writers who had visited Andalusia provided in their works favorable descriptions of casual juergas (like those seen in Cadalso's work) and the more formal dance performances they encountered in the theater, depicting the dancers as embodying a vibrancy that dancers on the French and British stages lacked. For example, although he is describing Spanish dancers in a theater in Seville, and not a juerga, Gautier does distill certain French views of Spanish dancers in this evocative passage: "Their style has not the least relation to that of the French school.... In Spain, the feet hardly leave the ground; there are none of those wide circular or spreading movements of the legs, which make a woman look like a pair of compasses stretched to its limits, and are considered down there revoltingly indecent. It is the body which dances, with curving motions of the hips, bending sides and a waist which twists and turns with the suppleness of a serpent or an Egyptian dance-girl."[43] Although the term flamenco was still not in vogue, the writers spoke of such dances as the olé, cachucha, fandango, and the Gypsy handkerchief dance. The staging, however, began to sound like an approximation of what would later be found in commercial cafés cantantes: a room (if not a stage) containing a lone guitarist or two, a few people clapping the rhythm, a singer who is often described as wailing, and a dancer or two, dancing "passionately" and sometimes "savagely."[44]

Between the 1830s and 1860s, performers on the northern side of the Pyrenees also aided in transforming traditional folk dances from Spain and creating an Andalusian dance genre for the European stage. Although some dancers from Spain showcased Spanish dance outside the country out of financial necessity after the death of Fernando VII in 1833, many dances thought to be of Spanish/gitano origin really took on new lives outside of Spain by non-Spanish dancers and then were transformed again when performed in Spain.[45] Dancers such as the Viennese Fanny Elssler, the French Marie Guy-Stéphan, and the Irish (but passed herself off as a Gypsy from Seville) Lola Montes popularized and introduced Europeans to their versions of the Spanish cachucha and bolero. They, among others, were responsible for creating a kind of Andalusian and Gypsy craze on the European stage, especially among the French. Then, in turn, these adaptations of Spanish forms of song and dance would be modified by Spanish dancers in theatrical productions on the Spanish stage, adapting their dances to what other European audiences wanted, and then Gypsy dancers transformed these theatrical dances for their urban audiences in places like Seville. The excitement for all things Andalusian provoked by a combination of the Continental reworking of Spanish dance and travel writers' titillating descriptions of juergas encouraged many people of means to travel to Spain to view these spectacles for themselves ... and then write about them some more.[46] Their orientalist disseminations helped the growth of an incipient tourist industry from the 1850s on and spurred the development of special schools of dance and cafés cantantes to accommodate both these visitors and new Spanish clientele who had both the means and leisure time to enjoy this novel form of mass culture.

Social and Cultural Changes within Spain Itself

Meanwhile, changes in Spanish culture and society acted in concert with these other transformations, which also aided in the development of a flamenco culture. While political turmoil swirled around Spain, industrialization began to reshape urban areas, both for better and for worse.[47] The nineteenth century saw slow and uneven industrial and urban development in Spain, with cities like Bilbao and Barcelona taking the economic lead. Although industrialization took place more slowly in Spain than in other parts of western Europe, it still forced significant numbers of the population to undergo startling transformations. Industrialization led to urbanization and all that that word implies: extreme poverty, overcrowding, filth, disease, and overall wretchedness. Toward the end of the nineteenth century, many Spanish cities began modernization/extension projects along the lines of Haussmannization in Paris, which further segregated the cities by wealth and class yet still did little to ameliorate the squalid and unsanitary conditions the working classes experienced on a daily basis.

Despite these real hardships, other transformations occurred that one could view more positively. With increased urbanization came an influx of workers ready to labor in factories and workshops and an increasing number of people from the middling and professional classes flexing their new economic muscle. As in the rest of Europe, Spanish cities housed a growing population that began to inhabit new spaces of sociability made possible by the creation of cheap and plentiful entertainment, and increased leisure time.[48] During the nineteenth century, cafés, bars, taverns, opera houses, and theaters dotted the European urban landscape, and different social classes segregated themselves among the various spaces and forms of entertainment. In Spain itself, similar recreational pursuits cropped up in urban areas. Spanish variants of these entertainments included the bullfight, the zarzuela, and the café cantante.[49]

In early nineteenth-century Spain, as in Britain, France, and other urbanizing countries, theaters, taverns, and cafés were spaces of urban sociability. At first leisure time and commercial entertainment belonged to the aristocracy and the upper-middle classes only. As cafés became more popular over the course of the century, they began to specialize in terms of form and function. Although some were places for men to congregate and engage in *tertulias* (formalized chats or debates), the others became sites for spectacles: *cafés conciertos* (usually cafés with short piano numbers and singing), *cafés líricos* (cafés for musical theater) and then, cafés cantantes (originally featuring a variety of musical numbers).[50] By the mid-nineteenth century, the café cantante emerged and began to flourish all around Spain, beginning in Seville and then moving up from Andalusia to Madrid, Barcelona, and other urban centers around the country.[51] Near the late nineteenth and early twentieth centuries, working-class men were able to partake of these forms of entertainment, in part because of commercial innovations begun in Madrid at the Café el Recreo theater in 1868. Eventually known as the *teatro por horas* (theater by the hour), this highly profitable pricing scheme involved staging lots of one-act plays instead of longer two- to three-hour plays and musicals. A spectator would therefore buy entertainment piecemeal, maybe two tickets for two one-act plays, but skip out on the third and meet a friend for a drink somewhere.[52] The cafés cantantes operated in a similar manner. In the late nineteenth century, the cafés were open from 8 p.m. until midnight, with a few shifts in the interim. The shifts would be priced differently, but all one had to pay to see a shift was the price of a drink. Male workers who wanted entertainment could go to the early shift (because they had to work the next day) or else wait until weekends and/or holidays to attend, while wealthier people could pay for all the shifts or attend the later ones.[53]

Flamenco Becomes Professionalized: The Attractions and Perils of the New Mass Culture

Increased urbanization and the beginnings of tourism helped solidify flamenco's place in the world of entertainment. By the mid-1800s, flamenco became professionalized and decidedly Spanish, much to the dismay of Spanish intellectuals and reformers who hoped to encourage a different sort of national identity. What we would now call the flamenco performance moved away solely from private celebrations in peoples' homes and small taverns to the more public space of the café cantante, where it could be enjoyed by a greater variety of people. A señorito could still hire a group of Gypsies to entertain his friends in a private juerga in the 1850s—and many Spanish aristocrats still did this—but flamenco performances could also be witnessed in dance academies, taverns, and the commercial cafés cantantes that had popped up not just in Andalusia but in urban areas throughout Spain. By the 1860s, those who managed to pay the (generally inexpensive) entry fee could share the entertainment once reserved for the upper classes only, and the café cantante became the most common place for larger numbers of people to watch a flamenco performance. By the end of the nineteenth century, the café cantante had flourished so successfully that many social critics set their sights on eliminating what they saw as this cancer on Spanish society.

Cafés cantantes did not begin to appear in any great number until the 1840s in Madrid and Andalusia. At about the same time, the foreign writers who popularized the Romantic image of Spain we are most familiar with began to visit Spain. While the café cantante began as a space where any type of singing could be performed, by midcentury there were many places that specialized in cante (and sometimes baile) flamenco. These cafés cantantes were essentially bars designed for watching musical entertainment, much in the vein of Britain's music halls and France's cabarets, only the Spanish variant housed flamenco performances. Some of the more famous ones were run by flamenco performers themselves, like cantaor Silverio Franconetti's Café Silverio in Seville. Professionalization set these places apart from the local tavern or dance academy. Performers were now contracted for a number of months or years before they continued on to other places in the concert circuit, and some of these singers and dancers toured outside Spain, achieving international acclaim.

By the second half of the nineteenth century, Spaniards flocked to these performances, but so too did foreigners, who through their travel narratives and then later travel guides made the flamenco singer and dancer the incarnation of the Spanish nation. Flamenco probably would not have endured without an incipient tourism fostered by prominent foreign writers and the occasional ordinary visitor who reported on their Spanish adventures, often in the most romanticized terms, contributing to an enduring notion that Spain was an exotic land within Europe. Flamenco dancing, or some approximate version thereof, became the coin of the tourist realm, as many hotel purveyors and gitanos in places like Seville and Granada quickly learned.

Much information about what tourists wanted to see or what they were steered to visit came from the travel narratives and newly emerging guidebooks that were first published in the nineteenth century, both from within and from without Spain. One must be careful in using these sources as reflections of what places were like, especially since foreign guidebook writers tended to assume a colonial voice and registered shock at Spanish food and customs, while Spanish guidebook writers tended to gloss over anything that might tarnish the reputation of the country. But these guidebooks and travel narratives give us a window into what elites of the period might have thought. For example, as early as 1865, a Spanish guidebook for Seville listed places where people could visit dancing schools, which was a rarity for Spanish guidebooks to do at the time because they generally focused on Spain's historical and artistic heritage.[54] Another Spanish guidebook for Granada depicted the gitanos living in the caves of the Sacromonte as people who "hassle foreigners with their dances and songs."[55] By the end of the century, foreign narratives and guidebooks recognized that flamenco was a lucrative commercial venture for bringing in foreign tourists. H. C. Chatfield-Taylor complained of these same gitanos whose "sole means of livelihood is fleecing the strangers" and who haggled with tourists until both parties were satisfied with the price agreed on for these "vulgar dancers."[56] Perhaps the most keen observation of the commercial and scripted nature of this performance for tourists came from the rare female observer who stripped bare what most writers of the time normally took at face value, that flamenco was somehow an unmediated expression of Gypsy passion: "While one gitana after another takes the stage, a crescent of men and women, seated behind, cheer her on with cries and clappings, strummings of the guitar, and frenzied beatings of the floor with staff and stool. Yet their excitement, even at its apparent height, never sweeps them out of their crafty selves. Beyond the dancer they see the audience. Disdain and dislike are in the atmosphere, and never more than when the rain of silver is at its richest."[57] Although the author could not mask her bigotry, her keen eye in this context noticed the performative imitation of passion for a credulous male audience.

Without national or regional tourist industries in Europe in the late-nineteenth century, guidebooks like Baedeker and the Michelin series, and tour groups like Cook's Tours (established in 1841) became thriving enterprises, guiding the new monied classes who had disposable income and some leisure time to see "what must be seen."[58] While most guides like those published by Thomas Cook Tours avoided mentioning dancing in their tourism literature, focusing instead on cultural and historical sites, the Baedeker guides included entertainment venues in addition to the practical information one usually found in a guide book. The Baedeker guides, which began to be published at the very end of the nineteenth century, even included information on cafés cantantes, which they understood to be sexually charged places. In Madrid they warned: "Those cafés in which, at an advanced hour of the evening, the so-called 'Flamenco' Songs and Dances are given should be avoided by ladies and visited by gentlemen only in company with a native friend," and in the gitano suburb of Seville they cautioned: "The performances in the suburb of Triana are of immemorial antiquity, but ladies are not advised to frequent them. This is the home of the genuine gipsies, known here as Flamencos, and they have preserved many of their characteristic, mainly Oriental dances and songs."[59] By the eve of World War I, the flamenco dancer was etched in the foreign imaginary as a fundamental part of Spanish national identity, so much so that the Michelin guide sprinkled tiny caricatures of the Michelin Man posing as various stock Spanish characters, including a flamenco dancer (see figure 6) and a stereotypical Andalusian man (see figure 7).

Figure 6. The Michelin Man as a flamenco dancer.
Illustrator: Ortíz.
Source: *Guía Michelin: España 1911* (Madrid: Sociedad Anónima del Neumático Michelin, 1911).
Image courtesy of Pau Medrano Bigas.

Figure 7. The Michelin Man with a stereotypical Andalusian woman.
Illustrator: Ortíz.
Source: *Guía Michelin: España 1913* (Madrid: Sociedad Anónima del Neumático Michelin, 1913).
Image courtesy of Pau Medrano Bigas.

Attitudes toward Flamenco Produced by Place

If we circle back to Cadalso, who appeared at the beginning of this chapter, he leads us to think about the location of flamenco performances, about how place and space transformed the spectacle over the years.[60] His work lets us peek at the juerga, which was always a private affair and tainted with the stain of vice. We also know that the songs and dances that would evolve into baile and cante flamenco had their public faces as well, at religious and civic fiestas, in the theater, in taverns, in cafés cantantes, and in front of foreign tourists. What emerged as flamenco in the nineteenth and early twentieth centuries, however, became more confined to smaller interior spaces within mostly working-class urban areas, which helped to solidify critics' convictions that flamenco had something to hide.[61]

Flamenco dancing and singing became targets for various people's racial, sexual, class, and national anxieties. Where one viewed the performances, how one viewed them, and who attended them often determined their moral judgments about the dances. For example, the dance academies run by brothers Miguel and Manuel de la Barrera in Seville functioned as places where "respectable" spectators of both sexes could learn about Spain's many forms of dance, with priority given to Andalusian folk dances and the national dance, the bolero. There, too, one could see cleaned-up versions of dances found in the taverns in Gypsy neighborhoods like Triana that would not offend the sensibilities of ladies, especially. Often guides from the European hotels would sell tickets to foreigners for functions at the dance academies or, barring that, would hire Gypsy performers to play in buildings rented out especially for those occasions.[62]

Eventually, these guides would bring tourists to places like Seville's Triana for what many believed to be an authentic Gypsy experience. The earlier shows in the dance academies and other rented halls were meant for mixed company, while gentlemen who wanted to see more sexually charged shows had to wait until after the ladies went home. Some, like Charles March, who saw a Gypsy performance via his guide, Mr. Peickler, spoke rapturously of the dances he had witnessed but balked when the dancers' manager offered to have his dancers demonstrate the fandango again: "The ladies by this time had all retired—and he said it could be now performed without the restriction their presence had imposed upon the dancers. I thanked him for his courtesy, and telling him that I could witness nothing too indelicate for ladies."[63] It

Inventing an Ancient Past for a Modern Form, 1789—1875 51

is obvious that already by the 1850s, what looks like an improvised and special show for a foreigner was elaborately staged for tourists' consumption.

While writers waxed rhapsodically over this staging of the juerga and other various gitano/flamenco performances, they were much less enthusiastic about other staged but less sanitized performances enacted by more realistic looking gitanos in their own barrios and homes. The most explicit example of this differential treatment occurred in Granada, in the Albaicín and in the caves of the Sacromonte neighborhood, where gitanos lived their segregated lives in harrowing poverty. Although writers of the mid to late nineteenth century knew that a visit to see and hear the gitanos perform in their cave homes was a necessary stop on the Córdoba, Seville, and Granada circuit, they often reacted poorly to the performers, conflating the gitanos with the poverty of their surroundings. It was one thing to attend a festive juerga and feel like one was slumming it in the Triana *barrio*; it was another to face the performers in the degrading surroundings of their homes.

> The gypsy quarter is unique in its suggestions of all that is disgusting and repulsive. They have burrowed into the hillside, and cut out holes in the rock. In these "dug-outs" they herd with pigs, chickens, and goats; and from such dens they come forth to prey by all the arts known to their cunning and unscrupulous race upon travellers and strangers in particular, and indiscriminately upon all whom they can deceive and plunder without too serious risk. The tourist who enters their holes might well expect to leave, not "hope," but all articles of value behind.[64]

Most of the writers who did venture to these parts of Granada had little favorable to say about the gitanos living there, and merely repeated the stereotypes they had heard or read before about them—that they were thieves, coarse, devious; every gitana, however, no matter how beautiful and/or how erotically she danced, remained steadfast in her chastity. Even the usually enthusiastic and sanguine Italian Edmondo de Amicis could not hide his disgust upon visiting the Albaicín, describing the gitanos as both animals and insects. There he encountered a "veritable cave of beasts" that "swarmed" with gitanos. They were, he said, "a people multiplying in the bowels of the mountain, poorer, blacker, and more savage than any seen before; another city, unknown to the greater part of Granada, inaccessible to the police, closed to the census-officers, ignorant of every law and of all government... foreign to the city, to Spain, and to modern civilization."[65] That he and others conceived of the population as a faceless swarm hidden from the authorities in the recesses of caves confirmed critics' notions that gitano performers had nothing of value for the civilized world—that, in fact, they threatened the morality of those who watched them. At best, they succeeded in parting a chump from his money.

By the 1890s, during the same period known as the golden age of the café cantante, the gitano dancers in Granada's Sacromonte had their own well-developed, although not state-sanctioned, tourism. But it is the contrast between how spectators viewed the gitano performers in the Sacromonte and those in the commercial establishments of the cafés cantantes in Seville that makes for the most compelling comparison. Although one can find these divergent viewpoints in many travelers' tales, H. C. Chatfield-Taylor expressed the contrast most explicitly. Of the gitano performances in Granada, he relied on ethnic stereotypes of gitanos as shifty crooks: "It is the stock in trade of the guides, and the dances organized there at exorbitant rates, are usually successful in entrapping the unwary traveler." Moreover, he caviled, the "dance he is to witness takes place in a dingy, foul smelling hut, with dirt floor and smoky walls.... Then the imposition begins. The dancing girls are fat, ugly creatures in gaudy cotton gowns, whose vulgarity excels anything seen in the Midway during the World's Fair, and as the performance progresses their movements become more and more objectionable."[66] Given that the Midway Plaisance of Chicago's World Exposition in 1893 had shocked much of the bourgeois world with its introduction of the "Egyptian belly dance" and the "hootchie cootchie," comparing the gitana dancers unfavorably even to that spectacle was truly saying something.[67] And yet move the gitanos and gitanas to Miguel Burrero's café cantante in Seville, and Chatfield-Taylor's tone changes to one of admiration: "But if you want to see lithe, quick movements, you must drop into the 'Burero' and watch the dancing girls as they dance the 'baile flamenco' to the twanging of guitars and the clapping of hands." Describing the view from the gallery, he compared the audience and stage favorably to a painting by the costumbrista painter Mariano Fortuny, with its "strong effects of lights and shadows—such brilliant colors." He remarked on one dancer's eyes that "glisten in the light of lamps," and seemed to be captivated by one dancer who, with "her head thrown back imperiously, her body writhing like a serpent, she dances the dance of the Gitanas, with the sensuous abandon of her race." Chatfield-Taylor did complain that as the night went on, the

Inventing an Ancient Past for a Modern Form, 1789—1875 53

Figure 8. Interior of the Café del Burrero, ca. 1881.
Photo by Emilo Beauchy Cano.
© ICAS-SAHP, Fototeca Municipal de Sevilla. Boele Van Hensbroek Archive. Emilio Beauchy Cano (1847–1928).

other dancers who took the stage were "plain and fat," but there was none of the disgust present that marred his view of the gitanos and gitanas in Granada.[68] For people like Chatfield-Taylor, the Cafe Burrero provided safe, enthralling entertainment under seemingly more sanitary and sanitized conditions than in the Gypsy neighborhoods of Granada. Professionalization of baile and cante flamenco worked to bring in spectators to these new urban spaces in a growing, but still relatively small, mass cultural market. Ironically enough, what people like Chatfield-Taylor imagined to be harmless entertainment in safe spaces were seen by many Spaniards as horrific dens of vice that needed to be eliminated from Spain's urban areas.

But where were these cafés cantantes actually located? Were they all really "landscapes of vice" situated in places with largely working-class populations? In some instances, as in the case of Barcelona, the answer is yes, as we shall see in chapter 3. But in Madrid and Seville, the answer is more complicated. The maps included here show the approximate locations of various cafés cantantes between roughly 1845 and 1939 as verified in print sources. A few cafés cantantes were not included because they were located much farther away from the commercial clusters pictured here. Moreover, the sites of flamenco performances that were clustered in the Gypsy barrio of Triana are not present on the Seville map because sources such as travel narratives and travel guides did not mention them by name nor provide any addresses. Finally, the locations of these sites are approximate because the street numbering changed many times between the nineteenth century and the present, but many of the street names are the same today as they were during the nineteenth century.

Whereas cafés cantantes could be found virtually anywhere in the older, central parts of Madrid and Seville, the pattern that emerged within these cities was quite different. In Madrid, as expected for a capital city, the commercial sites of flamenco were more numerous than elsewhere and the pattern was quite dispersed. They were common in the poor and working-class districts of Lavapiés, Embajadores, and La Latina, particularly along the Calle de Toledo and Calle de Embajadores and near the Gran Vía in the city center, and in Malasaña and Chueca. Still more were located near Sol between Calle Mayor and the Gran Via, all areas also known for their proliferation of prostitutes.[69] But there is a significant cluster around the Plaza de Santa Ana, the heart of this long-standing entertainment district. Of course, entertainment districts were often sites where sexual exchanges also occurred, but these exchanges were more subtly masked by class—aristocratic and bourgeois men might have "kept women," or might have sought out better outfitted courtesans rather than the more obvious street walkers of the Gran Vía.

In Seville during this period, by contrast, approximately two-thirds of the cafés cantantes within the almond-shaped Casco Antiguo were grouped in a linear pattern between the Plaza de San Francisco and the Alameda de Hércules. The Calles Sierpes, Tetuán, Velázquez, Trajano, and Amor de Dios, longtime centers of commerce in the districts of El Centro and Encarnación-Regina, were of particular importance. A few were located in San Bartolomé and in the poor barrio of La Macarena, and two on the Puente de Triana may be seen as riverside portals between different worlds on either side of the Guadalquivir. Neighborhoods close to the Alameda de Hércules housed some clandestine brothels, and there were sanctioned houses of prostitution concentrated on the Calle Atienza in the Encarnación-Regina neighborhood. Again, as in the case of Madrid, in Seville there is a good chance that

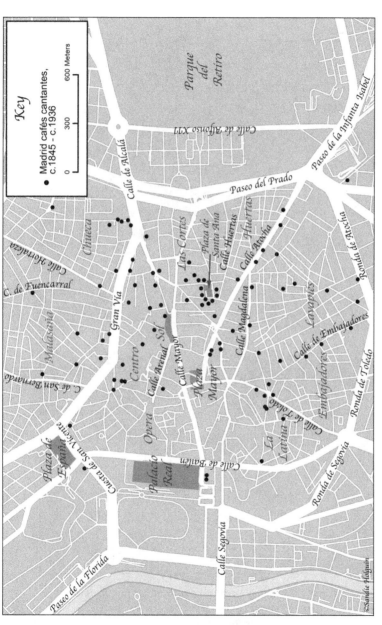

Map 3. Madrid. Locations of cafés cantantes, ca. 1845–1936. Scale is approximate. Café locations are approximate due to street numbering and street name changes.

Mapmaker: Todd Fagin. Map designer: Robert Rundstrom.

Sources: Map data compiled from José Blas Vega, *Los cafés cantantes de Madrid (1846–1936)* (Madrid: Ediciones Guillermo Blázquez, 2006), and Arie C. Sneeuw, *Flamenco en el Madrid del XIX* (Córdoba: Virgilio Márquez, 1989).

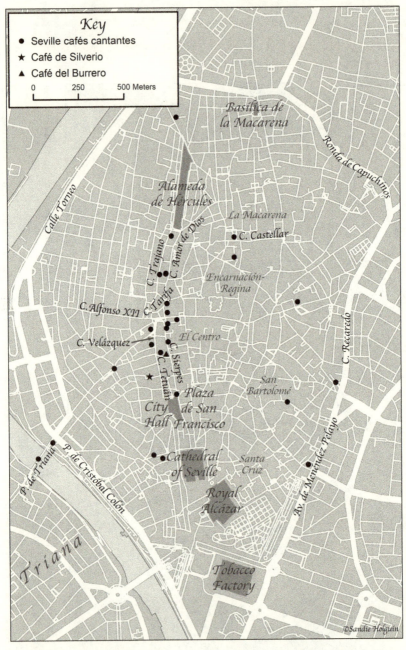

Map 4. Seville. Location of cafés cantantes, ca. 1845–1936. Scale is approximate. Café locations are approximate due to street numbering and street name changes.
Mapmaker: Todd Fagin. Map designer: Robert Rundstrom.
Source: Map data compiled from José Blas Vega, *Los cafés cantantes de Sevilla* (Madrid: Cinterco, 1987).

clandestine prostitution occurred near the sites of the cafés cantantes—or, if one is to believe some newspaper accounts of the time, within the cafés cantantes themselves—but that cannot be confirmed.[70] So, given these important caveats, spectators and social critics would have been more correct in assuming that cafés cantantes in Madrid were located in poor neighborhoods and associated with places of sexual exchange; they would have been less so in making such assumptions about the old center of Seville.

☙

Although it is extremely difficult to calculate the exact number of cafés cantantes that featured solely flamenco performances in this period, it becomes obvious through the antiflamenquista literature of this era that many people throughout Spain felt troubled by this incursion of mass culture.[71] Many of these entertainments had the whiff of vice about them, and as we will see in the next chapters, critics of flamenco (as performed in the cafés cantantes) would elide these forms of mass culture with prostitution, filth, and criminality—all traits associated with the working classes and, in the case of Barcelona, with the "foreign" Spanish.

But it is important to realize that not all of the complaints against flamenco and other forms of mass culture were the demented ravings of puritanical individuals who feared that "someone, somewhere may be happy."[72] This period, which we will explore in the next four chapters, witnessed the bourgeoning of a real culture of erotica and pornography, made possible by the cheap, mass production of erotic novelettes, postcards, and magazines sold in the major cities' local kiosks, and by the proliferation of short, inexpensive shows of all kinds—cabarets, cuplés, zarzuelas—*teatro ínfimo*—that pedaled (mostly) female skin and promises of sexual fulfillment. From around the 1890s until the beginning of the civil war, one could look around Spanish cities and find "a highly eroticized and irreverent Spain" that was carefully erased from public memory after the Spanish Civil War.[73] By the late nineteenth century, the dramatic increase in the number of cafés cantantes featuring flamenco performers in urban soundscapes all over Spain would have the double effect of incurring the wrath of social reformers and scolds and cementing Spain's national identity as an Andalusian one in the minds of foreigners everywhere. Let us now turn to these flamenco censurers.

2

The Perils of Flamenco in Restoration Spain, 1875—1923

Many foreign travelers' accounts of flamenco performers in the nineteenth and early twentieth centuries titillated their readers, inviting the uninitiated to experience the world of the café cantante through male predatory gazes. For spectators, the dances evoked sexual passion, even when the cantes spoke more of poverty and hardship than of sexual conquest. To see the effect of these performances on those who wrote about them, let us return again to Charles March, the American from the previous chapter who refused to witness dances that were "too indelicate for ladies."[1] His account of a woman performing the olé around 1856—when flamenco shows were beginning to appear with greater frequency on the stage and in cafés cantantes, taverns, and dance academies—captures both the attraction these performances held for some and the horror they provoked in others.

> With a sudden spring she approaches each man of her circle, as suddenly rebounds, again to return, surcharging him in her fierce career with that magnetic fluid which escapes like vapor from her excited system; and each man, as he feels this intoxicating fluid penetrate his veins, imbibes the feverish passions of the danseuse, and trembles when she trembles; respires to her

quick breath; groans with her moans; shouts with her cries, and stamps with her rage; in a delirium of transport returns, in tempestuous bravos and hoarse vociferation, the sounds which intoxicate and the glances which inflame him. I have witnessed the effects of opium, and the still more exciting hachich—but nothing of their influence equal to the delirium which seizes the Andalusians on the representation of this passionate dance.[2]

Likening the performance both to a group orgasm and a foray into psychedelic drugs, March unknowingly tapped into the fears that would permeate the writings of Spain's antiflamenquistas—that danger lurked inside for all those who dared enter the tavern or café cantante. For although males of all classes (and some females after the 1920s) entertained themselves by attending flamenco performances in all kinds of places, elites from various sectors of Spanish society aimed to cool flamenco fever.

With the exception of a few artists and intellectuals who would fight to legitimate the forms of flamenco they deemed authentic, most elites with access to a printing press would agitate against what they perceived as its evils. They divide into three main groups: the Catholic Church and its conservative allies, left-leaning intellectuals and politicians, and leaders from revolutionary workers' movements. All aimed their sights on the world of flamenco to critique Spain's political, economic, and cultural ills during the convulsive period between the Restoration and the beginning of the civil war (1875-1936). As we shall see, for the Catholic Church, flamenco was merely an offshoot of all kinds of mass cultural entertainments that led to immodesty, the breakdown of the family, and the weakening of the Patria. For many progressive intellectuals, flamenco, along with its twin scourge, bullfighting, kept Spaniards in a stranglehold of backwardness. They understood flamenco as a narcotic that turned Spaniards into Lotus-eaters, preventing them from solving the nation's numerous ills, including a corrupt political system, a wildly inadequate and unequal educational system, a lack of infrastructure and technological know-how, and vast inequalities of wealth. For working-class reformers and revolutionaries, flamenco and its concomitant lifestyle exploited people's poverty and diverted workers away from becoming full actors in the revolution that would end social, political, and economic inequality once and for all. In reality, all these groups railed against flamenco because it served as a vessel to contain their dissatisfaction with the ideological and structural changes that emerged out of the French and Industrial Revolutions. The resulting social and economic dislocations colored their impressions of flamenco. They viewed flamenco performances and the cultural practices that seemed to engulf them as the inevitable perverted outcome of increased secularization on the one hand, and the resistance to progress and modernization on the other. Certainly these sectors of Spanish society did not focus their disdain solely on cante and baile flamenco performances in the cafés cantantes. Too many other forms of mass culture competed for their ire. And Spain was not unique in its opposition to the growth of mass culture in an industrializing age.[3] But given that flamenco was native to Spain (albeit, to southern Spain), that it remained highly popular among a cross-section of Spanish society, and that foreigners flocked to flamenco performances looking for a "truly Spanish" experience, elites from across the political spectrum did save some of their more blistering critiques for flamenco. They penned many diatribes against this form of entertainment, deeming it a poor representative of what it meant to be Spanish and blaming it for the decline of the Spanish nation. What they were really complaining about, however, was the permeation of modern mass culture into the daily lives of everyday citizens. Critiques of flamenco converged and a variety of groups called for the regulation of cafés cantantes so as to minimize their detrimental effects on the nation, thus illustrating Ferrán Archilés's and Marta García Carrión's idea that nationalization projects during the Restoration led to a form of cultural homogenization. This homogenization arose "from civil society but developed within the framework established by the State."[4] That is, even those groups considered most revolutionary, like the working-classes, were still functioning within a discursive framework of nationalism, despite their dissatisfaction with the politics and policies of the nation-state. In order to understand the context that underlay these various groups' complaints, let us explore the historical circumstances that fed into their anxieties during the Restoration period.

Politics, Society, and Culture during the Restoration, 1875–1923

As we saw in the last chapter, stitching together a liberal state out of the torn fabric of absolutism and Catholicism proved troublesome for the various interested parties. The Revolution of 1868 and the following six years of mayhem reached their apogee during the First Republic (1873-74), when revolving presidents, a civil war with the Carlists, the

Cantonalist Revolts, and a war with Cuba posed numerous existential threats to the Spanish state. The intense disorder over such a small span of time became so entrenched in Spain's collective memory that mothers—it is said—would admonish their children: "Go clean up your room. It looks like a republic in here."[5]

Those were just the political struggles. Spain's economy also endured the birth pangs of liberalism, and the now seemingly predictable pattern of industrialization, urbanization, and social discontent led to the growth and radicalization of the working classes in urban areas and the awakening of revolutionary ideals in rural laborers. The Catholic Church struggled to maintain both power and relevance in a state that had stripped the church of many of its properties and had enacted some legislation to separate church from state. It seemed that calm eluded Spain. In the final month of 1874, however, the military used its time-honored strategy of the pronunciamento (military uprising) to restore public order, and, shortly thereafter, they installed the monarch Alfonso XII on the throne. Therefore, when the monarchy was restored and the Conservative prime minister Antonio Cánovas del Castillo embarked on a plan to stabilize Spain, many of the elites acquiesced.

Cánovas's strategy involved keeping dissident elements like the Carlists and the working classes at bay, weakening the political power of the military, diminishing the power of the church, strengthening the centralized state, and continuing to build, in a very limited fashion, on the liberal framework that had begun in 1812. Key to this program was the *turno pacífico* (peaceful turn), a strategy whereby two political parties led and run by civilian oligarchs, the Conservatives (conservative-liberals) and Liberals (only slightly less conservative than the Conservatives), would alternate power peacefully. When disorder threatened the state, the king would dissolve the Cortes and appoint the leader of the opposing party to rule. Elections were held, but the winners were already picked in advance via the system known as *caciquismo*, a not-so-delicate dance of machine politics and electoral fraud.[6] This political system remained in place—however tenuously—until 1923, when General Miguel Primo de Rivera upended the enterprise with his pronunciamento and subsequent dictatorship.

Cánovas del Castillo created the architecture for the turno pacífico in order to steady a volatile nation, but he also needed to tamp down on dissent. Working in concert, the king, the liberal oligarchy, and the military defeated the Carlists and ended the war in Cuba. The king and Cortes kept the generals, the church, and Catalan nationalists at arm's length, but they were less successful at quieting laborers' discontent, especially after the turn of the century. Superficially, it appeared that the machinery of government worked smoothly, and even if the majority of Spain's people were locked out of the political process, at least one could say that the government functioned as intended. Even the potentially precarious state of affairs created after the king's death in 1885, when María Cristina became queen regent for her soon-to-be-born son, Alfonso, stability prevailed.

While political turmoil swirled around Spain, social and cultural changes rapidly emerged, spurred on by slow and uneven industrial development and increased urbanization. As in much of the industrializing world, rural and industrial laborers sought gainful employment, a living wage, an eight-hour workday, and the legal right to bargain collectively. During the Restoration, at least three political/ideological groups vied for laborers' attention: anarchists, socialists, and republicans. Unlike anarchists, socialists and republicans fought to be included in the political system, but Cánovas's blueprint for governing consciously excluded them. In a similar fashion, the Restoration system kept nascent regional nationalisms at bay, especially Catalan nationalism, at a time when nationalisms surged all over Europe.

The social costs of urbanization and industrialization also fed the anxieties of people from all social classes and across the ideological spectrum. The steady increase of laborers into the major cities and the inability of the church and state to provide for the people who became destitute by the arbitrary forces of industrial capitalism made certain social conditions more visible. Such conditions, like homelessness, petty crime, women working outside the home, prostitution, and the weakening of family ties, troubled authorities, and these circumstances signaled a growing danger for the nation. Instead of blaming the state's changing economic structure for these ills, they castigated people's morals. Like industrializing nations across Europe, Spain had its own share of moral panics. Therefore, the state and religious institutions tried to police sexual practices and other forms of behavior they proclaimed immoderate, and the regulation usually involved women's bodies.[7]

Perhaps the Restoration system could have muddled along smoothly enough, keeping dissent under wraps—although probably not. After 1898 all bets were off. Spain's defeat in the Spanish-American War and the loss of its last colonial vestiges to the United States proved to be extraordinarily damaging to the Spanish collective psyche and shook many people's faith in the Restoration system. Spain's national "disaster" spurred a literature of reform coming from a wide spectrum of people who would become known as the regenerationists.

One can quibble with the term "regenerationists" to categorize a group of people who embodied a whole complex of ideas after Spain's defeat in the Spanish-American War, yet it can still serve as shorthand for outlining the broad concerns that numerous people expressed about Spanish identity in the first few decades of the twentieth century. Spain's ludicrously quick drubbing occasioned a parade of breast beaters willing to proclaim Spain's defects to anyone who would listen. Where did Spain go wrong? How did a once-grand empire tumble so ignominiously? The answers certainly varied, but Spain's social critics suggested at least three paths toward Spain's regeneration that could be applied to almost any perceived problem: look to industrialized, modern western Europe as a model to emulate; shut out all foreign elements and concentrate on distinctly Spanish historical examples and traditions as the road to salvation; capture those qualities that appear beneficial in modern western Europe and synthesize them with Spanish traditions to create a stronger, more vibrant Spain. Catholics and other conservatives tended to gaze backward and drew lessons from Spain's imperial, Catholic past, so perfectly embodied in the reigns of Ferdinand and Isabel, and Phillip II. For conservatives, Spain's push toward increased secularization in the nineteenth century had almost irreparably damaged the Spanish body politic. For these regenerationists, Spain's only hope lay in re-Christianizing the populace, reestablishing the coequal rule of church and state, and maintaining the hierarchies of old. Leftist regenerationists—that is, liberals and republicans outside the oligarchic political structure of the state—called for reformist measures that would help Spain compete in the new industrial economy and demanded the inclusion of more people in the political process. These measures included greater state secularization and centralization; universal and public primary education; a more complex infrastructure; land reform; and scientific and industrial education for elites, including universities that were capable of training these elites to succeed in this new industrial era. Leftist regenerationists sought to root out caciquismo once and for all and implement political reforms that would make the government truly inclusive and representative.[8]

Ever so slowly, the Restoration system began to crumble. The first hints of these fissures after "El desastre" came by way of anarchist violence that terrified elites in Barcelona and southern Spain especially but reverberated throughout the country. In Barcelona the Liceu bombing

(1893), the Corpus Christi bombing (1896), the successful political assassinations that cost the lives of three prime ministers (Cánovas, Canalejas, and Dato), and, most importantly, Tragic Week in 1909, whereby workers sacked and burned numerous monasteries, convents, and churches throughout Barcelona, resulted in the Spanish military and Catalan officials repressing the working classes there. Regional nationalists—the Catalans especially—reacted to working-class violence and the 1898 defeat most viscerally. Having sustained the most economic damage after the loss of Cuba and Puerto Rico, Catalan nationalists, who at the beginning of the century tended to be led by Catalonia's conservative industrial and clerical elites, blamed the incompetent government in Madrid (as well as the military) for the defeat and subsequent damage to its economy. They began to call for greater representation in the Cortes and local governance, and some even clamored for independence from Spain.

But it was after 1917 that the Restoration system began its steady tumble toward final dissolution, aided by pressure for reforms coming from three different groups: the military, Catalan nationalists, and the working classes. The junior army officer corps began agitating to form its own syndicalist group as a means to improve their material circumstances and command greater respect from the civilian population. The Catalan nationalists called for greater autonomy, and the socialists organized a nationwide general strike to improve wages and working conditions. While all these enterprises eventually failed, they signaled a political system in tatters. Matters only got worse. During the so-called Bolshevik Triennium (1918–20), interclass violence overtook industrial cities, culminating in Barcelona's era of *pistolerismo*, whereby gangs of anarchists and industry-paid thugs shot each other on the city's streets. Meanwhile, rural laborers in southern Spain also began to strike and, at times, destroyed property. Finally, the colonial war in the Rif in Morocco turned tragic for Spanish soldiers who were massacred by the thousands at the battle of Annual in 1921. This humiliating defeat contributed to the chaos of the early 1920s. The military felt under attack by those they perceived as domestic enemies—the working classes, political activists excluded from Restoration politics, and Catalan nationalists who appeared to be tearing at the fabric of national unity. The military responded via General Miguel Primo de Rivera, who staged a pronunciamento in Barcelona "to preserve order" and impose the military's version of regenerationism. Primo declared martial law, suspended the constitution, and dissolved all local governments and administrative bodies. Thus ended the carefully orchestrated Restoration system. It is within this context of a Restoration system under strain that we can now talk about the dynamics of flamenquismo and antiflamenquismo, which were shaped by a variety of pressure groups outside the political system.

The Church and Its Conservative Allies Combat Flamenco

Of all the groups troubled by the cultural transformations that accompanied a modern industrializing economy, the Catholic hierarchy found these changes most offensive and difficult to contend with. The entertainments associated with mass culture tended toward the secular and capitulated to the demands of a capitalist economy, seeming to reflect a loosening of moral strictures, especially in cities, where people, rent from their rural communities, formed new but looser bonds in urban areas. These cultural anxieties were not the sole purview of Spain's Church; in fact, the severe discomfort with modern cultural and social practices came straight from the top of the universal Catholic hierarchy, from a series of popes who saw their traditional, religious culture crumbling and reconfiguring into something disturbingly different right before their very eyes and who needed new shock troops to beat back the tide of immorality. The Spanish Church took this call to arms seriously and it labored to turn back the clock to a time when immodesty remained underground and most Spaniards respected the church's authority and its teachings. Despite receiving constitutional protections under the Restoration Constitution and maintaining authority within the Spanish educational system, the Spanish Church was fighting a losing battle to an increasingly secularizing—and in some cases, anticlerical—society.[9]

The church faced serious obstacles, such as declining attendance among the working classes, cosmopolitans in Madrid, Barcelona, and Seville, and the rural poor in Andalusia. Furthermore, republican, socialist, and anarchist activists fomented anticlerical antipathy, especially among the working classes. This confluence of events put the church on the defensive and forced its evangelists to find new ways to renew Spain's spiritual life out of its torpor. To this end they mobilized, establishing their own pressure/interest groups—especially among the youth and women—to concentrate on issues dear to them. Groups associated with Acción Católica (Catholic Action) and its various subsidiaries and the Asociación de Padres de Familia (Association of Heads of

Households) worked against Spain's secularizing tendencies and sought to police the populace's morals by marching in parades and street protests; lobbying politicians; generating newspaper articles, ads, and other forms of written propaganda; preaching sermons; and hosting numerous conferences.[10] As Frances Lannon has noted, "In spite of enormous state support . . . much of [the church's] art and literary culture were crudely propagandistic," and Catholic mobilization "rarely if ever addressed the fundamental problems of poverty and class conflict."[11] Instead, they concentrated on the ways that modern culture corrupted the youth, especially females—the traditional backbone of Catholic piety—and forced them away from Catholic spirituality and into dissolute lives.[12]

Cafés cantantes became one of their major foci of attacks. To them, the performances in these establishments belonged to a series of equally destructive forms of vice, on par with erotic novels, pornographic postcards, taverns, cabarets, movie theaters, dance halls, and contraception. This anxiety about cultural and spiritual decline was not unique to Spain's history. Europeans undergoing rapid industrialization and urbanization sounded the alarm against the rise of mass entertainments and the seemingly degenerate practices that came with them.[13] For the Catholic Church, the cafés cantantes, along with just about any other form of modern entertainment that included music that might be construed as sexually suggestive, represented the absolute decline of Spanish morality and, therefore, the Spanish nation. The spaces of flamenco performances often occupied neighborhoods that one might call seamy, and the entertainment attracted audiences across class lines. The owners, performers, and some of the audiences came from the uncontrollable working classes and, for the church, the establishments themselves reeked of disorder and vice. The spectacle of the café cantante, with its bailaoras and cantaoras, included women of uncertain moral status, clients and performers that often drank too much wine, and drunkenness that often led to brawls, broken furniture, and broken noses. These entertainments hid in dark alleyways, limited themselves to interior spaces, and remained open until the late hours of the night. Understanding that their influence over their parishioners' private lives was threatened and that free time was increasing for all social classes, the church aspired to control this increasingly unsupervised and secular leisure time.[14] Between the Restoration and the civil war, pressure groups emanating from and allying with the Spanish Catholic Church sought first to regulate and then to eliminate cafés cantantes and other offensive dance-like entertainments and tried to sublimate and redirect the spectators' sexual drives into more suitable Christian pursuits. Only then could the Spanish nation be strong once again, or so these groups thought.

Some of the early accounts from Spanish Catholic newspapers emphasized the criminality and sexual vice that seemed to accompany cafés cantantes and other forms of urban mass culture.[15] In 1884, in the "Calamities" column of the radically conservative Carlist newspaper, *El Siglo futuro*, an anonymous reporter excoriated the Valencians who frequented the new nighttime entertainments for disturbing the neighborhood's residents. Speaking of an uptick in crime, the author claimed that many "thugs and braggarts" took their "theater" out in public, that "gambling houses function with scandalous freedom," that prostitutes "walk around the streets too freely," and that the "cafés cantantes, with their love of flamenco, excite the audacity of the chulos."[16] Passersby belonging to "the good classes" often found themselves in the crossfire and, therefore, subject to danger. He claimed that "few nights pass without certain neighborhoods hearing shots, and newspapers report daily about these bloody encounters."[17] Another Catholic newspaper classified cafés cantantes and taverns as "dens of scandal and vice . . . where the most sinister of crimes, robberies, even including conspiracies against public order, are plotted."[18] This harangue against disturbances to "public order" would also turn up frequently in the attacks against the cafés cantantes as a dog whistle for those who feared the revolutionary potential of the working classes.

Catholic social critics harangued against the spread of cafés cantantes and other new popular forms of mass culture and blamed them for creating a new problem: the free mixing of classes. For example, when a young man who had married into an aristocratic family was shot in a café cantante on Hortaleza Street in Madrid, a Catholic journalist blamed the man's death on the series of "lowlifes" he cavorted with.[19] Another writer echoed this sentiment some years later when he complained about the practice of class intermingling that occurred most "especially in cafés cantantes." "Achulado gentlemen go to these places in Lavapiés [a working-class neighborhood in Madrid] and dress up in ways that they shouldn't," the writer proclaimed.[20] He then added a critique that would warm the hearts of those who felt strongly that patriarchal control of families was slipping away: "Youths who in other times would not have been outside their fathers' household, enjoy the liberty . . . to mix with people who constantly exhibit a constant, inconceivable degradation."[21] With the world and its social hierarchy all topsy-turvy and a population's inability to staunch the immoral flow, how could thinking, art, or regeneration occur? The author then made a final leap, linking class-mixing, mass culture, vice, and degeneracy to illiteracy in order to make a point about who should govern Spain: "A society that does not study cannot have culture, and without this, it is absurd to think that just anyone should intervene in the governing of the State, and more absurd still, that one should give weight to that opinion, that will be, at the very least, careless."[22] Thus a critique of the people who sought entertainment in the cafés cantantes became a primer on how to maintain class, patriarchal, and political authority.

Catholic newspapers frequently hurled yet another grievance against these cheap entertainments—namely, that they diverted a person away from both spiritual regeneration and other more serious pursuits. In a longish piece framed as a dialogue between a columnist and "El genio de España" (the spirit or genius of Spain), el genio remarks that he has lain dormant for a long time, but has now arisen because of the disturbances in Cuba. He laments that while Spain faces a grave crisis from the warfare and killing in Cuba and the Philippines, Spaniards on the mainland are spending all their free time entertaining themselves. In the capital especially, Madrileños waste time in entertainments designated for the masses, and in the process they are also "losing their body and soul." El genio catalogs the various entertainments: at least seven theaters, "one circus, two bullfighting rings, three or four pelota courts, cockfighting ... more than one thousand cafés and close to six thousand taverns ... [and the] many cafés that attract [men] with their cante flamenco and lewd dancing, and their dolled-up and provocative waitresses." Just like so many other offended moralists of the era, the genio conflates all of these entertainments and attacks them for promoting sexual immorality. He warns people that these places were merely "antechambers of brothels" that attract people who "worship lubricity." Then, in a rhetorical move typical of the church in this period, the genio supplies the "sole cause" of all this "nauseating trash" that has infected Spain—"the weakness of the faith, the State's paltry support of the Church, and irreligion"—and places the blame on outsiders, on "Masons, Jews, Protestants, rationalists, and spiritualists."[23] With all the corruption and irreligious behavior engulfing him, the genio of Spain offers Spaniards little hope for redemption. Similarly, Teofilo Nitram—speaking of the nameless, but very modern, "Town X," with its electric lights, other modern appurtenances, and entertainments, where "they make up for their lack of artistic talent with shameless, half-naked women"—complains that in contrast to the many diversions he has just listed, there are "only two Churches."[24] Religious critics of these forms of mass culture shared similar rhetorical techniques as progressive critics of flamenco, but their ends differed. The Church often linked the decline in the number of religious institutions to the increase in entertainment establishments, while progressives pointed out these same increases to decry the lack of secular educational institutions necessary to build a solid citizenry.

Because there had been so many complaints lodged from many quarters against cafés cantantes almost from their inception, enemies of these establishments, especially the Church and its conservative allies, began to agitate for legislation to regulate them.[25] Calls for regulation of entertainment establishments were not restricted to Spain, however. A European- and North American-wide phenomenon, spearheaded by leaders of social purity movements that detected vice everywhere in the big city, sought to police the activities of its citizens, especially those of the working classes and women.[26] Spanish authorities fell right into the regulatory mainstream. Thus it came as no surprise that when the Liberal minister of Interior, Segismundo Moret, signed a royal decree on November 28, 1888, curbing the perceived excesses of the cafés cantantes. The law began with a preamble that, with fine understatement, described cafés cantantes as "not always refined." Noting that these places fulfilled the "legal character of a public entertainment," the cafés cantantes' legal status needed to be spelled out. The complaints lodged in the preamble repeated many of the same ones hurled by antiflamenquistas of all stripes: spectators treated the (female) performers too familiarly, swearing and licentious language permeated the interiors, alcohol abuse and the outbreaks of violence that followed such inebriation led to "great scandals" and the need for "frequent intervention by authorities," and residents of these neighborhoods where these cafés cantantes permeated complained of excessive noise and other nuisances. Therefore, the Spanish government ventured to restore the "respect for morality and good manners, generally not observed in these establishments." In order to curb what were deemed immoral practices, the state subjected the cafés cantantes to new rules. These included but were not limited to requiring authorities to establish performance durations and closing times for these venues (but nothing could remain open after midnight); fining owners of said establishments who allow "obscene songs, lascivious dances, or whatever other act contrary to morals";

and suspending performances or closing establishments if an owner received three fines.[27]

While many Catholic writers praised this legislation as a good start, they still believed that the laws were not restrictive enough. One writer for the Catholic newspaper *La Unión Católica* lauded a French criminal tribunal's activities that sought to ban most women from French establishments similar to cafés cantantes and taverns unless they were related to the establishments' owners. He wished for such laws preventing immoral behavior to pass in Spain too in order to "uproot the abuses and crimes against honesty that are committed daily in the so-called cafés cantantes and other similar places."[28]

By 1909 many people wanted legislation with more teeth for cafés cantantes than could be found in the 1888 legislation. They registered their increasing discontent with café cantante owners who brazenly pedaled their performers' sexuality to their mostly male clientele. On March 17 of that year, a royal decree on cafés cantantes was published in the *Gaceta* and reprinted in newspapers across the countries. Most of the decree's stipulations centered around protecting young women's sexuality, hinting that cafés cantantes served as a cover for human trafficking and prostitution.[29] Owners of cafés cantantes and similar establishments could no longer house artists in said places, or anywhere nearby. In fact, the owners were forbidden from having anything to do with the artists' lodging. Performers were prohibited from contacting, talking, or mingling with their audiences during or after a performance, ostensibly to shield them from the customers' prying hands, lips, and other unwanted advances. In a similar vein, the architecture of these places had to be relatively open; in other words, there could not be separate areas where "some members of the audience are hidden from others," just as waitresses could not sit and eat with customers or serve them in rooms or compartments that were separate or isolated from the main establishments. Women had to be over sixteen and able to secure parental permission to work in the cafés cantantes. Once they reached the age of twenty-three, they could work without anybody's permission, but they had to be registered with the Registro de Higiene, the government's list of legally registered prostitutes, and had to supply their addresses for the previous two years, presumably to regulate their sexual hygiene and prevent illegal human trafficking. But forcing young women to register with the Registro de Higiene implied that officials did consider this work a form of prostitution, thus tainting the reputation of working-class women who tried to earn a living.[30] Finally, any owner who broke these rules had to pay increased fines for each offense. A third violation would force the café's closure.[31] By 1913 the *Gaceta* published the Reglamento de Policía de Espectáculos (Rules for the entertainment police), which established even more specific rules for public entertainments, outlining the proper behavior for the establishments' owners, performers, and spectators, and fining owners who allowed shows "contrary to decency" on their stages.[32] These regulations seemed to address some of the critics' concerns, but for some these rules fell far short. Only the "total and absolute suppression of these uncouth centers of corruption" would satisfy them.[33] Still, these shows continued, despite these laws, and it became apparent that flamenquismo offended people from many different quarters, although for different reasons. While very few groups could agree on what Spain's true identity should be or how Spain could regain its place among the European powerhouses, many acknowledged—some vehemently so—that flamenquismo was not the way to achieve Spanish greatness.

Until such time as these cafés cantantes could be completely abolished, Catholic activists used a multipronged approach to channel potential spectators—mostly middle-class and working-class people, and especially working-class women—into more spiritual pursuits. Their methods for re-Christianizing the populace included taking parishioners on excursions to the countryside, establishing Sunday schools for working-class girls, and emphasizing female modesty through various antipornography and anti-immodesty campaigns. The first of these approaches, which began before the 1909 café cantante legislation, entailed taking back Sundays, the traditional day of Christian worship. Industrialization had eroded Sunday church-going for the working classes because the new industrial factory required constant feeding (at least that is what the captains of industry believed), which meant that Sundays were no longer treated as sacred. Working-class activists had agitated for a forty-hour work week that paid at least subsistence wages, and they pressured the government to pass the Ley del descanso dominical (Sunday rest law), which eventually did pass in 1904. The law declared Sunday a work holiday for all except those workers most necessary for the functioning of the state.[34] While this legislation should have pleased church officials and practicing Catholics, it still allowed entertainment establishments like bullfighting rings, taverns, and cafés cantantes to remain open, leaving many religious figures apoplectic. One columnist, F. León, complained that some people were censuring Jesuits for using those free Sundays to take urban workers on excursions into the countryside for spiritual succor. He castigated working-class leaders as hypocrites who had agitated for leisure time under the pretense that it would replenish workers' spiritual lives, when in fact the leaders were encouraging workers to enjoy the pornographic pabulum of cafés and taverns, not the spiritual enrichment of Catholic catechisms.[35] Catholics may have been right to worry. As Jorge Uría contends, the Ley del descanso dominical did in fact open up opportunities for the working classes to participate in the entertainments previously reserved for the middle and upper classes, so much so that, as we shall soon see, working-class leaders would share many of the same concerns about the cafés cantantes and taverns as their Catholic and conservative counterparts.[36]

In the same vein, a priest by the name of Germán R. García advocated creating a number of Sunday schools to keep female workers away from the temptations of the flesh on their one day off. Hoping to end girls' and women's "prostitution of their souls with desire" in places like public dance halls, he envisioned a new social Catholic institution with three major ends: to have a place where workers could congregate safely away from the immoral delights of urban entertainments on Sundays and holidays, to fill laborers' days with moral teachings, and to instruct them in ways that fulfill the mission of the family.[37] Although García writes at the beginning of his essay about the corrupting influences of mass culture on the generic worker, he is much more concerned with the moral fragility of girls and women. For example, he envisioned these Sunday schools focusing on working-class girls over the age of twelve who would ideally receive lessons in proper Christian behavior from married middle-class women. In turn, both groups would benefit. Working-class girls would adopt Christian values and middle-class women would gain satisfaction from doing "useful and interesting work."[38] Once a network of Sunday schools could be successfully planted throughout urban Spain, this symbiotic relationship between middle-class and working-class females would solve two problems at once: girls would be removed from the decadent seductions of mass culture, and the "social problem" of working-class life would ease once these transformed girls started mirroring the modest and religious values of their middle-class teachers.[39] García thought this group of newly educated girls would became the beachhead from which to convert working-class men and bring them back into the Christian fold as well. In essence, García envisioned a world where the idealized conception of separate spheres would be made real: women would retire to the quiet domesticity of the home and church, while men would make their mark—soberly—in the working world.

But Sunday schools alone could not provide a sufficient bulwark against the tsunami of sin that rolled out from urban quarters, and so Catholic pressure groups began forming organizations and campaigns to eliminate these palaces of entertainment entirely and encourage more militant modesty in females. They also formed strategic alliances to stamp out this "pornography" with groups of people with whom they did not ordinarily agree, as we shall see later in this chapter. This does not mean, however, that Catholic pressure groups gave up on their antipornographic, antidance crusades, only that the more lurid displays of sexuality were more-or-less tolerated but exiled to the margins.[40] The international and Spanish Catholic hierarchy began concentrating feverishly to educate youths about the dangers of dancing in general and protect females from the establishments that tried to recruit them to a life of vice. Their efforts focused on promoting modesty in dress and customs, increasing the power of the father, and a redoubling of efforts to shut out modern influences that were carried to Spain by foreigners.

Regenerationists outside of the Political Process

Regenerationists outside the carefully structured Canovite political system shared some qualms with Catholics and other conservatives about the proliferation of cafés cantantes throughout Spain's urban areas. Like their conservative counterparts, regenerationist journalists, essayists, and novelists regarded these places as dens of vice and vectors for spreading national degeneration. But whereas the church's complaints focused more specifically on carnal sin, the loss of one's immortal soul, and the breakdown of social hierarchies, the regenerationists who leaned politically republican and socialist viewed the popularity of flamenco as symbolic of the greater problems facing Spanish politics and society. They fulminated against flamenquismo, and with it their perception that the whole Restoration political system, with its excess of political corruption, was rotting from the inside out. Their slanders against the flamenco world were not merely attacks against the state; they were also calls for modernization, for greater Europeanization, and for an end to cultural self-colonization. Not only did Spaniards have to contend with foreign travel writers who created stereotypes of an Andalusianized Spaniard but, they complained, Spaniards were also complicit in maintaining these stereotypes.[41]

Flamenquismo did not just mean a love of flamenco. It was also linked to a system that contained both the worlds of bullfighting and flamenco and a constellation of traits and lifestyles that were associated with the audiences who attended both spectacles.[42] In fact, some of the antiflamenquistas actually admired "authentic" flamenco performances.[43] They rejected flamenquismo, which for them included love of bullfights, frequent attendance at cafés cantantes, imitation of bullfighters' and flamenco dancers' dress, adoption of "gypsified" slang and gitano dress, love of violence—especially the use of knives—cockiness, hard partying, and, if we are to believe some writers, the love of white slavery and pornography.[44] Although many flamenquistas who dressed the part came from the laboring classes, many señoritos followed suit, culturally appropriating the manners and dress of their social inferiors. More importantly, these flamenquistas mixed in public places, breaking down the strict hierarchy of the social orders. Flamenquismo, rooted in the eighteenth-century phenomenon known as majismo, mutated to incorporate the cultural transformations imposed from both within and without during the late nineteenth and early twentieth centuries.[45] In fact, the greatest critics of flamenquismo shared complaints similar to their intellectual progenitors, the ilustrados, who in the previous century railed against the corroding effects of majismo.

Just as the eighteenth-century aristocracy adopted the cultural trappings of Madrid's majos, including their hypermasculinity and dangerous sexuality in opposition to the petimetre's/afrancesado's effeminacy, the nineteenth- and twentieth-century señoritos continued this trend, only in the posture of flamenquismo. Aristocrats took on the "tough guy" role of the flamenco much to the dismay of fin-de-siècle regenerationists, who desired to make Spain more "modern" and "European." Interestingly enough, this type of aristocratic alliance with Gypsy musicians played out in similar ways in Hungary.[46]

Some writers of the late nineteenth century resented Spaniards' self-colonization, the purposeful exhibition of a kitschy and salacious national identity framed by and for foreign consumption. For example, Gaspar Núñez de Arce, the president of Spain's Association of Artists and Writers, could not prevent the international congress of that association from being taken to a flamenco show at the Teatro de la Alhambra. Penning a letter of antiflamenco fury, he thundered, "It hurts us, and rightly so, that we are often presented as *the land of the castanets*, of majos and roguery; but we do not lose the opportunity... we grab it by the hair in order to present the cante jondo, soleá, and juergas to the foreigners who visit us." Given that Spaniards seemed to have lost no opportunity to showcase flamenco to any visitor, the writer wondered why Spaniards became upset when foreigners believed that the Spanish "passed their time among glasses of sherry, vihuela strummers, dancers, and singers." While acknowledging that most countries had some form of licentious spectacle created for domestic consumption, he said it was only in Spain where residents were "itching to show [foreigners] the conceited or ostentatious display of corruption that always boils in the background of human societies." If foreigners wanted to wallow in the misery and lewdness that these types of shows provided the spectator, he continued, they needed to "go alone or with a trusted friend," because no self-respecting patriot would want to present, let alone invite, somebody to see that face of their nation to others.[47]

Over the course of the late nineteenth century and until at least the beginning of World War I, other illustrious novelists/essayists like Emilia Pardo Bazán, Benito Pérez Galdós, Clarín, Azorín, Miguel de Unamuno, and Pío Baroja would register their disdain for flamenquismo and the political and social world it represented by satirizing it in their works. No one would do more to take the bull by the horns than the quirky, disaffected essayist and novelist Eugenio Noel (pseudonym of Eugenio Muñoz Díaz).[48] Although born of humble beginnings in Madrid and groomed for the seminary—something for which he had no calling, as he made obvious in his later anticlerical writings—he began making a name for himself as a writer after he volunteered for the Moroccan War in 1909 and sent dispatches detailing those wartime experiences to the daily newspaper *España nueva*. When he returned from battle he was jailed for espousing his republican views in print and criticizing Spain's boondoggle of a colonial war.[49] Friends with many writers of the so-called Generation of '98 and a lesser-known member of that group, he perceived himself as carrying on the regenerationist tradition of Joaquín Costa. In this spirit, he launched his antiflamenquismo campaign around 1911, which for him meant lambasting flamenco and bullfighting and the webs of significance that ensnared their aficionados. In his most fertile antiflamenco phase between 1912 and 1917, he wrote six books of essays and founded newspapers, all dedicated to eliminating the scourge of flamenquismo. He founded six antiflamenquista societies and, by his own account, all with no visible effect, but he remained undeterred in his quest to purify Spain of its Andalusian excesses.[50]

For Noel, Andalusia had become Spain's albatross, placed around the country's neck by impertinent foreigners and kept there by Spaniards who lacked the drive to free themselves of its rotting carcass. The stereotype of Spain as Andalusia distilled all that was wrong with Spain: ignorance, backwardness, militarism, corruption, bloodthirstiness, laziness, hypermasculinity and effeminacy—sometimes simultaneously—and a love of all things superficial (namely, bullfighting and flamenco).[51] The pageantry and posturing around both bullfighting and flamenco, he thought, anesthetized the populace from their own suffering and that of the people around them. As long as these two pastimes remained popular and drew in both foreign and domestic crowds, Spain would be unable to solve its very real problems. Get rid of flamenquismo and you get rid of the moribund political and social system too.

Less than the performers of these spectacles, it was the audiences and promoters who attracted most of Noel's ire, and even then, he vented his spleen more about the middle- and upper-class audiences than the poor ones, understanding that entertainment (and the alcohol and sex trade that often went with them) provided a balm for their miserable lives. Who were these people? The chulos, caciques, and señoritos, terms he often used interchangeably. They were men who could gamble, whore, and steal, if they liked, because their social status protected them: "Every cacique in his youth is a señorito chulo . . . when in his desire for pleasure he rapes a minor and the law absolves him, he rubs his hands in glee for having been born in a country where justice is an arm of politics. . . . It is not the señorito chulo who does violence to the law: it is the law that permits these shameful transgressions."[52] Hoping to dispel the idea that the señorito chulo was a stock character in the vast literature on Andalusia, a charming but essentially harmless fictive character, he asserted, "The señorito chulo is not a literary invention, but is a morbid type as abundant in Andalusia as olives," and then he cataloged the señoritos' numerous crimes.[53] His characterization of the señorito chulo verged on the anthropological, and like a cultural anthropologist might, Noel studied the chulo as part of a system—flamenquismo—with other actors like bullfighters, bandits, gitanos, flamenco performers, and laborers playing their roles. In trying to understand the system, he hoped to tear it down. He posited that señoritos chulos "envy the bullfighter and the bandit"—two prominent Andalusian stereotypes—"squandering" their fortunes on the elaborate clothing necessary to carry out the disguise. They "adopt the [bullfighter's and bandit's] manners, soiling them with their supposed aristocratic distinction, resulting many times in an inversion of the sex and always of the brain."[54] According to the language of his day, Noel viewed these men as degenerates (who reflected a degenerate and feminized Spain too), and try as they might to emulate the machismo of the bandit and bullfighter (and, by extension, the flamenco dancer), the señorito chulos weakened and feminized themselves through slavish imitation of the lower orders, just as aristocrats had aped the customs and dress of the previous century's majos.

While the señorito chulo admired and adopted the system of flamenquismo, he also did all he could to maintain it, according to Noel, and that is at the heart of his whole critique of Spain. Both systems, flamenquismo *and* Restoration Spain, required the various classes of society to participate willingly in them and avoid the hard work of reforming the nation. So, as Noel explained, an absentee landlord of large estates in Andalusia (a *latifundo*) did not really have to worry about a peasant uprising because he could channel their anger and defeat them with a bullfighter. Andalusians' and other poor Spaniards' idolization of bullfighting "has nothing to do with bravery or elegance, or skill, but rather the dazzling vision of a poor son of your womb, yesterday an urchin, dust, with nothing other than his will, and only by his force arises rapidly to tyrannize over the cacique as an equal, marrying his daughters[,] ... buying his estates, in whose threshold he slept when he endured the apprenticeship of the capes, conquering him, little by little, on his own land, man to man."[55] The gendered language of his critique and the social commentary about class envy is obvious: Mother Andalusia cannot support her poor son. But through the dint of struggle and hard work, he can rise above the all-powerful cacique and take the cacique's daughters and land, the booty of war and conquest, and now mother and son can regain their pride.[56] One class of cacique replaces another, and the bloodthirsty madness of Spain's "National celebration" continues on without end, leaving Spain no room for reflection on how to change.[57]

Like the bullfight, flamenco shows also yoked the señorito and the poor laborer together in pain and sorrow. When listening to Andalusian *coplas* (songs), they "drink from the same glass of wine filled with tears." Much to Noel's dismay, half of the songs "speak of adultery, fornication, [and] infidelity," but aficionados, he argues, proclaim the lyrics as passionate. Noel strips the veneer off, saying that "passion" is the word used to "cloak" the day-to-day misery of most of its inhabitants. "Pain," he insists, "is the natural daughter of impotence," and what better way to deflect pain than by fast living, alcohol, and other lubricious behaviors?[58] Some forms of flamenco song, like the cante jondo, had gained respect among some literary critics and artists, but for Noel, the themes expressed in such songs—dark nights of the soul, prison prayers, and curses—had escaped from the open markets and "pigsties" of the country and emerged victorious in the opera houses, theaters, and taverns of the big cities like Madrid, Seville, and Barcelona.

His mockery and disgust knew no bounds. *Bulerías*, the most festive and what he called the most representative of the flamenco palos, needed one to have certain skills: "To sing them you need a special quality in your voice, an exceptional mucousy membrane in the throat and an artistic taste so grotesquely crazy and absurd that reflect . . . a voluntary imbecility, and tones produced or accompanied by mysterious cramps."[59] All of the operatic emotions one heard and viewed in these performances were merely simulacra of real emotions. Flamenco music had lost its "spontaneous popular purposes" and was instead reconfigured and pulled away into "penitentiaries, taverns and brothels," where one could hear among the rot, sham imitations of "enchantments, remembrances, and the sad profundities of life."[60] We observe with Noel a critical thread that runs through many antiflamenquista writings: a vision of both regional and national culture that emerges organically and authentically from the rural populace. Once these forms of culture move to urban settings, they lose their purity and are perverted by touching the soil of commercial establishments. Although fundamentally anticlerical, Noel shared with Catholic conservatives a visceral disgust with the sites of mass culture.

Finally, Noel agitated against flamenco and bullfighting because, like other regenerationists, he deemed these entertainments as distractions from the ossified and inept politics of Restoration Spain. To pacify a restive population, the government substituted bread and circuses (well, really just circuses) for any concrete and desperately needed reform of the Spanish nation.[61] Noel lamented the state of Spanish politics, going so far as to publish a picture of a bull ring and call it "the true Spanish Parliament," whereby the people "pay much more attention to the election of bullfighters than to the election of their deputies."[62] He castigated newspapers for wasting column space on the latest bullfight and other mindless entertainments, juxtaposing that information with the knowledge that Madrid had "thirty neighborhoods without a school and fifteen with only one."⁶³ Spain needed intellectuals, hard workers, and an educated populace, not a bunch of dissolute drunks, dancers, and singers. Instead, when faced with any number of disasters, Spaniards did nothing tangible. Rather, they expressed their sorrow and frustration with a guitar, "and with delicious ease... [they] convert a kick into an accompaniment of soleares."⁶⁴ Despite his constant grousing about the evils of flamenquismo, he complained *because* he had faith that Spain could change. If Spaniards could examine themselves more critically, with cruelty even, then they could "define [them]selves as a nation with character."⁶⁵

Working-Class Antiflamenquismo

Antiflamenquistas like Noel probably shared more in common with socialist and anarchist antiflamenquistas than they did with Catholic and conservative ones, most likely because liberal regenerationists and revolutionary socialists and anarchists shared a faith in the Enlightenment tradition, and with it, the promise that education, science, and rationality would lead to human progress. As it turns out, socialist and anarchist intellectuals—those who founded, edited, and wrote in socialist and anarchist periodicals—were just as fervently opposed to the spread of flamenquismo in Spain as their less-than-revolutionary counterparts. Like the Catholic establishment and other conservatives, working-class leaders found the salacious atmosphere in many of the cafés cantantes offensive, but their moral objections to flamenquismo tended to stem from the conditions workers had to endure in order to survive under industrial capitalism. Working-class women danced and prostituted themselves in cafés cantantes and taverns because this labor provided them with an income their families needed; men plied themselves with alcohol and stooped to depths of soulless pleasure because the industrial system had taken away their humanity. Or so such leaders thought. They shared with people such as Noel the belief that official Spain kept the populace entertained in order to prevent greater social and economic changes.

Although the working classes had been deprived of representation in the Restoration system, we do know that government officials began to address the Social Question in the late nineteenth century, as worker agitation and violence intensified and the deplorable working and living conditions under which urban and rural workers labored become impossible to ignore.⁶⁶ In order to understand the depth and kinds of problems the working classes faced, the minister of the Interior, Segismundo Moret, headed the Commission of Social Reform (La Comisión de Reformas Sociales), a commission that worked nationwide to interview workers about their day-to-day lives at work, home, and leisure. This first commission existed from 1883 to 1903, and its canvassers asked its citizens standardized questions about the shelter they lived in, the food they ate, and the number of hours they worked, among other topics.[67] For our purposes here, the most important questions they asked were those that dealt with intellectual, artistic, moral, and religious culture.[68] Querying the people about the kinds of opportunities they had to participate in these aforementioned cultural activities, the interviewers discovered that laborers had little time or money to engage in educational or spiritual pursuits. To their surprise, many of the canvassers concluded that the working classes as a whole were not criminal or lazy; instead, vices like drinking and prostitution were prominent because these activities provided a brief respite from the bleak conditions of workers' lives. Yet in many of the regions that the government bureaucrats explored, many laborers could not afford even these vices.[69]

When the various reports came back to Madrid, those that did focus on workers' access to profligate entertainments blamed these problems on the inaccessibility to more cultivated activities. Conditions in the Andalusian mining town of Linares may have been among the worst. For example, according to reports, the town had no *ateneos* (cultural centers) and no choral societies (important sites of respectable working-class sociability, as we shall see in the next chapter). In fact, there was very little entertainment except for bullfights, casinos, and cafés cantantes, which "were always full." Workers preferred the gitana dances on the stage, and then once the show was over, "taking turns dancing with them" as the gitanas "moved from table to table." This all led to much talking, drinking, and breaking of things, and so often finished "with shots and stabbings inside and out of these establishments." Such activities, they thought, contributed to the decline of social mores not only because of the kinds of performances that were carried out in these places but because of the influence that came from the "continuous and free conversation with each other, with the women in these establishments and with the other unsavory characters."[70] In Vizcaya the commission blamed dances as exercising "the most pernicious influence" on the [male] workers' "domestic and social conditions," because the performances occurred at night, the "type of women who frequent[ed] them" were often "unregistered prostitutes," and "drunkenness and gluttony" often accompanied the dances. Again, high-status entertainments like the theater were scarce and unavailable for workers because of the steep price of tickets. Reformers argued that workers, therefore, gravitated to more illicit pursuits.[71]

Although these reports came from government bureaucrats tied to the Restoration system, their conclusions about the role of the café cantante in the lives of laborers did not differ so greatly from those of leading socialist and anarchist activists. Anarchist writers remarked less frequently about such things than socialists did, however. They did sometimes comment on the evils of alcohol and flamenquismo, but anarchists' literary magazines tended to use their pages to expose workers to the newest ideas in science, literature, and theories of revolution, believing that the ideas of elite culture could and should be made accessible to workers.[72] Socialists, however, showed no compunction about spilling ink over the problems of flamenquismo. Like so many of their contemporaries, socialist elites viewed participants in the world of flamenquismo as careening down the road to perdition.

The editorial board of *El socialista*, the main newspaper of the Socialist Party (PSOE) and the Socialist Labor Union (UGT), probably felt just as strongly as conservative Catholics about the deleterious effects of flamenquismo on the populace. Some of their frustration was evident in the way they lobbied for changes to the Ley del descanso dominical, announced by royal decree on March 3, 1904. As mentioned earlier, workers had fought for years to have a law like this passed, one that required most stores and industries to remain closed on Sundays in order to give workers one day of rest per week. Passed by the Cortes under the Conservative Antonio Maura, the law's reaches did not extend to bullfighting rings, taverns, and other entertainment spots like the cafés cantantes.

Just four months after the law passed, *El socialista* began publishing a series of articles—eighteen in nine months—most of them titled "Against Bullfights and Taverns."[73] The first one, from July 22, 1904, spoke of how representatives of some twenty thousand workers from Huelva and Madrid had sent numerous messages to the Institute of Social Reform, "applauding them" for passing a resolution to shut down bullfights and taverns in compliance with the Ley del descanso dominical. The column reiterated this demand, despite the antagonism coming from bullfight promoters and tavern owners. The writer called for the adoption of this measure as a means to diminish the crime rate, to improve the culture and health of workers, and to keep workers from a life of vice. The article ended by daring the government to support the resolution: "We'll see if the government supports it, or if they choose to please those who care nothing for the culture and health of the Spanish people."[74] Many of the articles that followed continued this same drumbeat, listing the worker representatives from various regions of Spain who wanted to close down the bullfights, taverns, and other entertainments on Sundays in order to save workers from alcohol and the sins that issued from its consumption. They tried shame as well, arguing that the great sums of money that could have been spent alleviating the plight of the poor and infirm were spent on spectacles that appealed most to the "uncultured" and "illiterate" of the population, reiterating Noel's idea that flamenquismo was but a form of bread and circuses perpetuated by the ruling classes to keep the working classes entertained and unconscious of their exploitation.[75]

Although not an official publication of the Socialist Party, *Vida socialista* (Socialist life), the short-lived weekly illustrated magazine founded by socialist militants Tomás Álvarez Agulo and Juan Almela Meliá, the stepson of PSOE founder Pablo Iglesias, took on flamenquismo and flamenco with excoriating prose.[76] The best example of this comes from an article titled "Crónica: El espectáculo nacional," by the intellectual José Alcina Navarrete. The title already plays with a couple of ideas. Usually the phrase *espectáculo nacional* refers to bullfighting, but in this case it was commenting on performances in a café cantante. Secondly, *espectáculo* can mean either entertainment or spectacle. Here it means both, as we shall see. The article begins by describing a place "where not a table is empty" and there is an anxious buzz in the room as people await eagerly for some kind of performance. In the crowd are "military men carefully collecting the tips of the frock coats for fear of dirtying them; obese gentlemen reclined lazily on soft couches; the occasional drunkard directing strange harangues at his fellow orgiasts; a group of gaudy men with hats full of dents . . . and a few vendors of kisses, huddled in dark shawls." This "mass of people . . . went to the café cantante late at night to entertain themselves by listening to the [cante jondo] and to tremble with excitement at the naked flesh of cupletistas."[77] He continues to evoke the excitement in the room until the curtain lifts and the audience becomes silent. One young dancer comes on the stage, performs, and then leaves. No one is moved. A second performer comes on, "a skinny woman cynically showing her nakedness and singing in a tuneless voice, which put the eardrums in complete anarchy." She is booed loudly off the stage, unable to finish her routine, and "the multitude, satisfied with its triumph, bursts into uproarious laughter." Next, a young man with a guitar and a "scrawny girl" appear and she sings a beautiful, gentle song that leaves the crowd in awe for a moment—a bit of art has passed through this crowd "drunk with lust." Finally, a "statuesque woman" with "voluptuously thick hips" and "naked white breasts wrapped in a flowered shawl" appears on the stage, moving to its center and eyes the crowd "cheekily." She begins the "carnal dance," "incessantly striking the floor with her feet," and driving the crowd crazy as they murmur all kinds of exclamations of approval, and she continues, seemingly intoxicated by their loud olés: "The audience shook, flush with desire. Waves of lust floated in the atmosphere."[78]

Why did Alcina Navarrete just re-create an evening at a café cantante? Was he hoping that his readers, in their excitement, would put down their newspapers and run to the nearest café cantante? One might expect this reaction at first glance. But no, he meant to shame his readers. What he described here was Spain's "espectáculo nacional." Those who attended this show were the same ones who went to bullfights, and they carried on in the same way at both places. Like the final lance of the sword that the torero plunges into the bull's back, Alcina Navarrete strikes the deathblow to his compatriots who amuse themselves at flamenco shows: "The Spanish race was represented among the audience who filled the café cantante. And the cowardly people, unable to roar about the brutalities of their tyrants, quickly get excited before the carnal dance of [this] lewd and shameless affair."[79] Once again, this socialist, like other progressive regenerationists, argued that Spaniards were being distracted to death. As long as they filled stadiums and concert halls, the powerful could be free to exploit the poor and illiterate.

Another short-lived weekly, socialist youth journal from the period, *Acción socialista*, commented on the backward state of Spanish political and economic affairs by echoing the trope of the *tipos populares* (popular types) that permeated the literary landscape of the nineteenth century and that enjoyed a brief renaissance in the twentieth. Part costumbrismo, part folklore, and part generalized kitsch, the tipos populares—images and descriptions of stock characters and peasants clothed in regional dress—became a quick if often erroneous way to sum up various parts of Spanish national character. The most famous of this kind of work was the two-volume *Los españoles pintados por sí mismos* (Spaniards drawn by themselves). The editor, Ignacio Boix, commissioned some of the best illustrators and writers of the day to create a compilation of sketches of the looks, habits, attitudes, and dress of the numerous types one could find in Spain, such as the bullfighter, the barber, or the boarding-house owner. Sometimes the portrayals were satirical, and other times not. Nevertheless, its great success spurred a veritable industry.[80] Late in the nineteenth century, popular illustrated magazines like *La ilustración española y americana* featured drawings and photographs of tipos populares for a mass audience. Even José Ortega y Gasset's first intellectual magazine, *España*, reprised its own very distilled version of *Los españoles pintados por sí mismos* for twentieth-century audiences, so the idiom of the tipos populares was available to a wide audience in Spain.

The editors of *Acción socialista* took the tipos populares and ran with them. Between August 29, 1914, and December 5, 1914, the magazine published ten full-page illustrations under the title "La fauna nacional" (National wildlife). The illustrated series prior to this one was "The International, illustrated," a series of laminates depicting workers' struggles around the world. In the August 22 issue, the editors announced that they were going to publish "La fauna nacional" next because they wanted to illustrate "other many characters that, sadly, are most representative of our country."[81] The title itself is relatively offensive in Spanish. Not only are the tipos populares associated with animals found running wild in the landscape, but the word "fauna" is also a colloquial expression for undesirable types and misfits.[82] And then, of course, by following a series depicting the heroic wonders of the working classes of the world with one that lambasted the "degenerate" stock characters of contemporary Spain, the pointed criticism is obvious. In chronological order, the collection included: the Inquistor, the Cacique, the Guapo, His Excellence the Picador, the Bailaora, the Flamenco, the Beggar, the Bandit, the Procuress, and the Gitana. For our purposes here, we shall limit ourselves to the Bailora, the Flamenco, and the Gitana.

Obviously, subtlety eludes the image of the Bailaora (figure 9), given that what focuses people's attention first is the naked breast and the hips that take center stage as well as the sense of movement in the image. We know that the dancer is a flamenco dancer by her dress, her shoes, her castanets, and, if one looks carefully, by the smoke outlining the shape of a flamingo head just above the castanet on her left arm.[83] The other dancers sitting down are obscured by her dress, but we see the male accompanists blowing smoke and staring at her legs with lust and perhaps reservoirs of anger about to burst forth. There is nothing in the image that evokes delight, neither the faces of the guitar players nor that of the dancer. Instead, the scene evokes the joylessness of a strip club.

In the second image of the Flamenco (figure 10), we see a man who wraps his large belly in garish clothing. He has a guitar in one hand, a

Figure 9. *La Bailaora*, part of the "National Wildlife" series illustrated by Tito for *Acción socialista*, 1914.
Illustrator: Tito.
Image courtesy of the newspaper archives of the Biblioteca Nacional de España. The image is owned by the Biblioteca Nacional de España.

Figure 10. *El Flamenco*, part of the "National Wildlife" series illustrated by Tito for *Acción socialista*, 1914.
Illustrator: Tito.
Image courtesy of the newspaper archives of the Biblioteca Nacional de España. The image is owned by the Biblioteca Nacional de España.

Figure 11. *La Gitana*, part of the "National Wildlife" series illustrated by Tito for *Acción socialista*, 1914.
Illustrator: Tito.
Image courtesy of the newspaper archives of the Biblioteca Nacional de España. The image is owned by the Biblioteca Nacional de España.

flamingo in the other, and the smoke he blows out of his cigarette takes the form of a bailaora. His hat looks to be the one sported by men from Jerez, a cradle of flamenco music. He represents over-the-top masculinity, as evidenced by the cigar and his too-tight pants that leave nothing to the imagination. By placing a plethora of bullrings in the background, the illustrator links this image to the system of flamenquismo that we have become familiar with in this era. For the illustrator Tito, the Flamenco is loud and boorish, yet another miserable animal in the zoo of Spanish misfits.

The final image, *La Gitana* (figure 11), counters many of the romanticized versions of Spanish Gypsies found in nineteenth-century travel narratives. Here the woman embodies all that the antiflamenquistas abhor, a bent crone of a woman with a tambourine and fortune-telling cards in her hand and money pinned to her ragged dress, the owl behind her in mockery. In the background a picturesque Andalusian campesino with a painfully thin burro is tending to the fields, but he is obscured by her sullen stare. Taken together, all three images bespeak a degenerate national identity rooted in the past, located in Andalusia, and dull and world-weary. Spaniards, these young socialists are saying, have become caricatures of themselves, doomed to extinction once the revolution occurs.

Cafés Cantantes as Pornography

One conclusion we can draw from exploring these various groups' antipathy toward flamenco and flamenquismo is that they shared certain anxieties about the effects of an industrializing and urbanizing world on the culture and morals of Spaniards. Cheap mass entertainments like those found in the cafés cantantes, they thought, blurred gender and class boundaries, weakened the father's authority, left females prey to sexual exploitation, and weakened the nation. Despite these groups' fundamental disagreements over how society should be organized, they could (and did) form alliances when necessary. For example, they assembled coalitions to stop pornography from corrupting the people of Spain.

Although today we might not readily categorize flamenco performances as pornographic, many antiflamenquistas did. Performances in cafés cantantes were subsumed under the umbrella of "theatrical" and "pornographic" entertainments so that when critics complained about the spread of pornography they were including cafés cantantes as part of the wider world of morally dangerous outlets, a world that included films, nude postcards, erotic novels, cabarets, and more. In other words, antiflamenquismo got folded into a much larger conversation about pornography that continued unabated through the Restoration, civil war, and immediate post–civil war era.[84]

Although complaints about the overwhelming influx of pornography into Spain began as early as the late nineteenth century, calls to stop its public display became louder in 1909 when the pope summoned Catholics to organize "morality leagues" to regulate the film industry, public entertainments, and other "shows of repugnant obscenity."[85] While this discussion based in Rome focused mostly on the film industry, Catholics in Spain followed Rome's command, forming a number of morality and antipornography leagues with wide-ranging goals. In Santander, for example, the Asociación de Señoras organized themselves against all things they deemed immoral, especially theatrical performances and films. Viewing themselves not as morality police but as a "morality army," they sought to ally with other groups across Spain and "work in the combat trenches against a pseudo-art that poisons the soul, destroys homes and ruins the Patria, all the while lining the pockets of their miserable exploiters." Here their arguments sound much like those one would hear from working-class activists. But the tenor changes when they link the "pornography" of cafés cantantes and other entertainments to what they perceive to be the constellation of ills besetting Spain, namely, the "atheistic state" and secular schools: "All are one and the same. Their end, at least, is the same. And their origin, too!"[86] Sexual exploitation *and* the destruction of the nation emerged from the loss of God in the home and in the schools, not from capitalist exploitation, as the working classes might contend. In an effort to combat the poisonous influence of highly sexualized forms of mass culture permeating modern European cities, Catholic activist groups like the Asociación de Señoras began organizing and assembling throughout Spain. Two years later, however, other people not necessarily associated with Catholic pressure groups would also spearhead attacks against cafés cantantes and other forms of entertainment deemed pornographic.

By April–May 1911, a diverse group of men—writers, academics, and laborers who would eventually spearhead the Liga Contra la Pornografía (Anti-pornography League)—met in Madrid's Academia de Jurisprudencia to discuss how to approach ending, or at least curbing, the easy flow of pornography into Spain, and how to use the laws already in existence to achieve these ends.[87] Headed by the sociologist

Adolfo A. Buylla, the group welcomed members of any political persuasion who were willing to fight the growth of pornography.[88] The nascent league's discussion of pornography took some very interesting turns, linking the free-flow of licentious materials to the weakening and disintegration of the mind, body, family, and, therefore, state. The group used other modern, industrialized European nations as cautionary tales for Spain. According to these "experts," France's depopulation problem guaranteed that there were insufficient numbers of men to fill necessary military positions; therefore, soldiers had to "enlist and re-enlist," straining an already weakened military and posing a crisis for France. In France's case, pornography clearly caused a once-powerful nation's decline. Not so for Germany. The emperor, in order to save his empire and stop "contagion" from infiltrating its borders, vaccinated against pornography by "adopting a medical-social plan," which included adding sports and physical fitness in the schools, something that, the antipornographers argued, the Spanish would also be wise to include in their curricula.[89]

The summary of the group's conference proceedings was more explicit about the consequences of pornography and the requirements for curbing its spread in Spain. According to this summary, which cites Wilhelm Van Brabant's work on the psychology of vice in children as corroboration, people's search for pleasure in mass cultural entertainments and lewd literature led to sexual infirmities. Visiting café cantantes and reading erotic novels, it was thought, would lead men to visit houses of prostitution, contract all manner of sexually transmitted diseases, and then pass these illnesses on to their innocent wives and children. Thus all things that were true and good—"patriotic feelings, religious faith, love of family, political ideals, honorable sexual love, respect for women"—withered away, perhaps forever, when a person embraced these kinds of vices.[90] To resist this onslaught of pornography and its decidedly detrimental effects on honorable Spaniards, the group posited two courses of action: prevention and repression. Their crusade included creating a Madrid-based league against pornography and "obscene shows" like those performed in cafés cantantes, with the hope of eventually forming a national antipornography league; making sure that officials would enforce the antipornography laws already on the books; fining establishments that offended "morals and public decency"; managing or working with the people who "through carelessness or neglect cooperate," even indirectly, with the propagators of pornography, such as bookstore owners or "owners of places that house cafés cantantes or indecent films"; "denouncing in the press" these aforementioned collaborators of pornography if they did not cease and desist in allying themselves with the flesh peddling industries; organizing meetings to oppose pornography; protesting scandalous dancing; and working across national borders with other countries trying to achieve similar ends.[91]

Eventually this Madrid-based group did get their wish for a national organization. On December 11, 1911, the Liga Contra la Pornografía) formed to counteract the "epidemic" and "plague" of pornography that had entered Spain, mostly, they claimed, through foreign channels.[92] Still headed by Adolfo A. Buylla, the league spelled out the goals they had outlined in the April meeting. They called on all people, "whatever their religious orientation, political affiliation or social class" in the spirit of "the eternal ideals of beauty, truth, and goodness," to provide the "material and moral support" and eliminate the decadent filth from the kiosks, bookstores, and entertainments that lined the city streets.[93]

Despite these various groups' dogged efforts to eliminate the stain of public entertainments like flamenco in the cafés cantantes, morality groups failed to curb audiences' appetites. These entertainments continued to grow apace, especially during and immediately following World War I, when performers from war-torn countries landed in neutral Spain to practice their arts. Foreign performers from as far away as Argentina and the United States introduced novel dances and musical forms such as the tango, the fox-trot, and jazz, which created even more anxiety about sexuality, class- and race-mixing, and the threat of revolution. Spaniards also created hybrid entertainments that incorporated aspects of the cabaret with more traditional elements of Spanish urban culture like flamenco, the most notable being the *cuplé*, a variety show that modernized two traditional Spanish forms, the theater and popular music.[94] Masses of people voted with their feet and ignored the moralist's proscriptions, filling the cafés and cabarets in Spain's urban centers. That is, until the civil war changed things.

After the chaotic years of the first two-thirds of the nineteenth century, when Spanish elites worked to implement a liberal state amid civil wars and colonial disturbances, Cánovas's Restoration system brought relative stability to Spain's political system, at least for its first thirty years. In doing so, it created the space and stability for sustained if uneven industrial and urban development. More people migrated to these cities in search of better fortune, and as happened in other European cities of the same period, new forms of entertainment cropped up to meet the needs of these growing audiences. In Spain, flamenco became the entertainment that maintained cross-class appeal, and because people of different classes and sexes inhabited the spaces of the cafés cantantes so openly and partook freely of intoxicating substances, Spanish regenerationists of many political persuasions went on the offensive. These antiflamenquistas worried about Spain's future in the aftermath of colonial defeat and in its perceived decline relative to other European powers. Moreover, the inability of the state to ameliorate the conditions of rural and urban laborers, burdened as it was by the effects of caciquismo, allowed social tensions to increase within Spain, further distressing these regenerationists. Flamenquismo became the target of their myriad complaints. Social and political turmoil would only increase during the final years of the Restoration and through the Spanish Civil War, and other groups within Spain and abroad would latch onto flamenquismo as a source of comfort or distress, depending on which identity one wanted to adopt. Whether we look at the perspectives of regional nationalists in Catalonia and Andalusia on the one hand, or foreign spectators on the other, flamenco would become further imprinted into Spain's identity over the following decades.

Part II

FLAMENCO ON THE REGIONAL AND INTERNATIONAL STAGE

The preceding chapters considered flamenco from the point of view of those elites who thought of themselves as guardians of Spanish national identity but who found themselves dismayed by the growth of flamenco as a popular spectacle for the masses. The next three chapters telescope *in* to the level of the region and *out* to the international stage to demonstrate the dynamic process by which flamenco connoted Spain in the public imagination. Chapters 3 and 4 examine the ways nationalists in Catalonia and Andalusia exploited a constellation of conflicting perceptions about flamenco to make their particular claims for regional nationalism and regionalism in the early twentieth century until the eve of the Spanish Civil War. Chapter 5 then moves to the international arena, namely to the World Expositions held between 1851 and 1937. Here I examine how the Spanish nation presented itself to the world, how the host nations displayed Spain to the world when they were in charge of entertainment, how foreigners and Spaniards viewed and digested these representations, and how these representations were then fed back to the Spanish populace by illustrious Andalusian composers and writers. In the end, these expositions became another key piece in the puzzle that was flamenco and Spanish identity.

In order to let the reader enjoy the narrative flow of chapters 3 and 4 without having to witness the theoretical foundations undergirding them, I am situating my general discussion of regional nationalism and regionalism in this short section.

While studies of nationalism and national identity have dominated much of the historiography of modern Europe since the 1980s, scholars have more recently begun to examine the ways that regional nationalism and regionalisms emerged to compete with centralizing nationalisms from about 1890 to 1939.[1] It is easy to fall into the trap of eliding the terms "regionalism" and "regional nationalism," because they are porous concepts. Regionalism can be seen as a neutral term, as Eric Storm does, to define a transnational movement in this period "that promoted the study, construction and reinforcement of regional identity," which emerged out of the latter stages of the centralizing nationalisms of the same period.[2] Xosé Manoel Núñez Seixas argues, however, that regionalism was "a very diffuse concept before 1914," and that by 1911 it "meant everything that questioned the 'excesses' of the state." In the end, he cannot even find a definition of region that does not begin to slip away from one's fingers before one can grasp it.[3] "Political regionalism" is defined by some scholars as the desire by a region's populace to obtain political autonomy or secede from the larger nation-state.[4] In contrast, regions that promote their cultural uniqueness while still maintaining their political ties to the larger nation-state were seen as fostering "cultural regionalism" or "regionalized nationalism."[5] Those sorts of regions tended to accentuate what they perceived to be the uniqueness of their regional folklore, music, dance, and architecture without feeling the need to differentiate themselves politically from the nation-state to which the region belonged. But, as Núñez Seixas points out, "regionalists do not claim their defined territory to be the subject of collective rights," and yet "historical reality contains several cases of greater complexity."[6] This complexity would have resonance in Spain.

The regions that I am focusing on in the next two chapters muddy the waters completely. Nationalism, regionalism / cultural regionalism, and regional nationalism / political regionalism weave in and out of the fabric of Spain between the Restoration and the civil war. For generally when historians of Spain focus on Catalonia, they speak of its nationalization as moving from cultural regionalism to political regionalism. That is, the Catalans became the most successful regionalists to promote their case for political autonomy at the beginning of the twentieth century, but they began their process of nationalization through cultural regionalism—the dissemination of Catalan culture in the nineteenth century. They created standardized dictionaries, taught Catalan language classes, established Catalan cultural centers, and promoted Catalan songs and dances. Eventually, Catalan nationalists began to call for political rights to pave the way for autonomy and possibly independence. This process adhered to the stages of nationalization Miroslav Hroch outlined in his foundational work on nationalism.[7] Catalan nationalists viewed themselves as different and separate from Spanish "foreigners." In contrast, by the late nineteenth century, Andalusia had appeared to many dismayed Spaniards as already too Spanish by half, and so to conceive of Andalusian regional nationalism in similar terms as Catalan regional nationalism fails. And yet, around the time of World War I, we can talk about a political regionalism in Andalusia—that is, a call for regional autonomy—that was still very much rooted in the unifying type of cultural regionalism, a "unity in diversity," to use a phrase beloved by the Spanish Falange in later years, that was meant to broaden Spain's "national heritage and provid[e] it with local roots."[8]

In the end, I have chosen to adopt the terms "regional nationalism" to talk about political aspirations for autonomy or independence and "cultural regionalism" to elucidate the ways in which regions defined their own cultural practices and cultural production in relation to the nation-state known as Spain. And more importantly, I will demonstrate how regional nationalists and cultural nationalists in both Catalonia and Andalusia would exploit public perceptions of flamenco for their own regionalist purposes.

3

Flamenco and Catalan Nationalism in Barcelona, 1900—1936

Around 1900 city councilor Guillermo López chronicled the many sins and hazards of life particular to Barcelona in the aptly titled *Barcelona sucia* (Filthy Barcelona). Besides the usual complaints lodged historically by urban critics of industrialized cities—that streets spewed with sewage, that drunks and prostitutes slunk unabashedly down dark alleyways—López saved his ire for one foe in particular. For him the proliferation of cafés cantantes, "the shame and scorn of modern cities," were the primary reason fewer people married, leading to "depopulation" and "the growth of tuberculosis, cancerous people, syphilitics and alcoholics." These "dens of vice" shocked López to his very core. Seemingly upstanding citizens participated in the life of the cafés cantantes, and this dishonored them. Their attendance led to a kind of "civil death" because they were "blinded by this flamenquismo that is so exotic in [their] beloved Catalan land."[1]

As we have already seen in the previous chapter, he was certainly not alone in his reactions. The cafés cantantes and flamenco, the music most often performed in them, aggravated social critics throughout Spain and in Barcelona in particular. No one was more visibly perturbed by these developments than the Catalan nationalists who worked aggressively to cultivate both a Catalan cultural and regional nationalism into Catalans' consciousness. For antiflamenquistas of all stripes, flamenco represented a backward Spain, too readily willing to fall into vice and laziness and too out of step with the modernizing, industrializing tendencies of western Europe. For Catalan antiflamenquistas in particular, flamenco was all this and more: it embodied the decaying, corrupt, and vice-ridden qualities of the incompetent and overpowerful centralizing state. Promoting the Catalan *sardana* dance and local choral societies (orfeóns and cants corals) became ways to inoculate against the flamenco virus.

The debates over musical forms, musical spaces, and their relation to national identity accelerated in late nineteenth- and early twentieth-century Barcelona. Perhaps that is to be expected, given that Catalan nationalism had increased in its intensity after the turbulence following the Revolution of 1868 and "El Desastre" of 1898. The meaning of these debates, however, has scarcely been explored by historians. Scholars have written some about the popularity of the café cantante in Barcelona, and others have written about the sardana and Catalan choral groups as important avenues for creating a Catalan national identity in opposition to a Castilian one, but little has been said about the interplay between the two identities and what they tell us about social relations and anxieties about the modern city.[2] Add to the mix foreign accounts of popular culture in Barcelona, and webs of identity become even more tangled.

This chapter, then, explores these complex webs of identity by situating flamenco, antiflamenquismo, and Catalan nationalism in Barcelona during the three decades leading up to the civil war. Catalan nationalists began to contest the kinds of music and dance that they heard and saw in public and in commercial spaces, and flamenco topped their list of musical forms that needed to be eradicated. They tried to solidify their identity in an increasingly polarized Spain by attacking cafés cantantes and promoting the sardana and Catalan choral societies. In doing so, they posited an identity that rejected the industrial system that Catalans themselves created and effaced the problems that came with it—namely, immigration, poverty, and worker unrest.[3] The problems Catalans blamed on flamenco were really the afflictions of modernity. But not wishing to cast aspersions on Barcelona's titans of industry, they aimed their displeasure at the "foreign" flamencos and their habitats, the cafés cantantes, and they did their best to keep these people and their entertainments cordoned off into specific, undesirable spaces of the city. In the end, however, the Catalan nationalists' attempts to render flamenco performers and their performances obsolete failed because foreigners and profit-seeking Catalans and Andalusians kept stoking the flames of an exoticized and dangerous Barcelona. Moreover, flamenco became an entrenched part of the Barcelona land- and soundscape, aided by the fact that spectators could now view flamenco performances in "safer" areas of Barcelona, such as at middle-class-oriented cafés cantantes and at the 1929 World Exposition. By the end of the 1920s, Barcelona could boast of cultivating an indigenous flamenco tradition that thrived side by side with new regional nationalist expressions of song and dance.

A Brief History of Modern Barcelona

With its mix of industrial grit, labor revolts that often led to violence, and splendid boulevards in the newer parts of the city, with its terrible beauty of *modernisme* architecture on the one hand, and shantytown slums on the other, *fin de siglo* Barcelona rivaled other world-class cities of the industrial era.[4] Sometimes called "the Manchester of the Mediterranean," or "the Paris of the South," Barcelona was the most industrial, most modern, and, some thought, the most "European" city in Spain. In fact, many travel writers at the turn of the century complained that Barcelona resembled other modern European cities too well and seemed to enjoy other Spanish cities that hewed more closely to the Spain of their imaginations.[5] Barcelona's modernity, as everywhere else, took a great social toll on its population.

When industrialization accelerated in the first quarter of the nineteenth century, Barcelona's population skyrocketed within the confines of a walled medieval city. Its population density was among the greatest in Europe—around 859 people per hectare—and there was nowhere to expand until after the walls were destroyed in 1854.[6] Industrialists set up factories in the area known historically as "El Raval," bureaucratically as "District V," and later, more colorfully, as "El Barrio Chino" (Chinatown).[7] The boundaries for El Raval were said to be between the Ramblas to the Calle Pelayo, the Ronda de San Antonio and Ronda de San Pablo, and the Paralelo and the Port (map 5). The working classes clustered in El Raval, as well as in the neighboring areas of Pueblo Seco and Sants.[8] After 1846 factory construction was forbidden in El Raval, and when the walls were destroyed in 1854, it ceased to be the industrial center of the city.

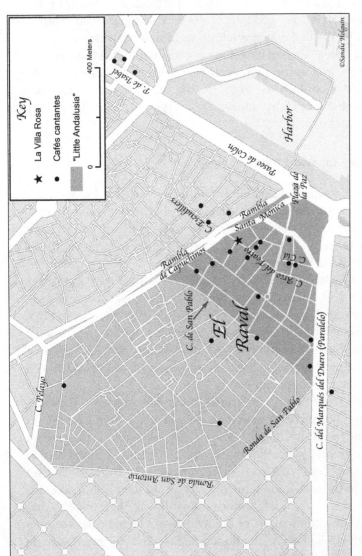

Map 5. Barcelona. Locations of cafés cantantes in the Raval, ca. 1875–1936. Scale is approximate. Café locations are approximate due to street numbering and name changes. Because toponyms transformed a few times in the period under study, they reflect the names and language used with greatest frequency between 1875 and 1936.
Mapmaker: Todd Fagin. Map designer: Robert Rundstrom.
Source: Map data compiled from José Blas Vega, "Recorrido por la Barcelona de los cafés cantantes y colmaos flamencos," *La Caña: Revista de flamenco* 25 (1999): 5–20, and Francisco Hidalgo Gómez, *Como en pocos lugares: Noticias del flamenco en Barcelona* (Barcelona: Carena, 2000).

Following the demolition of the walls in 1854, Barcelona underwent its own form of urban renewal on a scale with that of Paris under Baron Haussmann. Ildefons Cerdà designed the Eixample, a potentially infinite grid of wide city blocks fanning out north from the Plaza de Catalunya and broken up by thoroughfares such as the (currently named) Passeig de Gràcia and the Diagonal. Although Cerdà had designed his Eixample as a means to ameliorate the overcrowding, poor sanitation, and urban poverty of the medieval city by creating a series of blocks that furnished Barcelona with multiclass housing, the area became the dwelling place of "official Barcelona," the segregating line between bourgeoisie and working class. Barcelona's best-dressed set strolled the Passeig de Gràcia, while the working classes inhabited the medieval sections of the city. And thus, like Paris, London, and Vienna, Barcelona became more visibly segregated after the urban expansion projects of the late nineteenth century.[9]

Even after industry moved out of El Raval, the place remained a working-class neighborhood—even as the working classes expanded their presence in neighboring areas. Barcelona's population more than doubled between 1887 and 1920, from 272,000 to 710,000, and surpassed the million mark after 1930.[10] The majority of people who had migrated to Barcelona in the early and mid-nineteenth century had arrived from the Catalan countryside, but by 1900, nearly 27 percent of Barcelona's population was non-Catalan, and by the 1920s, the steady migration of people outside Catalonia swelled the non-Catalan ranks to around 35 percent.[11] Thus from the turn of the century onward, at least one-quarter of the urban population was distinctly Castilian, and the majority of the Castilian immigrants came from Murcia and Andalusia, the heart of flamenco country. It was this stream of non-Catalan immigrants into the working-class neighborhoods that heightened the Catalan nationalists' anxiety about the changing character of their city.

And its character had changed, as all cities do when rapid industrialization and urbanization take hold. Immigrants carried with them their cultural traditions from the countryside and other urban areas in Spain. They brought their language (Castilian) and their music, and their numbers added noise to the growing din of the city. To come back to our social critic Guillermo López, he grumbled how "the acoustic nerve of Barcelona suffers constantly from the treacherous aggression of these insolent howlers ... who invade all areas of the city causing grave harm to the tranquility and health of the neighborhood."[12] If it were only noise the immigrants brought with them, then perhaps social critics would have little to complain about. But with industrialization and urbanization came the usual problems: squalid living conditions for the poor and working classes, crime, prostitution, and, most important, violence, emanating from and directed toward the working classes.

While European cities outside of Spain contended with class conflict and, inevitably, violence, between 1870 and 1936, Barcelona had the reputation of being one of the most revolutionary cities in Europe—no doubt fueled by the numerous bombings and exchanges of gunfire between anarchists and the pistoleros hired by industrialists. Barcelona's other well-known nicknames, "La Rosa del Fuego" (the Rose of Fire) or "the City of Bombs," attest to that violence.[13] Unlike other European countries such as Germany, France, and even Britain, that had begun ever-so-slowly to incorporate the working classes into their political systems, Spain, as we witnessed in the previous chapter, had prevented most of its population from engaging in the political process through Antonio Cánovas's Restoration system. This meant that not only were the working classes excluded from this system, but so were the majority of Catalan nationalists. But Catalan nationalists, at least the more powerful and wealthier ones, had one distinct advantage: if they quieted their calls for Catalan autonomy or independence, they could rely on the Spanish military to quell revolutionary strikes in Barcelona. Therefore, Catalan nationalists struck an uneasy bargain with the central government in order to keep commerce running as smoothly as possible under tumultuous circumstances. The threat and real use of anarchist violence, always on or just below the surface of Barcelona's day-to-day life, brought great anxiety to official Barcelona, an anxiety that, at its worst, resulted in violent repression against the working classes and, at its best, manifested itself in diatribes against the vice-ridden lives of those in El Raval and those who partook of the life in cafés cantantes.

Entertainment Zones in Barcelona, 1900–1936

With the influx of workers into the Raval in the nineteenth century came places for workers to socialize and enjoy various forms of recreation. As early as the 1840s, numerous cafés, taverns, and other forms of entertainment clustered around Hospital, San Pablo, Unión, and Conde de Asalto (currently Nou de la Rambla) Streets.[14] The construction boom preceding the 1888 Exposition also contributed to the growing number of entertainment venues in the area, and the cafés cantantes became the most popular form of entertainment, heralding "the beginning of the golden age flamenco in Catalonia."[15] The spaces for entertainment expanded around 1900 into the region that would be known as the Paralelo, Barcelona's major entertainment artery,[16] bounded by the streets of Pueblo Seco, reaching to Montjuïc, to the walls of the Port, through the streets of El Raval to the Ronda de San Antonio, and reaching the end near the palaces of the Exposition in front of Cruz Cubierta.[17] According to Pere Gabriel, "It was between 1903 and 1914 when the street's true configuration emerged as an important urban element for the moral and cultural unification of the new Barcelona."[18]

Known by some as the Montmartre of Barcelona, the Paralelo was abuzz with entertainment at all hours of the day.[19] Sailors on leave, workers on break, and even the middle classes looking for adventure took in the various forms of entertainment available. From 1900 to 1936, it became the place to go to experience the cafés cantantes, zarzuelas, cabarets, and jazz performances, or to practice one's Charleston, cakewalk, tango—or whatever the latest dance craze—in the newly built dance halls. One working-class man remembers the Paralelo in its heyday of the 1920s.

> Going up the right side of the street there was ... the Frontón Nuevo, later there were the Casablanca and Arnau cabarets, later Tropezón, a dance hall of women where the [male] customers bought five tickets for a peseta to dance with the women they wanted. Down farther you could find the Teatro Español, the Café Victoria, the Café Rosales, the cabaret Concierto de Sevilla. ... Down farther was the Café Chicago, the Teatro Talía and farther up the movie theater Mistral. On the left side of the Paralelo was the Bataclán, the Teatro Apolo, inside the Atracciones Apolo and Frontón Apolo, and later the Teatro Nuevo, the café Barcelona and the Barcelona movie house with attractions and variety shows. Higher up we found the movie house Victoria, Molino, the Teatro Cómico, the Condal movie house, which had gardens in the back to go for refreshments, and finally, the América movie house.[20]

Although this region of Barcelona had at its core a distinctly working-class character, the Paralelo became a place where all classes could congregate. One could spot captains of industry, writers, scoundrels, and new immigrants mingling in these cultural spaces. Its character, however, retained the expression of the popular classes and reflected a new kind of urban culture. According to Pere Gabriel, the Paralelo's new urban culture had at least two distinct audiences, those who "combined the existence of a public attracted by the bohemian lifestyle and its fast-paced entertainment," and the other public, the majority, "who united flamenco, wine, and drink with the theater and the desire for sociability."[21]

The forms of entertainment changed over the decades leading up to the civil war, but the Paralelo remained *the place* to visit for locals and tourists alike. Jazz may have replaced the tango or the Charleston, but flamenco remained one of the few steady entertainments over the first three decades of the twentieth century. The location of the cafés cantantes were more limited, however, to the Barrio Chino section of the Paralelo.

The Flamenco Zone, or Little Andalusia

By the time of Barcelona's 1888 World's Exposition, the Barrio Chino began to have an Andalusian flavor. Cafés cantantes sprung up throughout this working-class district. The sites of flamenco were pretty well circumscribed by three streets in the rough shape of a triangle: starting at the Plaza de la Paz, and going up north to the Rambla de Santa Mónica and the Rambla de Capuchinos until San Pablo Street; then heading west on San Pablo to the Marqués del Duero Street (also known as the Paralelo); then south on the Paralelo and back to the Plaza de la Paz.[22] And within the greater triangle, Cid Street formed the heart of the Barrio Chino (see map 5).[23] Within this relatively small space, flamenco flourished and the barrio began to be seen as a "little Andalusia." Some made the claim that there were more flamenco shows, and more authentic ones at that, in this section of Barcelona than there were in the neighborhoods of El Perchel in Málaga, Triana in Seville, or the Sacromonte caves of Granada, although deciding what is or was "authentic" is always problematic.[24]

Despite being a local source of flamenco, the Barrio Chino, also called *los bajos fondos* (the underworld) was best known for being Barcelona's center of vice.[25] Prostitution and drug-dealing flourished here, especially on El Cid Street and across the Ramblas on Escudillers Street. *Cafés camareras*, where men could purchase drinks, food, and waitresses for assignations, were plentiful by 1900; and *meublées*, places where unmarried couples could rent rooms for illicit purposes, cropped up around dance halls and cabarets. Those who preferred entertainments that broke social norms even further could attend La Criolla or El Sacristán, clubs and cabarets for homosexuals and transvestites and the people who wanted to gawk at them.[26] Some establishments, like the Manco, were actually two places owned by the same person; one was a café cantante, and the other, a house of prostitution, and people were sometimes warned not to confuse the two entertainments.[27] In fact, social critics such as Francisco Madrid were both fascinated and appalled by the numerous juxtapositions of vice and virtue in los bajos fondos: "Here were united in an absurd and unique way the brothel with the dairy for the working classes[;] . . . the Cal Manco and the Casa del Pueblo Radical; the Santa Cruz Hospital and the Mina tavern; the Atarazana Barracks and the small second-hand book fair. . . . The good and the bad; civilization and *'hurdismo.'"*[28] And because of the proximity and sometimes interchangeability of musical entertainment with vice, citizens of Barcelona viewed the cafés cantantes as the "meeting point for prostitutes, Gypsies and bullfighters of little importance," among other figures of the underworld.[29] Given the atmosphere of the Barrio Chino, with its illicit underworld inhabited by a working-class population perceived to be among the most violent in the industrial world, it is no wonder that official Barcelona in general, and Catalan nationalists in particular, conflated the vices, corruption, and supposed decline of Barcelona with the cafés cantantes. Soon they would take steps to battle this scourge.

Of course, their complaints were no different from those of the Catholics, conservatives, progressive regenerationists, and working-class leaders that we encountered in the previous chapter, but they expressed their outrage in regional nationalist ways. What was it that made Catalan nationalists so despise the café cantante and flamenco? Certainly, there were plenty of attacks against the zarzuela, the most popular theatrical genre in late nineteenth-century Spain, including Barcelona. No one can deny that complaints against the zarzuela such as this one, "There is nothing so opposed to our manner of being and feeling, nothing as contrary to the Catalan spirit, as these coarse and vulgar little works that arrive here in bulk to be offered to the Barcelona public," were any different from the ones lodged against flamenco in the region.[30] But the condemnation against the zarzuela really only came after "El Desastre" of 1898. Regenerationists across Spain seized on the zarzuela's nationalistic lyrics as a symptom of Spain's degeneration and ultimate defeat at the hands of the United States. Therefore, it does not take a great leap of imagination to realize that Catalan nationalists would condemn the zarzuela's nationalistic lyrics and plots to distance themselves from the state that had failed everybody in 1898.[31] One could even understand the Catalan nationalists' complaints about the penetration of the zarzuela into the soundscape of Barcelona as a protest against the cultural imperialism of the capital, but the vilification of flamenco performances and the cafés cantantes that housed them seemed more rooted in social anxiety. Regional nationalists' apprehension focused instead on the moral makeup of the owners, performers, and audiences. As mentioned earlier, in Barcelona, flamenco performances occupied the same spaces as the transgressive Barrio Chino, and unlike the zarzuela, flamenco attracted aristocratic, bourgeois, and popular audiences. So morality, population, and genre became inextricably intertwined.

Nationality and class status also came into play. For one thing, most of Barcelona's cafés cantantes had originally been founded by Andalusians, who were already denigrated for their outsider status. All of these characteristics of the café cantante appeared to many Catalan nationalists as incompatible with the Catalan character and needed to be extirpated. According to noted Catalan nationalist Torras i Bages, the Castilian songs that arrived in Barcelona were "the Castilians' waste material," and although he complained about the numerous Castilian genres that had invaded Catalonia, he nonetheless saved his greatest disdain for flamenco: "But still it is more important to raise the cry against the performances, the songs and dances that commonly belong to the flamenco genre. There is nothing more antithetical than [flamenco] to the Catalan character, nor can one find another thing that is more destructive to the strictness and steadfastness of our race."[32] The painter Santiago de Rusiñol seemed to have conflicting views about flamenco and flamenquismo. On the one hand, he worried about the Catalans who were growing up hearing what he believed to be artificial and foreign songs sung by "bands of foreign street musicians, by minstrels . . . with the hoarse voice of the night, by degraded flamencos, who come to sing the odor of wine in place of the scent of the fig leaf, turning the green and beautiful vineyard into a tavern."[33] On the other hand, he took an interest in Andalusian music, especially when it was recast as something authentic, like the flamenco family of songs known as cante jondo.[34] What seemed to matter to him was place. What he perceived as a more authentic form of flamenco like the cante jondo reflected the world of Andalusia and, appropriately, it belonged there. But according to him and other like-minded people, the cante jondo resembled nothing like the musical performances one would find in a tavern or café cantante. Instead what we can see from Rusiñol's lament above is the fear that this invasive flamenco species overran and corrupted the natural beauty of Catalonia's primal land, thus destroying the very essence of Catalan identity.

Catalan Cultural Nationalism: La Sardana and El Orfeo

As studies of nationalism have demonstrated, a major component of creating or reviving nationalism requires an investment of time in cultural projects—that is, the promotion of hymns, songs, literature, and dances and the creation or revival of distinct languages that are supposed to capture a national spirit or a cultural genius. This is what is known in the field as "invented traditions."[35] In the case of Catalonia, Catalan nationalists gained prominence in the late nineteenth and early twentieth centuries. While all kinds of groups in Spain found themselves dissatisfied with Madrid's incompetence in this period, the Catalans' displeasure eventually evolved into a political movement, embodied in the Lliga Regionalista, that included calls for autonomy within or even independence from the rest of Spain. But undergirding the Catalan political nationalism was a cultural one. The influx of Spaniards from the south to work in Catalan factories and the spread of entertainment from Madrid and Andalusia in the forms of zarzuela and flamenco made a number of Catalan elites fearful that Catalan culture was disappearing under the weight of Castilian culture.[36] Josep Torras i Bages decried that all one heard in Catalonia were Castilian songs, "on the streets, in the schools, in the homes. You don't hear anything else, and all the beautiful and honest Catalan songs are forgotten."[37] Worse yet, the influx of flamenco could eventually kill Catalonia: "For all peoples, the public and social decline of morals that bring about the degeneration and death of a country have come from outside; the way that the outsider has introduced the seed of decadence: the loss of indigenous customs and the adoption of foreign ones signal the end of a race."[38] The Catalan nationalist writer and musician Josep Armengou used the common eugenicist and gendered argument blaming women for demographic decline. Calling Catalan women selfish and "self-destructive," he castigated them for being "dedicated to keeping their waistlines" while "immigrant women walk with pride and show their generous and throbbing wombs as infallible auguries of widespread victory."[39] Our social hygienist Guillermo López decried the 74 cafés cantantes (out of 244 cafés around town) for mortally wounding "family life, intellectual progress and the health of Barcelona." López, like Armengou and so many other antiflamenquistas, linked the sexually charged atmosphere of the cafés cantantes to the decline of the family in numerous ways: the husband who attended them strayed from the family fold and infected himself and his wife with sexually transmitted diseases; young men, disobeying their fathers, refused to marry because they could find their sexual outlets elsewhere; and young daughters, too, disobeying the patriarch, participated in this impure modern life, threatening their ability to find an honorable husband. The nation, built on the family unit, could not be strong if the family base was already rotten. Moreover, just as Eugenio Noel had done for Madrid, López provided statistics comparing the number of cafés cantantes with educational institutions, and in this juxtaposition, the educational institutions were found wanting.[40] Catalan national regeneration was therefore in order.

To combat Castilian cultural hegemony, Catalan elites, mostly from Barcelona and its surrounding areas, worked to solidify Catalans' ties to a homeland that was distinctly rural and conservative, and they did so by creating numerous cultural projects such as the Jocs Florals, the Excursionist Movement, and the Institute for Catalan Studies. Many of these projects focused on recovering the Catalan language, but some concentrated their efforts on song and dance. Music sung in orfeóns and in the cants corals, along with sardana dancing, played a more important role in disseminating the proper patriotic feelings toward the Catalan homeland. Certainly, many have written about the seminal role played by these community-oriented musical forms, but I want to draw a relationship between the dominance of the cafés cantantes in Barcelona with the sudden increase of orfeóns and sardana groups from 1900 on.[41]

As we already know, certain Catalan nationalists had been protesting the towering presences of the cafés cantantes in the Barcelona sound- and landscape. The only way to fight off this foreign intrusion was to solidify Catalans' commitment to traditional (however illusory that word might be) Catalan songs and dances that emanated from the countryside. But these songs and dances were disappearing, as they had been in much of industrializing Europe, and Catalan nationalists did what folklorists and composers all over Europe had begun to do in the nineteenth century: they traveled to remote areas to collect songs and dances from peasants, those who still—it was believed—retained vestiges of an authentic folk culture.[42] After choosing the songs assumed to represent an essential Catalan identity, Catalan nationalists would write down and standardize these songs, which they would then take to Catalonia's more urbanized, Castilianized, and modern cities to shore up what they perceived to be a dying identity. Urban dwellers in places like Barcelona could then repossess and reaffirm their Catalan identity, and transform themselves, however metaphorically, into embodiments of the values of rural Catalonia, values that included seriousness, hard work, simple tastes, and purity of body and spirit. The process for dispersing the songs to the Catalan masses came first through the orfeóns and cants corals and later through the sardana.[43]

The orfeón movement—that is, the establishment of choirs—as scholar Joan-Lluís Marfany claims, "was not a derivation of nationalism but was, on the contrary, a fundamental element in the genesis of Catalan nationalism and, above all, inseparable from its birth."[44] Some scholars also saw in the choirs the added benefit of taming the workers' revolutionary fervor.[45] The birth of orfeóns, as with most Catalan cultural projects, began in Barcelona. As early as 1850, the musical director and composer Josep Anselm Clavé formed a choral society for workers named La Fraternidad, which became La Sociedad Euterpa by 1857. By 1867 about four thousand workers belonged to this association of some eighty-five choral societies.[46] Although the Sociedad Euterpa was not always explicitly nationalist, the movement would become increasingly more so in the following decades. More unambiguously Catalan nationalist organizations emerged soon after with the Orfeó Català (1891), followed by the Societat Coral Catalunya Nova (1895) and the Institució Catalana de Música (1896), and in them, choirs sang liturgical music from the Renaissance and traditional Catalan songs. Over the next few years, orfeóns sprang up all over Barcelona and Catalonia. The importance of these institutions is best expressed by the fact that a special "palace" was constructed for the Orfeó Català in Barcelona. The gorgeous building, the Palau de la Música Catalana (the Catalan Music Palace), was designed by the architect of high Catalan modernisme Lluís Domènech i Montaner, thus linking together Catalan art and craftsmanship with a music that would also announce a Catalan identity to the world through song. As the number of these institutions grew, many Catalan nationalist social gatherings and meetings began with cants corals, and numerous organizations founded their own choruses, including sporting groups and Catalan workers' ateneos.[47] The songs themselves included a standard repertoire, usually a rendition of what would become the Catalan national anthem, "Els segadors," commemorating the Catalan peasants' Reapers War against Philip IV, and a sprinkling of reworked traditional folk songs that referenced the Catalan manse, the countryside, the heartiness of the peasant. The songs linked history and landscape, evoking what Anthony Smith calls "poetic spaces" in order to "integrate the homeland into a romantic drama of the progress of the nation."[48] Nowhere is this more noticeable than in Santiago Rusiñol's paean to Catalan folk songs: "Those of us who were born in Catalonia sing in Catalan. We sing and keep in mind that Greece's integrity and the French Revolution were made by a single song."[49]

Catalan composers and dramatists collaborated in creating a proliferation of Catalan-language versions of both popular Spanish as well as original Catalan-language zarzuelas. They also translated foreign (non-Castilian) chorale productions into Catalan. The Teatre Líric Català, founded in 1900, hosted its first performance in 1901 and specialized in Catalan-language productions only, written mostly by the most famous purveyors of modernisme—Serafí Pitarra, Ángel Guimerá, Santiago Rusiñol, Adriá Gual, and Apel-les Mestres—and whose themes centered on such things as pastoralism and the glorious Catalan past.[50] All these creations became important as a way to link language to narrative, to replace Spanish popular tunes with Catalan ones, to make Catalans feel the language in their bones. One of the founders of the Orfeó Catalá, Jascinto E. Tort y Daniel, understood the links among language, song, and human intimacy, and, by extension, nationalism, and the need to develop autochthonous Catalan music when he said, "By means of some song of the earth the Catalan individual ... discovers one's own personality even in the most vulgar acts of one's life."[51] But even outside observers made this link between choral singing and national unity. Describing a "fiesta of children and flowers" and contrasting that with the evils of the cafés cantantes, one writer explains, "This village has become accustomed to meeting in order to sing, and it knows well that it is in this way, feeling the heart nearby, that one understands and best unifies the collective ideal."[52]

At around the same time that the orfeóns popped up around Barcelona, the sardana began to be integrated into the Catalan nationalists' program. The sardana, a dance that is now celebrated as the national dance of Catalonia, certainly belongs to that body of cultural projects known as invented traditions. It is a recent dance that dates back to around 1850; in fact, its rise was contemporaneous with the professionalization of flamenco in cafés cantantes. As late as the turn of the twentieth century, the sardana was hardly popular. In fact, the esteemed poet Jacinto Verdaguer had seen it performed only once in 1884, and before 1900 most Barcelonans had not seen the sardana performed, except maybe in a bastardized version in the opera *Garín*, written by the decidedly non-Catalan Tomás Bretón.[53] But slowly, around 1902, Catalan nationalists began to embrace the sardana as their own, and by 1906 they hailed it as the national dance of Catalonia.[54]

So, what did the sardana and the cants corals offer to Catalan nationalists that cafés cantantes did not? For one thing, the sardana was a communal dance—some would even call it democratic—whereby the dancers formed a ring and passersby could join or leave the circle as desired. Unlike flamenco, which had to be hidden away in the dark recesses of the city, sardana dancers performed outdoors, in public squares, and without the need for special costumes. Those who joined the sardana circle displayed their desire to be part of a group that celebrated its Catalan identity. As the poet Joan Maragall said, "All of my patria fits in that ring." Similarly, a critic of the sardana wrote, "the Catalan nationalists' patriotism goes all the way down to their feet."[55] Although distinctly modern, the manner in which people danced the sardana appeared premodern, and thus masked the industrial nature of much of Catalonia, especially of Barcelona. In contrast, the café cantante represented commercialized leisure at its best, performed for a paying audience. The sardana was "spontaneous" and open to all Catalans, without money trading hands. The modern flamenco performance traded in the bodies of sexualized women and men, whereas the sardana, because it was perceived as a folk dance, radiated purity and innocence, and women of all classes could participate in the dance without fear of scandal. Like the sardana, the orfeóns and cants corals provided the means to display one's patriotism. The choirs sang in groups (as choirs do) and they chose patriotic songs that most often reinforced their Catalan identity, especially their ties to rural Catalonia. Whereas flamenco singers might wail about their personal pain—a lover's rejection, a life of poverty, a spate in jail—Catalans sang about fresh air, harvests, mountains, the vine. The themes embraced by these regional performers served antithetical functions. Flamenco singers and dancers performed cathartically by expressing the pain of urban life through song and dance; Catalan choir singers and sardana dancers conveyed joy in the values of rural Catalonia, thus negating the urban life that Catalans themselves had created. One form was entertainment, the other, spiritual succor.

But Catalan nationalists had their work cut out for them. While the sardana dancers may have had patriotism at their feet, most Catalans used their feet to head out to the entertainment zones to catch the cabarets and cafés cantantes.[56] And so began the difficult process of Catalanization through the sardana and the orfeóns. As one Catalan nationalist so succinctly declared, "The beautiful songs of the earth have to be the principal arm to combat flamenquismo."[57] The Centre Català Vilafranquí also began a campaign against what it saw as immorality by focusing on denouncing prostitution and flamenco song and dance.[58] But more than censuring flamenco and increasing the number of spaces outside the Barrio Chino for singing and dancing the "traditional" Catalan folk songs, Catalan nationalists raised their visibility through journals dedicated specifically to educating the populace about these Catalan musical forms.

Lluís Millet, the editor of one of the earliest and more prominent of these journals, the *Revista músical catalana*, the monthly bulletin of the Orfeò Català, carefully laid out the journal's program to its readers: to engender "the love and the feeling of the things of the earth, which are our own things until the end," as a "gloss" of Catalan songs, to "resuscitate" songs long forgotten in archives, to introduce readers to music from other countries, and, most especially, "to give an account of the movement of the Catalan chorale societies, especially of the most modern ones that follow the footsteps of the Catalan Orfeó ... to make noble Catalan art for Catalonia."[59]

Instilling Catalan nationalism was never far away from the thoughts of the writers in these magazines. Millet, again, in an article on the sardana, muses over the idea of regional or national music/dance in contrast with "universal" dance. He claims that dances that are now considered universal were once regional and that they reflected the "imitative expression characteristic of a race," but the process of universalizing these dances made them "washed out," losing their "healthy, primitive sincerity." Asking whether or not the sardana will ever become a universal dance, he proclaims a loud, "No"—"It must be ours and no one else's"; otherwise the dance will be an "unworthy" one. In fact, in what appears to be a slam against flamenco or flamenco-like dancing, he proclaims, "We have to want to make war on this crude and sensual dance, to preserve the sanctification of our youth and the happiness of our little ones." The sardana's "variety of rhythms" and other great qualities provide it with a certain "je ne sais quoi of primitivism and strength that rejects modern decadence!" Finally, for him,

Table 3.1. Music periodicals devoted to *sardanas*, *orfeóns*, and *cants corals* in Catalonia, 1900–1930

	1900	1910	1920	1930
sardanas and orfeóns	4	4	38	25
other forms of music	6	13	19	15

the sardana was a bulwark against modern decadent society: "Catalan musicians, new singers of the splendid renaissance of our land, make of the sardana a favored form of your inspiration; thus, in that glass there will be made fortified wine, as new wine in old skins, and it will take on the taste and smell of your land and will be protected from the sourness of modern decadence."[60] As we can see, in Catalonia antiflamenquismo served regional nationalist purposes. And while Catalan nationalists repeated many of the same arguments as other antiflamenquistas outside of Catalonia, they associated the decadent qualities of flamenco with non-Catalans—that is, with Spaniards.

Almost twenty years later, the fight to make the sardana *the* national dance continued. Other music journals such as *Ritme* explicitly set out their nationalistic goals of encouraging Catalans "who feel a yearning for brotherhood." "Contact with Catalan blood," it continued, "links [Catalans] spiritually and makes manifest the conscious duties of citizenship."[61] In fact, the period between 1900 and 1936 saw a proliferation of magazines designed to cultivate a love of Catalan song and dance. A sample of (translated) titles attests to this devotion: *Aurora: Organ of the Association of the Choruses of Clavé*; *New Catalonia*; *Renaissance: Spokesman of the Union of Coral and Orpheon Societies of Clavé*; *Bulletin of the Orpheon of Sants*; *Orpheo Levant*; *Catalan Music Magazine*; *Sardana*.[62] As shown in table 3.1, the numbers of music periodicals devoted to sardanas, orfeóns, and cants corals increased dramatically between 1900 and 1930.[63]

The Role of Foreigners in the Flamenco Boom

While the efforts of Catalan nationalists to foster a cultural Catalanism through coros and orfeóns achieved some great successes and did manage to imbue the Catalan population in Barcelona and the greater Catalonia with a strong Catalan identity, Barcelona's Andalusian identity did not die away. In fact, it was probably made stronger by the increased immigration of Andalusians and foreigners to Catalonia during World War I and by the installation in 1923 of the centralizing nationalist from Andalusia, Miguel Primo de Rivera, as dictator.[64] This confluence of people and events led to a Barcelona with a multifaceted identity: one that identified proudly as Catalan but also maintained an ambivalent and sometimes humorously resigned connection to flamenco.

The advent of World War I signaled another great transformation in Barcelona's character. Spain's neutrality during the war, coupled with Barcelona's location as a refuge for warring nations' displaced citizens, enabled many of Barcelona's inhabitants to enjoy relative economic prosperity and participate in new cosmopolitan forms of entertainment. Because Barcelona was the most industrialized city in Spain, it profited most by trade with the warring nations. Similarly, it became the city for European artists and performers to inhabit because it was one of the nonbelligerent cities closest to Paris, the cultural capital of Europe. The influx of foreigners brought new performers, novel forms of entertainment, and numerous cultural critics who would report their findings about Barcelona to their respective countries in fictional and nonfictional accounts that proliferated in the 1920s. And it was this contact with foreigners and the growth of different entertainment sectors that would highlight the various tensions in Catalan national identity. Catalan nationalists may have denigrated flamenco as too Spanish, too degenerate, and most un-Catalan, but the spectacles arriving from such places as Paris and the United States—cabarets, dance halls, jazz clubs, and so on—certainly outdid cafés cantantes in terms of lewd displays. Perhaps it was because Barcelonans viewed themselves as more European than Spanish that they were more willing to accept the cosmopolitan nature of cabarets and jazz clubs as distinctly urbane and forward-looking, whereas they understood cafés cantantes as belonging clearly to a degenerate, backward-looking Spain. In other words, Catalans in Barcelona occupied a contradictory identity. In some ways they enjoyed the cosmopolitan life as Mica Nava defines it, as a "structure of feeling associated with 'modernity' . . . [and] with a mood and historical moment which highlighted the fluidity and excitement of modern metropolitan life and culture [that] was characterised by a readiness to embrace the new." Additionally, cosmopolitanism "signalled a loosening of national identifications and a positive engagement with difference." Although Catalans in Barcelona may have acted as cosmopolitans by revolting against "'traditional' cultural forms" such as flamenco music and zarzuelas, their nationalist attempts to recapture and preserve

Catalan folk and song traditions bespoke a turn to the provincial and a rejection of the new.⁶⁵

The interplay between foreigners, Catalans, Castilians, and Andalusians in Barcelona during the interwar period created a kind of "feedback loop" with respect to flamenco. In other words, Catalan nationalists tried to cultivate and maintain a distinct national identity in opposition to the Castilianizing and Andalusianizing forces at work during the Primo regime.⁶⁶ At the same time, foreigners, especially the English and the French, whose fertile imaginations had been primed by years of reading accounts both of Andalusian culture and the bajos fondos of Barcelona, visited Barcelona, envisioning it to be Andalusia, and expected to participate (at least superficially) in the life of the Barrio Chino. Then they would write accounts detailing the spectacles of vice they encountered during their stay; others would read their accounts and come to Barcelona searching for the same experiences and ignoring anything that might counter their preconceived narratives about the city. The citizens of Barcelona, at least those with an eye toward profits, would then create spectacles to reinforce foreigners' conceptions of the Rosa de Fuego.⁶⁷ In his memoir, an anarchist, A. Bueso, recounted taking some friends to the Barrio Chino because they felt "the morbid curiosity that the so-called decent people feel to know how the 'petty criminals' live." His friend Alfredo "knew well that, in general, this entire neighborhood was staged like a theater to 'shock' the innocent."⁶⁸ And so people took advantage of the foreigners' desire to "slum it."

Catalan writers in the 1920s and 1930s complained about the damage done by foreign visitors/writers to Barcelona who focused solely on the vice of the city and/or some Andalusian stereotype of the place.⁶⁹ The Catalan journalist Andreu Avelí Artís recounted a story about a man who had planned out a wonderful itinerary for a French friend who was visiting Barcelona. It included some of the great sights of the city, such as churches, gardens, and Gaudí buildings, but all his friend wanted to do was go to La Criolla, the bar in the Barrio Chino that specialized in cabaret-type performances by homosexuals and transvestites. The journalist wrote, "We understood perfectly the wound that your civilized Barcelonan pride had received to see how a foreigner preferred to breathe in the atmosphere of a bar in the bajos fondos than become absorbed in the contemplation of our Romanesque paintings." Avelí Artís goes on to explain that, in addition to the flamenco shows that catered to tourists, writers such as René Bizet (*Avez-vos dans Barcelone*), Paul Morand ("Catalan Night"), Francis Carco (*Printemps d'Espagne*), and Henry de Montherland (*La petite infante de Castille*) contributed immensely to the foreigners' thirst for exotic Barcelona. He cited Paul Morand as the author who best made this famous "Barcelona cocktail that is served in the picturesque European bar. . . . Some drops of typical Andalusianism and some drops of anarchism, mixed with the murky liquid from the bajos fondos of the entire seaport. Shake it well and it's ready to serve."[70] Obviously he was not too far off the mark, as seen by this passage from Morand's "Catalan Night": "The detonations finally stopped. . . . Barcelona was once more what you see there, a city of money, and vice, the town of brothels full of girls underage, of obscene photographs, instruments of orthopedic pleasure, hiding her old inquisitionist soul behind illuminated advertisements, with her convents and her banks fortified . . . her confessionals defended from the poor by the same gilded gratings."[71] In one short paragraph Morand captured both the foreigners' fascination with Barcelona's underworld and their larger stereotypical conceits about Spain: the detonation of bombs, prostitution and pornography, and Catholic militancy and superstition.

Despite journalists' complaints about foreigners' attitudes toward Barcelona—and there were certainly other lamenters—enterprising Andalusians and Catalans counted on foreigners' thirst for Barcelona's "Andalusian mystique" and their desire to "slum it" to build entertainment palaces for the paying tourist.[72] The most famous of them all was La Villa Rosa, a large establishment founded by a Catalan flamenco guitarist, Miguel Borrull, and located on Calle Arco del Teatro 3, a liminal space between the Barrio Chino and the more respectable Ramblas (see map 5). Before 1915 the place was known as Can Maciá, a refuge for bullfighters and their entourages who lived in Barcelona. It was owned by a Gypsy who did not contract artists but who let those of his clients who were "aficionados of cante" go up to the stage and sing. Borrull, or as one writer called him, "also Gypsy, but completely commercialized," bought the place in 1915 and transformed it into a large café cantante for flamenco.[73] It reached its greatest heights in the 1920s and 1930s by hiring big-name talent from flamenco's professionalized theatrical circuit that was now becoming extremely popular in Spain and Latin America.[74] In fact, many journalists noted that La Villa Rosa had become a stop on every tourist's itinerary: "El Tibidabo, Montserrat, la Sagrada Familia, Montjuïc, la casa d'en Milà House . . . and Villa Rosa."[75] La Villa Rosa housed some of the greatest flamenco stars of the day, such as Juana "la Macarrona" and La Niña de los Peines, but for those who despised commercialism, or for those who wished that flamenco, its performers, and the tourists that came with it would just go away, La Villa Rosa played as one giant farce.[76]

According to those contemporaries who wrote about La Villa Rosa, the appeal of the place lay in its safety and commercialism. Although it was located right at the edge of the Raval and housed enough local color for tourists and members of "official Barcelona"—the street came with its share of darkness, dirty buildings, sidewalks redolent of urine, prostitutes soliciting their services, and mangy dogs and cats—it remained close enough to the Ramblas for any scared tourist to escape quickly if need be: "Villa Rosa is a magnificent concession that Barcelona makes for foreigners. It possesses all the mystery, all the discomfort and just the right lack of cleanliness so that the typical tourist doesn't feel defrauded."[77]

The critics who wrote about La Villa Rosa noted its staged quality in two ways: the performance took place on a stage and certain scenarios were staged by Borrull and his family to make the tourists feel as if they had enjoyed an authentic Barrio Chino experience.[78] The best illustration of La Villa Rosa's performative function comes from A. Bueso's account of "A Picturesque Interlude." Bueso sets up the *bronca* (fight) scene meant for wealthy foreigners: Usually a regular to the Villa Rosa who wanted to show a tourist a good time would pay a deposit ahead of time for the staged quarrel and for whatever damage might occur in the process. The person who paid for the setup had to be prepared to look surprised by the whole event. The set-up always occurred in the last performance of the show, around 2 a.m., because this was the most expensive one of the night. A dancer, usually a gitana who worked there, would sit down at the table of the "dazzled" (male) tourist and begin to talk, flirt, and so on. The tourist might touch her, and then she would protest because her "man was jealous and might get really angry." But the client still might continue to touch her. Then a gitano would approach the table and begin yelling at his "girlfriend," ordering her to leave the table. She would then protest and tell him to calm down, that these gentlemen were doing no harm. He repeated his "request." More shouts. The foreigners would now begin to understand what the quarrel was about, and the gentleman would try to be gallant and say that the gitana could have his seat. Then the fight would begin. The Gypsy "boyfriend" would take the gentleman by the jacket. Lots of chairs and tables would be overturned, glasses and bottles broken. Suddenly, a knife might come out, and the women would begin to scream, "For God's sake, Manuel, don't make us lose everything! Think of your kids! Don't lose it all for the sake of a bad woman!" Once the scene had run its course, Borrull would come out, place himself between the fighters, and order them to put down their weapons and go home. Then he would tell the customers to excuse the ruckus, but that it was dangerous to play with the gitanos' emotions. He would then offer to refund their money: "Go home. Nothing happened here." This usually ended all hostilities, and then Borrull and the customers often shared a drink together: "It was not unusual for the French, English or Americans to feel like brothers and kiss all the Gypsies on the cheeks, ending everything in the best manner possible." Sometimes this approach failed. The client would get upset, and Borrull would have to call the police from the nearby Atarazanas Barracks by the Plaza de la Paz. He would tell the cops not to be "too severe" with these clients after they paid up, so as not to sully the place's reputation. The police would let the clients go, as long as they had paid, and the clients felt that they had been let off pretty easily. Afterward, Borrull, the cops, and the performers would share a drink after the clients departed, and then Borrull would slip some money into the cops' hands as they left, thus ending that night's performance.[79] Tourists and members of official Barcelona who visited these prominent cafés cantantes left these establishments with stories of "authentic"—but not too dangerous—experiences of life in the rugged corners of Barcelona to share with other people. And thus, stereotypes of an Andalusian Barcelona continued to be perpetuated, despite Catalan nationalists' efforts to eradicate them.

The final step in the Andalusianization of Barcelona occurred with its hosting the 1929 World Exposition and the establishment of the Pueblo Español, a simulacra of Spain's rural regions, wherein each region displayed its crafts, songs, and food for the tourist who could now visit all of Spain without having to actually *visit* the entire country.[80] The exposition had already been planned for 1917, but World War I forced organizers to jettison that idea for a while. Planners for the pre-1917 exposition had already conceived of a type of Pueblo Español, but one that had emphasized Catalan architecture over other Spanish traditions. But when the exposition was reconceived during Primo's dictatorship, Spanish nationalism came to the forefront.[81] The official bulletin of the fair described the high praise the installation received: "All affirm its extraordinary category.... But there is something more. Something that fully satisfies both tourists and nontourists, the cultured and the uncultured, nationals and foreigners. It's the faithfulness to detail."[82] Although the numerous regions in Spain were represented in stereotypical form and with stunning detail, it was the Andalusian section of the display that seemed to get the most press.

The revised plans for the Pueblo Español originally lacked an Andalusian section because many on the planning commission feared that it would detract from the concurrent Ibero-American Exposition in Seville. King Alfonso XIII insisted, however, that Andalusia be represented in the picturesque tableau of Spanish regionalism.[83] Luckily for Spanish and Catalan tourism, the organizers obeyed the king's wishes and catered to the *españolada* tastes of domestic and foreign visitors. The Andalusian section included the Patio del Farolillo, which, according to the ironically amused journalist Josep Planes i Martí, played a brilliant role in the exposition: "It represents in one fell swoop all of the black legend and red legend of Spain: Carmen, guitars, manzanilla [sherry], flamencos and priests who are aficionados of bullfighting."[84] The Andalusian pavilion had a tablao on the inside for flamenco performances, and not surprisingly, it was the Borrull family of La Villa Rosa fame who had contracted the tablao and the talent within it. Borrull hired numerous Gypsies from the Somorrostro neighborhood of Barcelona (now destroyed), including the up-and-coming Catalan flamenco dancer Carmen Amaya and many of her relatives, to perform to excited crowds.[85] Some critics, even those Catalans like Sebastià Gasch who viewed themselves as flamenco aficionados, complained that these flamenco performances were merely kitschy enterprises for those tourists who "pay and pay well." The performers at the exposition were, well, performers. Gasch preferred the little-known singers and dancers in the dives of the bajos fondos who "sing and dance for themselves. Not for others."[86] But the Andalusian Pavilion seemed to be one of the most popular, leading Planes i Martí to comment that people in Barcelona should be extremely pleased with this folkloric and stereotypical pavilion. He saw cash aplenty coming from the exploitation of the españolada. It was, as he said, "good business." He admired Spain and Spaniards for doing this part of the pavilion correctly and he saw nothing wrong with exploiting a stereotype if it filled the proper coffers.[87]

And fill the coffers it did. Not only did the Andalusian pavilion and the tablao within it generate publicity and income for Catalans and Spaniards alike, but it achieved its success during a time when Spain entered yet another phase of political turmoil, the transition from Primo's dictatorship to the Second Republic. The Andalusian performances were so successful that a commission formed to create a cultural exchange between Andalusians and Catalans for the summer after the Barcelona and Ibero-American Expositions ended. During Corpus Christi week, 1930, the Barcelona Exposition site hosted an "Andalusia Week," with a series of flamenco performers and prominent teachers of flamenco dancing like Sr. Otero. And, of course, the director of this enterprise was none other than Miguel Borrull.[88] More importantly for flamenco and Barcelona's history, the patio Andaluz of the 1929 Exposition also launched Carmen Amaya, one of the most skilled and prominent flamenco dancers ever, onto the international stage. After her stint at the International Exposition, she toured internationally and starred in numerous films that displayed her talent to the wider world, leaving international audiences hungering for yet more flamenco performances. Amaya always identified herself as both a gitana with familial roots in Andalusia and as a citizen of Barcelona, thus she represented somebody who could embody both an Andalusian and a Catalan identity without eliciting anybody's rancor.[89]

In the brief years between Carmen Amaya's performance at the 1929 Exposition and the eve of the Spanish Civil War (1936), it was clear that baile and cante flamenco resided as comfortably in Barcelona as in Andalusia, and as naturally as the sardana and orfeó. Flamenco had become fully integrated into the Barcelona land- and soundscape, despite the efforts of Catalan nationalists. But the war changed things. Some flamenco performers still worked in Barcelona during the war, sometimes giving benefit concerts like the one sponsored by the Catalan Socialist Party (PSUC) and the Socialist Labor Union (UGT) in the Palau de la Música Catalana on January 24, 1937. The bailaora Imperio de Granada and the guitarists El Niño de Utrera and Sabicas were the headliner acts.[90] Unfortunately for the denizens of the café cantante scene, this cultural vibrancy would lose most of its luster after years of warfare and subsequent privations. As Francisco Hidalgo Gómez writes, the postwar years caused "a serious break in the relations between Catalonia and flamenco" because of the Franco regime's manipulation of Andalusian folklore and its suppression of Catalan culture.[91] Although the Spanish Civil War and its aftermath would change the forms of entertainment in Catalonia and Spain, the links between Catalonia and flamenco would not die completely. Eventually, by the early 1950s, the rumba catalana would emerge from the gitano neighborhoods of Barcelona, and with it, flamenco's resurgence. By 1966 statues representing the sardana and the flamenco dancer Carmen Amaya could occupy spaces near one another in Montjuïc Park without anyone looking askance.

But that is getting ahead of our story. Catalan nationalists in the period between the Restoration and the Spanish Civil War attempted to separate themselves from the cultural production emanating from Andalusia in order to differentiate themselves from the "foreigners" who kept Catalans from establishing their cultural and political sovereignty. Let us now look at how Andalusians employed flamenco to assert the strength of *their* regional identity.

4

The Marriage of Flamenco, Politics, and National Liberation, 1914—1936

Just months before World War I broke out, unleashing as never before the destructive forces of nationalism, the newspaper editor and writer Isidro de las Cagigas read his entry for the Juegos Florales in Sevilla's *Ateneo*. Like the Jocs Florals in Barcelona (see previous chapter), the Juegos Florales aimed to give writers and poets a forum for extolling their region's grandeur, and it became one among many springboards for launching an incipient Andalusian regionalism. As he spoke of Andalusia, he complained, "I believe, truly, that if Andalusia were a woman, she would be a woman of sound body who would offer herself with the exuberance of her sinews and with the jubilation of her temperament, without thinking that the river of life that she so gracefully offered up would tarnish her purity and sully her integrity."[1] The long essay that carried this statement, "Notes for a Study of Andalusian Regionalism," won the prize that year and was reprinted in Seville's regionalist magazine, *Bética*.[2] Finding strength in Andalusia's history and in the waves of migrations that rolled across the region over millennia, Cagigas became a booster for Andalusia's role in saving Spain from itself. He was aware, however, that in many quarters of Spain, Andalusia had become a laughingstock instead of a source of vibrancy, fodder for cheap stereotypes about flamenco dancers, bullfighters, and bandits. Despite his problematically sexualized rendering of Andalusia as a wholesome and vivacious woman whom others misconstrued as a trollop, Cagigas conveyed some of the ambivalent reactions Andalusian intellectuals felt about Andalusia's relationship to Spain as a whole.[3] On the one hand, as we have seen in previous chapters, many people found Andalusia and its inhabitants utterly charming and sometimes exotic; on the other hand, some foreigners and Andalusians themselves had projected a national identity onto Spain that reduced the whole of the nation to a cardboard cutout representing a dissolute nation in decline. From the eve of World War I until around 1936, Andalusian regionalists would wrestle more explicitly with their cultural and political heritage, seeing Andalusia as key to Spain's regeneration. Unlike the Catalan nationalists who argued for regional autonomy based on a rejection of cultural products they deemed foreign, like flamenco, Andalusian regionalists engaged with flamenco culture more ambivalently. Some rejected the Andalusia of flamenquismo, thinking, just as other regenerationists of that era had, that it reflected a backward and decadent Spain; others, most notably the Andalusian regional nationalist Blas Infante, embraced the stereotypes foisted on and internalized by Andalusians to argue for both Andalusian regional autonomy and Spanish regeneration.[4]

This chapter illustrates how Andalusian regional nationalism developed from the end of the nineteenth century until the beginning of the Spanish Civil War, with particular attention to the ways that flamenco was employed for regionalist purposes. Although I describe the ideas that some of the more well-known Andalusian cultural nationalists promoted, I focus primarily on the writings of Blas Infante, the most prominent of these figures; for it was he who forged a politics of regional nationalism for Andalusia *and* wrote seriously about the origins of flamenco music. Producing the majority of his works between 1914 and 1936, he made implicit a relationship between Andalusia's flamenco heritage and its political future.[5] Through a close reading of his works, I will demonstrate how Infante envisioned a libertarian politics rooted in the history of flamenco music.

A Brief History of the Course of Andalusian Regional Nationalism

Unlike the Catalans, who were able to make a case for regional autonomy based on a perceived historical incompatibility with and linguistic difference from the Castilian-centered Spanish state, Andalusians had a weaker case. What could one do with a place like Andalusia, a region firmly cemented into the building blocks of Spain? It had no special language. The region was tarred with the brush of Catholic fanaticism. It had flourished as the gateway to empire. Why would anybody claim special privileges for this region and how could they even entertain such notions? The answers again lie in regenerationist responses to Spain's political and economic circumstances. But those responses, which really began to blossom after 1914, took a distinctly marked turn away from the separatist ideas of Catalan and Basque nationalists, at least at first. Instead, they emphasized *Spain's* dependence on Andalusia, arguing that Spain and its civilization would be nothing without Andalusia's nutrients feeding the body of the sickened state, or to put a more positive spin on the matter, "Andalusia is Spain par excellence; all that is Andalusian becomes national and all that is national is Andalusian."[6]

Between about 1914 and 1936, most of the middle-class Andalusian nationalists envisioned a variety of paths for thinking about Andalusian regional nationalism. There were those who focused primarily on political regionalism undergirded by a federalist system of government, whereby an autonomous Andalusia would lead Spain out of its political, economic, and social morass. Others rejected political regionalism in favor of a cultural regionalism, which tied the fate of the region to service of the greater nation-state.[7] These regional nationalists adhered to the idea that Spaniards would have to disabuse themselves of the idea that Europe, especially northern Europe, was Spain's savior. They delved into Andalusia's history and culture before the final Reconquista and the first expulsion in 1492 to recover a usable past. The lessons gleaned from this era, known as the al-Andalus period, would be the source of Spanish regeneration. Finally, others refused binary choices and instead championed a regional nationalism that combined both cultural nationalism and political autonomy. Blas Infante would prove to be the most prominent of the regional nationalists forging this path. Although the ideas of the traditionally politically oriented regional nationalists are important in their own right, their ideas do not generally include the topic of flamenco. Instead, my goal here is to demonstrate how Infante's writings on flamenco married the ideas of cultural regional nationalism and political regional nationalism.

Some recent Andalusian nationalists begin the story of Andalusian nationalism in 1835 with the formation of the Junta de Andújar, a local governing body from various parts of Andalusia that organized to stave off the Carlist threat during the First Carlist War (1833–39), but as historian José Manuel Cuenca Toribio has pointed out, those who see in this

Junta a "milestone" for Andalusian regionalism are dealing more with a "novelistic category than a historiographical one."[8] A more credible beginning is the 1883 Asamblea Federalista de Antequera, in which some Andalusian Republicans drew up a constitution outlining the terms of an autonomous Andalusian state within a federation of states that made up Spain. Imagined as a secular, representative democratic republic and owing a great debt to the Federalist ideas of Francesc Pi i Margall via Pierre-Joseph Proudhon, this constitution called for a devolution of power, with decision-making generated at the level of municipality, then canton, then region. Although this attempt at implementing an autonomous federalist state failed, the act of having written a blueprint for Andalusian autonomy became an inspiration and starting point for Andalusian nationalists at the beginning of the twentieth century.

But an Andalusian political regionalism of any note did not really emerge until the eve of World War I.[9] Following the path of many traditional regionalist and nationalist movements of that time, Andalusian political regionalism was promoted by a small group of progressive middle-class intellectuals. The nationalists' writings point to both domestic and foreign events as influential over the ideas and course of their ideologies. Domestically, the Restoration system was beginning to careen out of control, as we have seen in earlier chapters. The working classes, progressives, Catholics, Catalan nationalists, and even the military expressed their disaffection with the liberal politics and caciquismo that maintained the moribund state. In Andalusia itself, economic conditions were among the worst in Spain. The latifundista economy functioned at the hands of absentee landlords who held large tracts of land and hired temporary laborers from a large pool of the unemployed to work it. Meanwhile the landholders resisted efforts to modernize agricultural practices with industrial machinery because of their access to cheap, abundant labor, thus exacerbating the land hunger and actual hunger of rural workers in the region. These particular social and economic conditions help explain the appeal of anarchism and Pi i Margall's brand of federal republicanism so prevalent in Andalusia.[10] The most influential Andalusian nationalists of the early twentieth century advanced a federalist political structure and advocated the economic ideas of Henry George, who believed that those who worked the land should own the fruits of that labor, but that the land's economic value—it's natural resources, for example—belonged to all members of the local community. Similarly, to counter the concentration of wealth in land, he argued that taxes should be abolished at every level of government, with the exception of a tax on rents.[11] This philosophy sat well with those who concerned themselves with ameliorating the great social and economic inequality of a latifundist economy that ravaged Andalusia.

The success of Catalan nationalism before 1923 and the blossoming of European nation-states in Europe after World War I provided maps to chart the course of Andalusian political nationalism. Under the leadership of Blas Infante, interested parties from various parts of Andalusia met in Ronda in January 1918 to establish a path toward regional autonomy along the lines of the proposed 1883 Antequera Constitution. Dubbing themselves the Regional Assembly of Ronda, they hitched their wagon to Wilson's Fourteen Points, especially its call for national self-determination. They continued pushing for their political movement the following year, meeting in Córdoba this time, fleshing out the means for decentralizing the Spanish state, creating a federation of autonomous regions, and ameliorating the economic hardships of urban laborers. Their efforts resulted in the Manifesto de Nacionalidad, but no concrete legislation resulted. Miguel Primo de Rivera's pronunciamento in 1923 temporarily quashed these dreams of autonomy. Then, with the advent of the Second Republic in 1931, Andalusian nationalists began again to push for their demands, especially after witnessing the Catalan nationalist triumphs; however, the civil war put an end to their dreams for the foreseeable future.

The Attractions of Cultural Nationalism

Although some Andalusian regional nationalists of the early twentieth century outlined and advocated for a detailed political and economic program moving toward regional autonomy, many were satisfied with promoting cultural regionalism only. Instead of rejecting the Romantic tropes imposed by foreigners and cultivated by purveyors of tourism, these regional nationalists turned stereotypes into strengths and delved into Andalusia's pre-Reconquest history in search of a usable past for Andalusia's and Spain's future.

The Sevillian Mario Méndez Bejarano was one of the first people to give shape to this form of cultural regional nationalism. A professor of literature and politics, he gave the inaugural speech of Seville's Juegos Florales in 1909, proclaiming that Andalusian regionalism was "healthy, fraternal, and patriotic" and that Andalusians were probably best suited to talk about the importance of their region to Spain.[12] He enumerated Andalusia's strengths—its varied landscape, its Mediterranean ports that could trade with both the Atlantic and Pacific worlds, its customs, artists, dress, and amusements—and concluded that only Andalusia had the resources to "live independently." And yet it did not. Not because it could not but because Andalusia was too important to Spain's vitality—it manifested the "authentic soul of Spain." Andalusia's culture became Spain's culture: "Andalusian games and entertainments, good or bad . . . quickly become national entertainments, capable of . . . attracting more press than any other political party, and fanaticizing the masses."[13] All that was good about Spain, however trivial it might seem, emerged from Andalusia, and Andalusia was key to saving Spain as a whole, he concluded.

Méndez Bejarano would continue over the following decades to dwell on the themes he outlined during these Juegos Florales, focusing especially on the importance of Andalusia's cultural treasures to the rest of Spain. Unlike the antiflamenquistas, Méndez Bejarano believed it important to address what others might conceive of as trivial matters, like bullfighting, dance, and song, but he was unwilling to credit ethnic minorities like the gitanos for creating any of Andalusia's cultural treasures. For example, in *Andalucía y ultramar*, he claimed that the Andalusian music collected in the canonical *Cantigas* composed during the reign of Alfonso the Wise (1252-84) "formed the base of [our] national music, of the cante jondo, which had nothing to do with Gypsies." Moreover, he continued, this Andalusian music with its "national instrument, the 'flamenco' guitar . . . [which] vibrates as a nervous system, as a human soul" inspired music and poems in Germany and France, and this "Arab-Andalusian poetry" went so far as to influence Dante's *Divine Comedy*. By the time Méndez Bejarano wrote this piece, which he published in 1929, he seems to have accepted as fact that a so-called genre within flamenco song, the cante jondo, had been legitimated as a serious art form after 1922. This artistic sanction occurred after intellectuals Manuel de Falla and Federico García Lorca organized the Cante Jondo Contest in Granada. Unlike these two intellectuals, however, Méndez Bejarano stripped the cante jondo of its "Gypsiness" and created a historical pedigree for this acceptable form of flamenco in the culture of al-Andalus.[14] The most renowned Andalusian nationalist, Blas Infante, would certainly adopt some of the ideas of cultural nationalism Méndez Bejarano advanced, but over the next two decades, Infante's understanding of Andalusian culture would align more closely with that of Isidro de las Cagigas, the regionalist discussed in the opening of this chapter.

Cagigas occupies a large space with Infante in the pantheon of Andalusian regionalists.[15] Although he shared some of Infante's political preoccupations, he was less enthusiastic about political autonomy. Instead, he advanced discussions of Andalusian regional and national identity by turning the perceived weaknesses of Andalusia into strengths, showcasing Andalusia's history and culture as remedies to cure the ills of Spain's political culture. Born in Seville but raised much of his early life in Granada, Cagigas studied law but seemed more drawn to Granada's literary and artistic life. He was cofounder of the literary magazine *España artística y literaria* and contributed many articles to regionalist newspapers and magazines like *El Alhambra* and *Bética*. Before 1914 he had already begun diving into archives from Andalusia's Islamic past, and it was there that he began to perceive links between that history and Andalusia's future, and by 1916 he had passed his civil service exams to become a diplomat. Soon thereafter, he labored in diplomatic posts in North Africa. He enters our story in 1914, after winning the prize for Seville's Juegos Florales. His speech on Andalusian regionalism was then published in *Bética* over the course of three months, and in it he elucidated the importance of Andalusian culture and history for saving Spain.

Like Méndez Bejarano before him, Cagigas noted how Andalusian regional culture could be found everywhere in Spain because Spain and Andalusia were inextricably tied together. A Catalan dancing a sardana would be out of place in Castile, whereas *sevillanas* could be danced anywhere. Andalusia acted as a life force, part of Spain's "vital organs, up to the point that it produces more influence within Spain than Castile." Foreigners, he argued, understood this better than Spaniards themselves: "Being that all of Spain is sentimentally Andalusian, and although nobody thinks that playing the bagpipes is [something Spaniards do], they believe that all Spaniards play the guitar and wear a broad-brimmed hat, not the classic outfit of the bandits of our highlands. And that which infuriates and annoys us Spaniards is nothing more than a virtual amplification of the real Spain." He took Andalusian culture seriously and mocked those he perceived would attack him for focusing on seemingly "trivial" details like bullfighting, dances, and women. Nationalists in Spain, he argued, always sought foreign experts who cited "serious" ideas in grand footnotes to help them deal with Spain's problems. He countered this Spanish and Andalusian self-loathing by elevating the role of these so-called trivial cultural practices: "Regionalism is not something that is invented and constructed with brilliant sentences in a piece of propaganda.... Regionalism has to be looked for in the intimacy of the people, in their most basic emotions, in their spontaneous demonstrations that skilled hands and exceptional minds can channel."[16] Although he rejected what scholars would now call the construction of regionalism and nationalism, the ways he outlined his views of Andalusian history and the "Spanish race" certainly point to a constructed usable past for the Andalusian region and the Spanish nation.

Cagigas rejected what regional nationalists in other parts of Spain kept trying to promote: a regional separatism based on readings of history that "proved" some kind of racial purity. Instead, he adopted a regionalism that recognized the beneficial effects of waves of invasions and migrations—Phoenicians, Romans, Greeks, Goths, Vandals, Muslims, Jews—leading to the conclusion that Andalusians were "a mixture of infinite heterogeneous elements, whose contributions came from all places, and principally from the Orient." They contained within them the unifying link "between the European and Semitic type."[17] Andalusians, who emerged as a fusion of races, gained their strength by opening themselves up to other cultures. Spain's (and Andalusia's) cultural decline, he insisted, began with the reconquest of Granada and the expulsion of Spain's Jews and Muslims. From these actions, "Andalusia lost all of its unity and all of its character."[18] Cagigas adopted a stance that was unpopular at the time but would later gain credence from the 1930s on, and it would certainly be promoted by Infante. That is, Spain's golden age was not, as many thought, achieved during its imperial height of the sixteenth and seventeenth centuries but rather in the centuries before 1492, when Muslims ruled Spain as al-Andalus.

With all these cultural and historical nationalist strands in place, Infante would become the great promoter first of Andalusian cultural nationalism, then of regional nationalism, and finally, of regional autonomy. As we shall see, he would take some of the ideas advocated by the regional nationalist thinkers above, mix them with particular economic and political arguments, and come up with his own ideas about the origins and strengths of flamenco and the people who created the art form.

Blas Infante and Regionalism

Blas Infante (1885-1936) was a man so inextricably tied to the history of Andalusian nationalism that his moniker, the "Father of the Andalusian nation," was officially enshrined in the preamble to the Andalusian

Autonomy Statute of 1980 and by the Spanish Cortes in 2002.[19] Inventor of the Andalusian flag, its coat of arms, and author of the Andalusian national anthem, Infante played oversized roles as both theoretician and activist for the incipient Andalusian nationalist movement.[20] His form of cultural nationalism also acted as a counterweight against the kinds of regional nationalisms promoted by the Catalans and Basques. More than anybody else, he would synthesize other regional nationalists' ideas and work to make them manifest in his writings, in his and Cagigas's creation of the cultural centers of Andalusia, and in his political operations. He, more than any other political and cultural regionalist, would clearly link flamenco music to Andalusian regionalist aspirations. His activities ceased abruptly when the Nationalists executed him during the first months of the civil war.

Already immersed in regional nationalist circles by 1909, five years later Infante wrote *El ideal andaluz* (The Andalusian ideal).[21] It was the first full-scale dissemination of his ideas about the Andalusian nation, its people, and its history, and in it he created a blueprint for awakening a regional nationalism that he claimed had lain dormant for hundreds of years. Once roused, Andalusians would take the lead in making Spain stronger. Although he revised some of his ideas over the following decades, the core principles remained until his death.

Unlike Catalan nationalism, which took northern and western Europe as its model for progress, Infante's Andalusian nationalism looked inward and backward in time. He declared, "The triumph of modern civilization is not Spanish."[22] Although he called for improving and intensifying the educational level of people in Spain to match the pace of other western European nations, he disapproved of the values those other modern nations taught—Taylorism, speed, atomization, for example. Infante grasped the obvious, that Andalusia had declined steeply since the Middle Ages, but, he averred, Andalusians still had their essence, their spirit. Mixing ideas that sounded like a combination of Henri Bergson's concept of élan vital and the doctor and anthropologist Federico Olóriz y Aguilera's modern racialist ideas crafted specifically for Spaniards, he claimed that the Andalusian spirit had been able to enrich itself through infusions of foreign blood without losing its own essence. Andalusians' "primitive vital energies have always been dominant; they have not been absorbed simply as nutritive elements by the life energies of a foreign blood."[23] He wrote of the importance of "racial fusion," a prevalent idea in Spain during Infante's lifetime. Indigenous Andalusians mixed with Tartesians, Africans from Carthage, Romans,

Goths, and Arabs, thus fusing into a stronger race, with the Andalusian features of the race most dominant.[24] He did not fear "the stigma of African origins" often imposed on Andalusia, making the radical argument for its time that all Europeans originally came from Africa. Heterogeneity, not purity, made Andalusians a stronger race.[25]

Andalusians' intellectual and cultural glories, and therefore Spain's, also came from all these invaders. Spain owed its civilization to Andalusia. The Greeks, he claimed, gave Andalusia democratic values, "the aristocracy of talent"; Bética, the Roman outposts in Andalusia, had the most free states, and in them indigenous Andalusians resisted Roman enslavement; the Arab Andalusians of the Middle Ages kept the light of ancient Greek and Roman knowledge alive while the rest of Europe remained unenlightened. Andalusian culture, the most prolific in Spain, came from the mixture of these immigrants and native peoples.[26] While he invoked the many stereotypes about Andalusians and their culture and turned them into strengths, he failed to mention one immigrant group that populated Andalusia—the gitanos—effectively cleansing the culture of their influence (this will change when he takes up flamenco in the 1930s). Only after the Spanish Reconquest, he remarked, with its reimposition of Christianity, Inquisitorial religious fanaticism, and the political tyranny that led to the expulsion of the Jews and Muslims, did Andalusia's decline begin: "The Andalusian spirit [was] scared silent. But it [was] not dead."[27] His critique undermined the narrative progressive regenerationists clung to, that Spain required the desire and capacity to modernize like northern Europe. Instead, Infante insisted, Spaniards needed to revisit Andalusia's pre-Reconquest history in order to pave the way for both Andalusia's and Spain's renaissance.

Andalusia's decline began when Ferdinand and Isabel yoked Andalusia to the centralizing Spanish kingdom, thus suppressing the spirit of its people. In order to recapture Andalusia's strength, contemporary Andalusians, Infante argued, needed to reform their political system to reflect the independent spirit of their people. This meant creating a kind of socialist federalism whereby power would be divided first among people in municipalities, and then provinces, and then regions. To end the economic misery of the day laborer, he called for cultivating the growth of a rural middle class, collectivizing land, and establishing rural banks, agricultural credit, and cooperatives. This would all be supported by educational reforms—hiring more teachers, combating illiteracy, educating parents, and creating a curriculum in agricultural and industrial education. Finally, he asserted, people had to destroy caciquismo to achieve these transformations.[28] But his most compelling arguments for the regeneration of Andalusia and Spain came from his interpretations of the role that flamenco played and continued to play in Spain's history.

Blas Infante's Synthesis of Regionalist Politics and Flamenco Heritage

Infante took the flamenco art form seriously, unlike many of his contemporaries who despised the ostensibly tawdry performances for intimate audiences in cafés cantantes or the sanitized versions for the masses in bullrings. Even though by 1922 people like composer Manuel de Falla and artistic polymath Federico García Lorca had already worked to legitimate cante jondo as an art form by uncoupling it from commercialized flamenco performances, most intellectuals refused to give the genre any kind of scholarly study. Infante was different, however. Steeped in musical scholarship and curious about the seemingly mysterious origins of flamenco, Infante continued and challenged the ideas of previous folklorists and musicologists like Demófilo, Hugo Schuchardt, and Felipe Pedrell. His work *Orígenes de lo flamenco y secreto del cante jondo* (The origins of flamenco and the secret of cante jondo), written in fragments between 1929 and 1933, was never finished or published in his lifetime; however, by 1931 Infante had begun to hint at some of his theories in his political tract *La verdad sobre el complot de Tablada y el Estado libre de Andalucía* (The truth about the Tablada Plot and the Free State of Andalusia), a work justifying the need for an Andalusian autonomy statute.[29] It becomes obvious in reading both works that Infante found it impossible to separate cultural production—in this case, flamenco—from Andalusian politics and society. The way he linked music and politics provides a window into his particular conception of Andalusian cultural nationalism and the "eternal essence" of his people.

In *La verdad*, Infante once again laid out his political aspirations for Andalusia: he desired a federalist system in Spain resembling that of the United States;[30] he advocated for land reform and workers' control of resources; and, more importantly, he spent time (again) arguing for Andalusia's role in lifting Spain out of the doldrums, precisely by avoiding any sort of affiliation with European ideals. He argued: "We cannot, do not desire, will never become Europeans." Although Andalusians might wear European clothes, underneath they were "Euro-Africans, Euro-Orientals, universalist men, a harmonic synthesis of men." Infante lambasted the "least Andalusian Andalusians," by whom he meant the "señoritos of the cities" and the children of immigrants from other parts of Spain for looking to Europe for answers. In contrast to the language of occupation that Catalan nationalists often evoked, Infante employed the language of colonization: "We have not been able to become Europeans, despite [Spain and Europe's] barbaric colonialism." What were these colonizing ideas? "The triumph of industrialism and Taylorism.... It is the useful—method separated from all the power of emotion." This triumph culminated "in that infirmity of the United States, in Detroit, in the barbarity of *standardization*, in the ROBOT." Andalusians, he continued, could not live life without enthusiasm or happiness; they refused to be lumped together as interchangeable parts of the mass machine. Andalusia represented "the individual for Humanity ... libertarian individualism" that bound itself to the community.[31]

By now, one might wonder how this discussion of colonialism, standardization, and libertarian individualism connects with flamenco. Infante began to hint at the links in *La verdad* but really fleshed them out in the compilation of writings that would become *Orígenes de lo flamenco*. In *La verdad* he put forth the idea that flamenco had a hidden history that only came out into the open in the mid-nineteenth century. Flamenco, he argued, "continued the authenticity of Andalusia, despite the European tyranny that Spain imposed.... The terrible and profane tragedy has been presided over by a funereal song: the cante jondo." He was speaking here of the reconquest and subsequent expulsion of Muslims, and he linked this tragedy to the musical form that would become flamenco, lambasting his contemporaries who sniggered at the art form:[32] "And you, you came to laugh at flamenco, as if it were some sort of musical or expressive contortion of your secular jester. And you, who turned the name of our tragedy into a pejorative word—all that the vanquished race creates is despicable—to express slang gestures or sex trafficking; a sarcastic name by which the conqueror's subconscious still gets angry at the subjected dogs."[33] What kind of cruel people, he intimated, would be so disrespectful of an art form that carried the pain and tragedy of generations of Andalusians?

The answer to this and other questions could be found in his then unpublished writings, *Orígenes de lo flamenco*. In it, he delved deeply into the musical scholarship on flamenco to see if he could discover where the mysterious word "flamenco" originated and why Andalusian music transformed from a chorale-based music in the Renaissance to a highly individualized form in the following centuries. His most simplistic response was this: "The music of the Andalusian songs is individualistic because the Andalusian people are also this way."[34] Obviously, he pushed his case further. Using a soft-shoe analysis akin to Karl Marx's concepts of base and superstructure, Infante theorized that flamenco flowed as an undercurrent of Andalusian music because it had to. A new type of music was required to arise "to express new emotional or conscious states" born of particular historical conditions. Thus this musical genre "developed . . . a new appropriate structure or form and a technique corresponding to this novel form. This, and nothing else, had to be the cause of the flamenco phenomenon."[35] His work aimed to chart the historical changes that provoked such a transformation in Andalusian music. Related to this structural approach to music was his conception of art's function in the world. Similar to Theodor Adorno's ideas about the purpose of art and music, Infante viewed art as "a protest against reality (not an escape from it or a simple reworking of it), inspired by the feeling of a superior reality out there that the artist experiences."[36] Art, he posited, comments critically on a world that needs repair and expresses new ways of mending it. It can be a reflection "of a world in another world," whereby "an unpleasant event becomes a pleasurable one if experienced through the mirror of another world. In the world of sound, color, movement, ruled by dominating rhythm[,] . . . [this] is how we get to see the reproach expressed by flamenco."[37] His aesthetic theories spoke of art as social critique, and he linked structural and thematic alterations in music and performance to historical changes. His mission, then, was to discover the relationship between historical circumstances in Andalusia and the evolution of flamenco over the centuries.

Like many aesthetic critics before and after him, Infante searched both for the etymology of the term "flamenco" and for the origins of the performance itself, especially since nobody had really heard the term commonly used before the mid-nineteenth century. He spent much of the book testing out various theories that had already been proposed by historians, musicologists, and folklorists, but he found most of their explanations lacking in scholarly rigor. For example, Infante admired Demófilo's work on cante jondo, but he points out that he spent much less energy studying flamenco dance. Many scholars, Infante argued, had studied medieval Andalusian music quite thoroughly. He even praised Julián Ribera y Tarragó, the academic Arabist who wrote copiously about Islamic culture under al-Andalus and traced various kinds of medieval music in Spain and Europe back to the Muslims of this earlier time and place. Ribera claimed Andalusia as the cradle and source of both elite and popular music. But, Infante added, Ribera barely mentioned flamenco, claiming that Ribera viewed it as part of the decline of Andalusian music after the Reconquest. Not afraid to smash icons, Infante also challenged the famous musicologist Felipe Pedrell, chastising him for merely describing flamenco and not analyzing it, for obfuscating—though not intentionally—flamenco's origins and development. He lambasted the great composer Manuel de Falla for insisting that the origins of flamenco could be found in cultures that came before al-Andalus, such as the Byzantines. Others, like Serafín Estébanez Calderón, who wrote *Escenas andaluzas*, a work that depicted some of the most famous flamenco singers and dancers of the mid-nineteenth century, insisted that gitanos or moriscos brought their music, music that developed into the flamenco genre, via North Africa.[38] Infante became frustrated by these hypotheses. He wanted to know: "When did flamenco appear? Why did it occur? How did it reveal itself?"[39] He dedicated the rest of his work to solving these mysteries.

He began his explorations with three premises: that using the word "flamenco" to denote a musical performance became popular only after 1850; that although the word—and by extension, the performance—was appropriated by gitanos, it originally had a more generalized and integrated meaning that included both gitanos and Andalusians; and that only those who belonged to this in-group could call themselves "flamencos."[40] With those premises in place, he began to debunk a whole host of theories about the origins of the word itself, starting with what I would call variants of the "Flemish/Flanders thesis."[41] Since one meaning of flamenco in Spanish is Flemish, or a person from Flanders, some musicologists linked flamenco to Spain's imperial history, when the Low Countries belonged to the Spanish crown. Some like Demófilo theorized that during Charles I's reign, troops from Flanders arrived in Spain with gitanos in tow. Spaniards hated these Flemish troops and, by extension, the gitanos who arrived with them; therefore, the soldiers and gitanos were lumped together as one group, flamencos, despised forever more. That particular meaning of flamenco, however, disappeared over the years, until the word became a metonym for gitanos only. Infante dismissed these various suppositions because he could not reconcile the fact that an epithet that supposedly emerged in the sixteenth century to express disdain for particular groups did not enter common parlance until the mid-nineteenth century. Moreover, Andalusians "did not hate the flamencos of Flanders," nor did they "loathe the gitanos," given that most gitanos in Spain resided in Andalusia. Despite what gitanos might have thought of Infante's portrait of a harmonious gitano/Andalusian coexistence at the time, Infante believed that nongitano Andalusians felt a "certain sympathy" with their gitano compatriots, and given all the evidence Infante had amassed, the Flanders theory made absolutely no sense.[42] Additionally, Infante's abiding love for native Andalusian culture, however defined, meant that he could not accept an origin story that might have emerged in another nation.

Infante entertained another proposal for the genealogy of the word flamenco but he it rejected it almost immediately. Again, the confusion emerges from the word's multiple meanings in Spanish. In this case, Infante considered flamenco as bird—the flamingo.[43] According to him, the Andalusian folklorist Federico Rodríguez Marín hypothesized in 1929 that bullfighters, señoritos, and gitanos dressed in short jackets and tight-fitting leggings looked identical to flamingos, and so people began calling these dandyish characters "flamencos."[44] Infante could barely hide his scorn. In fact, he suggested that if flamenco dancers had to choose a bird as their representative, they would be better off with a stork, since storks, at least, could actually be found in Andalusia.[45]

Infante returned again to Flanders as a source for investigating the forms, sounds, and rhythms of flamenco songs, but he did so mostly to criticize musicologists. Once again his ire fell on Felipe Pedrell, whom he accused of treating Andalusians and their musical heritage superficially, "as if Andalusians' psychological, ethological, or aesthetic problems were of less importance than the so-called savage or primitive races that so seriously occupy the attention of ethnologists." Andalusians and their culture, Infante proclaimed, deserved real scholarly attention, despite being a "bastard race, a conquered country."[46] And so Infante assigned this task to himself, first by dispensing with some of Pedrell's scattershot ideas about Bohemian Gypsy and Egyptian influences on flamenco. He decided to take Pedrell's ideas about flamenco at face value, that flamenco music originated in Flanders and was then transported and transformed via Bohemian Gypsies or some other group of people. According to Pedrell, during this migratory process, flamenco music lost almost all traces of its "primitive" character found in music "of the north." Infante rightly countered that if the music had removed all of its Flemish character, then the musical form that emerged would have been something brand new. He also observed that this Flemish music would have had to have been popular in order to "take" in Andalusia. Finally, if one were to look at Flemish music that was contemporary with music sung and performed in Andalusia during the Baroque period, their musical styles would have had to have been very similar in order to conform to Pedrell's thesis. Infante pointed out, however, that Flemish and Andalusian musical aesthetics in this period were completely different from one another.[47] And here is where things become interesting. In Infante's mind, musical forms acted dialectically with social and political conditions rooted in a specific place.

Relying on French musicologist Jules Combarieu's writings about Flemish music and combining them with historian Henri Michelet's depiction of "the Flemish character," Infante argued that "flamenco music" from the Low Countries specialized in "the science of counterpoint" that "socialized the melody" in choruses, in concert performances—it was music suited to aristocratic tastes. He declared: "Flanders, Michelet assures us, *is work*. All for one and one for all. The flamencos were *elite* workers for *musical work*. They [were] artisans before they [were] artists." In contrast, "the mysterious music of the Andalusian flamencos" differentiated themselves by their "irreducible individualism."[48] These apparent differences allowed Infante to conclude that there was an "incompatibility of ethos between a *socialist* music like the flamenco of Flanders, and another individualistic music, like the flamenco of Andalusia"; therefore, it was impossible for these two musical forms to be related.[49] Infante even went so far as to label Andalusian music "anarchist" (and not in a bad way), underscoring Andalusians' historical difficulty with organizing their people into chorales. If we remember the Catalans' efforts to create chorales as a unifying Catalan cultural force and as a bulwark against the encroachment of Castilian and Andalusian cultures (see previous chapter), we can see that Infante was trying to make certain claims about the Andalusian people and their social and political culture, and positing Andalusian culture in opposition not just to Flemish culture but to that of Catalonia as well. Andalusian/flamenco culture is "a Genre which cannot live, that asphyxiates and dies in the atmosphere of a Group, however free this group might be. To flourish it needs the fullness of liberty, which can only be attained with the development of the Individual. . . . Flamenco is a solitary music that in its loneliness, accentuates its individualistic character."[50] Flamenco required liberty, just as Andalusians did, because, lest we forget, Andalusians were libertarians who, through their individualism, tied themselves to the greater human community.[51]

Before sharing his theories about flamenco's secret origins, Infante had to confront one more problem: how to categorize and understand the concept of popular culture and flamenco's place within that framework. Infante understood that for people like Demófilo, Falla, and other folklorists and musicologists, flamenco did not qualify as popular music—especially something like cante jondo—because most people could not sing or dance this form of music and many were unfamiliar with it. Most of these folklorists and musicologists defined popular music as coming from the rural populace—urban culture could not, by definition, be popular. But Infante conceived of popular culture differently from many of his contemporaries. He observed the development of what we would now call mass culture and made the links between flamenco's popularity in urban centers and that of sports and other entertainments. He said, "Popularity does not necessarily mean universality.... Bullfights... and the exotic game of soccer are popular, for example, but nevertheless, few people have the ability or nature to become bullfighters or soccer players." The same argument could be made for flamenco. Infante preferred a different definition of popularity, "that which is accepted by or pleasing to the people." Did it matter that Andalusians might be unfamiliar with the name of an Andalusian palo? One could see, Infante noted, that a *copla flamenca* deeply moved Andalusian peasants and assured them of their Andalusianness every time they felt the music's vibrations moving through their bodies.[52] Something was popular if it could affect the emotions of those who most typically represented a particular people and if it could access those people's deepest feelings. The new flamenco singers were "the troubadours of the Andalusian people," those who represented "the most typical and expressive originality of this people, through their [different palos] that pain the heart." Underscoring the absolute importance of popular musical culture, Infante adds, "Ah, the copla flamenca is more accurate than electoral law for finding the true representatives of the Andalusian people!"[53] His understanding of music's ability to engender a sort of spiritual and *Völkish* awakening was nothing new—Richard Wagner had already cultivated and applied those ideas when he conceived of his "art of the future" in the nineteenth century. The novelty lay in his employment of flamenco music *in particular* to that purpose, especially given the disdain for flamenco that so many elites harbored.[54] And he insisted on belaboring that point.

Andalusian popular music, which for Infante encompassed a wide range of palos, contained "the historical essence of Andalusia." He equated this historical essence with "the deep or permanent spirit of the Andalusian people."[55] His understanding of flamenco music and its relationship to the Andalusian people and their spirit reflected the penetration of Romantic ideas as filtered through a Spanish variant of German idealist philosophy known as Krausism.[56] Unlike Demófilo, Falla, or García Lorca, who tended to separate out cante jondo from other Andalusian musical forms, viewing the former as belonging to gitanos and taking it more seriously as an art form than other permutations of cante or baile, Infante included more than a dozen palos in the flamenco genre, and he refused to distinguish between Andalusian and gitano music. They were all part of a whole. In a not very helpful explanation, he said, "These musical expressions, when they are flamencoized, belong to flamenco."[57] Trying to clarify the distinction between flamenco and other genres of music (in response to Demófilo's and others' desires to treat Andalusian and gitano music as separate from one another), Infante added, "There are not, according to popular sentiment, coplas gitanas and coplas andaluzas, only *modes* of singing the same copla, in a more or less gitano way."[58] He dispensed with what he conceived of Falla's false distinction between cante jondo and cante flamenco, whereby cante flamenco represented some kind of modern, commercialized, and bowdlerized version of the ancient cante jondo. Instead he insisted that flamenco existed long before cante jondo, that this distinction was a twentieth-century invention, and that it was a term whose meaning had been lost to the memory of the common people.[59] It was now up to him to uncover the origins of flamenco.

For Infante, flamenco, with its ancient roots, was a "complete lyrical organism" that offered up three forms of beautiful expression: "singing, guitar playing, and dance."[60] It also had the distinction of being a musical system that people treated and analyzed simultaneously as both European and non-European. He asserted that if people listened carefully enough to flamenco music they would be disconcerted because they would have to conclude that flamenco arose out of a great culture from the past, and that would be a difficult concept for serious people to comprehend and be comfortable with.

> What great culture would express itself through flamenco? Flamenco! Buffoonery, an exotic trinket, a tchotchke from the South.... But do Andalusian flamencos have this thing they call culture? Where is this live culture located?... On the surface of the fields with their constant tragic upheavals, on the stages of theaters and cafés, on the lonely streets of the rural villages and in the shadowy cities, at the moment when flamenco trembles in the air like a butterfly of sound. What great culture opens its lips in flamenco lamentation? Of course, neither the body, nor its shadow, nor its remains appear on the surface. Will it be a great underground culture? Is it that there are underground cultures, buried alive, groaning in the confinement of a tomb?[61]

Flamenco, although despised by many critics, embodies a once-great culture that had to hide in the shadows and mask its sorrows in song and dance. The songs, at least originally, were free of instrumental or choral accompaniment, and Infante equated this freedom with solitude, with loneliness.[62] Those who sang and continue to sing cante flamenco were doing it "not to please themselves but to liberate their imprisoned pain."[63] But what caused this pain? Exile and expulsion.

Infante posited that whoever created flamenco had to be a wandering people; that their music, rhythms, style, and so on, had to re-create stylistically the act of being banished to peripheries unknown; that these wandering people had to strip down their musical aesthetic expression to the melic (lyric) form. Finally, "they must have felt constrained in their movements, fearful of a strange power. The reduced scope of their melodies, their alternating progressions, come and go, in a narrow enclosure: the space of their dances says so: men in or near prison." He concludes that these wanderers must have been "profoundly sad" since the music's rhythm sounded like the "hours of grief," and the coplas registered "lyrical protests."[64] Putting this all together, Infante surmised that the great transformation in Andalusian music occurred between the last quarter of the sixteenth century—during the forced conversion and expulsion of the *moriscos*—and around the first quarter of the eighteenth century. The music that would become "flamencoizable" entered the royal court of Ferdinand and Isabel during the Renaissance. But Muslims in Spain, who had been the source of popular music at the time, remained the keepers of this culture, even if they had to conceal their religious background through forced conversions. These Muslims in hiding lived in Andalusia, and many were protected by fellow Andalusian laborers and nobles and, Infante suggested, gitanos who took them into their own communities.[65] In his final synthesis, Infante proclaimed that these "wandering bands, persecuted with fury . . . now roam from place to place and constitute communities ruled by leaders, and open to every desperate pilgrim, expelled from Society for misfortune and crime. All they need to do is be initiated to enter the group. It's the Gypsies. The hospitable wandering Gypsies, brothers of all persecuted[,] . . . a flock of Andalusians, the last descendants of men from the most beautiful cultures of the world; now fugitive laborers (in Arabic, *felamengu* means fugitive or expelled laborer). . . . Do you understand why the name flamenco has not been used in Spanish literature until the nineteenth century, and why although it has existed since [the sixteenth century], it did not appear in general usage?" Using this Arabic name, felamengu/flamenco became a code word to protect fugitive Moriscos, he continued.[66] These Andalusian exiles began to flee to the "mountains of Africa and Spain" and preserve "the music of the Fatherland," and in the process, "this music served to analyze their pain and affirm their spirit: the slow rhythm, the comatose exhaustion. The great creative legacy, reduced to the condition of Gypsies!"[67]

With this thesis, Infante solved for himself the mystery of the appearance of the word "flamenco" so late in the nineteenth century, when the many forms of flamenco song and dance seemed to have much earlier origins. His theory also accounted for what seemed to be the "Gypsification" of Andalusian music and for the "Arabic sounding" lamentations that could be detected in the flamenco genre. Oddly enough, his suppositions about the origins of flamenco did not include the other major group expelled from Spain—the Jews—even though the music shares some traces of medieval Sephardic music, and some musicologists claim that the *petenera* palo had Jewish roots.[68] Finally, his theory linked the musical form to historical and contemporary politics in Andalusia. And it is with this link that we must now conclude.

Tucked away between his discussion of the lonely and improvised character of flamenco performance and his historical explanation of flamenco as the music of a disposable people in hiding, Infante makes an astounding comparison between the character of Europeans, their political ideologies, and their urban spaces, on the one hand, and those of Seville, one of the most prominent flamenco cities, on the other. He lambastes the "West," with its "political democracies or individual tyrannies," for claiming that its people value individualism while they simultaneously mock flamenco. These supposed democracies impose uniform laws that go against nature. Reminiscent of his discussion of Europe, the United States, and Detroit in his earlier work, *El complot de Tablada*, Infante attacks the "the tyranny of the mass: the same perspectives, avenues with the same architecture, animated by the same inspiration from European cities." Andalusia, on the other hand, with its jewel city, Seville, brags "unequal streets, curves, each house with a different spirit, unheard of perspectives," blessed by God with grace. In Seville we have "the city of individualism." He argues that Europe is in decline, but that Andalusians with their song are the true free spirits, the true libertarians: "Here, the cante.... Each individual with a different vision, a distinct sound and an individual feel for humanity. Each individual, an expression of a world in the universe, who laughs when he feels like it. We, Andalusians!"[69] Given this analogy between Europe's uniform tyranny of the masses with political decline and Andalusians' nonstandardized cities and individualistic temperaments with political liberty, it is easy to see how Infante can make a teleological argument linking the history of flamenco and its oppressed peoples to a libertarian story of political salvation.

Unlike nationalists of any stripe and most intellectuals of his era, Blas Infante defended the popularity of flamenco, viewing it as an expression of the Andalusian—and, by extension, Spanish—soul. Unwilling to regard flamenco and the land from which it sprung as some kind of national joke or a representation of backwardness, he bestowed on it the power to heal Andalusia's social and political wounds. He made no meaningful distinction between the cante jondo and other flamenco song forms, although he imagined that what others termed cante jondo was a repository of pain carried across the generations. For him, flamenco, with its improvisational elements, echoed the independent spirit of a long-oppressed people. The history of Spain after the Reconquest, according to him, reflected Spain's decline and the pursuit of centralizing, corrupt power at the expense of the common people. Only through a recognition of Andalusia's historical and cultural importance to the Spanish nation-state would all of Spain thrive, and this recognition was best achieved through a federated system of autonomous communities. Andalusia would still be tied to the state, but, he believed, it would be strong and independent enough to improvise economic and political

The Marriage of Flamenco, Politics, & National Liberation, 1914—1936   143

solutions to local problems. His dreams of political autonomy for Andalusia failed to materialize, however, doomed as they were by the looming war, but in his writings we find a poetic marriage of flamenco, politics, and national liberation.

As we have seen in the preceding two chapters, Catalan and Andalusian nationalists manipulated people's different perceptions of flamenco to drive their own agendas about independence and autonomy. The next chapter will depart from the regional scale and move to the international one to see how Spaniards and foreigners—unwillingly and willingly—affixed flamenco to Spain's national identity.

5

Spain on Display Abroad and at Home, 1867—1922

Spain was all the rage at the 1889 Paris International Exposition. To hear tell of it, nobody could resist the fiery Gypsy women who bewitched men with their syncopated rhythms and strategically revealing costumes, nor the bullfights that exposed the seemingly primitive and bloodthirsty traits of the Spaniard. "Do you love the Spanish?" asked French musicologist and composer Julien Tiersot. "We have them everywhere. Bullfights on the right, bullfights on the left; a Spanish choral society here, Spanish shows there; at the Cirque d'hiver, major Spanish festivals, orchestra, dance[;] . . . at the Exposition, the Gypsies of Granada. Spain is over the top; indeed, it is too much for one man to contemplate and coldly analyze so many Spanish seductions!"[1] The French were seduced; Spanish elites, appalled. Once again with the tacit approval of Spanish authorities, the French became drunk with the liquor of Spanish Romanticism while elite Spaniards longed for a temperance movement to rid these fairs of the españolada.[2]

As many scholars have pointed out, International Expositions (or World's Fairs, in American parlance) provide a glimpse into the numerous ways that national identity is displayed to the wider world.[3] Less discussed is how the dynamic interplay between the host country, participating countries, and visitors to the fairs also help to construct and reify nations' identities. In cases like Spain's, the projection of national identity, like Spain's identity itself, remained highly fractured and contested. On the one hand, various Spanish governments took the goals of the World's Fairs seriously: to display the country's march toward progress through its industry, and later, its arts. Like many other nations, Spain deployed artisans to showcase their technological achievements and artisanal products.[4] On the other hand, when entertainment became a fundamental part of World's Fairs, official Spain had difficulty deciding what and how to represent Spain's diverse cultural heritage. Flamenco? Choruses? Classical music? Folk dances? Bullfights? Yes. Such decisions were complicated by the fact that visiting countries did not always choose the entertainment; sometimes host countries employed their own agents to contract performers directly from a particular nation for these world spectacles.[5] So for Spaniards there always seemed to be tensions that could not be resolved, some revolving around issues of class and nationalism and others around urban/rural divides, and perhaps this accounts for the mélange of entertainments that Spain produced for export to these expositions. Between exploiting the popularity of flamenquismo that foreigners seemed to crave and desiring to demonstrate the rich legacy of Spanish traditional folklore *and* a familiarity with European elite culture, Spanish organizers of various World's Fairs took a scattershot approach to entertainment. But mostly, they fell back on flamenquismo. The reactions to the gratuitous display of flamenquismo varied from audience to audience and eventually had repercussions for how flamenquismo and flamenco were perceived domestically.

This chapter explores the various dynamics that occurred among foreigners and Spaniards as they consumed Spanish entertainment via various World Expositions of the nineteenth and twentieth centuries. Spanish entertainment in these expositions cemented foreigners' idea of Spain as the land of Gypsies and flamenco dancers, much to the chagrin of many elite Spaniards. In fact, an incipient mass tourism industry outside of Spain began to take advantage of such stereotypes to lure tourists to Spain, even to parts of Spain that had no flamenco tradition.[6] Spanish elite visitors tended to cringe in shame at what they viewed as yet another depiction of Spanish exoticism, backwardness, and impotence but felt helpless to exorcise these powerful Romantic ghosts. At the same time, some of these flamenco shows—especially those performed in Paris—inspired non-Spanish avant-garde composers and artists to encourage Spanish composers and artists to draw from the flamenco/Andalusian idiom to create new masterpieces. As a result, members of the Spanish avant-garde began to stamp their artistic imprimatur on certain kinds of flamenco music, distinguishing between "commercialized" and "authentic" flamenco. This avant-garde would have its greatest impact on the now legendary 1922 Concurso de Cante Jondo (cante jondo contest) in Granada. To show how flamenco and Spanish national identity underwent this dual and simultaneous process of denigration and legitimation between the late nineteenth century and the Spanish Civil War, I delve into the world of entertainment at World's Fairs and related exhibitions held outside of Spain between 1851 and 1937, the majority of them located in Paris.[7]

A Brief History of World Expositions

Although most people mark the beginning of the era of World Expositions with the Great Exhibition of the Works of Industry of All Nations (London, 1851), world's expositions have an earlier history. Certainly, there are links between the European premodern fairs and markets, but the idea of more formalized exhibitions showcasing a nation's crafts and industries came from France in 1797 when the government of the Directory deemed it necessary to show the public that the French economy was still vibrant despite the ongoing Continental wars.[8] Still, London's Great Exhibition stood out for its size and scope, its heady displays marking the wonders of industrialization—the Crystal Palace, the big machines—its optimistic modernity, and its vision of British national and imperial power in the modern age, and so it is no wonder that the Great Exhibition represented a new way of displaying national ideologies. Every few years after that, it seems, various nations— mostly in Europe and the United States—held an exhibition, some spectacular, like London's 1851 Exhibition, and others more limited in their appeal, like Atlanta's 1881 International Cotton Exposition. Originally these post-1851 fairs concentrated on exposing visitors to the wonders of modern technology and the benefits of free trade. Later, as the popularity of these events grew and more economically diverse groups of people attended, the goals of these exhibitions slowly transformed. More and more exhibitions had pedagogical displays, and the hosts often held scholarly international conferences concurrently. By the 1870s, however, after World's Fairs had become routinized, many Europeans had become blasé about attending yet another exposition. To lure visitors in, exhibition organizers began to rely on promoting popular entertainment, so much so, that by the late 1880s entertainment became one of the most prominent features of these expositions.[9] As of 1900, entertainment became *the* reason many people came to the fair, and those who wished to expose visitors to educational matters or to the wonders of commerce had to clothe their exhibits in the garb of spectacle.

Popular culture's encroachment on fairgrounds was nothing new. Entertainments that we associate today with carnivals and county fairs— an assortment of food and drink, contests, stalls, and people-watching— had flourished in European fairs in the preindustrial age. But in the early years of the International Expositions, illegal entertainments popped up on the margins of the fairground sites. Once organizers of these fairs understood that people sought out the fairs for their entertainment value, they began to incorporate these diversions into the designs of the fairgrounds themselves, attempting to sanitize the spectacles for mass consumption along the way, although not always successfully.

The French encouraged this process in 1867 when they included designs for an amusement park and fairground in their original plans for the site on the Champ de Mars. The park, which surrounded the Exhibition Hall, was meant to hold exhibits too large for the building's interior; it also became the site for entertainment and non-European national pavilions.[10] Because the "exotic" pavilions' exhibits merged with the daily spectacles on the same grounds, the park became the focus of the exposition and "contributed to the transformation of the exhibition into a huge spectacle. With national pavilions displayed alongside amusement facilities such as café concerts, theaters, or Nadar's gas balloon, a visitor could not distinguish between entertainment and education, between amusement and information."[11] But the Paris Exposition of 1889 and Chicago's World Columbian Exposition of 1893 set the standard for integrating entertainment into the exhibits without shame and championing education through entertainment. Paris's Exposition, most famous for bequeathing us with the Eiffel Tower, transformed technological know-how into a "pleasurable distraction." Colonial pavilions provided glimpses into unknown peoples and "refreshment areas became exotic restaurants from far-off lands, serviced by equally exotic peoples."[12] Once Chicago's 1893 Exposition rolled around, there were no pretenses about what entertainment meant for fairgoers and fair organizers. Organizers set aside an entire mile-long expanse of land for the sole purpose of entertaining visitors, the place now famously known as the Midway Plaisance. Renowned for its Ferris wheel, Turkish bazaars, and, most scandalously, its Egyptian belly dancers, the Midway achieved unparalleled success.[13] From 1893 on, World's Fairs contained more hucksterism than innovation, more spectacle than edification, but as long as visitors could be entertained, they would keep coming to these fairs, promising the possibility of riches for host countries, which could make money through this incipient incarnation of modern tourism.[14] As we shall see, Spain featured prominently in these spectacles, holding a liminal space between European power and exotic Other, recalling for western Europeans a kind of noble and primitive preindustrial past, and for Spaniards a shameful national representation that rendered Spain weak and kept it from joining the European powerhouses.

Spanish Entertainment at the Fairs

As a western European power, Spain consistently participated in International Expositions from their very beginnings in 1851 until 1937, when the war-torn Republicans tried to rally the international community in Paris to aid them in defeating the Nationalists. Spain's officials and entrepreneurs treated the themes of each exposition seriously, poised to display the craft, industry, and art of the nation among the world of nations. Most often, their attempts to impress met with scorn or indifference, much to the dismay of the Spaniards who wrote about such things. But the entertainment—that was a different matter. Many of the foreign writers found much to admire in the songs and dances on display for the audiences who hungered for distraction. The music and dance came in many forms, often occurring at different places within each exposition site: there were classical music performances, operas, zarzuelas, and variations on flamenco. Although Spanish officials who organized these entertainments tended to promote classical performances and a wide variety of regional folk songs and dances, foreign audiences tended to stick to what they thought they knew about Spain—they clamored for Gypsies, flamenco, and as much Orientalism as one could muster.

The Universal Expositions of 1867 and 1878 in Paris began the process of incorporating entertainment into the fiber of the exhibitions themselves and, in the case of Spain, the French created simulacra of what they imagined Spaniards to be, and Spanish exhibitors cooperated, willingly or not. Eating began to be recognized as a form of entertainment too. The Exposition of 1867, where the national cafés and restaurants began to become permanent fixtures at these exhibitions, were designed to expose visitors to a variety of national cuisines, costumes, languages, and habits, but as one American pointed out, "two-thirds or more of the Tunisian, Roumanian, Spanish, Turkish, and other girls and garçons employed in the foreign restaurants of the Exhibition are actually French, and the real visitors from those countries are the last to discover it."[15] The illusion of delivering national authenticity through food prompted Carlos Frontaura, a novelist and correspondent for the satirical newspaper *El cascabal*, to mock the pretentious French visitors who thought they could know what Spain was really like after one visit to the "Spanish" café. Frontaura quotes their conversations in blistering detail for his Spanish readers. Visitors, he implied, competed to discover and point out the "real" bullfighters among the crowd. Another remarked on a diner who was *certainly* a Sevillian aristocratic dancer who would break out into a fandango as soon she finished her meal.[16] As to opinions of Spain's exhibit in the Exhibition Hall, we know little. A few sources hint at the dismay with which Spaniards felt about the displays that seemed shackled to the past and to distorted stereotypes: "Paris, being Paris, will ignore our books, our science, or our men of great achievements, but at the Universal Exhibition they will do justice to our progress, lauding bullfighter X enthusiastically . . . and the sword of bullfighter Z that felled the fiercest beast in one stroke."[17] Frontaura seemed so crushed by what he saw of Spain's exhibit that he could not write directly about it, using instead the words of the French writer Leon Plee to reflect Spain's "state of progress": "There was talk of circuses and great rides, and powerful and terrible emotions, and everyone expected to see bullfighters and chulos. . . . We already heard the . . . music, half Arab, half European, of the old Spain." Frontaura then adds, "The French are always the same when they speak of Spain; For them, Spain is a country where one thinks of nothing more than playing the castanets, highway bandits robbing, and lovers wooing."[18]

Even some of the entertainers at this exposition, although French, tried to masquerade as Spanish flamenco performers. Finding himself at one of the popular outdoor cafés-concerts where visitors spent their money downing beer and listening to crooners of all sorts, Frontaura laments the loss of his hard-earned money to singers attempting to capitalize on fantasies of Romantic Spain. In this instance, a woman appears on the stage whom he describes in unflattering terms as "ugly and ungainly," wearing a piece of tulle in imitation of a Spanish mantilla. She begins to sing in French, clumsily moving her arms, legs, and skirt, telling the tale of an Aragonese princess who falls in love with a bandit, much to the dismay of her father, who threatens her with a life in the convent. While the father searches for the local inquisitor (of course), the princess and her bandit lover perform a flamenco dance in Triana, the Gypsy quarter of Seville. The only Spanish utterance the performer injects into the production is a foulmouthed curse, which the French crowd repeats in great excitement. After one more zapateado flourish that leads to the dancer exposing her legs, Frontaura remarks on their comical shape and the bellows of laughter this elicits in her audience.[19] Although this performance is described in comical terms, it also reflects the tired stereotypes that Spaniards had to endure when others represented them.

Not much changed in 1878. Spanish government organizers banked on the popularity of Orientalism and offered up as its façade a partial replica of the Moorish Alhambra.[20] Writing in his diary on May 18, 1878, the Catalan literary critic Josep Yxart recounts the display of wares hanging in the interior of the pavilion: "The general impression one gets of the Spanish exhibit has been painful: neither wealth nor novelty . . . nor taste nor grandeur are to be found in their curation."[21] Foreign commentary on the Spanish Pavilion remained sparse, although French writers expressed admiration for the artistry of Spain's musical instruments, especially its "national instrument," the guitar, which Spanish lovers supposedly strummed under windows, played at every important festival, and even carried with them into battle.[22]

Despite Spanish intellectuals' disdain for the *pandereta* that passed for Spain's achievements in the world, Spanish officials and businessmen knew that pandereta paid the bills.[23] Even before the 1889 Paris Exposition, Spanish entrepreneurs sought to display their modernity to British audiences in a little-known Spanish Exhibition at London's Earl's Court (the summer of 1889). They knew, however, that they needed to lure the British in with the requisite spectacles.[24] One Spaniard who wrote to the foreign minister Segismundo Moret hoping to gin up support for the enterprise remarked on how Spaniards could display their exhibits and surpass the achievements of the Italians, who had gained much success in London the previous year: "With a simple parody of bullfights . . . with our rich repertoire of national music, our theater, our musical bands and characteristic dances, our colonial products, our own products, etc., . . . we must think about carrying out an enterprise that is not analogous or similar, but rather of such a magnitude of superiority that we leave behind . . . the Yankees with their

Indians, buffaloes, and automatic machines, and the Italians with their 'organ grinders' and 'macaroni.'"[25] The organizers were not afraid, it seems, of self-colonization, as long as they could do it better than the Americans and Italians. One privately circulated prospectus for this exhibition, which was meant to attract financial backers, called for around 650 people in addition to the 1,000 exhibitors for theatrical and musical entertainment, because "the Spanish people" were "essentially a musical race." They budgeted 66,000 pounds sterling for this "Spanish Contingent," which included "200 Musicians and Military Band, 40 Dancers . . . 20 Barbers in Figaro Costume . . . and 40 Bull-Fighters and Bandits of olden times."[26] This poorly organized, poorly funded exposition failed miserably on all counts, but success lay ahead for Spain in the 1889 Exposition, even if the achievements resided in its entertainments, not in its products or industry.[27]

Paris's Exposition Universelle of 1889 was probably Spain's most successful outside of Spain itself, notwithstanding Spanish elites' rejection of this version of their nation on display.[28] This fair stands out, too, for the importance of sound in the fairgoers' experiences, not just the visual spectacle. Not only did Thomas Edison's phonograph and telephone loom large in visitors' aural encounters; so did the clack of machines, the brassy notes of bands, and the symphonic concerts in the Palais du Trocadéro. Not until this fair had musicians successfully agitated to dedicate such a large portion of the fairgrounds to musical displays.[29] Musicologist Annegret Fauser notes that numerous people left behind documents commenting on the barrage of sound emanating from the fairgrounds. In fact, "music was so pervasive and inescapable that . . . it was perceived as being 'everywhere, raging with equal violence at the bandstand of the gypsies, under the tents of the Arabs, in the picturesque shacks of Morocco and Egypt.'"[30] Exoticism was the order of the day, whether the contributions came from the soundscape of the Javanese dancers, the Rue de Cairo and its "authentic" Arabs, Buffalo Bill's Wild West Show, or the Romanian Gypsies. As one can witness from Tiersot's commentary at the beginning of this chapter, Spain contributed significantly to the soundscape and visual spectacle with its choruses, symphonies, folk dances, and Gypsy performances. French newspapers had a field day with the Spaniards, feminizing the men, equating the dancers with non-Europeans, and sexualizing the women. All of these characterizations were best illustrated by the comic newspaper *La caricature* (see figures 12–14).[31] Inconveniently (for Spain) it could not project the kind of "serious" national music that might

Figure 12. One of a series of depictions of Spaniards at the 1889 Paris World's Exposition in *La caricature*, each titled "Tout à l'Espagne." The caption reads, "Oh the gitanas, what women! with their dance (but not like belly dancing, for example)! the Javanese of Spain, more lively than snakes . . . but the men! awful."

Illustrator: F. Bac.
Source: *La caricature*, September 24, 1889, 291.
Licensing of image courtesy of the Bibliothèque Nationale de France.

Figure 13. Spaniards at the 1889 Paris World's Exposition in *La caricature*. A sampling of the captions reads: "He tries to appear light and graceful; but he will have to make do, despite the native elegance, with his (female neighbor) across from him" (*below male dancer*); "She is the best! Look at her grace, such knowledgeable undulations of her skirt: the Spaniards never tire of it and neither do the Parisians" (*under dancer in center*); "Calm down, proud Spaniard, her turn will come soon" (*under dancer in upper right-hand corner*).

Illustrator: Drum.
Source: *La caricature*, September 24, 1889, 292.
Licensing of image courtesy of the Bibliothèque Nationale de France.

Spain on Display Abroad and at Home, 1867–1922 153

Figure 14. One of a series of depictions of Spaniards at the 1889 Paris World's Exposition in *La caricature*. Despite any evidence of female bullfighters at the Exposition, this caricaturist decided to portray one, warning the famous matadors Lagartijo, Frascuelo, and Ángel Pastor that they better watch out for this one. The caption below the flamenco dancer reads: "She turns and turns, clacking her castanets! She excites her public to the point of delirium by her captivating grace and her fiery glances! Olé! Olé and the clapping of hands accompany her! . . . She will dance until she is completely exhausted."

Illustrator: Drum.
Source: *La caricature*, September 24, 1889, 293.
Licensing of image courtesy of the Bibliothèque National de France.

obliterate the image of Carmen from the European imaginary once and for all—although it tried. Instead, Spaniards performed a great variety of music: classical European compositions, regional folk music, and flamenco exoticism. Spain's triumph lay in musical exoticism; its failure too. This potpourri of styles reflected the differing missions of various organizers—the Spanish government took charge of the official programming for its National Days and French organizers contracted the more "picturesque" entertainers for theaters, cafés, and restaurants.

The French organizers, with the help of the French government, took music very seriously in this exposition, both its composition and performance, creating a commission known as the Commission des Auditions Musicales to choose how and who should represent the music of nations. Split into four categories covering "'musical composition' (which dealt with all art music); orphéons and choral societies; brass and other bands; [and] military music," the commission, through a carefully selected series of performances and competitions, aimed "to showcase French music and its performance, and to engage in a friendly rivalry with other nations." Despite the lack of officially sanctioned participation, representatives of Spain were among the foreign countries to bid for concert space in the Trocadéro Palace, and they achieved those ends, joining Belgium, Finland, Italy, Norway, Russia, and the United States in the concert of nations.[32] Here, on August 20, 24, 29, and September 20, various regionally sponsored groups performed. The Orfeo Coruñés sang a series of songs, some Galician, some not, and included a medley of "Works of Spanish Composers, Popular Songs of Ancient European Iberia." A choir and *estudiantina* from San Sebastian sang a greater variety of regional songs, including sevillanas (Andalusia), seguidillas (Andalusia and Castile / La Mancha), the jota (Aragon), and the zortzico (Basque Country). The Unión Artístico Musical de Madrid performed pieces by Spanish classical composers, but they also nodded to the classical European tradition with their rendition of Mozart's *Turkish March*. Finally, they included a "procession and dances ... representing the nine regions of Spain."[33] These choices reveal an unspoken desire on the part of Spanish commercial interests to showcase the kinds of culture that both Spanish liberals and conservatives could rally around: a symphonic culture that aristocrats and aspirational aristocrats favored, and a popular, rural, folkloric culture that displayed the depth and variety of regional songs. Both of these traditions excluded the urban culture of flamenco. Flamenco still remained marginalized and discounted by Spanish elites, but it became one of the highlights for French and other non-Spanish audiences.

It was certainly ironic that the French organizers considered Gypsy musical performances as authentic representations of a nation's folk essence when, at least in the Spanish case, flamenco music was an urban phenomenon. As Fauser argues, Gypsies, because they were viewed by Europeans as a racialized Other who populated numerous countries while losing their own culture in the process of diaspora, gained in exchange an authentic popular voice through osmosis. Therefore, these blank cultural slates were able to imbibe their country-of-exile's folk essence and project it to the wider world. At least that was what non-gitano Europeans imagined. The "Spanish Gypsies from Granada" who performed at the Grand Téâtre de l'Exposition were thought to be tied to the natural world, and thus to the people of the Spanish heartland.[34] At the same time, exposition organizers and writers feminized them and lumped them in with the exotic Others of Africa and Asia (although closer in temperament to Africa, it seemed), placing Spain in the not-quite-European category, a classification that had sent Spaniards into fits of pique over the course of the century.

The Gypsies of Granada with their Capitán, a troupe of flamenco singers and dancers, became one of the grand sensations at the Grand Téâtre de l'Exposition (see figure 15). The performance group, according to French accounts, consisted at first of eleven people: "El Chivo," the head of the troupe and father to three of the female performers, Soledad (see figure 16), Matilda, and Viva; Pepa, Dolores, Lola, and Antonia, rounding out the females; and Antonio "El Pichiri" and Manuel, the male dancers.[35] Soon after their debut on July 11, and perhaps because of their success, the flamenco star—even by Spanish standards—Juana "La Macarrona" (spelled erroneously at times as La Maccarona and La Macarena) joined the group as its headliner, although Soledad also became a rising star during the course of the exposition. The most prominent male performer after El Chivo was Pichiri, and then some other minor dancers named Juana, Zola, Sánchez, and Concepción also performed.[36] The production, although carried out on a big theatrical stage, was similar to those found in cafés cantantes in Spain. The stage scenery simulated a humble Spanish inn. Once the curtain rose, the singers, dancers, and guitar players sat in a line with the men in the center and the women flanking them. The guitars, castanets, and clapping hands formed the "only orchestra." Then the singers and dancers performed many of the standard flamenco palos—tangos, alegrías, fandangos—as well as popular songs and dances found outside of Andalusia like the jota, seducing the spectators over the course of the show.[37] French commentary on the performances should not surprise us, given that it replicated many of the accounts written by travel writers earlier in the century. This time, however, the experience was open to all (including women) who could afford admission to the fair, not just select travelers. Female bodies took precedence over the music itself, although critics also remarked on the polyrhythmic sounds emanating from castanets and clapping palms, sounds that, from writers' descriptions, seemed both to mirror and quicken the pulse of sexually aroused spectators.

Figure 15. Poster advertising "The Gypsies of Granada at the Grand Théâtre de L'Exposition," 1889.
Bibliothèque Nationale de France, ENT DN-1 (LEVY, Emile/21)-ROUL.
Licensing of image courtesy of the Bibliothèque Nationale de France.

Figure 16. Young woman seated with a guitar, wearing a dark dress and shawl. The woman is thought to be Soledad, ca. 1889.
Photo by Emilio Beauchy Cano.
© ICAS-SAHP, Fototeca Municipal de Sevilla. Boele Van Hensbroek Archive. Emilio Beauchy Cano (1847–1928).

Although on the rare occasion the all-male critics would comment on the male dancers and singers, they focused their attention on the female form, sexualizing it and casting it into the natural world. The women sometimes surveyed audiences with "the languorous gaze of a gazelle."[38] But they were also imagined as predators ready to pounce on their unsuspecting prey. The dancers had "eyes on fire," "ardent looks," and "provocative smiles." Juana was "supple as a panther, her flexible torso, without corsets, and her swaying promises." Pepa had the "most beautiful arms in the world," while Teresa, "with her extra-Andalusian haunches, performed a certain belly dance that was more suggestive than the cold, mechanical crescendo of Cairo street."[39] The reviewer Paul Margueritte stripped down the performance this way: "I well understand. It's . . . carnal love they express. But with such naïveté! Such ingenuous and touching candor. There is nothing cynical about it; it is their instinct that shines through."[40] The sexualized treatment of the dancers linked them in critics' eyes to the other "exotic" non-European dancers and musicians of the fair, who were also perceived as being tied to Nature's kingdom. Margueritte, in grouping the Javanese, Spanish Gypsies, and Middle Eastern dancers together, said that "if one were to define the three great dances of the Exposition and to provide a reason to see them," it would be for the following reasons: "The Asian dance for the graceful flexions of the hands; the Spanish for their bodies, legs, and possessed arms: the Africans for their savage haunches—one could say that all three express love, the Javanese in incarnating the dream, the Gypsies desire, and the almées [belly dancers] satiety."[41]

The male dancers were often feminized, much in the way that male colonized subjects were feminized through the process of Orientalization.[42] Although the Gypsy men were sometimes referred to as "swarthy looking," they became linked in some writings to the broad category of almées. For example, Pichiri's "slender, lean legs, a coquettishly tight body in a short jacket, assail his companions with lightness and grace and twists in such a way as to recall the contortions of the Eastern almées. . . . Pichiri, executing the belly dance, is unsurpassable."[43] Another anonymous writer echoed Lenótre's sentiments, calling Pichiri's "contortions" "astonishing," likening his success to those movements that borrowed from the almées.[44] So although Pichiri when dancing in tandem with a female dancer could represent sexual desire and the sexual act, when dancing solo he became feminized, more controllable under the critics' gaze.

Taken together, the female and male performers of the Spanish gitano troupe served as reminders to French audiences (and presumably other foreigners) of a mythical European past depicting "man in his natural state," before the trapping of civilization masked the pulsating sexuality that lay beneath the surface of the skin. In fact, one reviewer said as much after the troupe's premiere. Calling the Gypsies "almost savage," he implied that they were plucked straight out of "the escarpment in which they habitually dwell" (the Sacromonte, no doubt) and whisked away to Paris, where somebody had to find them appropriate clothing for a "civilized" country, all in the space of a week. "Who," he asked, "would not wish to see the troupe, yesterday still clothed in rags, perform the dances so characteristic of their tribe today, before a refined audience, accompanied by wild songs and howls?"[45] Despite the musicians' and dancers' professional credentials and the fact that most of them came from Seville, not Granada, much of the French press during the exposition characterized the performers as having sprung out of the earth sui generis, ready to entertain those Europeans who had long lost their souls to civilization.[46]

By showering so much attention on the Gypsies, the French managed to transform the Spanish into colonial subjects within Europe. Nowhere is this more apparent than in the cartoon by F. Bac with a caption that reads, "Oh the gitanas, what women! with their dance (but nothing of the belly, for example)! the Javanese of Spain, even more lively than snakes . . . but the men! awful." Those short sentences managed simultaneously to Orientalize the performers, transform them into animals, and denigrate the men (see figure 12). Characterizing flamenco music and its performers as the embodiment of a world grounded in nature and animal sexuality enabled French critics to paint Spain as exotic, savage, and non-European, despite the country's location just south of the French border and distinctly within the European continent. Equally important, depicting the female dancers as sexually animalistic—one might venture to say, virile—and the male dancers as feminine, could lead one to imagine an emasculated Spain unfit for the task of being a ruling power. This hierarchy of nations is apparent in the way that critics often grouped the Spanish gitanos with the Javanese dancers and the various Middle Eastern performers, emphasizing the commonality of their "intoxicating" and "timeless" music, their performers, and their national spirits.[47] Flamenco performances achieved the careful balance necessary to convince Europeans that it was the true music of the Spanish people—Western enough not to alienate the European ear but Eastern enough so as to sound both foreign and authentic. As Fauser has noted, European spectators craved exoticism in their music and dance but became uncomfortable if they heard sounds that conflicted with their expectations of what music *should* sound like. So, for example, the other great musical sensation of the fair, the Javanese dancers, remained visually exotic while maintaining enough of a Western sound to satisfy European audiences, while the Vietnamese dancers' exoticism could not overcome the decisively discordant sounds—to European ears, anyway—that emanated from a non-Western tuning and scale.[48] Conversely, performances of North African, Middle Eastern, and Sudanese music sometimes repelled spectators and critics because the music at the fair sounded different from the purported "Arabic music" that had been filtered through French composers. To complicate matters further, some critics like Tiersot discounted the "Arabic music" for being too Gallicized and too urban and, therefore, inauthentic.[49] The gitanos' music, however, hit the sweet spot for French critics, and they responded by proclaiming its authenticity, extolling its ancient roots, and insisting on its pervasiveness throughout Spain.[50]

While the French went agog over the gitanos, Spanish writers recorded their embarrassment over what passed for Spanish entertainment at the fair. Both novelists Emilia Pardo Bazán and Benito Pérez Galdós concluded that French audiences especially had been bamboozled into believing that the flamenquismo they witnessed on stage reflected any real artistry or authenticity. Neither one dismissed flamenco altogether—they seemed to distinguish an artistic form of flamenco that they never actually defined from some other bastardized one that one might see in a local café cantante. Pardo Bazán may have been disappointed that Spain had nothing distinctive to offer in terms of industry at the fair, but she was even more dismayed by the sheer gaudiness of the performances she witnessed.[51] She first discussed the Javanese dancers (she approved), moved on to the Egyptian belly dancers (she called belly dancing "flamenco in its larval state"), and then saved her real fire for the Gitanos de Granada. She called the women "ugly, brazen, ragpickers, unable to dance, with alcoholically hoarse voices."[52] La Macarrona may have been a bit better than the rest of the dancers, but she and the other dancers were not the kind of bailaoras one might find in Seville's famous Café Silverio, a place, she conceded, where one could view some flamenco virtuosas. In reality, however, La Macarrona *did* cut her teeth in Silverio's café cantante and had been on the professional circuit for years.[53] While the French elevated the gitanas to the level of paradisiacal virgins, Bazán demoted them to trollops, commenting on their rudeness and overexaggerated mannerisms. She remained both puzzled and appalled by the enthusiastic reception they received, especially among the "most illustrious and celebrated European ladies." And then, to top it all off, these performers were not even staying true to the flamenco art; instead, they filled their repertoire with old zarzuela standards and other folk songs, sung in the most formal way possible.[54] Pérez Galdós shared similar sentiments. One letter in a series he wrote for Argentina's *La prensa* spoke of the Spanish entertainments—bullfights, flamenco dancers, and Gypsies—in terms reminiscent of Tiersot, likening them to "an invasion." The French, he proclaimed, "lick their fingers with delight upon seeing our bullfights, our Gypsy dancers, our cante jondo, or whatever (because, truthfully, I have difficulty classifying the Gypsy crooning, as they have styled it here)."[55] Like Pardo Bazán, he judged these dances revolting, examples of "the worst" kind of performance "one finds in the cafés cantantes in Madrid or Seville," and proceeds to name one such awful place, Madrid's El Imparcial. He remarked that there were two kinds of flamenquismo, one "refined" and the other "coarse," but in this instance, this group had sunk in his estimation to a lower level of crudity still. The audience lapped up the troupe's performance, thinking them "the best" and "most authentic gitanas," "and they confuse[d] the indecent contortion of their torso with the graceful sway of the hips that impresses itself in the Oriental character of that which is truly flamenco." And given that the spectators did not know any better, they were "left with the illusion that they have enjoyed the quintessence of Spanish charm."[56] Pardo Bazán's and Galdós's reviews provide us with enough information to conclude that they had at least a passing familiarity with the variety of music that fell under the heading of flamenco and that there were elements of that genre that passed artistic muster—it is just that the performances they witnessed did not measure up to those standards.

Perhaps the harshest critiques of the show came from the journalist José de Castro y Serrano, originally from Granada, whose rebukes might reflect a certain pride in an Andalusia devoid of gitanos. De Castro repeats the usual antiflamenquismo complaints about scandalous female sexuality on the stage and the performers' alcoholic tendencies, even going so far as to say that the only link between the flamenco genre and the Flemish people (*los flamencos*) is their "propensity to get drunk." But then he moves directly to racial categories and stereotypes to register his distaste for the genre—something most critics avoided doing, even if their criticisms did sometimes reveal covert racism against gitanos. He appears particularly perturbed by the spectators' admiration for all things Gypsy—for their dress, their attitudes, and their turns of phrase—and yet, he asks, "Who really wants to cultivate a friendship with a Gypsy? What mother would give up her son to a Gypsy? Who would be honored to be related to a Gypsy?" For de Castro, the idea defies comprehension. He goes beyond mere slander to set up a scenario for aspiring female flamenco performers reminiscent of the climactic scene in Dostoevsky's *Notes from the Underground*.[57] De Castro describes the lives of young gitanas with the "unfortunate luck to be born beautiful," and having the requisite bodies and voices to match. They are given castanets at an early age and lured into performing their lascivious dances with the illusion that they will receive great admiration and riches. Instead, as the years pass in these bars and cafés, the women lose their beauty, their voices, and their "feminine charm." The attributes that could have snagged them a "good husband" landed them instead in "a hospital bed or in the sad job of sending other poor women to their perdition."⁵⁸ The commercialization of their bodies through music, he implies, lands them in the same place as the common prostitute.

The French romanticization of gitanos and flamenco dancers galls him, especially because the French keep insisting that they embody Spain's true essence. He counters that, like the French, probably 90 percent of Spaniards know little to nothing about flamenco. He asks, "Would somebody dare tell us why all disorderly song and dance in our country is called flamenco?" His irritation lies in a few places, with the performers' seemingly coarse behavior, the music's origins, and the location of the performances. Like many of his compatriots, de Castro distinguishes between Andalusian and flamenco music. For him, Andalusian music is spontaneous, born of the people, and certainly not commercialized. He is not there to criticize Andalusian music, for what he views on the exposition stage is not Andalusian: "Andalusian song and dance enrapture us; but we are not enchanted by salaried Andalusians who sing and dance." True Andalusian songs and dances do not "emerge from the land of wine cellars: they are purely Oriental and, consequently, from regions where they don't drink wine . . . they don't need immoral methods to translate their songs and dances into language that expresses the joys of mourning and the laments of pleasure."⁵⁹ In these few phrases he has managed to express his reverence for a music located in the Orient and linked to Andalusia's Muslim past, a music far removed from the vulgar displays at the Grand Téâtre de l'Exposition and the café cantante. He joined the ranks of those Andalusian regionalists who looked to valorize Andalusia's Islamic past, but unlike Blas Infante, de Castro was unwilling to link flamenco to that proud tradition.⁶⁰

De Castro does not mind Orientalizing certain Spanish dancers, but he disapproves of the kind of Orientalizing done by the French organizers and press—one that relegates Spain to the savage world. He is aware that the gitanos are lumped together with the "semibarbarian people" of Egypt, Nubia, Indonesia, and South Africa, and complains that the trinket and costume shops scattered around the park do not contain the music or folk crafts of Hungarians or Neapolitans. Instead, visitors gaze at "Nubians, Persians, and Ethiopians, howling with pleasure and displaying their naked flesh," among whom the "miserable Spanish flamencos are confused." The Spaniards had been shackled together with the semibarbarians of the world, he thought, instead of joining their rightful place beside the other people of Europe. He would be more willing to accept the presence of flamenco performers and bullfighters at the fair if the organizers had also displayed more of Spain's industry, arts, and scientific discoveries. Instead, the French chose to highlight flamenco, leaving Europe deceived about Spain and "satisfy[ing] its absurd" notions about what it meant to be Spanish. The French, it seemed to him, were unpersuadable.[61]

The year 1889 opened up the musical world for Universal Expositions, but the 1893 World's Columbian Exposition (Chicago World's Fair) raised the bar for spectacles by including an entire territory spread out for amusements and musical entertainment, the Midway Plaisance. Given that the justification for this fair was to commemorate Columbus's voyage across the Atlantic (why Chicago would be the place to commemorate such a thing is a bit of a mystery), Spain played a highly visible role, just not in terms of its music. The Spanish government sent replicas of Columbus's caravels and some letters written by the explorer to the site, and the Infanta Eulalia appeared as Spain's emissary. The pavilion was a replica of the Rábida Convent in Huelva, the port from which Christopher Columbus sailed across the Atlantic. The Spanish government sent "historical" music to the fair, meaning instruments from the time of Columbus. The music was going to be reproduced in the same manner in which troubadours and jongleurs played "at the meeting between Ferdinand and Boabdil," as the *Chicago Daily Tribune* so evocatively described the fateful 1492 defeat of the last Muslim ruler of the Emirate of Granada by Ferdinand and Isabel.[62] Although there was one reference in the Spanish press to flamenco performers being contracted for the fair, there seems to be no evidence that they actually ever made it there.[63] Instead, Spain was vaguely exoticized and conflated with other "Oriental" cultures in the Midway Plaissance's Moorish Palace, which had a section that replicated the Alhambra, and where "through the opening of the arches and beyond the galleries the visitors catch glimpses of various points along the picturesque coast of Tangier. . . . In one of its parts is located THE HAREM."[64] As at other World's Fairs, when the Spanish government was allowed to decide what they would contribute to represent themselves, they did not include flamenco performers. When others got to decide the entertainment, they often included flamenco dancers and other vaguely Orientalized versions of Spanish culture that drew on a North African idiom. Yet again, foreigners conflated Spain with Africa. Such was the case again with France in 1900.

French and Spanish critics' observations about Spanish participation at the fair reinforced those they made in 1889. In fact, some who wrote in 1889 would return to the same themes in 1900. This time, however, Spanish participation was clouded by its recent defeat and loss of colonies in 1898. Certainly the sting of "El Desastre" remained sharp, especially since other European powers had recently begun their colonial expansion in Africa. Spanish organizers hoped to remedy this embarrassment by presenting themselves as modern, cultured Europeans.[65] So although the Spanish organizers showcased examples of art and industry, and Spanish painters like Joaquín Sorolla won the Medal of Honor in the Fine Arts competition, Spaniards could not shake off the dishonor of flamenquismo and all things Andalusian.[66] The French organizers insisted on imprisoning them in Moorish palaces.

The French created a section in the Trocadéro called Andalusia in the Days of the Moors, with vague echoes of Cairo Street from the 1889 Exposition. An Orientalist's dream, it was replete with bullfighting rings, replicas of the Sacromonte and the Alhambra, Gypsy weddings, flamenco dancers, Moors on horseback, an African neighborhood, and, among many other accoutrements, a replica of Seville's landmark tower, the Giralda.[67] Once again, according to reports, the spectacle drew large crowds, much to the horror of Spaniards who wrote about it. The journalist Alfonso de Mar described the installation as a bunch of "flamenco calamities" whose only strength lay in being the only Spanish exhibit to arrive at the exposition on time. He bemoaned the españolismo that became etched permanently on the French psyche during the previous Parisian Exposition, claiming that it "now stinks and provokes only a grimace of poorly disguised boredom and contempt among the French and foreigners who view it."[68] Embarrassment ran deep. Emilia Pardo Bazán could barely hide her disgust (again) with the parade of Spanish stereotypes, the "poorly educated" employees, and, on the day she visited, a "wise elephant" ambling through the picturesque scene.[69]

In addition to the Andalusian street, a café cantante modeled on Seville's famous Café Burrero from Seville was situated on the lower floors of the Spanish Pavilion (see figure 10 in chapter 1). This made journalist and literary figure Valero de Tornos none too happy. He noted, "The [Spanish] Commission giving further proof of its good sense, rented the underside of our pavilion to a French company which... has succeeded in exploiting Spanish specialties, and being that it's Paris, it is clear that these specialties can only be flamenco."[70] Expelling what must have been some pent-up regenerationist bile, he wryly asserted, "We will have lost our colonies; but guitar and beer, never. We complain that they think of us as a country of . . . majas, monks, and bullfighters, but the first thing one finds everywhere is cante flamenco."[71] And it is this that mortified Spanish critics, that foreigners affixed these identities onto Spain, locking the country into an ossified past and a failed present rather than a modernity that International Expositions were meant to reflect.

Pardo Bazán and Valero de Tornos both remark on the displays inside the Spanish Pavilion, and even the building's architecture itself, as remaining stuck in the past, projecting an air of melancholy to those who passed through its halls.[72] The exhibits are scarcely attended, and the wares for sale in the stalls include the usual menagerie of fans, mantillas, and hats. To them, Spain's representation at the fair reflects Spain's decline as a world power. The link between Spain's presentation at this exposition and its post-1898 battered fortunes can be found in César Sillo Cortés and Angel Guerra's not-so-subtly titled book, *Otro desastre más: España en París* (Another disaster: Spain in Paris).[73] They comment on the pavilion, which emulated a kind of generic Renaissance-style filled with tapestries and armor, a time capsule of the sixteenth century. They remark that a foreigner passing through might think, "'How great Spain was then! But, Spain today? . . . Is there a Spain today?'" The authors continue, "We have no present or future. Can't we present ourselves to the world as any more than as an evocation of the past?" The writers wander through the exposition's Hall of Colonies and remark on Spain's colonial losses, noting that "our greatness was as great as our neglect and our abandonment." Instead, all that Spain is left with, all that Spain can offer spectators, is "Andalusia in the Time of the Moors," with its "strumming guitars and cantaoras . . . reminding people that this is a petrified nation and not a living people."[74] Despite the shame Spanish writers felt about this foreign projection of Spain onto the world, it did have certain positive effects over the next couple of decades, at least in terms of Spanish artistic creation, as we shall soon see.

After the Paris 1900 Exposition, the more celebrated World's Fairs seem to have shifted their center of gravity from Europe to the United States, at least until the interwar period, and although Spain participated in some of the expositions across the Atlantic, financial straits and political disintegration prevented Spain from participating in more than a nominal way. This does not imply that the World's Fairs no longer made their mark on Spanish identity. They did. In fact, the role played by the expositions through 1900 (and buttressed by Spain's

1929 International Exhibitions in Barcelona and Seville) helped cultivate a European avant-garde's musical appreciation for flamenco/Andalusian music that would influence the Spanish avant-garde in its quest to refashion flamenco for its own purposes. The synthesis of a more general European avant-garde aesthetic with that of Spain's avant-garde cropped out the most embarrassing and unsavory bits of flamenco. In the process they sanctified cante jondo as the only flamenco form that could be deemed art. At the same time, the expositions, acting as microcosms of the world, fed into a burgeoning European tourist industry that would continue to render Spain as a land of flamenco.

Musical Fusion, Purity, and the Concurso de Cante Jondo

What would have happened if in 1889 the French composer Claude Debussy had missed the Gypsies of Granada with Their Capitán and bypassed La Macarrona and Soledad? It is highly likely that Spanish musical history would be different today. But Debussy did take careful notice of them, and of the other unfamiliar musical acts that year, borrowing elements of the "primitive" and the folkloric from their work, incorporating them into his own musical compositions, and becoming one of the leaders of the European musical avant-garde in the process. He was but one of many composers who adapted folk music for symphonic purposes, although many of his contemporaries, like Béla Bartók, mined music from their own nations' heartlands to compose nationalistic works.[75] Debussy differed from other composers in that he expanded his own musical range by going outside of Europe for his inspiration, much as Vincent Van Gogh had appropriated Japanese prints, and Pablo Picasso, African masks. Debussy's experimental music attracted to Paris musicians from across the continent and, wittingly or not, influenced the music of some of Spain's most canonized composers. Those who heard the Parisian siren call included Enrique Granados, Isaac Albéniz, Ricardo Viñas, Joaquín Turina, and, most important for our story, Manuel de Falla, who began his musical career steeped in the sounds of Andalusia by way of French and Russian influences and who used what he learned from these Europeans to bring luster to some elements of flamenco.[76]

Falla resided in Paris from 1907 to 1914, and there he not only mixed with expatriate musicians from Spain, he also moved in musical circles that included European composers such as Maurice Ravel and Igor Stravinsky, who were part of the group known as Les Apaches, originally formed to pay homage to Debussy. As part of Les Apaches, Falla sought ways to incorporate Debussy's style into his own, convinced that Debussy's "Latinate" and "impressionist" style meshed well with Spain's. Debussy, on the other hand, had become enamored of the gitanos he had heard perform at the Universal Expositions held in Paris in 1889 and 1900.[77] His encounters with the flamencoized music inside and outside the Spanish Pavilions in Paris convinced him that Spanish music had something of the exotic to offer the world. Debussy's musical adaptations reinforced Falla's predilection to assimilate echoes of that Gypsy music into his own compositions.[78]

When World War I reached France, Falla moved back to Spain and began what would become a very fecund musical period that paid homage to Andalusia. In collaboration with María Martínez Sierra, Falla wrote the score for the ballet *El amor brujo*. In composing it he synthesized Andalusian folk songs and rhythms with those of French modernist music. He also cast "real Gypsies" in his work, most notably the flamenco dancer Pastora Imperio, who, although not trained formally in dance, lent an indigenous authenticity to Falla's concert hall work. Although this work succeeded internationally, it fell flat for most Spanish critics because they believed it lacked "Spanish soul," too colored as it was by the French modernist strains of Debussy and Ravel.

Falla's views about Andalusian music were also shaped by Russian ballet's 1916 arrival in Spain (followed by Stravinsky in the 1920s). When the Russian ballet began its tour in 1916, Falla drew on these innovative compositions and choreographies for his next big work, while some of the Russians who were on this tour and subsequent ones incorporated the Spanish music they witnessed in cafés cantantes to enrich their own choreographic imaginations. This cross-cultural fertilization resulted in *El sombrero de tres picos* (1919), a retelling of a classic Spanish novel with a modernist aesthetic. Some of the finest artists of the European avant-garde collaborated on this ballet. But Falla and Russians like Stravinsky shared something else: a belief that popular music from their respective homelands had their origins in something broadly defined as "the Orient."[79] For the Russians, this Oriental music came from Byzantium; for Spaniards, it arrived, they thought, by way of Egypt and North Africa and could be heard most distinctly in the wails of cante jondo emanating from Andalusia's narrow, cobbled streets.

Falla found new ways to draw on what he saw as the rich heritage of Andalusian music to create modernist musical compositions, but he also feared that this heritage was disappearing before his very eyes. It is with a sense of panic that in 1922 he helped organize the Concurso de Cante Jondo (Cante Jondo Competition) with Federico García Lorca, the legendary poet and playwright, and Fernando de los Ríos, the Socialist politician and later minister during Spain's Second Republic. This competition has become legendary and widely chronicled in the various accounts of twentieth-century flamenco, especially as it pertains to giving cante jondo an intellectual sanction that was missing from most discussions of flamenco until that time.[80] Given that, those details will only appear here in broad outline. More pertinent to this narrative is how the organizers' conceptions of authenticity, folklore, and mass culture clashed with observations held by antiflamenquistas such as Eugenio Noel, by ambivalent flamenco audiences such as Emilia Pardo Bazán and Benito Pérez Galdós—who, if we remember, witnessed the same musical acts as Debussy—and even by flamencophiles like Blas Infante. By segmenting out cante jondo from the rest of flamenco and sanitizing flamenco's eroticized elements, the organizers hoped to bring serious study and appreciation to a form of music they perceived as ancient, mysterious, and rich with melodies for modern audiences, while dispatching once and for all with the more salacious aspects of the music that one might find in the local tablao and café cantante.

Both Falla and his friend and protégé García Lorca found themselves trying to understand the roots of the music they had both grown up hearing from servants around the house, in the streets of Granada, and in the local taverns. To them this music was purely Andalusian, its sounds and rhythms inflected with strains of the Orient, with the history of al-Andalus, and with the suffering of diasporic gitanos. Moreover, as Samuel Llano has recently argued, they sought to portray a positive image of gitanos in the face of racist fears and a vast literature that deemed them criminals and degenerates.[81] Cante jondo, they believed, achieved its authenticity by being rooted in place—in the home, in the plaza, along the banks of the river, but never in a commercialized establishment. Commercialization had only led to the degeneration of their maternal music, to the flamenquismo that they and so many other elites despised. This contest, then, was meant to begin a process of cultivating young talent who could then teach others how the music was supposed to be interpreted and sung and to return to some older form of musical purity. It was both a kind of salvage ethnomusicology along the lines of Frances Desmore's and Alan Lomax's undertakings in the United States and an incubator to nurture new talent. It also aimed to demonstrate to all Europeans (and to Spaniards themselves) the culture-worthiness of a sometimes-despised art form. Echoing the ideas taught at the Institución Libre de Enseñanza (ILE) about the role of folklore and other forms of cultural production in the service of national regeneration—all the major supporters of the Concurso had deep ties to the ILE—Falla argued for "the preservation of [these] primitive songs . . . in many parts almost completely forgotten." Although many of his contemporaries scorned this music because, he believed, they misunderstood it and "consider[ed] it an inferior art," he asserted that, "on the contrary, it is one of Europe's most valuable popular artistic expressions."[82] García Lorca, too, sounded the alarm bells: "Gentlemen, the musical soul of the people is in grave danger!" The organizers of this competition were undertaking "patriotic work" in trying to save this dying art form that had become associated with "immoral things, the tavern, the juerga, the tablao of the café . . . the españolada." Their mission, then, involved saving both Andalusia and Spain from national embarrassment, "to unite the patriotic idea with the artistic one" in holding this competition.[83]

In order to attract this talent, they had to have some idea about what they were looking for, and they had to sell their ideas to the broader intelligentsia, which García Lorca would do on February 19, 1922, in a conference at Granada's Centro Artístico.[84] His ideas replicated many of those posited by Falla in his essay "El cante jondo (canto primitivo andaluz)." This meant defining cante jondo and differentiating it from other forms of music that had earned the despicable name "flamenco." Although there would be dancing at this competition, rarely did the organizers speak of dance, focused as they were on the singing and the poetry behind the song. According to them, the music had a distant origin in India from "primitive Oriental races," which mixed with an autochthonous Andalusian music and transformed it into what would become the cante jondo. According to Falla, as García Lorca interpreted him, there were three processes by which cante jondo came into being: first, the Spanish Church's adoption of liturgical songs; second, the "Saracen invasion"; and third, the arrival of Gypsies with the Saracens via Egypt to Andalusia. The Gypsies then conserved the Andalusian song form known as the *siguiriya* and gave it, as Falla termed it, "a new modality" that would become cante jondo.[85] This form of song retained old roots, unlike flamenco, which, they declared, had its origins in the eighteenth century. According to them, Andalusian songs that were related to the siguiriya gitana—palos like *martinetes*, *polos*, and *soleares*—could be grouped into the cante jondo family. This type of Andalusian song, Falla claimed, "is perhaps the only European type that retains the structural and stylistic purity, the highest qualities inherent in the primitive song of the Oriental people." Flamenco song, in contrast, had "adulterated and modernized" it ("What a horror," Falla claimed.). Cantaores could barely summon the necessary skill to convey the depth of the songs' expression, relying instead on artifice and ornament, and what remained of "the Andalusian song is nothing more than a sad and lamentable shadow of what was." Their vocal range limited them to "only two modern scales, those that monopolized European music for more than two centuries: the phrase, grossly metrified, is losing daily that rhythmic flexibility that was one of its greatest beauties."[86] Thus any forms of music that fell outside the categories outlined above were marked as "not cante jondo" and, therefore, disqualified from the contest.

Interestingly enough, both Falla and García Lorca used European composers like Glinka and Debussy to demonstrate their own bona fides.[87] And here is where the ironies abound. Falla recounted how Debussy acquired his knowledge about both cante and baile jondo from the Gypsies of Seville and Granada during the 1889 and 1900 Paris Expositions. García Lorca, in a similar vein, tried to convey the importance of cante jondo to the development of contemporary European music, also through Debussy. According to García Lorca's account, at the 1900 Paris Exposition, Debussy heard "a group of gitanos who sang cante jondo in all its purity." After the young Debussy heard the singers, he "who had his soul and spirit open to the four winds was impregnated by the ancient Orient of our melodies."[88] Let us not forget that these performers were the very same ones who Pardo Bazán and Galdós had lambasted as tawdry imitators of authentic flamenco performers. But because well-respected European composers had anointed these Gypsy performers as artists, they became artists to the usually self-flagellating Spaniards. This feedback loop created by members of the European avant-garde outside Spain succeeded in convincing some Spanish elites to prize an ethnic group they had formerly held in contempt. Foreigners thus imposed their ideas about Spanish national identity on Spanish composers, and Spanish composers in turn transformed these ideas, reifying the Gypsy and cante jondo as emblematic vessels that contained within them the Spanish cultural traditions in danger of being lost to posterity.

Despite the rumblings of some intellectuals who feared this competition would just replicate the same tired españolada that the organizers were desperately trying to avoid, the contest got the green light and funding from the authorities in Granada.[89] Some of the requirements for entering the contest were as follows: It was open to singers of both sexes. Anyone over the age of twenty-one who sang professionally was forbidden from entering the contest. Accompanying guitarists could be professionals, and all contestants had to begin by singing a siguiriya gitana in the first round of competition. After the initial tryouts, the selection committee would decide which finalists would take part in the actual contest and celebration on July 13–14.[90]

The competition attracted an amazing group of Spanish (and a few foreign) intellectual and artistic luminaries as spectators, and some of them as judges, including but not limited to the composers Joaquín Turina, Felipe Pedrell, Andrés Segovia, Stravinsky, and Ravel; literati Juan Ramón Jiménez, Ramón Gómez de la Serna, and the Machado brothers; and painters Santiago Rusiñol and Ignacio Zuluoga (who decorated the fiesta site).[91] The singers performed under the light of a waning moon at the Plaza de los Aljibes, located on the grounds of the Alhambra Palace.[92] Not all of the singers and dancers were young or amateurs, but those who could not meet the specific qualifications spelled out in the contest rules were forbidden to compete for prize money. Instead, as experienced practitioners of cante y baile jondo, they sang, played guitar, and danced in the noncompetitive parts of the festivities. Names made famous during the golden age of flamenco, such as the singers Antonio Chacón and Pastora Pavón ("La Niña de los Peines") and dancer Juana La Macarrona, performed as honored guests. Legend also has it that an elderly gitana surprised everybody by rising from the crowd and dancing a soleares with such perfection that she left the crowd awestruck. Only later did the organizers find out that she was "La Golondrina," a famous Granadian dancer on the performing circuit back in the day, who was said to have danced at London's Great Exhibition of 1851.[93] It turned out to be difficult to find young, unprofessional talent, but a few people emerged, and the first prize was shared by two people. The first, twelve-year-old Manolo Ortega, who went by the stage name "El Caracol," would spend the next decades enjoying great success as a cantaor, despite, as many people thought, of having sold out over the years by singing less "pure" forms of flamenco. The second winner, a complete surprise, was seventy-two-year-old Diego Bermúdez ("El Tío Tenazas"), a cantaor whose singing career was cut short early in life after being stabbed in the lungs.[94]

Flamencologists mark the Concurso de Cante Jondo as a major turning point in the history of flamenco. It was, as Timothy Mitchell disparagingly writes, when "flamenco became art."[95] And it is true that

Figure 17. Juana Vargas, "La Macarrona," dancing in the Pasaje del Duque restaurant, June 1935, some forty-six years after performing in the 1889 Paris World Exposition.
© ICAS-SAHP, Fototeca Municipal de Sevilla, Serrano Archive.

what these intellectuals ended up defining as cante jondo did achieve a certain grudging respect from many members of the European artistic avant-garde and some intellectuals (although nobody would ever be able to convince somebody like Eugenio Noel that any part of this musical form had artistic value). Cante jondo, at least, could be saved from the commercialization that, they contended, had cheapened this most enduring legacy that Andalusia had given to Spain and the world. But it was not saved, at least not in the way the organizers had meant it to be. Yes, cante jondo garnered respect, but their definition of what constituted cante jondo was purely arbitrary, restricting the wide palette of flamenco forms to a narrow range of music that evoked pain, sorrow, and seriousness, relinquishing the rest of the music to the seedy margins. These excluded forms continued to thrive and evolve, however, despite Falla's and García Lorca's admonishments. They tried to petrify cante jondo in amber, not realizing, as many scholars have pointed out, that it was precisely the commercialization and professionalization of other "inauthentic" forms of flamenco music in the taverns and cafés cantantes that kept any form of flamenco alive.[96] They could not save Spain from flamenco.

Part III
FLAMENCO AND THE FRANCO REGIME

The previous three chapters of this book dipped in and out of three major temporal divides in Spanish history, just skirting the edges of the Primo de Rivera Regime (1923–30), the Second Republic (1931–36), and the Spanish Civil War (1936–39) but focused instead on spatial and conceptual categories—the regional, the national, and the international. This organization was a conscious decision, made chiefly because cultural trends do not always correspond with major historical turning points. Those temporal breaks based on political turning points do not necessarily tell us anything about the cultural milieu people lived in. For those who participated in the life of flamenco, whether as spectator or performer, not much changed between 1923 and 1936. Major flamenco stars might have performed in cafés cantantes and in larger venues like bullfighting rings and amphitheaters, while lesser-known figures still performed in cafés cantantes and taverns. Flamenco dwindled some in popularity, making way for jazz and other new forms of entertainment, but it did not die out.

The Spanish Civil War, however, did change things for the world of flamenco and for many other sorts of entertainment. War does that sort of thing. But whereas in other countries these kinds of mass entertainments might flourish again after wartime, they did not in Spain, at least not for more than a decade. When war broke out in July 1936, most of the flamenco performers on the professional circuit were already working in the major cities, the majority of them in Madrid and Seville, and many continued to perform in these cities, despite the fact that the former was under Republican control and the latter under Nationalist rule. Still, when they could, performers in Seville tried to retreat to their villages. Quite a few performers of *ópera flamenca* happened to be in Jaén when fighting began, and they stayed there for most of the war. Those performers with means, like Sabicas, El Niño Utrera, and Carmen Amaya, fled to places like Argentina, France, and the United States. Some managed to avoid fighting in the war by employing their artistic talents behind the lines, and some entertained the troops on the battlefront, whether they wanted to or not. In major cities like Madrid and Barcelona, flamenco entertainers continued to work (for lower wartime pay) in the theater and some performed benefits for the war effort, but they could only do so in the early evenings, given that blackouts were enforced to prevent nighttime air raids.

After the war, the flamenco performers' fates, like everybody else's, depended on what side of the war they were associated with. People who had been too open in their enthusiasm for the Republican side could be denounced and sent to concentration camps.[1] Most could not find work in their professions, except for the lucky few who did temporary work in the summer and maybe a handful who could work at the (very) few places that existed after the war.[2]

Whatever the fascination or aversion that regional nationalists, Spanish nationalists, and foreigners felt toward flamenco in the first four decades of the twentieth century, none of that would matter by 1939. The Spanish Civil War (1936–39) ended the culture of the cafés cantantes, tablaos, and ópera flamenca for a time. The 1940s were grim for most people living in Spain. In addition to physically repressing the vanquished through imprisonment, starvation, and executions, the war's victors also actively sought to suppress any elements of modern culture lingering in Spain since, according to them, modern cosmopolitan culture had helped bring about the civil war in the first place. Two foundations of the Franco regime—the church and the Falange—worked on campaigns to purify Spanish culture and to remake it according to the tenets of National Catholicism. For the early years of the Franco regime, this meant that flamenco would

Part III: Flamenco and the Franco Regime

play a much less prominent role as a symbol of Spanishness, and other regional folk songs and dances would prevail in its stead. As the regime consolidated its power and opened Spain up to foreign investment and tourism in the 1950s, flamenco served a more decisive role in shoring up that foreign investment. The next two chapters trace how the flamenco genre rose from pariah to eminence once the Franco regime gained confidence in its ability to maintain power.

6
Rebuilding the Fractured Nation, 1939—1953

When the Spanish Civil War ended in 1939, the Nationalists took their victory as a mandate to extirpate ideas they deemed foreign to Spanish national identity and to repress, if not kill, the numerous enemies of the state. To discuss music and dance in the context of the nationwide repression that followed the civil war may appear to trivialize people's suffering under a dictatorship. But if one takes seriously the power of art both to transform and to be transformed by politics, then the leap from political repression to cultural analysis is not so unfathomable. The Franco regime had to undertake postwar reconstruction, but given that the Spanish people had undergone the trauma of civil war and that Franco and his regime brooked no dissent, his regime was tasked with facilitating both the physical reconstruction of the built environment and the cultural construction of a unified national identity, wherever that identity could be shaped.

The nature of Spain's single or plural identity proved to be one of the major fault lines of the Spanish Civil War.[1] While the Republican side made allowances for regional nationalities, the Nationalist band understood Spain to have lost its moorings in the modern era because a succession of leaders had squandered the vast Spanish empire through incompetence, spinelessness, and lack of religious fervor. Moreover, they contended, foreign ideologies and traitorous regional nationalists had already weakened and were on the verge of destroying what little of the Spanish nation remained. The Nationalists harked back to Spain's pinnacle of power, when the monarchs Ferdinand and Isabel, and later, Philip II, ascended the throne, enforced religious purity, and spread Catholicism and the Castilian language to an empire across the sea. After the civil war, wishing to return to Spain's glory days of unification by sword and faith, the Nationalists strove to enforce unity through violence, which meant that they executed and jailed regional nationalists and eliminated regional languages in state and municipal institutions. The Nationalists took their victory as a mandate to extirpate ideas they deemed foreign to Spanish national identity, by any means necessary.

Violence was not the only way to shape this identity, however, and the regime could use softer forms of persuasion through cultural practices. Just as the revolutionary Left in the interwar period viewed cultural artifacts and the performing arts as intrinsic to a society's transformation, so too did the revolutionary and conservative Right. As revealed in numerous scholarly works, Fascist Italy and Nazi Germany strove to create fascist cultures that would channel the revolutionary tendencies of the working classes into acceptable avenues.[2] Franco's Spain was surely no different in this regard. While the Franco regime never adhered to some strict definition of fascism, it most assuredly brought elements of fascist aesthetics and ideology to the table with a heaping dollop of Catholicism. This fusion of hypernationalism with conservative Catholicism—known as National Catholicism—colored all aspects of Spanish cultural, political, and even economic life. Two pillars of the Franco regime—the Falange and the church—worked on campaigns to purify Spanish culture (in its many incarnations) and to remake it according to the tenets of National Catholicism.[3]

For the early years of the Franco regime, this meant "purifying" Spanish song and dance. Therefore, the regime strove to make flamenco play a much less prominent role as a symbol of Spanishness. The Catholic Church aimed to eliminate almost all forms of dance, taking as a cautionary tale the maxim that dancing represented "a vertical expression of a horizontal desire."[4] The Falange, however, had some uses for a limited range of songs and dances. Under the auspices of the Sección Femenina (SF, the female cohort of the Spanish Falange), the regime systematically cultivated an identity of "unity in diversity," employing Spain's regional songs and dances for the cause of Spanish nationalism. They did this consciously and more effectively than the progressive reformers before them.[5] The SF's Coros y Danzas de España programs ostensibly served two purposes: to domesticate regionalist aspirations through the folklorization of these regional differences and, I would argue, to untether Spain from its associations with flamenco. Their attempts to extirpate flamenco from the landscape would fail, especially when the regime opened Spain up to foreign investment and tourism in the 1950s. But in the early years of the Franco regime, various players had the political and legislative heft to move flamenco (and other forms of modern song and dance) away from the front of the domestic and international stage. In fact, one could say that this chapter is decidedly *not* about flamenco. Rather, it is about the way the forces of the Franco regime tried to make Spaniards and foreigners forget about flamenco as a marker of Spanish national identity by concentrating on other forms of cultural expression. From 1939 until the early 1950s, through a combination of terror, repression, and propaganda, the regime worked to consolidate its vision of a nationalist, Catholic state from top to bottom. Music and dance became a means by which the regime could continue and expand on the efforts launched by the Catholic Church in the early twentieth century to create a new Spain scrubbed free of secularist "pornography" like flamenco. The Spanish nation would now be reinscribed on women's dancing bodies and singing voices. The women belonging to the SF's Coros y Danzas de España would inhabit regionalist garb to perform the Spanish nation and, in the process—the regime's allies hoped—exile flamenco from Spain once and for all.

The Catholic Church and Dance, 1923–1936

As discussed in chapter 2, the Catholic Church and other conservatives fought the scourge of flamenco and other forms of modern song and dance with all the tools at their disposal, using a combination of legislation and modern mass media to warn the populace about the dangers of these expressions of modernity. After the dictator Miguel Primo de Rivera seized power in 1923, the church had in him its strongest ally in decades and began rallying the faithful to battle these modern ills. Most of the fight would take place over the bodies and souls of women. Women would be blamed consistently for the loosening of morals and would be deemed responsible for upholding the honor of the family and the nation. At the beginning of the Second Republic (1931), the Catholic Church was stripped of much of its legislative power, but it still had enough political savvy to employ mass media for its own purposes. Finally, when civil war began in 1936, the church threw its weight behind the Nationalists and emerged victorious, enabling them to reenact and consolidate their moral authority over a weakened and frayed populace.

The Spanish Catholic Church's crusade against modern culture did not emerge from Spain itself but rather from the Vatican, where it trickled down to the Spanish Catholic hierarchy. Because church-state relations were more closely integrated in Spain than elsewhere, the Spanish Catholic Church received more political support than most other nations to attempt the measures the Vatican proposed. As early as 1914, Pope Pius X weighed in on the tango (he did not much care for it), and by 1921 Pope Benedict XV in one small part of his encyclical *Sacra Propedium* called for a fight against the ills of modernity, chief among them the "unlimited desire for riches and an insatiable thirst for pleasures." Arguing that this pursuit of wealth and other forms of corruption kindled class hatred, the pope moved somewhat abruptly to female modesty: "So many women of every age and condition . . . do not see to what a degree the indecency of their clothing shocks every honest man, and offends God. . . . And We speak not of those exotic and barbarous dances recently imported into fashionable circles, one more shocking than the other; one cannot imagine anything more suitable for banishing all the remains of modesty."[6] This short passage in the encyclical illustrates that the onus fell on women to act modestly in order to curb the sexual appetites of the men around them. In a similar vein, most of the Catholic hierarchy's pronouncements would focus on female modesty as the corrective force against men's inability to control their own sexual drives.

Spanish Catholics took these commands seriously. While various groups under the umbrella of Acción Católica continued to work against the tide of modernity after World War I, the Catholic hierarchy's anxiety about sexual promiscuity and blurred gender roles reached a more fevered pitch by 1926, at the height of the Primo regime. The 1926 Pastoral letter from the Spanish bishops, "Metropolitan Spaniards: Collective Pastoral [letter] on Immodesty and Public Customs," took issue with the trappings of modern cosmopolitan life and their penchant for eroding good Christian values. The letter decried Spaniards' spiritual alienation from Jesus Christ and blamed it on the influence of "intense" and "cosmopolitan" corruption of traditional customs. Early on in the letter the archbishops blamed "immodest [female] fashions" for "fomenting this invasion of sensuality." How did Spaniards, especially the youth, come to choose the path toward damnation? *Modernist foreignness*. That was the neologism the bishops created to describe this process of encroaching secularism and cosmopolitanism. Modernist foreignness, in contrast to traditional, "profoundly Christian" Spanishness, "perverted Spanish customs" and put traditional Spaniards in grave danger. These new foreign and modern customs forced children and women to lose their "decency and modesty" and were now "opening a wide breach where pornography [can] penetrate, which is the precursor to faith's ruin."[7] Foreigners, they claimed, were responsible for making it seem normal that the sexes should feel comfortable in each other's company, and they argued that it would be best for Spaniards not to follow the same secular and cosmopolitan path as other countries.

Abstention from these forms of mass culture was the only way traditional Catholics could combat this seemingly impossible overflow of foreign, modern culture, this "pornography of the theater, movie house, cabarets, books and novels, or whatever indecent form it [took]." Good Christians had to avoid attending "shows that glorify vice" and shun immodest women, especially those who led "scandalous lives." But mostly, girls and women had to learn modesty, and that modesty was best taught by the head of household, the father.[8]

From about 1926 on, those conservatives concerned with the proliferation of the various forms of pornography, which certainly had increased substantially in the 1920s, focused on using legal strategies and moral pronouncements to prevent girls and young women from sliding down a slippery slope—from working in cafés cantantes and other similar establishments down to the depths of prostitution. Some of their efforts were aided by an international treaty signed in Geneva in 1923, to which Spain was a signatory, banning the circulation of pornographic materials. Under Articles 456 and 586 of the Spanish Penal Code, people could be charged with circulating such materials, and by 1926 people were increasingly prosecuted for this crime, broadly speaking, especially in Barcelona.[9] The first national meeting of the Assembly against Public Immorality (Asamblea Contra la Pública Inmoralidad), which covered all manner of vice, including immorality in "public entertainments," hoped to petition King Alfonso XIII for a variety of changes that might help decrease Spain's immoral behavior, such as providing incentives for property owners if they stopped using their establishments for "prostitution . . . cabarets, halls with immoral shows like dances and cafés cantaores, and generally, houses of ill repute, licentious customs or immoral trafficking."[10] By 1928 a magazine dedicated to Catholic workers, the *Revista Católica de cuestiones sociales*, called for a revision of the 1913 Reglamento de Policía de Espectáculos in order to prevent young women between sixteen and twenty-three from being able to work in these entertainment industries, period, because for these reformers, "The fight against prostitution cannot be limited to the said evil that one is trying to fight. It is necessary to attack it in its origins, near and far ... the license [given these] entertainments are without a doubt causes and effects of the corruption of customs that maintain and foment this abominable trafficking."[11]

In the first years following the founding of the Second Republic on April 14, 1931, Republicans and Socialists stripped the church of much of its power in Spain. Despite their diminished influence, Catholics formally and informally conducted morality, austerity, and modesty campaigns, all with the aim of achieving the goals they outlined during the Primo regime. They even had allies in what seemed like unlikely places, like the general governor of Catalonia, Juan Selvas, who had already seized "more than a million pornographic publications" in Barcelona and who wanted to increase government oversight over dance academies.[12] Still, although groups like Acción Católica agitated for campaigns against (female) immodesty as early as 1933 so as to continue the work begun by earlier antipornography leagues, their campaigns did not reach their full force until after the civil war and the Franco regime's consolidation.[13]

The Catholic Church, Dance, and Postwar Cultural Reconstruction

As an institution the Catholic Church benefited the most from the Nationalist victory. Having thrown its lot in with the Nationalists at the beginning of the war, the Nationalists handsomely rewarded the Catholic hierarchy for its support. The Franco regime reversed the anticlerical legislation initiated during the Republic and handed the reins of education and morality over to the church's leadership. Following Franco's wishes for autarky after the civil war, the church encouraged spiritual autarky by working to eliminate the foreign virus of modernity that had permeated Spanish borders since at least 1789. Ideologically speaking, this meant reimposing Catholic values on a populace that had been sometimes inching, sometimes lurching, toward greater secularization. This reimposition took many forms: controlling primary and secondary education; censoring entertainments such as movies, plays, and festivals; and regulating female sexuality and dress.

As we have already seen, the Spanish Catholic Church fulminated against the loose morals brought on by the modern age, especially with the advent of those incubators of sexual desire, the cinema and dance hall. Critiques of mass culture were not the monopoly of the Catholic Church and traditional conservatives, and they could certainly be heard coming from people who possessed quite different ideologies.[14] But the church had more tangible power now. Whereas before the civil war the church could only denounce these transgressors of Catholic morality, after the war the church had full license to prosecute them. Under Acción Católica's Comisión Episcopal de Ortodoxia y Moralidad (Episcopal Commission of Orthodoxy and Morality, hereafter known as CEOM), the Oficina Nacional Permanente de Vigilancia de Espectáculos (Permanent National Office of Surveillance over Entertainment) became the umbrella organization for Catholic groups to monitor, criticize, and sanction entertainment, especially with respect to their suitability for women and minors. For example, groups such as the Confederación Católica Nacional de Padres de Familia (CONCAPA) and the Marian Congregations published newspapers such as *Filmor* and *Sipe*, which evaluated and provided Catholic rating systems for films and plays, as did magazines like *Ecclesia* and *Signo*, published by Acción Católica.[15] For these arbiters of morality, films came in for the greatest amount of scrutiny and condemnation, given their depictions of romance and sexuality and their blatant disregard for family and religious traditions. Although not surveilled as much as films and plays, dance also fell under the watchful eye of Catholic officialdom. Dances became something to regulate and ban. For the Falange, dance had to be monitored, but it could still be put to useful purposes—something the Catholic Church very much doubted.

The church's prosecution against most public dancing began in earnest immediately after the war with the recrudescence of austerity and modesty campaigns and the publication of religious pamphlets that outlined in almost catechismic form the dangers of dancing for the younger generations. These various campaigns focused once again on women's modesty, the foreignness and cosmopolitanism of modern dance and the immoral behaviors that sprung forth from it, and the need to recuperate and revitalize regional folk dances.[16]

Planning for more campaigns of austerity and modesty began in 1939, and there is evidence that at least one city, Bilbao, held such a campaign.[17] Acción Católica printed up a series of talking points for preachers, public speakers, conference goers, radio, and the press to distribute their message widely about necessary Catholic behavior covering five categories: fashion, customs, sports, film and other entertainments, and beaches and pools. One such topic under the customs category was "foreign and regional dance."[18] Slogans introduced for this year included "Woman, become inspired to dress in Spain. To sing and dance in Spain" and "Young campesina: neither immoral dances, nor immodest clothing, nor uncovered legs, nor pagan customs. Regional clothing that is decent. Regional clothing that is modest. The patriarchal custom that is healthy. Forge the Caudillo's Spain!"[19] Archbishops in various dioceses answered survey questions about the moral state of their particular dioceses, especially with respect to the five categories listed above. The biggest complaint that religious leaders lodged against their dioceses had to do with young women walking arm-in-arm with young men and being allowed to go out of the house alone. Dancing ranked a distant third.[20]

Publications for this campaign like "Lo extranjerizante" (The fondness for foreign things) provide us with a window into the ideology that Acción Católica intended to disseminate during the first years of the regime. This work blamed many of Spain's ills on Spaniards' desire to ape foreign cultures, forgetting their own wholesome culture in the process. Well-heeled Spaniards, the writer claimed, hired French and British nannies to care for their children and, in the process, these caretakers "de-Spanishified" their charges in the process. Additionally, the gentlemen's practice of sending their daughters off to London or Paris for "finishing" completed the effect of turning Spanish women against Spain, for they now judged everything Spanish to be "backward" and "out of fashion."[21] The supposed "proscription against Spanish dance" also posed a "violation of Spain's heart." Echoing the anticommercial, antimodern language and sentiments that Manuel de Falla and Federico García Lorca had employed to justify their revitalization of the cante jondo almost two decades earlier, Catholic writers like Flores de Romeral bemoaned the death of these "essential elements of the race" and called for reestablishing regional Spanish folk dances.[22] He complained that Spaniards had given the people of Latin America their song and dance but, in exchange, brought back to Spain the "exotic range of pirouettes, contortions, [and] dislocations given to us by decaying and savage people, bringing them to the most remote corners of our nation."[23] Pure Spanish dance had been forgotten by Spaniards and it had been perverted and/or lost by the influx of foreigners: "The boiling cuplés, shameless and pornographic, came to us from abroad; the tangos, brittle, agonizing . . . and sensuous, came to us from abroad; epileptic jazz, jungle-like, Aborigines with the taste of papaya and the smell of the pigsty, came to us from abroad."[24] Not only did the language iterated here paint a picture of dances and songs that were out of control (and uncontrollable); it employed a specifically racialized, bestial language, linking modern music to (black) savages in ways reminiscent of Nazi Germany's racialized discourse around jazz, and it certainly mimicked the language many writers had consistently used to describe the very Spanish but modern flamenco performers.[25] The only solution to this perceived problem of Spanish degeneration, it seemed, was for Spaniards to learn regional folk dances and songs. Such a focus would restore female modesty and rebuild a greater Spain purified of foreign influences.

The church's fixation on fighting modern dance and cultivating regional dances would continue through the 1940s and 1950s through various publications and campaigns for modesty and austerity. A couple of tracts written in the 1940s covered the dos and don'ts of dancing for young Catholics, concentrating again mostly on young women's necessary role in discouraging such activities. Carlos Salicrú Puigvert's *¿Es lícito bailar?* (Is dancing permissible?) and Rufino Villalobos Bote and Sebastián Jiménez's *¿Es pecado bailar? ¿No es pecado bailar?* (Is dancing sinful? Is dancing not sinful?) expressed similar arguments against modern dance and its corrupting values and promoted religious and regional folk dances instead.[26] In many instances their language is almost identical, and that could be because they plagiarized large swaths of a sermon translated into Spanish given some twenty years earlier by a French Dominican monk, Ferdinand-Anton Vuillermet.[27]

Both writers stressed that some dancing was permissible, as long as certain rules of decorum were maintained. For example, dances could express certain emotions and passions that other art forms could not, but in order for dance to reach an artistic and spiritual plane, the physical gestures had to be "measured," and their movements expressed "rhythmically" and "harmoniously."[28] This kind of dancing could be found in some of the ancient societies represented in the Bible, although not in all of them. Biblical dances like those performed after religious triumphs like David's defeat of Goliath or Judith's over Holofernes were perfectly respectable dances—the two sexes did not mix and the dances' content honored the religiously stalwart. Other biblical dances, such as those found in the books of Job, Ezekiel, and Exodus, were not because the dancers were dangerous and dishonest, and both sexes danced in mixed groups.[29] Regional dances like the jota were the one exception where men and women could dance together—although not all official members of the clergy believed this.[30] Again, the reasons for the church's deep distrust of modern dances arose chiefly from the idea that modern dances led to sexual temptation, the eventual corruption of men's and women's morals, and the decline of the family and patriarchal authority.[31] Even though these Catholic authors agreed that the dancing one could find in cafés, bars, theaters, and dance halls was inherently immoral, Salicrú Puigvert even went so far as to castigate those who participated in the so-called cultured dances of high society because these dances just masked the lascivious feelings of its dancers behind class, and, he believed, "concupiscence can be harbored just as easily in the modest dress of the proletariat as in a percale gown."[32]

Modern dances also countermanded the hierarchical order established by the church and placed Spanish individuals and families on par with the "savage," "uncontrollable races" that the Spanish empire had tried to "civilize." These writers ignored flamenco here, since flamenco songs and dances tended to be performed on stage rather than among couples in dance halls, but we know that the church's attempts to regulate the "pornography" of cafés cantantes shared the same racial discourse as their campaigns to discipline dancing among Spain's tender youth. These disorderly, immodest dances included waltzes, mazurkas, tangos, fox-trots, and the boogie-woogie, among many others prevalent during the earlier Jazz Age. The "embarrassing" jazz bands, or as Salicrú Puigvert dubbed them, "Negro art," displayed "so much dissonance, so many epileptic contortions, so many syncopated melodies," that one should could only consider the music a joke.[33] Villalobos Bote and Jiménez felt compelled to quote the Galician novelist José María de Pereda to illustrate his disgust for most modern dance (and modern democracy) and the harm they committed to women's modesty and the patriarchal order: "Dance is a republic in which nobody has authority nor law, neither fathers nor husbands over their daughters and wives. . . . In this republic of dance the man has only rights: the woman, only obligations."[34] Obviously, dancing was a dangerous proposition, so much so, that the last sentence of ¿Es pecado bailar? proclaimed "Death before dancing" to its vulnerable readers.[35]

As we have seen, these tracts, as well as Acción Católica's modesty and austerity campaigns, laid some of the ideological cover for the Franco regime's construction of the National Catholic state. They focused on rendering foreign cultural importations as toxic while underscoring the wholesomeness of regional folk music and dance.[36] They could justify the recuperation of Spain's regional dances, costumes, and songs because the sexes rarely mixed and the dancers moved about in graceful steps out in the open, in plazas, with full views to the public, in contrast to flamenco performances hidden in the crime-ridden sections of cities and attended by people characterized as reprobates. It would take the Women's Section of the Falange (the SF) to institutionalize the performance of regional songs and dances in the hopes of recuperating Spain's culture and its women's modesty.

Coros y Danzas

Given the Franco regime's almost systematic approach to rooting out regional nationalism and enforcing a Castilian- and Catholic-based nationalism, it is odd to contemplate why they would support a cultural program like the SF's Coros y Danzas, which seemed to complicate their notion of a unitary national identity. Why would Francoists promote folkloric dance and choral groups that represented the diverse regions of Spain immediately after having fought a war to eradicate such diversity? Part of this seemingly confusing attitude toward regional diversity had to do with the leadership and legacy of the Falange Española. Founded in 1933 by José Antonio Primo de Rivera, the Falange played the revolutionary vanguard to Franco's traditional Catholic conservatism. In their 1934 revolutionary platform that criticized both the excesses of capitalism and the bloody strife implicit in the socialist conception of class struggle, the Falange wrote of strengthening the nation's power by subordinating individual wills to a greater collective good. Most of all, they believed, national unity was the "supreme reality of Spain." Using an evocative phrase that to this day is surprisingly vague but which José Antonio's sister repeated ad infinitum, the Falange exclaimed, "Spain is a unity of destiny in the universal." The Falange's meaning was stated more clearly in the sentences that followed: "All conspiracy against this unity is abhorrent. All separatism is a crime we shall not pardon. The current constitution, insofar as it promotes disintegration, attacks the unity of Spain's destiny."[37] The cultivation of Spanish unity remained a primary goal of the Franco regime, even after José Antonio's death early in the war.

José Antonio's sister, Pilar, served as female helpmeet to José Antonio's Falange, and she carried out her understanding of his ideas after his death.[38] Setting up a parallel organization known as the Sección

Femenina de la Falange Española (1934), Pilar organized women to help in the war effort by making clothes for soldiers, tending the wounded in hospitals, and taking care of orphans and widows devastated by the war. Once the war ended, the SF became an official branch of the Franco regime—still headed by Pilar—which served to inculcate the values of National Catholicism in Spain's girls and women by employing various outreach programs and teaching home economics in elementary and secondary schools. From 1939 to 1977, unmarried Spanish girls between the ages of seventeen and thirty-five who wanted any form of advancement or privilege such as government jobs, entrance into a university and subsequent professional careers, or access to a passport, had to serve six months in the Social Auxiliary of the SF. Once in the service, they were required to learn home economics, female comportment, childcare, and other domestic arts. Thus the SF became a way for the regime to honor the memory of José Antonio through his sister's contribution to the new state and, more importantly, mold Spanish girls into paragons of femininity that borrowed from traditional Catholicism and modern fascism.[39]

One of the most important legacies of the SF was the Coros y Danzas de España (Songs and Dances of Spain). What may have seemed inconceivable when Pilar imagined it in 1939 flowered into international success by the 1950s. Begun first as a means to achieve domestic unification, it later developed as a launching pad for cultural diplomacy.[40] In addition to performing at many official functions within Spain, the Coros y Danzas featured representatives in such international organizations as the United Nations, UNESCO, the European Conference of Agriculture, and the International Federation of Folkloric Groups.[41]

The Coros y Danzas served many purposes, but for Pilar these groups operated primarily to unify Spain. The SF's mandate, according to their statutes, was "to foster in the Spanish woman love of the Patria, the State, and the glorious traditions of [the Spanish] nation," as well as to support the male Falangists in their "fight against the anti-Spain."[42] To achieve these goals, the organizers of the Coros y Danzas tied music and dance to the people and to the land from which they had sprung. Pilar had an almost mystical conception of music, including it as a sacred prong in a Holy Trinity that also incorporated "National Syndicalist doctrine" and "the land."[43]

Because music evokes a range of emotional states and memories through sensory stimulation, Pilar imagined music as *the* great facilitator of national unity,[44] and she conceived of the Coros y Danzas as a representation of her catchphrase "unity in plurality": "When Castilians know the [Catalan] Sardanas and know how the [Basque] 'chistu' is played, when everybody understands all the depth and philosophy within Andalusian song, instead of understanding it through the zarzuela stages[,] . . . when fifty or sixty thousand voices come together to sing the same song, then yes we will have achieved the unity between the people and the lands of Spain."[45] At first glance this reliance on regional music to connect the populace to a transcendent national spirit seems like a renunciation of her brother José Antonio's Falangist nationalism. José Antonio maintained the position that a nationalism tied to the poetic spaces evoked by land and song was a squishy and weak sort of nationalism that did not reflect well on a nation's people: "It is the kind of love that invites you to dissolve. To soften. To cry. The one dissolves into melancholy when the bagpipe weeps. . . . All that is very sweet, like a sweet wine. But also, drunkenness and indolence are hidden, just as they are in wine." Therefore, he deemed it best to drink in the wine of song in moderation "without revealing our secrets [, because] all that is sensual is ephemeral."[46] But as Beatriz Martínez del Fresno argues, at least at the beginning of the regime, Pilar employed the SF "to overcome localism and wipe out any trace of regional identity in the songs and dances by repeatedly exchanging and deterritorialising them within the national boundaries."[47] That is, singers and dancers learned and performed music outside of their natal region. But by the 1950s, the SF had changed its policies altogether about who could and could not perform regional songs and dances—women were now required to perform music from their home province only.[48] In this context of the growing strength and consolidation of the Franco regime, regional diversity became unproblematic because the Coros y Danzas found a way to domesticate political regionalist aspirations in the service of the Spanish state. Or, as scholar Carmen Ortíz puts it, "Regional differences were folklorized."[49]

In addition to its contributions toward the expression of Spanish unity in diversity, the Coros y Danzas promoted a whole complex of values near and dear to fascist and Catholic hearts. Regional dances embodied the characteristics of their requisite lands and the authentic expression of their peoples, thereby promoting a positive contrast to the commercialized songs and dances deemed dangerously "exotic" and "foreign"; folkloric songs and dances represented the expression of the group, not the individual; the performers, plucked from various occupations and social classes, closed the gap between urban and rural

Spain (although rural values always prevailed in the Coros y Danzas); the diversity of regional songs and dances negated the primacy of Andalusia as *the* representation of Spain once and for all; the performances radiated "authenticity" and warded off the taint of commercialism because amateurs performed them and well-meaning and low-paid staff researched the songs and dances;[50] and the dancers, females vetted by the SF, presented themselves as chaste and modest, eliminating the kinds of complaints about sexual suggestiveness lodged against modern dance. Finally, by researching, preserving, and performing these songs and dances with the aid of musicologists like Manuel García Matos and literary scholars like Ramón Menéndez y Pidal, the organizers of the Coros y Danzas imagined themselves as recovering a world almost lost to modernity, completing their historical mission by disseminating these performances to the greater world.[51] This desire to save an artistic form perceived to be dying should now sound familiar to the reader, given that these ideas were expressed by people of various political outlooks in the eighteenth and nineteenth centuries, by the organizers of the *Concurso de cante jondo* (1922), and by Republicans who promoted the Misiones Pedagógicas as late as the Second Republic (1931–36).[52]

As early as the civil war, the SF established various bureaucracies within the scope of Nationalist organizations. It created the Servicio de Cultura y Formación de Jerarquías de la Sección Femenina in January 1938. Under this umbrella organization, the SF planned to develop programs to disseminate music and folklore throughout Spain for patriotic purposes. Following the Nationalist victory in April 1939, the SF organized groups of singers and dancers to perform for Francisco Franco and members of the Nationalist army at the new headquarters of the SF, the Castillo de la Mota in Medina del Campo (Valladolid).[53] Between 1939 and 1942, as the Franco regime worked to rebuild Spain in its own image, the SF also began to create a place for itself in this new Spain. The recovery of traditional dances, music, and folklore featured prominently in the SF's agenda under the Coros y Danzas program, and, more importantly, the regime indulged the SF here—perhaps because the program was not perceived as threatening—for some incarnation of the Coros y Danzas appeared at a variety of official state functions from 1939 on.

In 1942 the SF first began organizing provincial, then regional, and then national competitions to pick the best exemplars of traditional regional songs and dances.[54] Between 1942 and 1976 the SF held about twenty of these contests in Spain, and according to Pilar, what began as a contest with three thousand participants in 1942 grew to "more than sixty thousand" at its height.[55] When the first national competition began to be publicized, newspapers parroted the SF's messaging. For example, *ABC* exclaimed that spectators had watched the dancers performing in Madrid "with indescribable enthusiasm that denotes the magnificent disposition of the Spanish public to like something that is authentically theirs." The SF, continued *ABC*, held these contests "to resuscitate Spain's true folklore in songs, dances, and costumes," and to "bring to the public conscience the great beauty of Spain's folklore, when so many exotic dances and so many strange songs try to supplant them."[56] They hammered home the idea that the Coros y Danzas represented Spanish authenticity and diversity. Contemporary newspapers, films put out by the Franco regime, and propaganda written by the SF continuously emphasized the songs' and dances' fragility in the face of modernity.[57]

Another theme that began to emerge more consistently after the Coros y Danzas traveled internationally was that Spanish folklore, its music, and its dancing encompassed much more diversity than the Andalusian flamenco so beloved by foreigners. In the fascist journal *Vértice*, the folklorist Nieves de Hoyos Sancho wrote of the Coros y Danzas, "Our Andalusian dancers don't present anything that we could call flamenco. Why? Without a doubt it is because the showy flamenco invaded tablaos and stages for a long time." She continued to denounce flamenco for its commercialism and inauthenticity and stated that the Coros y Danzas refused to reproduce a flamencoized concept of Andalusia, given that there were so many other authentic Andalusian songs and dances Spain could export. She still managed to essentialize Andalusians and their dances, however, in much the same manner that foreigners had done for so long: "The soleares and peteneras music that they dance is like a collection of all of Andalusia; they have not learned to dance; they do it by instinct, by race, their movements do not have studied rigidity, but the flexibility and ease of the natural and unconscious."[58] Tellingly enough, the influence of Manuel de Falla's categories of the cante jondo had managed to penetrate the Coros y Danzas. *Soleares* and peteneras were (and still are) considered part of the flamenco repertoire, but they achieved respectability by being deemed cante jondo forms of expression.

With a brief exception in 1942 for a visit to Germany, the Coros y Danzas at first seemed destined to fulfill domestic educational purposes only. That is, folklorists and performers strove to educate the

Spanish populace about their own folkloric traditions that the educators perceived to be threatened by modernity. As one journalist put it, the SF was not performing to "tell stories" but rather to "practice History."[59] First, it helps to remember that the SF viewed themselves as menders of the national fabric that had been riven both by modernity and civil war. Their dissemination of Spanish folklore would therefore aid in national reconciliation. Second, the Franco regime's policy of autarky after the war and the UN's political and economic isolation of Spain after 1945 prevented Spaniards from engaging in much contact outside the country. This situation would change in 1947, after Argentina proved willing to defy the UN's embargo by sending President Juan Perón's wife, Eva, to Madrid to deliver food and other economic aid to starving Spaniards. In gratitude for this grand gesture of humanitarianism, the Spanish government sent the Coros y Danzas on a tour that began in Argentina but also continued to Brazil and Portugal.[60] From 1948 on, when the Coros y Danzas were not inaugurating some sort of festival or special event in Spain, they traveled much of the world, either as performers or competitors and, in the process, became cultural ambassadors for the Franco regime.

Cultivating Spain's Image Abroad through Folkloric Song and Dance

The voyage to Argentina launched the Coros y Danzas to international success.[61] What began as a goodwill mission of thanks became a way for the SF to reconnect with an exiled people and reestablish cultural links with Spain's historic imperial subjects. Additionally, the Coros y Danzas organizers began to view themselves as powerful cultural intermediaries who could teach foreigners about Spain. This meant rewriting the narratives perpetrated and perpetuated by foreigners, who conflated all Spanish dance with flamenco. Despite the Coros y Danzas' numerous attempts to educate foreigners about the abundant diversity of Spanish song and dance, foreigners most often commented on and gravitated toward the Andalusian ones.

In the memoir she wrote toward the end of her life, Pilar spoke of the SF's need to spread its ideology to the greater world. But this political program could not work in Europe, she insisted, because Europeans treated Spain with "contempt." Instead, by following the path of "History," the SF concluded that their ideological and political program "should be directed at the Hispano-American world." Pilar stated this sentiment boldly and without regret, delineating the various ways that the SF attempted to strengthen the links between Spain and its former empire.[62] By expressing this desire to renew the broken cultural, linguistic, historical, and religious bonds between the Madre Patria (literally, the Mother Fatherland) and the former colonies, she was harking back to the doctrine of Hispanidad, which had become a core belief of conservative and radical-right Spaniards since the turn of the twentieth century and that hardened into dogma during the Franco regime.[63]

The Coros y Danzas became the means by which to soften the fascist image abroad and reconnect with the old colonies and the Spanish exiles within them. In her farewell speech to the first group of Coros y Danzas to leave Spain for the shores of Argentina, Pilar reminded the young women of their duty: "To recover for Spain the Argentines' interest and to bring to the Spaniards who live there the authentic tradition of the faraway Patria." She explicitly stated that the Coros y Danzas, acting as a kind of embassy, were on a "Universal" and "Historical" mission, and that it was their duty to complete these missions as a part of this "politics that the Caudillo [Franco] directs." Finally, she cautioned the young women to remember that this trip was not some sort of tourist holiday but rather "an act of service carried out with the usual austerity and with the happy discipline that the Falange imposes on us."[64] And serve they did.

In April 1948, 150 people representing the Coros y Danzas set sail on the *Monte Albertía* from Cádiz for a three-month excursion to Argentina and Brazil, with a stop in Portugal on the way back home. Groups from Bilbao, Logroño, Asturias, La Coruña, Seville, Lérida, Cáceres, Málaga and Zaragoza, under the care and direction of Eulalia Ridruejo and María Josefa Hernández Sempelayo, initiated Spain's charm offensive to the wider world.[65] Here was the opportunity to change the Franco regime's image as a cruel, oppressive, fascistic state—a Black Legend for the modern era—to a much more benevolent one, replete with happy, smiling dancers who reflected Spain's beauty, diversity, and order.

Every move the Coros y Danzas made was cultivated to remind Spaniards, exiled Spaniards, and Latin Americans of the historical and cultural bonds that no one could rend asunder. During the first stop in Luján, Argentina, the dancers disembarked from their ship and went to the Basilica to "pray before the [Marian] image that the Conquistadors brought from Spain four hundred years ago."[66] During other stops along that tour and subsequent ones, the performers provided both symbolic and explicit links between Spain and Latin America through the conduits of colonialism and Catholicism, and then attempted to strengthen these bonds through language and music. For example, in 1949, while in Lima Peru, the Coros y Danzas placed flowers on the grave of the conquistador Francisco Pizarro on their way out to Chile. While in Santiago, Chile, they attended a mass at the Church of San Francisco, and the women of Badajoz placed flowers on a marker commemorating Pedro de Valdivia, the conquistador, founder of Santiago, and first royal governor of Chile.[67] Whenever possible, it seems, the Coros y Danzas attended masses and placed themselves in locations that would make Latin Americans and exiled Spaniards see the historical and cultural links between the Madre Patria and the former colonies. In fact, the leaders of the SF made no attempt to hide their neocolonial longings. Pilar, in an undated speech—presumably to a Latin American audience—spoke of music's power to unite peoples from distant lands: "The Falange, which is above all about unity, has preferred music, better than any other means, to unite our spirits, and the most accessible part of music for everybody has been chosen: song. Song, that which we [Latin] Americans and Spaniards sing in the same language." Then, echoing a previous speech she gave to the SF in Zamora in 1939 to encourage Spanish unity, she imagined some fifty to sixty thousand Latin American and Spanish voices singing the same songs together so that their souls would be united, nurturing mutual understanding and love. What distinguishes this speech from the one in Zamora was her blithe willingness to compress time, history, and space in order to (re)incorporate the defunct Spanish Empire into the new Spanish state: "So the sea which separates us will be an accident of Geography only, that will serve to bring from here to there and from there to here the culture of your Republics and of our Patria."[68] Music, in other words, might conquer where armies could not. An Argentinean official reinforced this sentiment when he apparently called the young women of the Coros y Danzas the "'new conquistadors' because they came to snatch the heart and soul of the Argentineans."[69] Finally, the film *Ronda española* (1951), the lighthearted, propaganda piece about the Coros y Danzas' tour of Latin America, filtered through the trope of romantic comedy, explicitly linked the dancers and the conquistadors by filming the dancers dressed in their regional garb dancing on a map of Latin America.[70]

With a strong belief in the power of music to heal all manner of wounds, the Coros y Danzas, through international tours and folklore competitions, used its troupes to break down the barriers remaining between hostile nations and Spain, and exiled Spaniards and the Franco regime. After the first two tours of Latin America, the Coros y Danzas rapidly expanded their scope to other parts of the world, including Switzerland (1949), Lebanon (1950), Belgium (1951), France (1951), England (1952), and the United States (1950, 1953). One of the first narratives the SF hoped to rewrite with the help of its enthusiastic performers was the course and outcome of the Spanish Civil War.

First they began with the Spanish exiles. Accounts written by the people allied with the SF and the Coros y Danzas emphasize the power of nostalgia to bring about national reconciliation with the Republican exiles of the Spanish Civil War.[71] Their accounts overflow with stories of expatriates weeping after watching and hearing the Spanish young women perform songs and dances from the numerous regions of Spain that the exiles had been forced to leave. Pilar reported that when the Coros y Danzas visited a dying Catalan man in the hospital, he asked "to hear a sardana before leaving this world." The group from Lérida complied with this request. Another exile supposedly kept his distance when meeting the women from the Coros y Danzas. He sported a jacket with a Republican insignia, but a woman from the group quickly covered it up with a carnation. Soon thereafter, "he began to cry and he later became the most enthusiastic supporter of the Coros y Danzas."[72] In these accounts, the exiles were always shy, sometimes openly hostile (but eventually won over), and always nostalgic for the Spain to which they could never return. These accounts never actually say that the refugees from the war could never return, but Pilar hints at their status when she refers to the exiles' relationship to "the lost Patria." It is obvious, however, given the repressive and vindictive policies of the Franco regime, that open supporters of the Republican cause would have been jailed or killed on their return to Spain.[73]

But this appeal to nostalgia also served the SF's purposes of creating a revisionist account of the war and of the Franco regime itself. They solidly placed the sole blame for the war at the feet of the Republicans and simultaneously offered themselves up as the healers of the breach between Republicans and Nationalists, since "the two sides in battle sang the same ancient songs of the people, the two sides, the same songs."[74] Suárez Fernández stated this message more clearly when recounting the Coros y Danzas' performance in Colombia (1950). According to him, the invitation to dance apparently came from the exiles themselves, who wanted to welcome this new generation of Spaniards. Although he was willing to remark on the warm reconciliation made possible by the Coros y Danzas, he could not necessarily forgive the exiled Spaniards their trespasses, for although there was a desire to "overcome the bitterness and madness of a civil war," he declared, Republican sympathizers such as these exiles "had been at the point of placing Spain under a Soviet Regime."[75] Later, when recounting Ladislow Vajda's Ronda española, he wrote about the film's "double message": "In the end, there is a bond among all humans that happiness can awaken; in Spain there no longer exists a Spain of conquerors and conquered, only one of brothers on the path to reconciliation."[76] Suárez Fernández's memory of the war's meaning follows the narrative path outlined by Michael Richards; that is, in the early decades after the war, the Franco regime constructed warring sides as the victors and vanquished of a crusade against the forces of Communism and atheism, but by the 1960s, the narrative had been softened to a "fratricidal conflict," a kinder metaphor evoking the misunderstandings that can sometimes overtake family members who love one another deeply.[77]

Reconciliation could be difficult in the postwar era. Certainly, hostility met the dancers in the form of protests at almost every stop on their foreign tours. During their first tour in Santiago, Chile, a group of students in the audience shouted, "Die, fascist scum!"[78] In London's Stoll Theatre, protesters threw leaflets from the balconies to the spectators below and then shouted, "Down with Franco" and "Franco the Assassin" as they left the theater.[79] In New York, "the hall was copiously picketed by anti-Franco organizations."[80] Demonstrators also awaited the dancers in San Francisco.[81] Dissenters even crossed the threshold into violence in Mexico City, where a bomb exploded in the middle of a performance by the group from Santander.[82] Despite the jeers they faced from some hostile people in the crowd, the Coros y Danzas, flush from the twin successes of their first Latin American tour and their competition in the International Folk Festival in Llangollen, Wales, became emboldened to tour more widely and conduct cultural diplomacy during a time when Spain was a pariah among the world's great powers. They knew that they were not universally loved, but their strategy was to decouple aesthetics from politics, even if some spectators refused to go along with that plan. To domestic audiences, especially in written and filmed accounts meant explicitly for consumption in Spain, the SF bragged about the gracious receptions audiences gave them and explained how foreigners could now see that Spanish exiles and enemies of the state had misrepresented what Spain was like under the Franco regime. To foreign audiences they presented themselves solely as reflections of a beautiful and variegated folkloric tradition, with nary a hint that that the dancers and singers were tied to the regime. Sometimes they had to deceive.[83] For example, in 1950 they performed a benefit concert in Santa Barbara, California, at a time before representatives of the Franco regime were allowed in the United States. The person introducing them said that the dancers were sent by "a Spanish civic organization interested in the care and welfare of underprivileged children of Spain—as well as in the preservation of the beautiful folklore of Spain."[84] Nowhere in this introduction was the name Falange Española to be found.

For the most part, their strategy succeeded. For example, one newspaper critic for the *Times of London* wrote, "This organization may possibly have political affiliations, which may have been the cause of the unmannerly welcome from a section of the audience determined to distribute some leaflets, but whether political or no it is obviously a national organization concerned to preserve regional traditions."[85] In New York, where the Coros y Danzas played a benefit concert for cancer research, the columnist writing for the *New York Times* acknowledged that the troupes must have been vetted by the Spanish government, and that the person who organized the U.S. portion of the tour, Harry Sokol, wanted to improve "Hispano-American relations." While "unpleasant political overtones could not be avoided," the columnist writes, "what was seen on the stage, however, was an age-old expression of the genius of the Spanish people, who possess one of the richest of all dance cultures. It has existed since centuries before Franco and the Falange were ever thought of and will doubtless continue to exist after both have become part of the long-forgotten past."[86] Success followed the Coros y Danzas to Los Angeles as well. A *Los Angeles Times* review generally praised the variety of songs and dances performed to enthusiastic Spanish-speaking audiences. The columnist opened the column, however, by explaining that the troupe represented itself as the "Coros y Danzas de España, while picketers handed out leaflets calling the group by its full name, the Coros y Danzas de la Sección Femenina de la Falange de España, warning the possibly naive spectators that the Coros y Danzas masked their fascist foundations under colorful costumes.[87]

The SF also salted the mines by providing newspapers with information that parroted the lines that the SF often publicized in domestic newspapers and journals and by finding reviewers who were favorable to the regime.[88] For example, a column that was supposed to appear in *La revue francaise* comments on how the traditional dances of Spain were being lost to the modern accoutrements of film and radio and how these amateurs were reviving the traditional songs and dances of Spain, adding that they were also trying to disabuse foreigners of the notion that all Spanish popular art could be "reduced to Gypsy 'flamenco.'"[89] Another writer, whose past publications indicated that she was supportive of the Franco regime, wrote a summary and history of the work done by the Coros y Danzas for the journal *Ballet* in London, again mimicking the main talking points of the SF, including the idea that all of the performers were amateurs.[90] Most explicitly, the Spanish ambassador to Belgium wrote to María Victoria Eiroa, cofounder of the SF and head of its delegation in Galicia, to say that the director of the *Journal des beaux arts* wanted to publish an article about the Coros y Danzas (who were going to perform in Brussels the following month) and was asking for somebody to send the following information immediately: "A good article written by an important Spanish folklorist that touches on ... [how] Spanish folklore, contrary to what foreigners think, is not only about Andalusian folklore or flamenco folklore. Spain, for a series of reasons—geographic, ethnographic, etc., is a country with one of the most varied and rich folklores of the world."[91] Once again, the Coros y Danzas pushed a program reminiscent of what nineteenth-century nationalists of all persuasions in Spain had attempted to create during the nineteenth century and the early decades of the twentieth century. Like their forbears, they worked to catalog, present, and educate audiences about the cultural treasures of rural Spain, imagining that the essential values of Spain lay in its heartland, not in the corrupt cultures of its urban centers. The Coros y Danzas had already served up this platter of "unity in diversity" to its domestic audiences. The point now was to convince international audiences of the same thing.

These are but some of the numerous examples that demonstrate that the SF knew that the Coros y Danzas furnished the means to soften the Francoist image abroad. Pilar referred to them as "a cultural embassy in permanent circulation."[92] According to Suárez Fernández, when asked if the Coros y Danzas had achieved any real successes after three years of intense touring around the world, Spanish diplomats answered that they had done "excellent" work with respect to international relations because they put forth "a friendly image of Spain."[93] A Brazilian journalist supposedly remarked that "the flying skirts of these girls do as much for Spain as the embroidery on the jackets of the diplomats."[94] Sometimes, however, even those who promoted the benefits of the

Coros y Danzas as cultural ambassadors undercut their own messages about the Franco regime. When Suárez Fernández recounted the exiled Spaniards' reactions to the dancers, he remarked that the exiles closed their minds to politics and opened up their hearts: "Those who lived [in Argentina] in exile did not have before them the image of Francoist Spain; rather, they had the accents and dances of their own land."[95] Of course, by calling attention to the idea that the dancers consciously diverted the exiled Spaniards' attention away from the politics of the Franco regime, Suárez Fernández implied, however unconsciously, that there was something legitimate about the exiles' criticism of the regime. Suárez Fernández chose instead to remember the Spanish exiles as having bathed themselves in the warmth of patriotism, nostalgic for a Spain that would be forever lost to them.

The Didacticism of the Coros y Danzas

As illustrated in both the numerous newspaper columns describing the Coros y Danzas' performances as well as the Coros y Danzas' own prolific publications, didacticism remained one of the chief goals of these productions and tours. They sought especially to disabuse foreigners of their erroneous conceptions of Spain's history, traditions, and people. Tired of the old saw that Spain *was* Andalusia (and vice versa), the Coros y Danzas took every opportunity to puncture that myth, even as they sometimes reinforced Andalusian exoticism. For example, Suárez Fernández expressed his joy that audiences were shown a splendid variety of Spanish folklore that "demonstrated the falsity of this Gypsy pseudo-flamenco to which people have wanted to reduce the Spanish."[96] Another commentator eagerly exclaimed that the Coros y Danzas effectively dispelled the Andalusian stereotypes of Spain: "For many of the English, above all those who believed that Spain was no more than sun, carnations, tambourines, guitars, bulls, and olés . . . the dances and songs of the north were a revelation."[97]

Because the Coros y Danzas concerned themselves with shattering the stereotypes foreigners held about Spanish song and dance, they took great care to have narrators describe the dances during the performances and created illustrated programs that explained the various regional dances, although at least one knowledgeable dance critic caught errors in both the written translation and the descriptions of the dances listed in the program.[98] As their confidence grew from the 1950s to the mid-1960s, the Coros y Danzas felt it less necessary to defend their project against the forces of andalucísmo. We can see this transition most clearly between the programs for the early 1950s and for 1965.[99] By 1965 the Coros y Danzas registered a confidence about Spain's multiple folkloric forms, mainly because they had triumphed on the international stage. That confidence, coupled with the tourist boom in Spain, allowed them to address flamenco, at least in passing.

One important feature of the Sección Femenina's conception of their folklore was their steadfast notion that one could not separate the songs, rhythms, and steps of each region's music from the land from which they sprung. With an essentialized understanding of geography, the SF connected the regional songs and dances to the land, whether through text, maps, or photographs and films of the women dancing on the specific land to which they belonged. The dancers *became* the land they represented, and the SF hoped that by displaying the various regional dancers and singers, people would begin to realize that the unity of Spain became even stronger because of its diversity; thus in the various musical programs that the SF produced for the Coros y Danzas, the singers and dancers were described according to a set of geographically determined characteristics. For example, Galicia, the land in northwestern Spain from which some dancers came, was described as "sweet and wet as Brittany and Ireland." Their favored instrument, the *gaita* (bagpipes) hinted at the traces of their Celtic roots, but when they danced the regional *muiñera,* one could "see how the southern influence has partially infiltrated [this music] to make it happier." Echoing a long-standing literature about Castile as a harsh but sober place, the "daughters of Castile" are characterized as "serious" and "noble" in their performance, "even in their happiness."[100]

The introduction to the 1953 program begins by disabusing the audience of the idea that Spanish song and dance is only Andalusian song and dance, but then it manages to valorize Andalusian folk music by rooting it in ancient history, all the while minimizing flamenco's commercial impact. The written program begins with the standard claim that when foreigners imagine Spanish dance, they conjure up images of a female Andalusian dancer, "a dark, beautiful woman with a smile on her lips, a red flower in her black hair, the body swaying and the arms raised" in the pose of a flamenco dancer. This image overshadows other Andalusian dances, the narrative continues, even though flamenco and these other regional dances come from the same source, "the fruit of an ancient civilization that developed in Southern Spain in the era of the

Moorish kingdoms." Those who wrote the descriptions of the Andalusian regional songs and dances for this program fell into the same Orientalist clichés as everybody else who tried to describe Andalusian music. Careful listeners, they contended, could hear echoes of Arabic songs in the refrains of soleares or cante jondo, although, according to this account, other Spanish songs from this region were both "more quiet" and "more sparkling" than their flamencoized counterparts. The music all stemmed from the same "nostalgic depths, the same wild and profound poetry," or so they claimed. The dances, too, "evoke . . . the women of ancient Islam," and when audiences hear the combined rhythms, castanets, and guitar, their imaginations are supposed to take them to the "era in which the Caliphs of Cordoba forgot their worries" when the women performed their "millenarian" dances.[101] Instead of negating the stereotypes that foreigners may have had about flamenco, these descriptions reinforced them. The women were made into mysterious and enticing ciphers onto which men could project their own desires. Like Manuel de Falla, García Lorca, and the Andalusian nationalists of the early nineteenth century, these program writers set the origins of Andalusian music in an Oriental past, thus eliminating the "problematic" gitanos from this narrative. Strangely, they chose to situate the origins of the music in the history of al-Andalus, given the embarrassing fact—for a National Catholic state, that is—that Muslims dominated the region in that era.

By the late Franco regime, however, the defensive posture with respect to Andalusia diminished significantly. The reasons are many. First, the regime was now sufficiently consolidated, especially when it received financial and military support from the United States after signing the 1953 Madrid Pact and gaining full membership in the UN in 1955. Second, partially as a result of these mended political and economic relationships, the Franco regime was able to open Spain up to tourism, and the Coros y Danzas could play a role in marshaling enthusiasm for all things Spanish. These developments helped the regime and its supporters display themselves with confidence and even allow them to embrace the Andalusian identity that they once rejected. By 1965, when the Coros y Danzas made daily appearances at the New York World's Fair, they had perfected their presentation to the world, proud to display the variety of Spanish folk dances and accepting of Andalusia's oversized role in Spanish folk culture. In a demonstration of loosening Catholic strictures, women and men danced together, more realistically approximating how the dances might have been performed in the past. The song and dance programs that audiences could read were much more detailed, covering the history and landscapes from which a dizzying array of regional dances sprung.

In programs published in 1965, the writers appealed again to the ancientness of Spain's cultural heritage, claiming that "the oldest depiction of men engaged in dancing that has been found in Europe is the wall-paintings of the cave of Cogul, in Lérida province." Then, in typical fashion, geographical essentialism followed, with an explanation that, generally speaking, "the dances of the East are feminine, while those of the West are unmistakably masculine," and thus concluding that in eastern Spain, the dances "are ceremonious and delicate; those of the south, lively and bold; those of the north[,] ... warlike in tone."[102] In a section titled "Regions, Costumes and Dances," all three are covered in supreme detail. Andalusia is the first region that appears, introduced to the audience through the poetry of Manuel Machado, the Machado brother who sided with the Nationalists during the civil war.[103] Then begins a brief explication of the poem and what it means for the region and for Spain: "Andalusia is the great enigma, the sphinx that surprises the poets, maddens the painters, tortures the musicians, each and every one of them incapable of really interpreting her. Yet all of her is contained in her dances."[104] Flamenco is still ignored, but the protestations one read and heard in earlier versions of the Coros y Danzas programs were now gone from this 1965 edition. Instead, there are more photographs of dancers and more detailed descriptions of the regions, musical instruments, costumes, and histories of the places that these singers and dancers come from. The program reflects a greater joy and confidence in Spain's place in the world of nations. It even takes a few risks, like saying that some believe that the jota, the second most popular folk dance form outside of Andalusia, is really nothing more than a fandango in disguise: "This is perhaps why there are no jotas in flamenca Andalusia." By referring to the fandango, they called into being the idea of flamenco, something they had tried so hard in the past to banish from audiences' understanding of the place. They also acknowledged the presence of gitanos in Spanish culture in the alegrías: "It is not a gypsy dance, but the gypsies endow it with a special grace, a verve, a touch of light."[105] What emerges from the 1965 program is the culmination of the SF's goals of claiming all regional dances as Spanish, domesticating them by folklorizing them. If we remember the politics of the Catalan sardana in chapter 3, we can see how the SF successfully co-opted the dance for national purposes. Catalonia is hailed as "single and multiple," reflecting "in its songs and dances both unity and variety." Catalonia has become Spain writ small. The sardana becomes "one of the great Spanish dances, originating in the Ampurdán and now extended to all of Catalonia" with a "very ancient, perhaps... Greek, origin, like nearly all the Catalan dances."[106] By submerging the dance into an ancient history and linking Catalonia's songs and dances to the SF slogan of "Unity in diversity," the SF was able to take the sting out of regional nationalism and invent an ancient history for Spain's cultural and national identity.

The differences between the 1953 and 1965 programs for the Coros y Danzas demonstrate the ways that the Coros y Danzas had succeeded in projecting an antimodern, promodesty, and pro-Spain ideology sought by both the Catholic Church and the SF. They succeeded, superficially at least, in counteracting the Andalusian narrative imposed from outside. But their vision of a variegated Spanish culture was less resilient than they had imagined. For when the tourism boom began to materialize in the 1950s, flamenco and Andalusia would rise again in the following decades; and it is there, to flamenco and tourism, where our next chapter leads us.

7

Tourism and the Return of Flamenco, 1953—1975

In his 1953 plan for how best to promote tourism in Spain, Carlos González Cuesta wrote, "The tourist looks for comfort and ease in his travels . . . good food in restaurants, better wine and españoladas: bulls, flamenco dance, cante, gitanos, . . . Seville, Cordoba, Granada. . . . We have to resign ourselves touristically to be a country of pandereta, because the day we lose the pandereta, we will have lost ninety percent of our attraction for tourists."[1] And although he suggests a host of other types of tourist draws and destinations in Spain, one can almost envision him holding his head in his hands with the century-long accumulated frustration of Spanish elites when he adds, "But how these bulls, cante, and majas weigh us down!"[2] The embattled resignation—if one can say such a thing—with the Spain of pandereta has a long history, as we know. This troika of majas, bulls, and cante all sprang from Andalusia, of course, and Spanish tourism promoters certainly understood that for most foreigners, Andalusia *was* Spain. And so began again the dilemma for those who longed to open Spain up to the world in the age of mass tourism: should tourist boards promote Spain as the land of pandereta or should it present itself as a modern country (although one steeped in Catholic tradition) with diverse landscapes, people, and traditions?

The Franco regime's Ministry of Tourism and Information decided not to choose.

Europe's and the United States' postwar economic boom created the conditions for the growth of mass tourism beginning in the 1950s, but there was certainly no guarantee that Spain would share in the riches that came from it. Because of its ideological (but unofficial) alliance with the Axis powers during World War II, Spain did not benefit like other European nations from the postwar reconstruction efforts. Exiled Spanish Republicans and antifascist partisans pressured the international community to keep Spain politically and economically isolated in the hopes that the Franco regime would crumble.[3] Consequently, Spain did not receive Marshall Plan aid, nor did it gain immediate entrance into the UN. But with the intensification of the Cold War in the early 1950s, Spain, with its prime location on the Mediterranean, became useful to the United States as a bulwark against communism. The Spanish government needed cash and respectability and the United States government coveted a place to construct military bases. Both governments sealed their relationship with the 1953 Bases Treaty. The treaty provided an infusion of currency into Spain and rehabilitated the nation's good name, ensuring the Franco regime's survival.

But survival did not mean acceptance or prosperity. If Spain were going to be brought into the international family fold again and thrive, it would need to both transform its image abroad and keep the money flowing into the country. Throughout the 1950s and 1960s, the Franco regime developed a multipronged strategy to achieve both these goals. It would concentrate on international cultural exchanges such as those represented by the Coros y Danzas, and it would marshal its resources to develop a vibrant tourist industry that would at first rely on selling the Spain of pandereta, with flamenco and folklore at the forefront.[4] The success of these strategies culminated in Spain's participation in the 1964–65 New York World's Fair and the portable tourist exhibit that traveled worldwide, the Expotur. Meanwhile, foreign tourist industries would continue to employ old tropes about Spain in their own promotional materials, thus continuing the same dynamic we witnessed some seventy-five years or so earlier, whereby foreign conceptions of Spanish national identity contributed to the reification of these stereotypes within Spain itself. Once again, enterprising Spaniards colonized themselves for material gain.

Flamenco, therefore, became a major star in the production of

Spanish tourism despite the antiflamenco sentiments that had permeated the writings and pronouncements of Spanish elites since flamenco's inception. Although these elites often savaged flamenco because they perceived it to be a commercial venture that catered to the base tastes of the masses by engendering their lust, flamenco's distinctly commercial appeal eventually persuaded those in power to hitch their wagon to that moneymaking star. To save face, cultural promoters of the regime ended up playing a sort of double-game by projecting simultaneously conflicting identities of Spain to foreign and domestic audiences. The Ministry of Tourism and Information promoted both a Spain of pandereta, as exemplified by the "Spain is different" campaign, and a Spain of diversity, that had something for every kind of tourist—hunter, skier, sunbather, and art enthusiast.[5] Flamenco became part of the bait that drew in tourists. Tourism organizers and promoters within Spain stripped flamenco away from its roots as a mass cultural spectacle with sordid origins and folklorized it, making it easier to buy and sell it as a symbol of Spanishness to foreign visitors.

Early Tourism and Flamenco in Spain, 1905–1950

As we learned in chapter 1, Andalusia became the first region in Spain to be populated and popularized by prominent foreign writers and the occasional tourist who reported on the land's contours and its people, often in the most romanticized terms, contributing to an enduring notion that Spain was an Oriental land filled with happy people and beautiful dancing women wielding castanets—that is, when they were not attending a bullfight or fending off bandits. Flamenco dancing, or some approximate version thereof, became the coin of the tourist realm, as many hotel purveyors and gitanos in places like Seville and Granada quickly learned, so much so, that they began staging dances for eager audiences.

The earliest cultivation of domestic tourism in Spain came from excursionist societies and bicycling clubs at the turn of the century, but early in the twentieth century, Spanish officials began to contemplate developing a state-run industry dedicated to promoting tourism within Spain and abroad.[6] The year 1905 saw the creation of the National Tourism Commission to Promote Tourist and Recreational Excursions of the Foreign Public, designed to build on the foundations of already developed historical and cultural tourism in selected regions of Spain. It commissioned studies, created publications, and dreamed up infrastructure projects aimed to develop a Spanish tourist industry that would market itself mainly to foreigners, although its effects were extremely limited. Soon thereafter in 1911, a royal decree announced the formation of a Royal Commission of Tourism and Artistic Culture (1911–28), headed by Benigno de la Vega Inclán, a member of King Alfonso XIII's inner court, to "promote the development of tourism and the dissemination of popular culture."[7] The commission sought to encourage (official) cultural tourism above all, steering both domestic and international tourists to Spain's greatest artistic treasures and historical monuments as well as to its diverse regional attractions, and it attempted to create the infrastructure necessary to support such endeavors.

Spanish travel guides published under the auspices of this commission reflected Vega Inclán's vision of the Spain he wanted tourists to encounter. While foreign guidebooks might have continued to emphasize what they called the "Oriental" and other stereotypical aspects of Spanish culture and civilization, the guidebooks put out under the auspices of Vega Inclán's commission almost always avoided the Spain of pandereta. Instead, they focused on the Spanish art, culture, and history that could be displayed in "civilized" fashion—that is, the culture carefully showcased in museums. They highlighted the diversity of Spain. Even when describing Spanish dance, guidebooks such as F. Sánchez Cantón's cited Andalusian dances as merely a small part of the numerous Spanish dances that included collective dances like "the sardana in Cataluna, the aurrescu in Navarre . . . the jotas in Valencia and Murcia—and [dances] of a more personal character—like the Andalusian dances, all varied and distinct."[8] In contrast to the foreign guidebooks that wanted to reduce Spanish national identity to Andalusia and its requisite cante and baile flamenco, Spanish guidebooks like Sánchez Cantón's compelled readers to notice Spanish variety and recast the national dance as the jota, not baile flamenco.

But when the commission tried to take its show on the road to London on the eve of World War I, it fell unwittingly into the pandereta trap once again. Their exhibit, Sunny Spain (May–October 1914), located at Earl's Court and funded by the Spanish government, was intended to attract tourists to Spain by displaying the country's complex history, varied cultural production, and diverse population.[9] Advertisements in London for the exhibition featured an Andalusian woman against a backdrop of Granada's iconic landscapes. The centerpiece of the exhibition was a panorama of thirty-three landscape murals and, twice daily, Spanish folk dancers representing five provinces and clad in regional costumes performed their songs and dances for British audiences against those backdrops of the Spanish countryside. Once again, however, the Andalusian dancers proved more popular, and after all the other folk dancers had left by the end of June, the Andalusians stayed until the exhibition's closure. But for elites at home, the Sunny Spain Exhibition proved to be a national embarrassment, as summed up by a conservative politician who lamented the "flamenco ridiculousness we are exhibiting in London." Ramiro de Maeztu concurred, observing that the exhibit failed to demonstrate to foreigners that "Spain today has good hotels and trains and truly urbanized cities" that could provide travelers with both the comforts of travel and the "historical and natural beauty of Spain."[10] The scandal at home was so devastating that it neutered Vega Inclán's power and that of his commission.

In addition to the "Sunny Spain" debacle, budgetary problems and administrative constraints—like the fact that Vega Inclán's project for Spanish tourism was almost a one-man show with little administrative support from the state—limited this commission's ability to deploy all the necessary firepower to enact the kind of tourist industry that Vega Inclán envisioned. This situation changed finally in 1928, when the Primo regime in conjunction with the king's royal decree finally created a state-run organization dedicated to the development and marketing of tourism. Known as the Patronato Nacional de Turismo (PNT, 1928–39) this National Tourist Board began in Primo's regime but continued under different organizational structures during the Republic and civil war (1931–39). It professionalized tourism, tackling the various impediments necessary to clear the way to making tourism a big business—launching hotels, marketing the country using advertisements and brochures, setting up travel agencies in foreign countries, making connections with municipal and provincial officials, and so on.[11] The PNT also expanded its definition of cultural tourism to include regional folk arts and cuisine and piggybacked on the nineteenth-century concept of seaside tourism, including not only new beach resorts but other forms of nature tourism like hiking in the mountains and hunting.[12] Finally, the growth of sports' cultures in industrialized parts of the world opened a path for creating sports' tourism, although the sports promoted—skiing, fishing, golfing, boat racing—were still the purview of the upper classes. The PNT avoided marketing the stereotypical images of Spain—the flamenco dancer and bullfighter—although foreign tourist agencies like Thomas Cook continued to sell Spain this way, even in places like

Figure 18. An out-of-place flamenco dancer is an advertising draw for Thomas Cook Tours, 1936.
Source: Spain: Make It San Sebastian, pamphlet/brochure, 1936. Image courtesy of Thomas Cook Archives.

San Sebastian, the seaside resort located in the Basque Country, not exactly known for its flamenco dancers (see figure 18).[13] Instead, the Spanish government hoped to cultivate the kind of tourism that would enable visitors to take Spain seriously for its history, culture, and natural wonders.

Unfortunately, the untimely dual conflagrations of the civil war and World War II crushed the Spanish government's ability to maintain a thriving tourist industry. During the war itself, the Republicans maintained a skeletal PNT, which spent its energies promoting anti-Nationalist propaganda in the form of brochures and posters, accusing the Nationalists of bombing Spain's cultural and artistic heritage. The Nationalists, under the auspices of the Servicio Nacional de Turismo (1938—renamed the Dirección General de Turismo in 1939), returned the propagandistic fire with their own pamphlets and posters highlighting the atrocities Republicans had committed against religious cultural treasures.[14]

After the civil war and throughout the 1940s, a tourism infrastructure was merely nominal, given the wartime destruction both within Spain and the rest of Europe, Spain's autarkic economy, and the difficult work of building a new state and consolidating a new regime from the ashes of war. Railroad networks and tourist lodgings had been destroyed, so the strictly monitored tours the Dirección General de Turismo conducted had to take place on whatever highways still existed. Continental Europe's wartime dislocation and the "hungry years" of the 1940s prevented most people outside of and within Spain from traveling, ensuring that whatever rare tours remained were limited to political elites and the wealthy. The era of mass tourism emerged only after Europe and the United States experienced the postwar economic boom, allowing the working and middle classes, groups of people who previously neither had the financial means nor the leisure time to travel, to explore regions outside their usual ken. The 1950s saw the Franco regime's attempts to regain legitimacy for Spain in the eyes of the Allies that had defeated the fascist Axis powers and acquire the necessary cash to rebuild its still-tattered state. In order to do so, the Franco regime worked to clean up its tarnished image as a fascist state by employing cultural diplomacy and the soft power of tourism.[15]

Creating the Spanish Tourist Boom

Spain's tourist boom in the late 1950s and 1960s owed much of its success to Spain's and the United States' economic and military interdependence. That is not to say that other European powers did not play a major part in increasing the flow of tourists into Spain, but the United States' new role as one of two superpowers in the postwar era made receiving its administration's blessing (and dollars) all that more important in a world that had become bifurcated in the Cold War era. Although Spain did not receive any financial aid through the Marshall Plan, eventually relations between Spain and other Western powers thawed when the country's location at the crossroads of the Mediterranean became seen as strategically important in the fight against Soviet communism. By 1950 Spain had negotiated a currency exchange agreement with Great Britain, and by 1951 it had exchanged ambassadors with the United States and opened up its first American Express office in Madrid, both within days of each other.[16] That same year saw the Franco regime's elevation of tourism to cabinet status under the auspices of the Ministry of Information and Tourism (MIT). At first tourism played a secondary role to the other departments under its control, such as the press and other propaganda outlets, but it would soon be an equal if not superior partner.[17] The following year, the MIT began devising its National Plan for Tourism, whose aim was to revamp its tourist industry and create new forms of tourism and a new tourist infrastructure to supplement the industry's former emphasis on monumental, historical, and folkloric tourism with "high-volume, low cost tourism . . . centered on what were seen as 'modern' tourist tastes . . . such as sunshine, beaches and popular customs."[18]

Spain's transformation from pariah state to tourist paradise in the Cold War era occurred after 1953. This year began the trajectory that would make Spain one of the most popular tourist destinations in the world. First, the Pact of Madrid, signed by Spain and the United States, provided Spain with economic and military aid in exchange for the United States' rights to construct and employ air and naval bases on Spanish territory. Although this funneling of cash did not yet end the Franco regime's autarkic economic policies, it did prop up the economy enough to keep the regime from crumbling. The agreement also communicated at least some kind of rapprochement between Spain and the rest of the West, signaling to businesses like American Express, Cook's Tours, and the Hilton Hotel chain that Spain was safe again and ripe for moneymaking opportunities.[19] Although there is no explicit link between the Pact of Madrid and the National Plan for Tourism, it is reasonable to believe that the promise of American dollars and, one would imagine, American tourists, would spur Spanish officials to begin plans to rethink their tourist industry. In fact, as we shall see, there is substantial evidence to show that the MIT wanted to cultivate North American tourists above all.

In 1953 the MIT asked for proposals from the public on how best to market Spain to the world. Those who submitted proposals were well aware of the changes that had taken place in the tourist industry since the end of World War II—namely, the "democratization of tourism," whereby even working-class people had paid vacations and some disposable income at hand. But as one writer commented, North Americans provided the most tantalizing opportunities for tourist growth in Spain: "It should, however, be emphasized that the large number of American tourists who are currently visiting Europe is the clear consequence of a

Figure 19. Iberia Airlines advertisement for Andalusia with a flamenco dancer taking center stage in the image, 1958.
Image courtesy of Iberia.

democratized movement of tourism. Now, the 'democratic American,' in any case, has more money than the 'democratic European.' This circumstance, accompanied by the fact that 'Spain' is truly 'in fashion' as a tourist destination in the United States, requires a special and in-depth advertising campaign."[20] Of course the MIT did not focus solely on the United States—it cast its net wide throughout Europe, Latin America, and even East and Southeast Asia—but the United States and, to a lesser degree, Great Britain, would be deluged with advertising in the form of brochures and targeted ads in major newspapers, magazines, and the trade journals of airline, cruise ship, and tourist industries.[21] In fact, the Spanish airline, Iberia, certainly contributed to the promotion of stereotypical imagery in the first decades of the Spanish tourist boom (see figures 19 and 20).

A sampling of these reports demonstrates the dilemma the regime faced: should the advertising reflect what the administration wanted

Figure 20. Iberia Airlines advertisement with the flamenco iconography stripped bare—just a chair, a guitar, and a sombrero, 1968.
Image courtesy of Iberia.

tourists to see (a land of picturesque beauty coupled with an array of modern cities, striking historical monuments, and fabulous art) or what they believed tourists wanted to experience (bullfights, folklore, and flamenco)? Their proposals struck a sort of compromise, echoing what González Cuesta, the man whose words opened this chapter, suggested. Advertisements should pander to those tourists who imagined Spain as the land of castanets, luring them in with promises of bullfighters and flamenco dancers, and then once tourists arrived in Spain, they could be awestruck by Spain's other wonders: the monuments, beaches, mountains, art, and so on.[22] In the 1950s the MIT promoted some version or another of the slogan "Spain is Different," emphasizing the folkloric aspects of Spain that Spaniards believed foreigners wanted to sample. Although there were subtle nods to flamenco, the MIT tended to highlight the diverse folk customs from all around Spain, reflecting the ideologies promoted by such groups as the Coros y Danzas.[23] They also tried to reassure tourists that visitors to Spain could enjoy the country's exotic qualities while still maintaining their creature comforts. It was a place, as a 1957 tourist pamphlet declared, "where the charm of the Orient and the comfort of the West lived together harmoniously; where the joyful survival of a traditional past does not impede today's progress and dynamism." This tourist brochure pandered some to its imagined audience, mentioning the Oriental charm of southern Spain, accompanied by a picture of female villagers in whitewashed villages, dressed in clothes reminiscent of those worn by North African women, while on the opposite page flamenco dancers appear. The word "flamenco" is never mentioned, however; instead the illustration is meant to represent the folklore described in the text of that page.[24]

Similarly, in 1957 Rafael Calleja, a longtime publicist for the state tourism agency, the Dirección General de Turismo (DGT), issued a new and revised edition of his 1943 *Apología turística de España*. The 1957 version reflected the Spanish state's mission to portray Spain as both "different" and modern, and it included many more descriptions, drawings, and photographs of españoladas than the 1943 version. The 1943 book for tourists had explanatory text about each region and 439 photographs of "landscapes, monuments, and typical Spanish qualities"—meaning photographs of people in regional costumes—highlighting the "rich, varied, multiform Spain."[25] It also gestured at tourists' love of flamenco and bullfights by presenting a couple of sketches of these subjects in the Andalusia section, but there was no discussion whatsoever of flamenco. The 1957 *Nueva apología turística de España*, however, ramped up the folklore and flamenco, although it tried to give flamenco a greater air of respectability by calling the singing *cante hondo* (the alternative spelling of cante jondo) and the dancing *baile Andaluz* (Andalusian dancing). Its descriptions of Spanish song and dance mirrored the ideology perpetrated by the Coros y Danzas: "Regional dances (the Aragonese jota, the Catalan sardana, the Galician muiñera, the typical dances of the Basque lands, of Leon, Castile, Valencia, etc.) are of extraordinary interest. Andalusian dances have traveled all around the world, but only in their native natural surroundings does their charm shine. The popular songs of rich splendor and variety stand out as among the most personal and valuable characteristics that are typically Spanish. And . . . the Andalusian ones—cante hondo—the most renowned."[26] The illustrations are even more illuminating in this revised text. The drawing of a flamenco dancer actually uses the preferred flamenco term, referring to her as a "bailaora."[27] Two pages later we see a drawing of a couple dancing in a flamenco pose and the back of a man accompanying them on his guitar. The caption here reads, "Andalusian dance."[28] Finally, in the section describing Granada and Córdoba, the illustration shows one man singing, passion etched on his face, while a guitarist plays alongside him. Here the caption says, "Cante hondo."[29] The second part of the book has, like the original edition, hundreds of photographs of landscapes and monuments, but it has also added pictures of city life—ostensibly, to portray Spain as a modern country—and more space dedicated to "typical" Spanish types, mimicking (not ironically, however) the colonial idea of photographing "natives in their natural habitat." This time, however, one person who represents *La andaluza* (the female Andalusian type) is photographed from behind from the torso up, with her hands in a pose familiar to flamenco dancers.[30] Taken together, all these images suggest a turning away from the antiflamenquismo of the early Franco regime and to a realization that flamenco and other similar stereotypes could sell Spain to tourists. They were careful, however, to emphasize the flamenco form that intellectuals deemed art during the 1922 Concurso de Cante Jondo in Granada, that is, the cante jondo. It was reinvigorated shortly before the publication of the second edition of Calleja's book by the reemergence of the First National Cante Jondo Contest in Córdoba in 1956, the first such contest since 1922.[31]

Among the many efforts to jump-start the Spanish tourist industry in the early 1950s was the opening of nightclubs, especially in the coastal regions where tourists flocked, which offered a place for people to drink, perhaps dance, and watch some form of entertainment. Some of these places were rebranded as tablaos, another name for the intimate clubs where flamenco was performed, functioning much like the nineteenth-century cafés cantantes. There were close to three hundred such places in 1952 in the entire country, although they did not solely serve tourists. Some, like the Cortijo El Guajiro, one of the first tablaos to open in Triana, Seville (it opened in 1952), nurtured the careers of such acclaimed performers as Fosforito, Trini España, Matilde Corral, El Farruco, Manuela Vargas, and Rafael El Negro (see figures 21 and 22).[32] What these businesses (re)discovered is that flamenco brought in tourists, so if they could find a way to include flamenco in their slate of entertainments, they could achieve great financial success.[33] Once more tourist locales developed in the late 1950s and early 1960s along places like the Costa Brava and the Costa Blanca, these resorts would serve up flamenco on a platter, completely divorced from the regions where the performances originated.[34] Flamenco's popularity in nightclubs did not

Figure 21. Entrance to the Cortijo El Guajiro tablao, 1960s.
© ICAS-SAHP, Fototeca Municipal de Sevilla, Cubiles Archive.

escape promoters' eyes, and so official tourism posters took flamenquismo and ran with it, tempting foreigners with images of the cultural world of flamenco or bullfights in nearly one-third of its tourist posters between 1950 and 1960.[35]

Foreign tour groups like Thomas Cook Tours participated in the feedback loop of national identity, manipulating the stereotypes of Spain, as did the Spanish firms like Iberia Airlines that advertised in

Figure 22. El Moro, Pepe Lucena, El Chocolate, El Negro, and Matilde Corral performing a show in the Cortijo El Guajiro, ca. 1955–60.
© ICAS-SAHP, Fototeca Municipal de Sevilla, Cubiles Archive.

their brochures. Feeling little pressure, it seems, to promote Spain as a modern land, except in its accommodations, a 1950 Thomas Cook brochure remarked on the "special charm of this old-world corner of Europe" where British "holidaymakers" could experience "the land of the ox-cart, the toreador, the castanet dancers and the typical architecture of white buildings in the southern sun" while staying in the "up-to-date comfort of excellent hotels offering the best of two worlds."[36] One year later, the brochure for the same tour featured on its cover an illustration of flamenco dancers in black and white, dancing in front of a blood-red background, evoking, perhaps, a bullfighter's cape or the color of passion (see figure 23).[37] The year 1952 marked the beginning of advertisements from Iberia Airlines in the Thomas Cook brochures, which in the first years prominently displayed flamenco dancers while promoting Spanish sunshine (see figures 24 and 25).[38] An Iberia Airlines black-and-white advertisement from 1954 hit all the españolada bases. "Fly with us to Spain. Iberia Spanish Airlines," was embedded in a background strewn with flowers. Above the text, taking up half the advertisement, is a Spanish fan with illustrations printed on it of Don Quixote and Sancho Panza riding a wooden horse, a pair of flamenco dancers, Seville's iconic Giralda, and a bullfighter. Right above the fan

HOLIDAYS IN
SPAIN
PORTUGAL
BALEARIC ISLANDS, MALTA, GIBRALTAR AND CYPRUS

1951

Advertisements

FLY TO SPAIN
with IBERIA
SPANISH AIR LINES

REGULAR
"SKYMASTER SERVICE"
TO
MADRID
BARCELONA
PALMA
VALENCIA
SEVILLE
CANARY ISLES

4 CONDUIT ST. LONDON, W.I.   GROsvenor 6131.

Figure 25. Iberia Airlines advertisement in a Thomas Cook brochure. This time a flamenco-dancing couple promises good times in Spain.
Source: *Summer Holidays in Spain and Portugal, Balearic Islands, Malta, Gibraltar and Cyprus*, 1953, pamphlet/brochure.
Image courtesy of Thomas Cook Archives.

Figure 23 (*top left*). A flamenco-dancing couple graces the cover of the summer brochure advertising a tour for the Iberian Peninsula and a variety of Mediterranean islands.
Source: *Summer Holidays in Spain, Portugal, Balearic Islands, Malta, Gibraltar and Cyprus*, pamphlet/brochure, 1951.
Image courtesy of Thomas Cook Archives.

Figure 24 (*bottom left*). Iberia Airlines advertisement in a Thomas Cook brochure. A flamenco dancer figures prominently.
Source: *Winter Sunshine*, 1952–53, pamphlet/brochure.
Image courtesy of Thomas Cook Archives.

Figure 26. Iberia Airlines advertisement in a Thomas Cook brochure. Replete with Spanish stereotypes and icons, it features Don Quijote and Sancho Panza, flamenco dancers, La Giralda of Seville, and a bullfighter.

Source: *Holidays in Spain and Portugal, Balearic Isles, Andorra, Madeira, Malta, Gibraltar, Cyprus*, 1954, pamphlet/brochure.

Image courtesy of Thomas Cook Archives.

flies a small Iberia Airlines airplane (see figure 26).[39] Obviously, Iberia airlines knew its potential audience, and it followed the timeworn strategy of advertisers, building on the dreams of those to whom it was trying to market. In this case, the advertisers imagined that Britons wanted pandereta, and pandereta they would get. But over the course of the late 1950s and through the 1960s, tour groups like Thomas Cook would shift their focus more on festive adventures at prepackaged beach resorts and a bit less on flamenco fantasies.

The Boom Arrives (Late 1950s–1960s)

Spanish tourism took off in the late 1950s, aided by the expansion of charter travel, a more streamlined and open border patrol, and the 1959 Stabilization Plan that forced the Spanish government to devalue the peseta and open up trade and investment to the international market.[40] The result was what is now referred to as the Spanish tourist boom, which began around 1957 and exploded after 1962, when Manuel Fraga took the helm of the MIT, reorganized its administrative structure and transformed the Spanish tourist industry into a world-class powerhouse.[41] Fraga strove to make Spanish tourism ever more professional and profitable and encouraged the maintenance and building of more resorts like those in the Costa Brava and Costa Blanca and rezoning land for touristic purposes.[42]

By the late 1950s and early 1960s, some elements from within the tourist industry began to chafe at the portrayal of Spain as the land of pandereta and sunshine, and began calling for more modern and less hackneyed images of Spain. As Sasha Pack notes, in 1962 the DGT commissioned a study on how to develop and market pilgrimage tours, commenting, "In recent years, the majority of the [promotional] efforts have been based on climate, beaches, sun and sea, Andalusian folklore, and other such motifs that, though they continue to be effective and relevant, are becoming a cliché." Spain needed to "present in a massive and dignified way attractions of another type, in order to compete with the countries of central Europe, which, perhaps for their lack of attractive climate, have capitalized on more cultural themes."[43] Recognizing the need to expand its marketing strategy, elements of the Spanish tourist industry began to limit the promotional materials that featured andalucismo and flamenquismo. In fact, only one of the Spanish tourism promotional posters produced between 1964 and 1969 featured flamenco dancers.[44]

That does not mean that foreign tourism operators dropped flamenco from their tourist brochures, nor does it mean that flamenco died out as a tourist attraction once people came to Spain. In fact, flamenco flourished all over the country, even in places where historically it had never been. Foreign tour operators, airline companies, and domestic resorts milked flamenquismo for all they could—they just presented it as one of many opportunities available when visiting Spain.

Thomas Cook Tours was but one of many British tour companies that flooded Spain in the 1950s and 1960s, and its brochures and the films produced for its use over those two decades reflect the changing nature of Spanish tourism. Thomas Cook Tours had promoted travel for the comfortable middle and upper classes at seaside resorts like San Sebastian and Santander since at least 1934, but after 1955 the company began to emphasize sunshine and beaches for a greater number of rain-beleaguered Britons, especially as the MIT began allowing the development of resorts, mostly with the help of foreign investment, on the Costa Brava, Costa Blanca, and Costa del Sol. Thomas Cook's relationship with flamenco was decidedly confused. On the one hand, a brochure from 1955 advertising "holidays in Spain and Portugal" had an image of flamenco dancers in its "General Information" section and recognized that flamenco singing took place in the south; on the other hand, a tour that same year advertising the warmth and sun of the Costa Brava and Mallorca claimed that visitors could "spend the day lolling in the sun or swimming from one of the many pure white sandy beaches on the island. At night you will be thrilled by the Mallorquin folk dances and exhilarated by the wild Andalusian flamenco." Thus, one imagines that at whatever resort Thomas Cook had contracted with, people approximating flamenco dancers had been hired to entertain tourists. Tour brochurs in 1957 (see figure 27) return to the misplaced imagery of flamenco dancers in San Sebastian as well as a focus on seaside bathers, and a 1958 tour to the same place repeats the theme, but with a different illustration of flamenco dancers.[45] Beginning in 1959 the covers of their brochures and booklets to Spain and Portugal changed to photographs, many of which showed people splayed out on beaches or portrayals of peaceful seaside towns, but the brochures' interiors jar one's sensibilities, showing flamenco dancers popping up in the most unlikely of places, like the one from "Big, Gay San Sebastian," where a tiny flamenco dancer is superimposed on a beachside scene (see figure 28).[46] In 1963 a flamenco dancer is located in between Madrid and Valencia on a tourist map of Spain (see figure 29).[47] These oddly placed images of flamenco continue throughout the early 1960s,

Figure 27. Flamenco dancers in San Sebastian. Flamenco is not usually associated with this area of Spain.
Source: "In Spain They Say, 'Aquí está su casa,'" and "San Sebastian: Gateway to Romantic Spain," *Holidaymaking*, 1957, magazine.
Image courtesy of Thomas Cook Archives.

Figure 28. A tiny flamenco dancer dances among the sunbathers.
Source: "Big, Gay, San Sebastian—But See How Inexpensive!" *Holidaymaking*, 1959, magazine.
Image courtesy of Thomas Cook Archives.

Figure 29. Tourist map of Spain, where the flamenco dancers are decidedly not in Andalusia.
Source: *Holidaymaking*, 1963, magazine.
Image courtesy of Thomas Cook Archives.

perhaps assuring tourists that they could still experience southern Spain, even if they really just wanted to lie out in the sun. Ironically enough, 1963 marked the beginning of what Cooks Motor Coach Tours called "the Flamenco Tour," looping tourists south and west through Madrid, down to Andalusia, and back up north along Spain's eastern coast, but the tour never actually advertised any excursion to flamenco clubs during their stops in Córdoba, Seville, or Granada—three places historically known for flamenco. And, oddly, this brochure lacked any photographs of flamenco dancers. It is as if flamenco had become so prevalent in the social imaginary of Spain that tourists no longer needed a reminder of that fact.[48]

Films meant to attract tourists to Spain also provide a window into the conflicting ways that foreigners and Spaniards presented Spain and its identities. A film produced sometime in the 1950s, *Holiday in Spain*, "presented by" Spain's state-owned corporation that facilitated bookings for transportation and lodging, ATESA (Autotransporte Turístico Español), begins in Madrid, showing views of the modern city along with the Royal Palace. It then hits the highlights of Spain—Toledo, El Escorial, Segovia, and so on—and focuses on religious processions and pastoral scenes, before moving on to the Costa Brava and other beach resorts (interspersed are mini ads for ATESA bus and car rentals). The film finally ends at the Madrid airport, from where the sated tourist will depart. The scenes embody the Spain that Spanish officials wanted represented to foreign eyes—a land of beauty, modernity, and enough tradition to pique visitors' interests. Nary a flamenco performer was to be found.[49]

Films presented by the British, however, reflected a much different place, a country of endless entertainments that one still finds in resort towns built mainly for tourists' bacchanalian adventures. The early 1950s *Costa Brava* begins immediately with a scene of flamenco dancers dancing outside, a dance the narrator calls a fandango (but it sounds more like a malagueña), and a voice-over that declares, "You are in Spain, and may your holiday be as colorful as the dance you're certain to see there performed to wild Gypsy music, the Spanish fandango." Our narrator guides us through the Costa Brava, highlighting the various sights, and the film ends again with dancers.[50] *Majorca—Stay in the Sun* (1958) also begins with flamenco dancers, this time on a stage near a hotel pool, in broad daylight, outside the highway that runs along the beach. After this artistic desecration, the usual touristy sights of hotels, pools, sunbathing, and shopping are laid before the viewer. The film ends with regional dancers in their folkloric costumes.[51] By the 1960s we see how truly commercialized the Spanish resorts have become. *Magic of Majorca* begins with an aircraft landing at Majorca, followed by passengers disembarking and heading to the Kontiki hotel, where in the middle of the day a flamenco dancer emerges from an outside fountain and begins to dance for the hotel guests (this all happens within the first three minutes of the film). By the ninth minute of the film, one witnesses more flamenco dancing, followed by a scene in a disco, a market, and, soon thereafter, a tapas bar.[52] It is important to emphasize that Majorca and the Costa Brava were never centers of flamenco, but the people managing a rapidly growing tourist industry for a mass market understood that tourists wanted to be entertained, and flamenco could easily be marketed for these purposes because tourists already had preconceived notions that Spain meant flamenco dancers. They would not necessarily be incorrect in thinking that way, given that Spanish nightclubs far from Andalusia and Madrid advertised their own flamenco entertainments.

By the late 1960s and early 1970s, tour companies like Thomas Cook really accelerated their promotion of Spanish beaches and party life, and although one could sometimes find photographs of flamenco dancers in their brochures, the company was starting to move away from this particular clichéd portrayal of Spain, as Spain itself was experiencing the economic boom that was catapulting it into the category of "modern European nation." Meanwhile in Spain, various parts of the tourist industry were finding their way to feed the economic maw by increasing still more the number of tourists who entered the country. They did this by marketing the country at special events like the 1964-65 New York World's Fair and traveling tourism exhibits like Expotur. In the process, they played the double game of presenting Spain as both modern and the country of pandereta.

The 1964–1965 World's Fair

As discussed in chapter 5, world's fairs played a prominent role in showcasing and molding national identity, but that national identity was created by the interplay of exhibitors and spectators. World's fairs had vanished from the European landscape during World War II and the subsequent European reconstruction. They returned to Europe, Brussels specifically, in 1958. Highlighting the science and industry of the atomic age, the Belgian theme, "Building the World for the Modern Man," seemed to be a kind of balm for life in the nuclear era. Spain, once again considered part of the family of nations, participated in this fair and provided entertainment in the form of the Coros y Danzas and Zambra, the flamenco troupe headed by Rosa Durán, named after the eponymous tablao in Madrid.[53] The Spanish Pavilion in Brussels did not make a great impression compared to those of the United States, the Soviet Union, and France, but the Spanish government was able to use that exposition as a way to reaffirm its place on the international stage.[54] After dipping its toes in Belgium, the Spanish government, in close collaboration with the MIT, worked deliberately and meticulously to guarantee that Spain would make a giant splash when New York City hosted its world's fair in 1964-65. Putting together all the resources they had at their disposal, they created a dazzling display to ensure that Spain would become one of the world's greatest tourist destinations.

The theme of the 1964-65 New York World's Fair, "Peace through Understanding," provided an optimistic counterpoint to the negative reality of the Cold War. New countries created out of the violence of decolonization could introduce themselves to the world's stage in a nonthreatening manner, and old countries like Spain, with reputations to mend, could engage in a whirlwind of cultural diplomacy. The New York World's Fair was Spain's coming-out party. It provided a stage for the Franco regime to create, refine, and package its national identity for both foreign and domestic consumption, especially because 1964 also marked the "25 Years of Peace" commemoration within Spain.[55] The "real Spain," therefore, was not repressive, theocratic, backward, and mindlessly conformist; instead, as Miguel García de Sáez, the commissioner of the pavilion of Spain gracefully put it, "The real Spain [was] gay and hardworking, sunny, following the path of her history with faith and optimism."[56]

Despite the fact that the number of tourists to Spain had already increased by approximately 160 percent between 1959 and 1963, the World's Fair created a great opportunity to increase Spain's share of European tourism even more.[57] To achieve this transition from fascist Spain to sunny Spain, the Franco regime spent the equivalent in pesetas of $7 million to create an array of spectacles intended in their totality to dazzle audiences and reshape their thinking about the country.[58] In doing so they hoped to entice tourists to visit Spain and flood it with money. As we well know, this transition did not begin just in 1964. But the 1964 World's Fair became the perfect place to project to the world a more multifaceted national identity. The fair provided what Spain needed at this moment: time (close to two years), space (a pavilion with eighty thousand square feet of exhibition space), and an eager audience (around 25 million people visited the Spanish pavilion by the close of the fair in 1965).[59] At home, the regime represented Spain's participation as a fully modern state, a player in the world that had something to teach the "newer" nations about civilization and culture. Spain—the narrative went—had blessed much of the world with its language, its civilization, its art, its food, its music, and it was time that the world was reminded of Spain's contributions to these areas. While there is much to discuss about the contents of the Spanish pavilion—the food, art, historical artifacts—the chief focus here is on the dance performances in the pavilion, for these performances represented both the Franco regime's multivalent rendering of its national identity and its ambivalence about such a rendering.[60]

Individual dance stars rotated in and out of the pavilion over the course of two years, but there were two types of performances that remained constant throughout the pavilion's tenure: the amateur Coros y Danzas of the Sección Femenina and professional flamenco dancing. The prominence of both these types of dance in the Spanish pavilion reflects the Franco regime's decision to project, on the one hand, a Spanish identity that was rural, timeless, folkloric, and unified by regional plurality (the Coros y Danzas) and, on the other hand, a national identity that the regime (rightly) imagined that tourists wanted: an Andalusian-based Spain represented by orientalized, exotic flamenco dancers and singers. In Spain itself, however, the regime presented the Coros y Danzas as the cultural victor over the hearts and minds of Spaniard and foreigner alike.

Coros y Danzas in the Spanish Pavilion

As discussed in the previous chapter, by 1965 the Coros y Danzas had successfully advanced a version of Francoism with a (female) human face at home and abroad. They continued to embody the idea of "unity in diversity," emphasizing folkloric and traditional values, reflecting one part of the regime's enforced identity. Although the organizers of the Coros y Danzas seemed to fear flamenco far less than they had in the 1950s, their role remained the same as it had been over the previous two decades, to "find, discover, interpret and reveal to all, that immense Spanish treasure of folk songs and dances, and take them to every corner of the Motherland as well as carrying them abroad for the joy and admiration of the all the countries of the world."[61] In other words, the Coros y Danzas represented the "true" image of a timeless Spain that could hold together the country's disparate parts, and as it had done in earlier years, it was tasked with being the conduit through which the Spanish government displayed and softened for foreigners its most important and oppressive institutions, the military and the Catholic Church. The Coros y Danzas were trotted out for special occasions related to Spain and the World's Fair, but they seemed to function more for domestic (Spanish) than for foreign consumption, given that these displays were meticulously detailed in Spanish newspapers and magazines. They paraded along Fifth Avenue during "Spain Week," a week coinciding with Columbus Day and commemorating the Spanish gifts of "culture and civilization."[62] They greeted the Spanish naval training ship, *Juan Sebastian de Elcano*, with traditional sailing and fishing songs when it docked at Pier 86 of the Hudson River and then met the naval cadets the next day when they attended Mass at St. Patrick's Cathedral.[63] They danced in the lobby with members of the Spanish Civil Guard before the New York Philharmonic played its "Spanish set" for its Promenade

Series in June 1965.[64] By their mere physical proximity to representatives of the Spanish military and Spanish Church, the Coros y Danzas transformed symbolically into the representatives of Spanish culture and the Spanish state. This becomes clearer in the Spanish press. In the popular magazine *Blanco y negro*, the Coros y Danzas are referred to as "the spice of Spain."[65] Along with the hostesses of the Spanish pavilion, the dancers acted as ambassadors for heads of state and social lubricants for foreigners unfamiliar with Spanish culture. On the inaugural evening of the fair, April 22, 1964, the dancers entertained American and Spanish officials in the Spanish pavilion. According to *Blanco y negro*, the combination of festive dancers, attractive hostesses, and great food made this "'Spanish Night' . . . the most important cultural and social gathering of the Fair."[66]

The Spanish press continued to portray the Coros y Danzas as the reflection of a multicultural Spain that was greater than the sum of its parts and more representative of the entire country than Andalusia. Although the Coros y Danzas performed daily in the courtyard of the Spanish pavilion from eleven in the morning until 7:30 at night, and twice a day at the theater, the Spanish press downplayed the fact that most of the performances took place in the courtyard. Instead, they focused on those performances that took place in the larger theater, intimating a greater popularity than might have existed: "A theater of some 700 or 800 seats permits the Coros y Danzas, as fantastic as always, to present to spectators a Spain that is not only Andalusia, but also Extremadura, Aragon, the Basque Country, Salamanca, Valencia, Catalonia and all these regions of Spain that are as serious and noble as Andalusia is charming and happy-go-lucky." Just in case an Andalusian might be offended by the author's take on the Coros y Danzas, the author did explain that the maestro flamenco and ballet performer Antonio Gades was more than "enough to represent our South." Although this writer, Enrique Menenes, repeated the party line about the Coros y Danzas' successes at the World's Fair, they never achieved the flamenco dancers' fame with audiences and critics. But this issue was not nearly as important as the implications of attracting throngs of people to the pavilion. The Spanish press understood the financial rewards of displaying a friendly, colorful Spain to their audiences. Given that there were over ten million visitors to the fair, and given that millions would pass through the Spanish pavilion, Spain would "see the payback in the years to come."[67]

Flamenco Takes Center Stage

In contrast to the Coros y Danzas' shows, the performances in the Teatro Español, mainly flamenco and some forms of Spanish classical dance and guitar, appeared to satisfy spectators' expectations of Spanish identity. The main performers were the international stars Rosa Durán of the Tablao Zambra, Manuela Vargas, and Antonio Gades. The majority of the dances showcased flamenco in its many incarnations. Both Durán and Vargas had competed and won the "best dancer" award at Paris's International Festival of Dancers in 1963 and 1964, respectively, and Antonio Gades had already begun appearing in Hollywood films like *The Pleasure Seekers* in 1964.[68] The Catalan self-made man F. Estrada Saladich, a booster both for Spain and for Spanish and U.S. business exchanges, emphasized the passions these dancers could evoke: "After a good drink, a magnificent dinner, and the magic of the lights, dances, and rhythm[,] . . . the public, whether Nordic or Anglo-Saxon, have enough blood [coursing through their veins] to rise from their seats with the entire company's stomping and final palmas."[69] He was but one of many Spaniards who knew that foreigners loved to consume flamenco entertainment, and he felt no shame in promoting it because business in Spain would prosper by cultivating such cultural spectacles.

Although the performers certainly expected audiences to become caught up in flamenco's syncopated rhythms, the shows' organizers also appeared to want to educate audiences about the meaning and roots of flamenco music, even if the history of flamenco and Spanish dance was crafted to suit promotional ends. They achieved this education through the programs that accompanied Antonio Gades's, Manuela Vargas's, and Rosa Duran's Tablao Zambra's performances.[70] They sought to explain to audiences how to interpret the various flamenco songs and dances, and they served to promote these dancers to the pantheon of world-class dancing.

Edgar Neville, the Spanish filmmaker, music critic, and much-lauded director of the seminal flamenco documentary *Duende y misterio de flamenco* (1953), wrote an essay in the Gades program explaining the history of Spanish dance, especially the bolero, and described Pilar López's role in improving Spanish dance by "bringing order and discipline to our explosive percussion dancing, to the Andalusian dancing, to the dance of the Gypsies." She then passed the torch to Antonio Gades—now dancing at the pavilion—who, Neville claimed, elevated both Spanish classical dance and flamenco: "Gades is a great academic dancer . . . with an extraordinary faculty for dancing the type of flamenco preferred in the world today, which is a flamenco danced by an artist possessing the faculties of a classical ballet dancer." His choreography "adds, as it were, 'literature' to dancing."[71] Neville argued that by synthesizing flamenco with classical ballet, Gades had modernized the art form, creating a flamenco that was more cosmopolitan, literary, and *accessible* to a much wider audience.

In contrast, the program for Tablao Zambra projected foreign stereotypes of Andalusian Orientalism while still trying to give audiences formalized ways of seeing the dance. In what appears to be the pinnacle of Francoist chutzpah, the program begins by co-opting the work of Federico García Lorca, one of the civil war's first victims. It reprinted excerpts from his 1922 essay, "El cante jondo," which was meant to provide justification for the Concurso de cante jondo and that, as we have already learned, gave an intellectual imprimatur to a small set of songs from the flamenco genre.[72] The excerpt drew on the parts that evoked the mysticism of cante jondo and rooted the music in a racialized Andalusia: "This chant, soul of our soul, lyric river bed through which escape all the aches and ritual expressions of our race."[73] It reinforced the ancientness of the song: "The 'Cante jondo' has nurtured itself from time immemorial." It also repeated the section of García Lorca's essay that illustrated the draw the music had for classical composers such as Manuel de Falla, the modern Russian school, and Debussy—especially after he saw the gitanos perform in the 1900 World's Fair—thus reinforcing García Lorca's earlier message that Spanish music had influenced the work of canonical European composers. The Spanish Ministry of Tourism and Information used an essay that had been written some thirty years earlier, but without any contextual information except for the author's name and essay title. Without any temporal context, the text sounded like it could have been written in 1964, especially since the last paragraph used direct speech, "See for yourselves the transcendental quality the 'cante jondo' hold [sic], and how great the exactness of our people in calling it just that."[74] By choosing García Lorca as the messenger, the Franco regime could reclaim for Spain the artist who was world renowned for his literary genius. It seemed to matter little in the context of the program produced for Zambra Tablao Flamenco that García Lorca's life was cut short by Nationalists' bullets. Additionally, by distilling the essay down to a few spare points, the Ministry of

Tourism and Information could rehabilitate the musical form that had been denigrated in the 1940s and 1950s in ways that were similar to those employed by de Falla and García Lorca in 1922.

After guiding the audience through García Lorca's homage to the cante jondo and providing some "Facts about Flamenco," the program elucidated the purported role of the Tablao Zambra in the life of Madrid. According to the literature, the Tablao Zambra was founded in 1954 "as a school for flamenco song and dance, to afford Spaniards a place to watch and listen to the old Andalusian song and dances that were slowly being lost, performed again in all their purity."[75] Oddly, these were the same arguments used in the past to elevate the Coros y Danzas while disparaging the contributions of flamenco to Spain's identity. Times had obviously changed. Although the Tablao Zambra *did* eventually become the place in Madrid where many famous flamenco artists worked to perfect their craft, the tablao itself seems to have been set up primarily to attract foreign tourists and their money, given its original name, "Zambra" Spanish Tourist Club, and its location near the Paseo del Prado and the Retiro Park at the edge of the tony Salamanca District.[76] The Spanish Ministry of Tourism and Information could not concern itself with origin stories that might undercut its investiture of Tablao Zambra with the robes of flamenco authenticity; instead, it authorized this troupe the rights to claim an ur-flamenco pedigree that had not been tainted by modern mass culture. After establishing Tablao Zambra's bona fides, the program provided a discussion of flamenco's historical roots but carefully placed them many centuries back rather than in the heart of the nineteenth century, and it made sure to distinguish between Andalusian and Gypsy flamenco. The writer deemed the former "more moderate, characterized by more rhythmic and profound expressions," while proclaiming the latter to be "less formal" and "full of those carefree expressions reflecting the character of their race." Finally, in drawing out flamenco's history, the writer stuck to the Orientalizing script that had worked so well in the past with foreigners: "The Andalusian flamenco is also the only Spanish folklore that preserves in all its originality the highest primitive characteristics of the song and dances of oriental peoples."[77] In one short essay, the Tablao Zambra managed to recolonize itself as the European exotic other.

While the Spanish government offered spectators at least two versions of Spain through dance, one diverse but unified, timeless, and rural, and the other the embodiment of Andalusian mysticism so beloved by foreigners, the reactions by the American press tended to ignore or politely tolerate the first group of dances (the Coros y Danzas) and reinforce the Orientalism and perceived ancientness of the professional flamenco dances.

Unlike the Spanish sources, which touted Coros y Danzas' ability to charm audiences, American critics were not so impressed.[78] After the opening of the fair, dance critic Nelson Lansdale wrote that there were more people onstage of the Coros y Danzas than in the audience and that, "costuming aside, there was no way for a non-specialist to distinguish the dances of Andalusia from those of Catalonia, Galicia or any other province."[79] More wry in his critique was Charles Boultenhouse of *Ballet Review*: "There also appeared a company claiming to be engaged in 'preserving' the folk dances of Spain which was actually a very charming-looking group of youngsters of the Spanish middle class enjoying themselves. Their dancing was only charming and lacked the ritual intensity and peasant solidity of gesture and sheer presence necessary to the proper performance of folk dances."[80] The critics found the Coros y Danzas colorful and festive but not spectacular. Sadly, for American audiences, these dancers could not hold a torch to flamenco dancers.

In contrast, the flamenco performers dazzled most American critics, and that enchantment came partly from a willful misunderstanding of the art and partly from the carefully constructed narrative posed by Spaniards themselves, as noted above in the performance brochures. American audiences would not relinquish the stereotypes they formed of Spaniards and they were rarely disabused of their stereotypes by Spanish officials. Therefore, the audiences and critics tended to focus on what they saw as the mysterious, timeless, Oriental, and sexy aspects of flamenco dance, and by extension, the unfathomable but desirable nature of Spain itself.

The Othering of Spanish flamenco seemed to come quite naturally to the various critics, and they did not appear to be embarrassed by the purple prose or the condescending colonial language that left their pens: "The flamenco voice is hoarse, cracked, with a tone of too many cigarettes and too much wine. Yet the broken lament can endlessly sustain, flatten, and vibrate notes in passionate appeal like no other vocal sounds outside of a mosque or synagogue."[81] Going back even further in time and place than the Near East, Boultenhouse wrote, "The power of flamenco is mysterious. There are theories of its ritual origin, of its ancientness; surely some dark flame of neolithic times must still live in the intensity of stamping feet and clapping hands."[82] Romantic, yes; neolithic, no. Flamenco performers also connected with the supernatural world: "They begin seated, clapping hands, waiting like mediums for the spirit to strike."[83] Commentators could not resist compounding the myths of Spanish primitiveness and mystical superstitiousness that had been pedaled for centuries before them and that were now reinforced by the official material distributed during the performances.

Once the (male) writers established the exotic appeal of the flamenco dancers, the sex appeal followed, much as occurred when foreigners writing in the nineteenth century witnessed the dancers in the cafés cantantes. Manuela Vargas and her troupe were praised for their "raw, unbridled passion." Vargas had "Goyaesque good looks, arching back," "rippling feet," and possessed the dangerous sexuality of the predator with her "serpentine arms" and "spidery hands."[84] The most fulsome praise of Vargas came from *Newsweek* magazine, which rated her as "quintessentially feminine" and viewed flamenco as "sensual," with "women [who] constantly flirt with their skirts and real lacy underwear."[85] Rosa Durán of Tablao Zambra received similar treatment from the priapic Boultenhouse: "Sometimes Rosa Duran would look like a Minoan goddess. How one longed to see her in Minoan costume, with her breasts exposed and snakes in her hands."[86] Antonio Gades, though male, also received his share of comments about his masculinity and sexuality, a change from foreigners' feminized portrayals of male dancers in the previous century: "Gades can do a lightning double turn, drop to one knee in a masterful split second, and then [rising?] to an insouciant pose, hand on hip, head thrown back, face proud. Sometimes he walks away from the achievement, as a torero walks away from the bull."[87] Still, the writer felt the need to link Gades's masculinity to the long-enduring stereotype of the macho bullfighter. Everything written about the flamenco performers was constructed as primal femininity and masculinity, as premodern bullfighting, as Oriental mosques and synagogues. The American press's sparkling reviews of the flamenco performances in contrast to their mostly tepid reviews of the Coros y Danzas performances reveal that no matter how good the Coros y Danzas might have been, foreign spectators preferred flamenco and they chose to imagine Spain as a passionate, premodern place with Old World charm that posed little threat to anybody.

The association of Spain with flamenco dancers and not, mind you, with flamenco singers was further reinforced by advertisements placed in major American newspapers and within the official catalog of the Spanish pavilion. The Spanish pavilion became one of the most popular pavilions of the fair; so much so, that *Life* magazine dubbed it "The

Figure 30. Advertisement for Corelli's shoes, shoes that "find new fashions in flamenco."
Source: *Harper's Bazaar*, January 1965.
Photo courtesy of Caleres, Inc., St. Louis, MO.

Jewel of the Fair."[88] The Spanish Ministry of Tourism also prepared the way for such enthusiasm by employing a multipronged advertising strategy and tapping sympathetic newspaper and magazine columnists to promote the Spanish pavilion's attractions. So it seems once fairgoers became primed to visit the Spanish pavilion by publicity that Spanish officials curated, advertisers fed that desire for all things Spanish and advertised their wares in the flamenco idiom. For example, in the January issue of *Harper's Bazaar*, which had a special edition focused on Spain, Corelli's Shoes (with an advertisement tie-in to Iberia Airlines) "finds new fashions in flamenco" and offers up styles like "Toreador," "Granada," "Madrid," and "Matador" (see figure 30), while Bergdorf Goodman delights in telling us, "A passion for flamenco stirs Miss B. to the tips of her dancing toes." Not to be outdone, Arnel laid out its Spirit of Spain fashion spread, featuring models in bored flamenco-ish poses,

Figure 31. Advertisement for Arnel fashions, one of many advertisements tying in with *Harper's Bazaar*'s special edition on Spain.
Source: Harper's Bazaar, January 1965.
Photo courtesy of Celanese Corporation.

with a text that read, "Arnel captures the Spirit of Spain . . . dazzle in the colors of stained glass . . . move with the easy grace of a flamenco dancer . . . and take your own Spirit of Spain south for the winter."[89] (See figure 31 for an example of that photo spread.) Not surprisingly, advertisements in the *New Official Guide* for the pavilion of Spain also took advantage of flamenco fever. The Bates textiles company featured a fetchingly posed young woman, rose in mouth, with a ruby red bedspread draped over her body to form the likeness of a flamenco dress with its *bata de cola* (see figure 32). The text beckons us to "fall in love with Spain—and Bates' 'Flamenca!'" and encourages us to discover "fashion's new passion in bedspreads . . . rich tapestry weaving inspired by Spain . . . each bedspread smoldering with two tones of a hot-blooded color. It's 'Flamenca!,' the new bed glamour from Bates. Completely reversible, even to the swirling, sinuous fringe. Warning: after

Figure 32. Advertisement for Bates' Flamenca line of bedspreads, the bedspread that would make one as passionate as a flamenco dancer.
Source: Comisaría General para la Feria Mundial de Nueva York, *New Official Guide: Pavilion of Spain* (New York: Office of the Commissioner of the Pavilion of Spain for the New York World's Fair 1964–65, 1965).
Image courtesy of Maine Heritage Weavers / Bates Mill Store.

'Flamenca!' things may never be the same!"[90] Even the name of this bedspread line could not simply be called "Flamenca"—it had to have an exclamation point attached to it in order to signify the over-the-top passion foreigners had been led to expect of flamenco dancers. There was no question about it; given the publicity fostered by Spanish officials and American advertisers, in American minds, at least, Spain equaled flamenco. The Spanish government and its representative tourist industry may have wanted to present foreigners with a more complex vision of the Spanish nation, one that demonstrated great regional variation, but they undercut this vision at every turn. Instead, they gave the public what it wanted, the exoticism of flamenco, thus making Andalusia the representation of Spain once again.

But *this* particular representation of Spain had its merits. It certainly softened Spain's image abroad. The carefully curated pavilion of Spain led many to forget that Spain was run by a dictator and had been closely allied with the Fascist Axis in World War II. The Spanish Pavilion was dubbed "the Jewel of the Fair," blithely erasing Spain's brutal regime.[91] American newspapers and magazines fell in love with the Spanish pavilion and the dancers in it, and once the pavilion gained a following, there was little mention of the Franco dictatorship or Spain's past alliance with fascism. Spanish officials certainly felt that their gamble had paid off. After the fair closed on October 17, 1965, with a farewell performance by Manuela Vargas and her flamenco troupe, the Spanish Foreign Ministry's official bulletin for U.S. audiences, the *Spanish Newsletter*, proclaimed the pavilion's success: "Its exceptional architectural and artistic qualities ... its unrivaled song and dance groups ... all combined to create an unforgettable impression in the minds of millions of Americans. As a result, the image of Spain is now all the stronger. The urge to visit, invest or to learn more about Spain is immeasurably greater."[92] That last sentence indicated the Spanish government's desire to link the pavilion to increased tourism, and on that score, the fair did seem to dramatically increase tourism to Spain—it rose 30 percent alone between 1964 and 1965, at least according to the admittedly propagandistic *Spanish Newsletter*.[93] The Spanish Ministry of Tourism and Information may have convinced those who once might have hesitated to visit a country run by a dictatorship to pack up their bags and see a kinder, gentler Spain. Spain's success at the fair emboldened the Ministry of Tourism to take the most portable and exportable parts of the pavilion and tour around the world with them to garner even more potential tourists to Spain. Thus began the traveling tourism exhibition known as Expotur.

Expotur: Portable Tourism

Expotur, part nineteenth-century exhibition and part twentieth-century marketing strategy for mass tourism, had been conceived prior to the New York World's Fair but seems to have been another prong in the strategy to bring ever more tourists to Spain. Like the Spanish Pavilion, Expotur dedicated itself to mounting exhibits that included posters, films, photographs, and samples of artisanal products from various regions of Spain. The series of images and products were portable enough to be carried on tour around the world and demonstrated to the world once and for all how much variety Spain had to offer the tourist.[94] This portable exhibit became the basis for the tourism show known as Expotur. It began its dry run in Madrid in 1963, and then some of those materials were also presented in the tourism section of the Spanish pavilion in New York.[95] Expotur achieved its goals to lure tourists to Spain and continued its tours until the early 1970s, traveling widely in Europe, Latin America, the United States, and as far away as Pakistan.[96] One of the stated goals of the tour was to combat *"lo pintoresco,"* the typical folkloric stereotypes that Spaniards had been contending with for a century. The evidence from numerous NO-DO films and press clippings that cataloged the successes of Expotur, however, reveals that Expotur reinforced *"lo pintoresco"* at every turn.

The official state news and propaganda films, the *Noticieros y Documentales* (commonly known as NO-DO), which were edited for brevity and positive spin, showed various opening days of Expotur, which usually required the attendance of important dignitaries who would walk through the exhibit, gazing intently at posters and artifacts. After that part of the display ended, spectators walked to a small replica of a tablao where a flamenco ensemble would perform a few songs. Meanwhile, the audience dined on tapas, and waiters who were dressed in what appeared to be Andalusian regional folk wear retrieved what looked to be sherry from large barrels and poured it with great fanfare into the spectators' glasses.[97] Newspaper clippings of the Expotur in Rome and Rio de Janeiro reveal the same pattern: a sampling of various forms of tourism available in Spain, a brief discussion of Spain's history and contributions to civilization, and a prepared feast in an "Andalusian patio" or a tablao where flamenco dancers performed for their sated guests.[98] Even Spanish journalists were not immune to the allure of the flamenco-dancer-as-tourist-attraction: under the headline "Against All Predictions (and in spite of the Italian 'forces') 200,000 people visited Expotur in Five Days," Antonio Diolano wrote, "Spain's sun has decidedly warmed the French cold winter. . . . The 'true' flamenco represented by four fabulous artists also contributes to this success."[99] This pride in Spain's flamenco performers is a good reminder of how far flamenco had risen in stature. Once viewed by official Spain as the representation of vice and the perilous outcome of unbridled modernity, in the latter part of the Franco regime, flamenco became a source of Spanish confidence. By erasing the more sordid-seeming origins of flamenco, inventing an ancient pedigree for the art form, and contending with the need to attract hordes of tourists to Spain, the Franco regime helped weave flamenco into the fabric of Spanish national identity. Although groups like the Sección Femenina's Coros y Danzas worked to create and propagate the idea of a Spain that built strong national unity through its diverse regional songs and dances, they failed to convince outsiders of that fact.

It appears that by the late 1950s, the Coros y Danzas served as propaganda for domestic purposes, while the flamenco performances appeased foreign audiences' preferences. NO-DO, for example, made a series of documentary films cataloguing all of the regional dances performed by the Coros y Danzas.[100] They also filmed numerous clips for their weekly distributions at movie theaters, highlighting the numerous successes of the Coros y Danzas in international dance festivals and at exhibitions like the New York World's Fair, while paying less attention to flamenco performers.[101] Presumably, Spaniards were meant to feel proud of their countrywomen's representation of the Spanish nation. Conversely, to attract foreigners to Spain, the Ministry of Tourism always managed to showcase flamenco performances, either in big theatrical productions or in more intimate tablao-like settings whenever it sponsored exhibitions abroad.

Once the Franco regime distanced itself from its earlier policy of autarky, it almost had to promote the Spain of pandereta that Carlos Gonzalez Cuesta had so perspicaciously articulated in 1953. Tourism is often about selling dreams and stereotypes to foreigners—otherwise, why leave home? Foreigners who visited Spain during the great tourist boom wanted beaches *and* flamenco. Their desire for the exotic Other had to be slaked. The tourism and image producers under the Franco regime realized that they could play both narratives out at once, Spain as multiregional and Spain as Andalusia, without harming anyone in the process. In the end, business concerns trumped ideology, and flamenco as an art form continued to achieve worldwide recognition for Spain despite the numerous attempts to quash its influence in the twentieth century. After Franco's death in 1975, the role of flamenco changed dramatically. The nearly simultaneous movements for regional autonomy within Spain and the growth of a world music culture would complicate flamenco's function as a marker of Spanish national identity.

Coda

Passionate, sophisticated and devoted to living the good life, Spain is both a stereotype come to life and a country more diverse than you ever imagined.
Lonely Planet travel guide for Spain, online version

Nineteenth-century European writers and painters had mythologized Spain as the quintessential romantic country. It was the land of Moors and Gypsies, of swirling flamenco skirts and narrow-hipped matadors. . . . The funny thing is that it's all still true—it's just not the whole truth. As the old Saturday Night Live routine goes, Franco is still dead. But Spain is very much alive. . . . A flamenco beat still drives it, but Spain is now a country of high-speed trains and cutting-edge Web technology.
Frommer's Spain, online version

For all the talk of Spain's history, this is a country that lives very much in the present and there's a reason "fiesta" is one of the best-known words in the Spanish language—life itself is a fiesta. . . . Perhaps you'll sense it along a crowded, post-midnight street. . . . Or maybe that moment will come when a flamenco performer touches something deep in your soul. Whenever it happens, you'll find yourself nodding in recognition: *this* is Spain.

Frommer's Spain, online version

Outsiders, as we can infer from the snippets of tourist-guide patter registered above, cannot refrain from defining the Spanish national character. They have done so for centuries. And although tourist guide books and tourism websites are designed to peddle fantasies to the traveler hankering for a novel experience, one wishes they could draw on a wider array of subjects. These guides gesture at Spain's modernity, at its diversity, but then the colonial voice reemerges to assert the familiar: "a stereotype come to life," "a country driven by a flamenco beat." Really? *This* is Spain? The Spanish Tourist Office still sells romance: "Do you believe in love at first sight? A study says that it's possible to fall in love just by staring at someone for a few seconds. Something very similar to what you feel each time you visit Spain." It insists, however, on highlighting much more than the romantic Andalusian stereotypes foreigners and tourism purveyors called forth ad nauseam that we have witnessed in this book. Instead, the spotlight shines on a variety of people who have made their mark internationally, bringing together the local and the global, the modern buzz and the historical mystique.[1] For those who focus on describing flamenco performances, however, it seems that not that much has changed over the course of two centuries. Even when writers are trying to understand flamenco performance on its own terms and avoid the overtly sexualized language we encountered from the tourist whose reflections began this book, they still cannot help themselves from employing hackneyed Orientalist metaphors. A 2017 *New York Times* travel writer had this to say of a flamenco performance in Seville at the Casa de la Guitarra: "A vocalist began to cry out a song of pain or lost love—folk melodies in harsh quarter-tones, like a muezzin issuing a call to prayer at a mosque."[2] And although the writer probably did not create the article's headline, "Vibrant and Seductive Seville, Easy on the Wallet," it evokes that image Isidro de las Cagigas railed against in the early twentieth century of Seville as an exuberant woman whose openness leads others to assume she will trade sex for cash.[3]

Taken together, these and other common portrayals of Spain's identity encapsulate many of the problems I have elucidated in this book.

There is the recognition—long fought for—that Spain's landscape and culture are far more diverse than one might imagine, despite the constant bombardment of Andalusian flamenco (and bullfighting) images. Many people realize that the era when Spain and its people were typecast as inhabitants of some nineteenth-century fantasyland of bandits, bullfighters, buffoons, and bailaoras is now gone, and yet these clichés are difficult to dispel. When the *Frommers* writers try to dismiss the Romantic image of flamenco-skirt-twirling Gypsies—among other stock characters—they hedge their bets. The spirit of the stereotype is true, they surmise, even if the letter is not. And although Spaniards have tried since the inception of the café cantante to direct the masculine and colonial gaze away from the image of the passionate gitana and toward people considered more respectable, and toward tamer cultural sites and profound historical traditions, neither the producer nor the consumer of tourism desires to let go of the stereotype of Spain as passionately premodern and exotic.

That image continues successfully to fulfill tourists' fantasies while filling Spain's coffers. To look seriously behind the flamenco curtain and discover political and social struggles between elites and the masses, regional nationalisms, class warfare, ethnic and gender oppression, colonialism, and culture wars, as I have attempted to do here, would undo years of careful practice and complicate simple slogans. And tourism functions best on simplicity.

The depiction of Spain as the land of flamenco, the not-quite-European country with the Oriental/Gypsy soul has captured the imagination of people living outside Spain and has been exploited by entrepreneurial spirits within Spain. That is not to say that flamenco flourishes today only to serve the interests of commerce. Artists, scholars, and historical preservationists have chosen to undertake serious study of the art form and to promote its historical and artistic significance to both Spain and Andalusia. In fact, one could say that there has been a bifurcation in the way that flamenco is treated within Spain: it has undergone both kitschification *and* renewed artistic and academic respect.

The Waning of Nacional-flamenquismo

Although concluding my narrative about flamenco with Francisco Franco's death in 1975 might seem like an arbitrary cut-off point, the politics and culture of Spain changed dramatically enough after the transition to democracy that writing about the relationship between these transformations and the reception and promotion of flamenco would require yet another book. And others have begun to do just that.[4] Instead, I chose to explore the complicated journey that flamenco took from its early, seemingly shady roots in the late eighteenth century to its widespread acceptance and celebration in the latter years of the twentieth. When flamenco began to become popular in urban centers like Seville, Madrid, and Barcelona in the second half of the nineteenth century, and when foreigners began to amplify its popularity through their writings, encouraging an incipient tourist industry based on this form of entertainment, flamenco became affixed to Spain's national identity. But Spanish elites across the political spectrum and in different regions of the country mostly rejected this characterization, which they perceived as toxic, and they sought to promote a variegated Spain, usually modern, and less tied to Andalusian stereotypes. But generally, the more elites fought these stereotypes, the more the stereotypes were called into being. For a short period in the early years of the Franco regime, when much of the country was shell-shocked from the war and subsequent terror and while the Franco regime and its ideological allies were consolidating their power, flamenco's influence within Spain waned and its forms of expression were shunned, although performers-in-exile like Carmen Amaya (see figure 33) still captivated audiences on the international stage and, like many other exiles, promoted the image of the passionate flamenco dancer in a variety of Hollywood films. Flamenco's exile from Spain's cultural milieu did not last for long, however. Once the Franco regime forged diplomatic and economic ties with Western powers like the United States, Britain, and France, and began to lose its outcast status, the Spanish government was able to attract money to its shores in the form of mass tourism. Flamenco became key to advancing that industry, so much so, that flamenco scholars refer scornfully to this period of flamenco promotion in the 1950s as *nacional-flamenquismo*, a riff on the zealous ideologies of National Catholicism and National Syndicalism enforced by the Catholic Church and Falange respectively.[5] In the case of nacional-flamenquismo, the state appropriated Andalusian flamenco performances for the tourist nation, sanitized them, and turned them into kitschy expressions of Andalusian folklore that tourists lapped up with alacrity. Despite flamenco's nadir in this period, as flamencologists have characterized it, there were hints in the 1950s and 1960s that a scholarly and artistic appreciation of the art form and its performance was beginning to emerge.

One could point to Edgar Neville's 1952 documentary *Duende y misterio del flamenco* (known in English simply as *Flamenco*) as a bridge

Figure 33. Carmen Amaya in the autumn festivals of 1958.
© ICAS-SAHP, Fototeca, Municipal de Sevilla, Cubiles Archive.

between nacional-flamenquismo and a scholarly appreciation of the performance. Neville, a filmmaker and writer, was perhaps most of all a flamenco enthusiast.[6] He directed and wrote the screenplay for this film, which highlighted some of the most critically acclaimed flamenco singers and dancers of the day, such as the cantaores Fernanda de Utrera and Antonio Mairena and the bailaoras Antonio, Pilar López, and María Luz. The film captures singers and dancers performing various flamenco palos in different parts of Spain and presents them in ways reminiscent of the films created to showcase the Coros y Danzas.[7] For example, one segment follows the dancer María Luz as she performs a soleares on a platform mounted "on a hill near the Alhambra of Granada." A couple of minutes later, the focus moves to the outskirts of Madrid where two male dancers dressed in stylized Andalusian clothes reminiscent of bullfighters' costumes perform in front of other people dressed in folk costumes from the eighteenth century. The narrator (actor Fernando Rey) remarks that they are dancing in "a view of Madrid immortalized by Goya."[8] It becomes apparent that the dancers and filmmaker are performing a dynamic tableau vivant in homage to Francisco Goya's *Pradera de San Isidro* (1788). Like the photographs, films, and documentaries produced by the Coros y Danzas, *Duende y misterio del flamenco* works to tie particular songs and dances to specific Spanish terrains but it also deepens the "Spanishness" of these performances by linking them to other luminaries of Spanish culture like Goya. Despite the film's touristic qualities, Neville's work ventures to provide an unschooled audience with some context for understanding the various flamenco palos.

But four key events within the space of only four years launched a different trajectory for flamenco than the one represented by nacionalflamenquismo and the tourism industry. In 1954 Roger Wild, a Swiss citizen of Spanish parentage, convinced flamenco guitar maestro Perico el del Lunar to gather together a group of the finest flamenco singers to create an album. Together they recruited, directed, and recorded some of the most beloved and historically important "traditional" flamenco singers, like Pericón de Cádiz, Pepe el de la Matrona, and Bernardo el de los Lobitos. The album, *Antología del cante flamenco*, was first produced and distributed in Paris. Only later, in 1958, did it get marketed and sold within Spain under the Hispavox label. This anthology ended up canonizing flamenco singers who had begun their careers in the early part of the twentieth century.[9] One short year later, Anselmo González Climent, an Argentine by birth whose parents hailed from Cadiz, wrote *Flamencología*, a scholarly study of flamenco music in all of its forms, reminiscent in some ways of the work Demófilo attempted in the nineteenth century.[10] With this title, Gónzalez Climent created the neologism that is in use to this day to denote the scholarly study of flamenco. His work so touched the poet Ricardo Molina that Molina sought his collaboration in reprising a cante jondo competition, invoking the 1922 Concurso de Cante Jondo.[11] Thus in 1956 the Concurso Nacional de Cante Jondo was born. This competition, centered in Córdoba, continues to this day as a triennial event, although it is now called the Concurso Nacional de Arte Flamenco. Finally, in 1958 a Chair of Flamencología was established in Jerez de la Frontera for the "study, research, conservation, promotion and defense of the genuine Flamenco Art."[12] This constellation of flamenco phenomena hastened the development of flamenco studies and was soon followed by another foundational work, *Mundo y formas del cante flamenco*, by Ricardo Molina and Antonio Mairena, who crystallized the idea that "pure" flamenco originated before the nineteenth century among insular gitano communities who had kept their music secret from other Andalusians. Flamenco music escaped the confines of these communities in the early decades of the nineteenth century, only to be corrupted by the explosion of the commercialized café cantante scene in the second half of that century.[13] Molina and Mairena's vision of flamenco history remained dominant until the late twentieth century.

Flamenco's sanctification also received a boost by the state-run television station RTVE when it ran an ambitious documentary series titled *Rito y geografía del cante* (Rite and geography of cante) during the last gasps of the Franco regime. Airing weekly on television from October 23, 1971, to October 29, 1973, the one hundred thirty-minute programs showcased flamenco singers—many unknown to general audiences—performing in bars, in tablaos, in homes, and at fiestas in their respective Andalusian homelands, with special attention to places like Seville, Jerez de la Frontera, and Cadiz.[14] As William Washabaugh notes, "The first 40 programs concentrated on geographical regions and the flamenco forms that were favored in those regions. The next 50 programs profiled individual artists, and the final ten programs developed miscellaneous topics."[15] As such, the series itself follows the formula viewers had come to expect during the Franco era from early works on the Coros y Danzas and the aforementioned *Duende y misterio del flamenco*: didactic documentaries made to highlight Spain's cultural treasures, lands, and customs, mainly for tourists' consumption. One startling difference here, however, is that these programs were geared toward Spanish, not foreign, audiences. Washabaugh makes a compelling case for the series as an anti-Francoist creation that employed Francoist documentary tropes while simultaneously breaking down the centralizing ideology of the regime. For example, it focuses on the less flashy types of flamenco performers in humble settings—people thick of waist, teeth missing, and blind—and amplifies the message Molina and Mairena propagated about the "secret" gitano origins of cante flamenco.[16] Thus, Washabaugh argues, by making Andalusia and gitanos (both famous and unknown) the central foci of the series, "these films are not just about music and Andalusian culture. They are also about opposing Franco's centralist politics and advancing a regionalist andalucismo."[17]

But just at the moment when these flamencologists pushed to restrict the canon and delineate who or what could be called authentic flamenco, others began to break down these barriers again and redefine the meaning of the art form. In the 1950s, gitano neighborhoods like Gràcia, Hostafrancs, and El Raval in Barcelona became the center of the very popular rumba catalana, a melding of flamenco rumba (itself a nineteenth-century fusion with Cuban rumba) with elements of rock 'n' roll and still other Cuban rhythms. It has been described as the "fusion of Andalusian-Catalan songs in a light style with Afro-Cuban features," demonstrating once again that musical "purity" cannot be contained by regional or national borders.[18] In other quarters, the cantaor Enrique Morente started his career singing traditional flamenco palos in his 1968 recording, *Cante flamenco*, which earned him recognition by the Cátedra de Flamencología in 1969.[19] Then, in the early 1970s, just as Franco was skirting death's edges, Morente tested the waters of political resistance to Franco by setting the poetry of Miguel Hernández and García Lorca to music—both of these poets lost their lives in the civil war as enemies of the Nationalists. Lauded by members of Franco's left-wing opposition for his skillful interpretations of traditional palos and for his quiet but open resistance to the regime via his choice of poets to commit to cante, Morente was later condemned for "corrupting" cante flamenco with his increasing interest in fusing flamenco palos with jazz and rock 'n' roll.[20] Similarly, the world-famous tocaor Paco de Lucía made his name by inflecting flamenco with jazz and classical music.

Flamenco since the Transition (1980s–Present): Nested Identities and Globalization

Flamenco, as I have demonstrated throughout this book, has been imagined by outsiders as a symbol of Spain's national identity, while people within Spain have often resisted this depiction, relegating this identity to Andalusia alone. But flamenco diffused successfully beyond Andalusia in the nineteenth and early twentieth centuries, especially to other major cities of Spain. Performers went to Madrid (and still do) if they wanted success on the flamenco circuit, and to Barcelona, where communities of gitanos cultivated the art form in contradistinction to the sardana. Both places became important centers for flamenco. As I have argued in this book, this dissemination was aided by foreigners who wrote about their experiences watching the performances, the popularity of World's Fairs, and the rise of mass culture in industrializing cities. After declining in the early years of the Franco regime, flamenco became a necessary part of Spain's identity. Once the Franco regime transformed the Spanish tourist industry into one of its top priorities, flamenco became a chief economic engine of Spain's tourist economy and served to solidify flamenco as a major component of Spain's national identity.

With its national identity in flux, Spain remade itself in the post-Franco era by casting aside, bit by bit, the culture and politics of dictatorship and National Catholicism. Mechanisms for political devolution emerged, despite both the Franco regime's insistence on national unity for Spain and the remaining forces of centralization, militarism, and Catholicism found in the 1978 constitution. Politicians and others pushed for decentralizing the state and granting autonomy to some regions. The constitution held in tense balance the forces of centralization and decentralization, announcing "the indissoluble unity of the Spanish Nation, the common and indivisible homeland of all Spaniards," while still guaranteeing "the right to self-government of the nationalities and regions of which it is composed and the solidarity among them all." This precarious balance of power-sharing has proved problematic to this day.[21] But the constitution did allow for the eventual devolution of powers to the autonomous communities, seventeen in all, based at first on the historical regionalist aspirations of Catalonia, the Basque Country, and Galicia, although Andalusia pushed successfully to become included in the first autonomy statutes enacted in 1981. The rights granted to autonomous regions varied, making the powers of each region asymmetrical with respect to the central government and to each other, and autonomous regions, including Andalusia, have renegotiated their statutes from time to time. Whereas the effects of these statutes are numerous and beyond the scope of this book, the implications of certain forms of power-sharing are relevant to the cultivation and maintenance of what Yuko Aoyama has termed the "flamenco art complex."[22]

Complications associated with the new post-Franco autonomy statutes had an influence on the diffusion and popularity of flamenco. These complications arose from the disparate allocations of resources and the competing political and cultural identities that befall a state that aims to be both unitary and plural. Spain's national tourism organization, Turespaña, has a finite amount of money it has to spend on the promotion of Spanish tourism both domestically and internationally, and it certainly has succeeded in cultivating the flamenco and bullfighting identities—among numerous other ones—as major draws for foreigners. Although one would rightly expect an intense promotion of flamenco within Andalusia, many businesses in places like Madrid also thrive on these stereotypes, as witnessed by the souvenir stands with all kinds of flamenco regalia in their stores, the flamenco and bullfighting

Figure 34. This restaurant in Toledo, which specializes in potatoes, dresses up potatoes in flamenco costumes, 2010.
Photo by author.

mockups one can pose for in the Plaza Mayor, and the prevalence of flamenco ticket hawkers constantly haranguing passersby in the Plaza de Santa Ana and other parts of central Madrid. Even one restaurant in Toledo has taken advantage of flamenco's popularity (see figure 34). But Turespaña also has to promote other regions in Spain and other forms of tourism, whether it's sun-and-beach, gastronomy, or pilgrimage tourism, thus spreading financial resources across Spain. Individual autonomous regions also compete for tourists and their money, and they too must choose their focus. The Junta de Andalucía, Andalusia's autonomous government, has chosen to promote flamenco tourism as part of its (regional) national identity, and it has sunk considerable money into the preservation and dissemination of this art form.[23]

Andalusia's 1981 Autonomy Statute set up the administrative structure of the region and declared Blas Infante the "Father of the Andalusian nation." His green and white design for the flag, his national anthem, and his motto for the Andalusian nation, "Andalusia for itself, for Spain, and for humanity," were all made official as well.[24] The 1981 statute outlined the region's responsibilities for "protecting and developing" Andalusia's "historical-artistic patrimony" but said nothing about flamenco.[25] However, it took consistent pressure from scholars during the 1990s to reconfigure Andalusia's administrative and political structures so as to institutionalize the study and promotion of flamenco as national heritage. In 2005 the Junta de Andalucía created the Andalusian Institute of Flamenco as part of the Andalusian Department of Culture and Sport, which "is charged solely with the development of flamenco within and outside the region." More important to the adoption of flamenco as Andalusia's birthright was the 2007 revised Statute of Autonomy, especially Article 68. It claimed for the autonomous community the "exclusive competency [responsibility] regarding the knowledge, research, development, promotion and diffusion of flamenco as a unique element of Andalusian cultural heritage."[26] The autonomous government of Andalusia received another boost to its mission when in 2010 UNESCO inscribed flamenco on its Representative List of the Intangible Cultural Heritage of Humanity.[27] UNESCO thus categorized flamenco as part of Spain's intangible heritage. By centering "the heartland of Flamenco" in Andalusia, it had the practical effect of justifying the institutionalization of the flamenco industry within the confines of the autonomous region of Andalusia.[28]

The autonomous community of Andalusia has taken this mission seriously, centralizing and dominating the production of flamenco's infrastructure, and has pumped a considerable amount of money into this venture.[29] But as ethnomusicologist Matthew Manchin-Autenriet contends, this centralization of the flamenco infrastructure has begun to anger flamenco artists who are not on the professionalized flamenco festival circuit. There has been some pushback. Andalusians, especially those living in the eastern half of the region, have charged the regional government with implementing a version of nacional-flamenquismo writ small. Some in this area reject flamenco as part of their national/regional identity.[30]

Flamenco's successes and its perceived failures are tied to a series of nested identities that are glued together financially, traveling up and down in scale from the municipal to the global.[31] Although flamenco purists disdain what they perceive to be the overcommercialization of flamenco and its remove from traditional gitano flamenco performer dynasties, flamenco probably could not have survived without the interplay of an international tourist market and the infrastructure that municipalities, regions, and the Spanish state provide. But this is nothing new. As Mercedes Gómez-García Plata argues, when the cafés cantantes reached their height at the end of the nineteenth century, critics were already complaining that flamenco had lost its purity. The professionalization of flamenco actually helped diffuse the art form to urban areas in Spain, thus cultivating its popularity both domestically and internationally.[32] And so it goes today. The geographer Aoyama contends that the "global demand for cultural commodities," linked to the "rise of cosmopolitan consumerism," as in the case of world music, has helped keep the flamenco art-complex alive.[33] Several sources of commercial interests centered primarily but not exclusively in Andalusia have also intersected to keep flamenco popular throughout Spain. These interests include local flamenco artists who perform in tablaos and theaters; businesses like flamenco shoe, guitar, and dress shops; peñas flamencas, community-sponsored organizations where students, professionals, and sometimes tourists meet to hone their craft or watch others practicing it; flamenco schools; and, finally, state-, regional-, and municipal-sponsored festivals.[34]

A quick search of the festival listings from the Centro Andaluz de Flamenco's website, a cultural organ of the Junta de Andalucía, reveals the vast network of flamenco festivals and contests held in one year throughout Spain and beyond: 748 listings, with 497 of them in Andalusia, 187 in the rest of Spain, and 64 outside Spain, as of this writing. Readers learn of very specific competitions and festivals, like *saeta* contests, sponsored by a local town or organization, as well as larger flamenco festivals like the internationally renowned and multilevel sponsorship of the Bienal del Arte Flamenco de Sevilla. A search refined to include the word "festival" yields a total of 313 listings, with 182 of them in Andalusia, 76 in the rest of Spain, and 55 outside of Spain.[35] And while these statistics demonstrate that the focus of flamenco promotion rests in Andalusia, the Spanish state still plays a large role in keeping flamenco national and promoting it globally to keep the tourists coming. Spain's commercial brand, known officially as Marca España, represents a state-sponsored policy that "has as its objective to improve the image of the country abroad and among Spaniards."[36] Highlighting the importance of the Marca España as a means of introducing international tourists to Spain, a recent book targets different ways to brand Spain. Among them, of course, is flamenco dance. A chapter titled "Flamenco Dance to Reinforce the Marca España" features an interview with the internationally famous bailaora Cristina Hoyos, founder of the Flamenco Dance Museum in Seville. In describing her, the author writes that "she and other artists contributed to the notion that one could know Spain through dance. In short, constructing the Spanish Brand."[37]

There is no doubt that flamenco in all its forms is an economic driver of the Spanish and Andalusian tourist industry, an entertainment juggernaut that continues to draw international tourists to Spain's shores. To give but one example, the last major flamenco festival for which we have statistics, the internationally acclaimed Bienal de Flamenco de Sevilla, which took place from September 8 to October 2, 2016, generated 6.3 million Euros solely from tourists originating *outside of Spain*. This statistic does not include the 34 percent of visitors who came from within Spain. About one-third of the total visitors to the festival came from France (16.7 percent), the United States (8.4 percent), and Japan (7.6 percent).[38] Of those foreigners interviewed via a questionnaire commissioned by the Bienal, 90.5 percent said that they intended to come back to Andalusia, and 38.9 percent of those said that it was flamenco that made them want to return.[39] By any measure, Spain and Andalusia have succeeded in marketing the flamenco phenomenon, even as this success has left many residents bitter about their towns and cities becoming consumed by commercial behemoths that seem to erode their local cultures.[40]

This book began in nineteenth-century Seville, where a naïve American sought to relieve the boredom of martial law by visiting a staged musical performance in the protoflamenco style, only to discover that the dancer who caught his fancy had also been capable of inciting violence when faced with injustice. Let's end the book in Seville too. Although much of the contemporary flamenco art complex has sanitized flamenco performances to reach broader audiences and to collect more revenue, there are still remnants of that activist past that rears its head in times of social crisis. Two powerful examples of such protest come to mind, one that employs flamenco dance to perpetuate historical memory and another that uses flamenco song and dance to register both an economic protest and a critique. Both also served to link contemporary performers to their counterparts in the past.

On May 24, 2013, to commemorate the International Day of Women for Peace and Disarmament, a group of about thirty women, mostly dressed in mourning black, marched through the streets of the Barrio de Macarena in Seville, singing a variety of songs, although not cante flamenco. They were reclaiming the streets for women who had been erased by the violence of the Spanish Civil War and the subsequent Francoist repression. They stopped in key locations to allow one or two women to dance alone in the flamenco idiom. Parts of this march were filmed. A filmed segment on YouTube titled "We Women Do Not Forget, 1936–2013" is summarized this way: "Act of Historical Memory in homage to the women who faced reprisals at the orders of General Queipo de Llano during the Francoist repression, celebrated in the Barrio Macarena in Seville, on May 24, 2013. One can find this war criminal buried in the Basilica of the Macarena Church."[41]

General Queipo de Llano, often referred to by the moniker the Butcher of Seville, was responsible for the brutal terror waged on Seville's citizens, especially in the first weeks of the war. Citizens from the working-class neighborhoods of Triana and La Macarena tried unsuccessfully to resist the uprising and were met by Queipo's forces with executions, jail terms, and other forms of repression. In recent years there has been a movement to have his remains removed from the Basilica of the Macarena Church.[42]

The protestors, ostensibly descendants of Queipo's victims, are reclaiming the streets for themselves both by walking through them and by renaming the streets using printed placards bearing the new names. They erect a placard beneath the Pastora Divina Street sign, renaming it Old Ana and Teadora Street. The new sign reads:

> Teadora played the harp and defended the Republic when her sister Ana was assassinated and her husband imprisoned. One she mourned and to the other she brought food every day in jail. When the coal with which she cooked and the money with which to buy it ran out, she made wood chips from the furniture in her house. She began by cutting the legs off the chairs, and after having worked her way through tables, wardrobes and cupboards, finished dismantling her harp bit by bit. Her starving husband, the silence of her house and of the entire country, finally killed her.[43]

The women continue through the streets, singing and stopping, erecting street signs dedicated to Manuela Beltrán Gómez, a young working-class woman in her twenties who was shot by Queipo's forces in 1936, and to Ángeles García Palacios, a teacher during the Second Republic who was banned from teaching during the entire Franco regime. Then they raise a more general street sign named "Reprisals against Women," which names the Nationalists' collective crimes: "Thousands of women suffered the horror of atrocious fascist and patriarchal repression because of their politics and because they were women. They wanted to change the world and their place in it. They were crammed into prisons and concentration camps, dishonored, had their babies stolen from them, killed, tortured, raped. More still, they were silenced in History with the consent of the Military, Church, and Political powers. Now and forever, we will not forget." Finally, they move to the Basilica of the Macarena Church, where we see some women encircle the grave marker of General Queipo de Llano and silently lay a wreath on it with the words "We women do not forget." Outside the basilica there is a loudspeaker blaring Queipo's inflammatory words about the "reds" that originally terrorized much of Seville's population when they emanated via radio broadcasts in 1936. Meanwhile, outside, more women gather around a wooden replica of Queipo's grave marker, surrounding two women who dance without musical accompaniment on Quiepo's simulated grave. Striking their feet in flamenco rhythms, they use their bodies to hit at the source of their ancestors' oppression. The depth of their anger and sorrow is palpable. Then, in what seems to be a move of reconciliation, the group of women begin singing again as one of them lays a wreath made of household linens and other objects, including a photograph of a dead woman and a clock. There is catharsis in the embodied act of remembrance.[44]

Flamenco song and dance has also been put in the service of economic protest against the forces of unbridled capitalism. Beginning around 2010 and peaking around 2014, the self-described "activist-artistic-situationist-performative-folkloric collective" known as Flo6×8 has employed a variety of flamenco palos to protest the austerity measures, unemployment, and bank failures produced by the Great Recession of 2008, which hit Spain and especially Andalusia very hard. Based in Seville and documented in news reports and on YouTube, Flo6×8 view themselves as "a group of ordinary people who have a series of common concerns [and] who share a love of flamenco art and a criticism of the financial system." They "practice civil disobedience by the direct action of singing and dancing in bank offices and in front of ATM machines."[45] They began their nonviolent guerrilla flash mobs in Andalusia but have performed as far north as Barcelona. Their general method is to show up unannounced at a bank and begin dancing and/or singing, bellowing lyrics that reflect the sorrows of a people destroyed by financial institutions, stupefying bank workers and customers in the process.[46]

For example, in 2011 approximately twenty people targeted the Banco de Santander in Seville with their "Rumba Rave 'Banquero.'" They occupied the bank lobby and began to dance while recorded music blared out lyrics like "You got a wallet / I've got a problem. / Ay, no money / Banker, banker, banker. / You have cash / I have debt. / It's looking bleak out there / Banker, banker, banker." The singing continues, chastising the bankers for absconding with wads of cash while the people suffer the pains of inflation and debt, and the people who suffer are told, "Don't think—work, spend—and pay, of course / Don't think—just eat, sleep, work / eat, sleep, work / eat, sleep, work . . ." Meanwhile, the dancers empty out their pockets, pantomiming the gesture that declares that they do not have even a coin to rub between their fingers. In the midst of all the dancing, a man costumed as a cow runs in between the dancers. The bank tellers become alarmed and call security to get the group out of the bank.[47] In June 2012 Flo6x8 entered a Bankia building in Seville to protest the Spanish government's bailout of this bank with taxpayers' money, performing a *bulerías* once inside, "Bankia, pulmones, y branquías" (Bankia, lungs, and gills). This time there was a live singer among the dancers who wailed, "You have lowered my salary while you raise the price of everything. / In order to survive I even had to pawn my parrot and I had to sell my house." The bank is called out by name in the song (as is the bank president, Rodrigo Rato) and its greed lay bare: "Bankia, Bankia, Bankia. / For you six lungs / For me, not even a few fish gills."[48]

The group is completely aware that they cannot topple the banking system—they see themselves as Lilliputians fighting giant monsters, knowing full well that their attacks on the banks are about as effective as "picking at cracks in the ice with a cardboard ax." Instead, they view themselves as gadflies representing the woes of a populace that has been impoverished by people who were meant to represent them and protect their interests. Nowhere was this clearer than when a few of their members emerged from the public galleries of the Andalusian Parliament as a politician began to speak, ostensibly about economic matters. A woman stands up and begins her cante jondo: "Begging, on my knees is how you like to see me / or emigrating / begging for a shitty job. / While you in indulge in dodgy deals / You are the foremen of the Troika." She is escorted out by security, and the politician begins to speak again. This time a man bellows, "Let the whole world hear it / Andalusia is a rich land. / Let the whole world hear it / You give away our money while you sell us out. / You serve the Troika." He is escorted out also. The politician tries to regain her voice after sipping some water. She begins to speak yet again, and a third woman arises and sings, "And now please get it right / Nobody above anybody. / And now please get it right / Stand up to capitalism. / A new law of laws." She, too, is gently led away from the gallery.[49]

Such disruptive gestures remind us of what Blas Infante saw in flamenco music—an improvised, individualized cry of anguish and dissent against the powers of the state and its representatives.[50] Although his version of flamenco's history does not necessarily pass scholarly muster today, he saw reflected in the art form the brilliance of a people who could turn their despair into art. So despite flamenco's nineteenth-century journey from the poor neighborhoods of urban Andalusia to the more comfortable commercial establishments, from its revival and hypercommercialization in tourist resorts in the Franco era to its dissemination through the global markets of the twenty-first century, flamenco music, because of its malleability and improvised character, still has the power to do more than entertain. Flamenco music can, when given the right set of circumstances, bear witness to human suffering.

Glossary

Al-andalus: The name given to the parts of the Iberian Peninsula that were under Muslim political and cultural rule during the Middle Ages. Territory shifted greatly between 711 and 1492. Córdoba was the seat of economic and cultural power in Al-andalus.
bailaor/bailaora: A male/female flamenco dancer.
bata de cola: The long train of a flamenco dancer's dress.
bolero: A dance made famous in the eighteenth century. It was considered by many to be the national dance of Spain.
cafés cantantes: Small clubs modeled after the French *café chantant*, where singing occurred. In Spain, many *cafés cantantes* became places for flamenco performances only.
cantaor/cantaora: A male/female flamenco singer.
cante: Singing/song.
cante jondo: The literal translation is "deep song." The family of songs known as *siguiriyas* and *soleares* are now considered part of the *cante jondo* idiom.
cants corals: Chorales created in Catalonia. They reached their greatest popularity at the beginning of the twentieth century.

chulo: The literal translation is "pimp," but generally meant a youth of the lower classes who dressed in flashy clothing and engaged in raucous, gangster-like behaviors that challenged the authority of the dominant classes.

cigarrera: A woman who worked in the tobacco factory.

copla: A popular form of verse, usually with four stanzas, which is often set to music.

Coros y Danzas de España: The folk singing and folk dancing group composed of people from diverse regions of Spain, organized and run by the Sección Feminina of the Falange Española.

costumbrismo: A literary movement, especially prominent during the nineteenth century, that sought to depict rural customs and rural life. The movement contributed some to the creation of Spanish stereotypes.

españolada: Related to *costumbrismo* and *pandereta*, it is a derogatory word used to describe music, art, and other artistic expressions that stereotype Spaniards. These works usually evoke the worst stereotypes from Andalusia.

flamenquismo: A love for all things related to flamenco. It was also linked to a system that contained both the worlds of bullfighting and flamenco and a constellation of traits and lifestyles that were associated with the audiences who attended both spectacles.

ilustrados: Spanish intellectuals and reformers who believed in the principles of the Enlightenment.

jaleo: The call and response and basic hell-raising during a flamenco performance.

juerga: A raucous party or celebration, usually involving lots of alcohol.

majismo: The act of being a *majo* or *maja*.

majo/maja: Working-class men / women from Madrid (although they were prominent in Andalusia too) in the eighteenth century who dressed flamboyantly, suggesting a certain sexual freedom and opposition to what they saw as the feminized, French-influenced court culture.

orfeón: A Catalan choral society.

palmas: Polyrhythmic hand-clapping that is essential to flamenco music.

palos: A family of songs.

pandereta: Literally means "tambourine." Shorthand for the stereotypical images of Spain created by and for tourists. It is closely related to the term *españolada*.

pintoresco (lo): Picturesque, colorful. Depending on context, it can denote *pandereta*.

pitos: Rhythmic finger-snapping.

pregones: The cries coming from vendors hawking their wares.

sardana: In the family of circle dances, it is now considered to be the national dance of Catalonia.

Sección Femenina: The female version of the Falange Española, the Spanish Fascist Party.

Glossary

señorito: Pejorative word used to describe a wealthy and/or aristocratic man. Señoritos were said to like attending (and paying for) raucous flamenco gatherings.

tablaos: The mid-twentieth-century version of the *café cantante*. *Tablaos* sprung up all over Spain at the beginning of the tourist boom in the 1950s.

tocaor/tocaora: A male/female flamenco guitar player.

toque: Guitar playing.

voz afillá: A frayed and hoarse-sounding voice. It takes its name and meaning from the nineteenth-century *cantaor* Diego el Fillo, who made the sound famous.

zarzuela: A Spanish form of light opera and/or musical theater. It reached its greatest popularity in the nineteenth century.

Notes

Introduction

1. S. Teackle Wallis, *Glimpses of Spain; Or, Notes of an Unfinished Tour in 1847* (New York: Harper & Bros., 1849), 181–84.
2. Ibid., 186–87.
3. One of the pioneers of gender history in the United States, Temma Kaplan, recognized that it was not odd for working-class women to break away from stereotypical gender norms when the family's health and survival were at stake. The cigarreras' political activism in the case above fits Kaplan's analysis perfectly. Temma Kaplan, "Female Consciousness and Collective Action: The Case of Barcelona, 1910–1918," *Signs: Journal of Women in Culture and Society* 7, no. 3 (1982): 545–66. For a discussion of tobacco workers' strikes in the late nineteenth century as well as representations of tobacco workers in popular culture and the press, see Rosa María Capel Martínez, "Life and Work in the Tobacco Factories: Female Industrial Workers in the Twentieth Century," in *Constructing Spanish Womanhood: Female Identity in Modern Spain*, ed. Victoria Lorée Enders and Pamela Beth Radcliff (Albany: State University of New York Press, 1999), 131–50; D. J. O'Connor, "Representations of Women Workers: Tobacco Strikers

in the 1890s," in *Constructing Spanish Womanhood: Female Identity in Modern Spain*, ed. Victoria Lorée Enders and Pamela Beth Radcliff (Albany: State University of New York Press, 1999), 131–33, respectively. In fact, female tobacco workers' storied militancy is reflected in a comment by the writer Carmen de Burgos, when she claimed, "Their strikes are feared by the public authorities, as the populace is always on their side." Cited in Capel Martínez, "Life and Work," 133.

4. One of the first people to thoroughly document the link between disorder and flamenco, at least in the newspapers of Seville, was José Luis Ortiz Nuevo, *¿Se sabe algo? Viaje al conocimiento del arte flamenco según los testimonios de la prensa sevillana del XIX, desde comienzos del siglo hasta el año en que murió Silverio Franconetti (1812–1889)* (Seville: Ediciones El Carro de la Nieve, 1991).

5. Luis Palma et al., "Live Flamenco in Spain: A Dynamic Analysis of Supply, with Managerial Implications," *International Journal of Arts Management* 19, no. 3 (2017): 61.

6. "Flamenco Cleaning Services," accessed October 29, 2017, http://www.flamencocleaningservices.com. Playa Flamenca is located near Torrevieja, Alicante. Michael Billig, *Banal Nationalism* (Thousand Oaks, CA: SAGE, 1995).

7. I will be using the terms "Gypsy" and *gitano/gitana* interchangeably instead of "Romani" or "Roma" because Spanish Gypsies commonly refer to themselves as Gypsies. In flamenco performances it is highly complimentary to exclaim, "What a Gypsy!" to a performer on the stage.

8. Gerhard Steingress and Enrique Jesús Rodríguez Baltanás, *Flamenco y nacionalismo: Aportaciones para una sociología política del flamenco; Actas del I y II Seminario Teórico sobre arte, mentalidad e identidad colectiva (Sevilla, junio de 1995 y 1997)* (Seville: Fundación Machado, 1998).

9. The big exception to this rule is the sociologist/flamencologist Gerhard Steingress.

10. Génesis García Gómez, *Cante flamenco, cante minero: Una interpretación sociocultural* (Barcelona: Editorial Anthropos, 1993).

11. Norberto Torres Cortés, *Historia de la guitarra flamenca: El surco, el ritmo y el compás* (Córdoba: Almuzara, 2005).

12. Steingress and Rodríguez Baltanás, *Flamenco y nacionalismo*.

13. Cristina Cruces Roldán, *Más allá de la música: Antropología y flamenco*, vol. 1; *Sociabilidad, transmisión y patrimonio* (Seville: Signatura Ediciones de Andalucía, 2002); Cristina Cruces Roldán, *El flamenco y la música andalusí: Argumentos para un encuentro* (Barcelona: Ediciones Carena, 2003); William Washabaugh, *Flamenco: Passion, Politics and Popular Culture* (Oxford: Berg, 1996); William Washabaugh, *Flamenco Music and National Identity in Spain* (London: Routledge, 2016).

14. Timothy Mitchell, *Flamenco Deep Song* (New Haven, CT: Yale University Press, 1994); José Luis Navarro and Eulalia Pablo, *El baile flamenco: Una aproximación histórica* (Córdoba: Almuzara, 2005).

15. K. Meira Goldberg, Ninotchka Bennahum, and Michelle Heffner Hayes, *Flamenco on the Global Stage: Historical, Critical and Theoretical Perspectives* (Jefferson, NC: McFarland, 2015); Ninotchka Bennahum, *Antonia Mercé, "La Argentina": Flamenco and the Spanish Avant garde* (Hanover, NH: University Press of New England, 2000); Michelle Heffner Hayes, *Flamenco: Conflicting Histories of the Dance* (Jefferson, NC: McFarland, 2009).

16. Ángel Álvarez Caballero, *Gitanos, payos y flamencos en los origines del flamenco* (Madrid: Editorial Cinterco, 1988); Ángel Álvarez Caballero, *El cante flamenco* (Madrid: Alianza, 1998); José Blas Vega, *El flamenco en Madrid* (Córdoba: Almuzara, 2006); José Manuel Gamboa, *Una historia del flamenco* (Pozuelo de Alarcón, Madrid: Espasa Calpe, 2005); Navarro and Pablo, *El baile flamenco*; Daniel Pineda Novo, "El flamenco, tradición y vanguardia," *Revista de flamencología* 5, no. 9 (1999): 81–84; Manuel Ríos Ruiz, *El gran libro del flamenco* (Madrid: Calambur, 2002).

17. Rocío Plaza Orellana, *El flamenco y los románticos: Un viaje entre el mito y la realidad* (Seville: Bienal de Arte Flamenco, 1999); Rocío Plaza Orellana, *Los bailes españoles en Europa: El espectáculo de los bailes de España en el siglo XIX* (Córdoba: Almuzara, 2013). Of all the flamencologists, she is the one who most closely writes as a traditional historian would.

18. Bernard Leblon, *Gypsies and Flamenco: The Emergence of the Art of Flamenco in Andalusia* (Hatfield: University of Hertfordshire Press, 2003); D. E. Pohren, *The Art of Flamenco* (Morón de la Frontera: Society of Spanish Studies, 1967).

19. For a discussion of how stereotypes about Spaniards remained the same over centuries while their meaning changed depending on historical context, see José Álvarez Junco, "España: El peso del estereotipo," *Claves de razón práctica* 48 (1994): 3–12. Adrian Shubert was one of the first contemporary historians to take on the history of bullfighting. Adrian Shubert, *Death and Money in the Afternoon: A History of the Spanish Bullfight* (New York: Oxford University Press, 1999).

20. The concept of degeneration, which had its heyday in the 1890s after the publication of Max Nordau's *Degeneration* and through the early decades of the twentieth century in Europe, has been explored in numerous works. Max Nordau, *Degeneration* (New York: D. Appleton, 1905). The classic scholarly works on the issue include: Daniel Pick, *Faces of Degeneration: A European Disorder, c.1848–c. 1914* (Cambridge: Cambridge University Press, 1989); J. Edward Chamberlain and Sander L. Gilman, eds., *Degeneration: The Dark Side of Progress* (New York: Columbia University Press, 1985). For a recent work on the concept of degeneration in the Spanish visual arts, see Oscar E. Vázquez, *The End Again: Degeneration and Visual Culture in Modern Spain* (University Park: Penn State University Press, 2017).

21. Some scholars refer to the flamenco music of this period as *nacionalflamenquismo*, hinting at its ideological centralization during the Franco regime.

22. Washabaugh, *Flamenco Music*, 9.

23. Francisco León Fernández, "Frasquillo" (1898–1940) was, according to Clara Chinoy, "the first person to formally teach flamenco independently from other Spanish dance styles." Clara Chinoy, "The First Academy of Flamenco Dance: Frasquillo and the 'Broken Dance' of the Gitanos," in *Flamenco on the Global Stage*, ed. K. Meira Goldberg, Ninotchka Bennahum, and Michelle Heffner Hayes (Jefferson, NC: McFarland, 2015), 143. For the origins of flamenco guitar, see Torres Cortés, *Historia de la guitarra flamenca*, 13.

24. "Flamenco—History," accessed October 4, 2017, http://www.andalucia.com/flamenco/history.htm.

25. My information about the staging comes from looking at various historical photos and reading various historical accounts of flamenco performances in the late nineteenth and early twentieth centuries.

26. Margot Molina, "La reina de la bata de cola," *El País*, April 6, 2003, https://elpais.com/diario/2003/04/06/andalucia/1049581344_850215.html.

27. See chapter 4 for a detailed synopsis of these theories.

28. Steingress, *Sociología del cante flamenco*, 2nd ed. (Seville: Signatura, 2006). One of the most recent attempts to understand the etymology of the term comes from William Sayers, "Spanish *Flamenco*: Origin, Loan Translation, and In- and Out-Group Evolution (Romani, Caló, Castilian)," *Romance Notes* 48, no. 1 (2007): 13–22.

29. Until recently, the term was thought to be used first in the Madrid press in 1853, as discovered by Arie C Sneeuw, *Flamenco en el Madrid del XIX* (Córdoba: Virgilio Márquez, 1989), 22, although recently my colleague Bruce Boggs discovered another earlier incarnation, also in a Madrid newspaper, *El espectador*, in 1847. See chapter 1 in Bruce A. Boggs, "Riffing in Spanish: Flamencos and Flamenquismo in the Popular Theater" (unfinished manuscript). The word "flamenco" can also confound one because it has at least three meanings in Spanish: Flemish, flamingo, and flamenco performance.

30. See chapter 4.

31. Payos refers to peasants, but for gitanos, payos are merely nongitanos. When used by gitanos, the term is often derogatory.

32. Variations of this argument can be found in Félix Grande, *Memoria del flamenco* (Madrid: Espasa-Calpe, 1979); Antonio Machado y Álvarez, *Colección de cantes flamencos, recogidos y anotados por Demófilo*, ed. Enrique Baltanás (Seville: Signatura Ediciones, 1999); Ricardo Molina and Antonio Mairena, *Mundo y formas del cante flamenco* (Madrid: Revista de Occidente, 1963); Anselmo González Climent, *Flamencología* (Córdoba: Ayuntamiento de Córdoba, 1989).

33. Variations of this argument can be found in Cruces Roldán, *Más allá de la música*; Mitchell, *Flamenco Deep Song*; Steingress, *Sociología del cante flamenco*; García Gómez, *Cante flamenco, cante minero*.

34. Mercedes Gómez-García Plata, "El género flamenco: estampa finisecular de la España de pandereta," in *La escena española en la encrucijada, 1890-1910*, ed. Serge Salaün, Evelyne Ricci, and Marie Salgues (Madrid: Editorial Fundamentos, 2005), 121; Washabaugh, *Flamenco Music*, 9.

35. A small sampling of those scholars includes Plaza Orellana, *Los bailes españoles en Europa*; Steingress, *Sociología del cante flamenco*; Washabaugh, *Flamenco Music*.

36. Génesis García Gómez, "Volksgeist y género español," in *Flamenco y nacionalismo: Aportaciones para una sociología política del flamenco*, ed. Gerhard Steingress and Enrique Baltanás (Seville: Fundación el Monte, 1998), 193–206; Mitchell, *Flamenco Deep Song*; Plaza Orellana, *Los bailes españoles en Europa*; Steingress, *Sociología del cante flamenco*; Gerhard Steingress, . . . *Y Carmen se fue a París: Un estudio sobre la construcción artística del género flamenco (1833–1865)* (Córdoba: Editorial Almuzara, 2006); Gerhard Steingress, *Flamenco postmoderno: Entre tradición y heterodoxia; Un diagnóstico sociomusicológico (escritos 1989–2006)* (Seville: Signatura, 2007).

37. Estela Zatañía gives more credence to the rural roots of flamenco, however. Estela Zatañía, *Flamencos de Gañanía: Una mirada al flamenco en los cortijos históricos del bajo Guadalquivir* (Seville: Ediciones Giralda, 2008).

38. For a discussion of how the bullfight was a modern form of mass culture in Spain, see Shubert, *Death and Money*.

39. Michelle Heffner Hayes, *Flamenco*, 29–31.

40. Lou Charnon-Deutsch, *The Spanish Gyspy: The History of a European Obsession* (University Park: Penn State Press, 2004); Plaza Orellana, *El flamenco y los románticos*; Steingress, *Sociología del cante flamenco*; Steingress, . . . *Y Carmen se fue a París*; James Parakilas, "How Spain Got a Soul," in *The Exotic in Western Music*, ed. Jonathan Bellman (Boston: Northeastern University Press, 1998), 137–93; Trinidad Pardo Ballester, *Flamenco: Orientalismo, exotismo y la identidad nacional española* (Granada: Universidad de Granada, 2017).

41. Benedict R. Anderson, *Imagined Communities: Reflections on the Origin and Spread of Nationalism* (New York: Verso, 1991); E. J. Hobsbawm, T. O. Ranger, *The Invention of Tradition* (Cambridge: Cambridge University Press, 1992); Ernest Gellner, *Nations and Nationalism* (Ithaca, NY: Cornell University Press, 1983).

42. For works that make the argument that nationalism is a premodern phenomenon, or where traces of nationalism can be found earlier than in the post-Enlightenment era, see Prasenjit Duara, *Rescuing History from the Nation: Questioning Narratives of Modern China* (Chicago: University of Chicago Press, 1995); Aviel Roshwald, *The Endurance of Nationalism: Ancient Roots and Modern Dilemmas* (Cambridge: Cambridge University Press, 2006); Anthony D Smith, *The Ethnic Origins of Nations* (New York: Blackwell, 1987). For a selection from the modernist school, see Anderson, *Imagined Communities*; John Breuilly, *Nationalism and the State* (Chicago: University of Chicago Press, 1994); Gellner, *Nations and Nationalism*; E. J. Hobsbawm and T. O. Ranger, *The Invention of Tradition*; Miroslav Hroch, *Social Preconditions of National Revival in Europe: A Comparative Analysis of the Social Composition of Patriotic Groups among the Smaller European Nations* (New York: Cambridge University Press, 1984).

43. Alejandro Quiroga, "The Three Spheres: A Theoretical Model of Mass

Nationalisation: The Case of Spain," *Nations and Nationalism* 20, no. 4 (2014): 684.

44. See, for example, Maarten Ginderachter and Marnix Bayen, eds., *Nationhood from Below: Europe in the Long Nineteenth Century* (Basingstoke: Palgrave Macmillan, 2012); Nira Yuval-Davis, *Gender and Nation* (London: Sage, 1997).

45. For discussions of regionalism, see Xosé-Manoel Núñez, "The Region as *Essence* of the Fatherland: Regionalist Variants of Spanish Nationalism (1840-1936)," *European History Quarterly* 31, no. 4 (2001): 483-518; Eric Storm, *The Culture of Regionalism: Art, Architecture and International Exhibitions in France, Germany and Spain, 1890-1939* (Manchester: Manchester University Press, 2010); Joost Augusteijn and Eric Storm, eds., *Region and State in Nineteenth-Century Europe: Nation-Building, Regional Identities and Separatism* (New York: Palgrave Macmillan, 2012).

46. Joep Leerssen, "Nationalism and the Cultivation of Culture," *Nations and Nationalism* 12, no. 4 (2006): 564.

47. See, for example, José Álvarez Junco, *Mater Dolorosa: La idea de España en el siglo XIX* (Madrid: Taurus, 2001). This work has appeared in a condensed English version as *Spanish Identities in the Age of Nations* (Manchester: Manchester University Press, 2011). See also Borja de Riquer i Permanyer, "La débil nacionalización española del siglo XIX," *Historia social* 20, no. 20 (1994): 97-114.

48. For some of the more recent scholarship on national identity in Spain, see the essays in Javier Moreno et al., *Construir España: Nacionalismo español y procesos de nacionalización* (Madrid: Centro de Estudios Políticos y Constitucionales, 2007); Javier Moreno Luzón and Xosé M. Núñez Seixas, *Los colores de la patria: Símbolos nacionales en la España contemporánea* (Madrid: Tecnos, 2017); Javier Moreno Luzón and Xosé M. Núñez Seixas, *Metaphors of Spain: Representations of Spanish National Identity in the Twentieth Century* (New York: Berghahn, 2017). See also Ferrán Archilés and Manuel Martí, "Un país tan extraño como cualquier otro: La construcción de la identidad nacional española contemporánea," in *El siglo XX: Historiografía e historia*, ed. María Cruz Romeo and Ismael Saz (Valencia: Universitat de València, 2002), 245-78; Ferrán Archilés and Marta García Carrión, "En la sombra del estado: Esfera pública nacional y homogenización cultural en la España de la Restauración," *Historia Contemporánea* 45 (2012): 483-518.

49. Marnix Beyen and Maarten Van Ginderachter, "General Introduction: Writing the Mass into a Mass Phenomenon," in *Nationhood from Below*, ed. Marnix Beyen and Maarten Van Ginderachter (Basingstoke: Palgrave Macmillan, 2012), 14.

50. Many travel narratives from the nineteenth century produced by British, French, and American writers reflect these attitudes. To see how many of these Romantic ideals got attached to Spain, see Xavier Andreu Miralles, *El descubrimiento de España: Mito romántico e identidad nacional* (Barcelona: Taurus, 2016).

51. The Black Legend refers to the negative propaganda begun around the sixteenth century and spread by Spain's French and British rivals. It characterized Spain as the land of cruel Inquisitors, sadistic colonial rulers, repressive politicians, and intellectual and artistic yokels.

52. Statistics from the nineteenth century are not always reliable, but one can still make educated guesses based on the number of advertisements in newspapers and magazines and on comparative statistics for other types of spectacles in the same period.

53. Beyen and Van Ginderachter, "General Introduction," 8.

54. Luis García Berlanga, dir., *Bienvenido Mr. Marshall*, 1953.

55. Some good examples of musicological studies include Philip Vilas Bohlman, *The Music of European Nationalism: Cultural Identity and Modern History* (Santa Barbara, CA: ABC-CLIO, 2004); Benjamin W. Curtis, *Music Makes the Nation: Nationalist Composers and Nation Building in Nineteenth-century Europe* (Amherst, NY: Cambria Press, 2008); Annegret Fauser, *Musical Encounters at the 1889 Paris World's Fair* (Rochester: University of Rochester Press, 2005); Marina Frolova-Walker, *Russian Music and Nationalism: From Glinka to Stalin* (New Haven, CT: Yale University Press, 2007); Harry White and Michael Murphy, eds., *Musical Constructions of Nationalism: Essays on the History and Ideology of European Musical Culture 1800–1945* (Cork, Ireland: Cork University Press, 2001). For Spanish music during this period, see Carol A Hess, *Manuel de Falla and Modernism in Spain: 1898–1936* (Chicago: University of Chicago Press, 2001); Josep Martí, "Folk Music Studies and Ethnomusicology in Spain," *Yearbook for Traditional Music* 29 (1997): 107–40; Pedro Ordóñez Eslava, "Qualities of Flamenco in the Francoism: Between the Renaissance and the Conscience of Protest," in *Music and Francoism*, ed. Gemma Pérez Zalduondo and Germán Gan Quesada (Turnhout: Brepols, 2013), 265–83; Serge Salaün, *El cuplé (1900–1936)* (Madrid: Espasa Calpe, 1990); Federico Sopeña Ibáñez, *Historia de la música española contemporánea* (Madrid: Ediciones Rialp, 1958).

56. J. Connell and C. Gibson, *Sound Tracks: Popular Music, Identity and Place*, Critical Geographies (London: Routledge, 2002), 45.

57. See, for example, Celia Applegate and Pamela Maxine Potter, *Music and German National Identity* (Chicago: University of Chicago Press, 2002); Celia Applegate, *Bach in Berlin: Nation and Culture in Mendelssohn's Revival of the "St. Matthew Passion"* (Ithaca, NY: Cornell University Press, 2014); Jeffrey H. Jackson, "Making Jazz French: The Reception of Jazz Music in Paris, 1927–1934," *French Historical Studies* 25, no. 1 (2002): 149–70; James H. Johnson, *Listening in Paris: A Cultural History* (Berkeley: University of California Press, 1996); Samuel Llano, *Whose Spain? Negotiating "Spanish Music" in Paris, 1908–1929* (Oxford: Oxford University Press, 2012); Clinton A. Young, *Music Theater and Popular Nationalism in Spain, 1880–1930* (Baton Rouge: Louisiana State University Press, 2016). Jeffrey H. Jackson and Stanley C. Pelkey, *Music and History: Bridging the Disciplines* (Jackson: University Press of Mississippi, 2005), explicitly works to connect the

two disciplines. A recent work on ballet and national identity that demonstrates similar concerns as mine is Ilyana Karthas, *When Ballet Became French: Modern Ballet and the Cultural Politics of France, 1909–1939* (Montreal: McGill-Queen's University Press, 2015).

58. Krisztina Lajosi, "National Stereotypes and Music," *Nations and Nationalism* 20, no. 4 (2014): 629. Her work provides an excellent discussion of how a musical style became national in the Hungarian context.

59. Curtis, *Music Makes the Nation*, 31; Carl Dahlhaus, "Nationalism and Music," in *Between Romanticism and Modernism: Four Studies in the Music of the Later Nineteenth Century*, trans. Mary Whittall (Berkeley: University of California Press, 1980), 86–87. See also Bohlman, *The Music of European Nationalism*.

60. Curtis, *Music Makes the Nation*, 32–33.

61. For histories of Spanish symphonic orchestras and more general discussions of Spanish music, see Carlos Gómez Amat, Joaquín Turina Gómez, and Alicia de Larrocha, *La Orquesta Sinfónica de Madrid: Noventa años de historia* (Madrid: Alianza Editorial, 1994); Tomás Marco, *Spanish Music in the Twentieth Century* (Cambridge, MA: Harvard University Press, 1993). For a discussion of the bourgeois makeup of symphonic audiences in other parts of Europe, see William Weber, *Music and the Middle Class: The Social Structure of Concert Life in London, Paris and Vienna between 1830 and 1848* (London: Routledge, 2017).

62. Young, *Music Theater*.

63. Joshua Goode, *Impurity of Blood: Defining Race in Spain, 1870–1930* (Baton Rouge: Louisiana State University Press, 2009), 15.

64. Ibid., 166–68.

65. Lou Charnon-Deutsch, *The Spanish Gypsy*, 12.

66. I will not distinguish between lowercase and uppercase *g* when I talk about Gypsies. In keeping consistent with English and Spanish grammar, when I use the English variant, I will capitalize it; when I use the Spanish one, I will not capitalize.

67. The conflation of flamenco performers with mysterious, sensual, and closer-to-nature Gypsies illustrates Neil MacMaster's thesis about racial thought in the nineteenth and early twentieth centuries—that is, it was "fundamentally an expression of cultural attitudes that were recoded through the methodologies and discourse of 'objective' and empirical research.... In this sense all racism was cultural." Neil MacMaster, *Racism in Europe: 1870–2000* (New York: Palgrave Macmillan, 2001), 193, cited in Goode, *Impurity of Blood*, 7.

68. For more discussion of these ideas, see Andreu Miralles, *El descubrimiento de España*; Jesús Torrecilla, *España exótica: La formación de la imagen española moderna* (Boulder, CO: Society of Spanish and Spanish-American Studies, 2004).

69. Edward W. Said, *Orientalism* (New York: Vintage Books, 2003); Charnon-Deutsch, *The Spanish Gypsy*, 10. See also Parakilas, "How Spain Got a Soul," esp. 139–43.

70. For example, during the Enlightenment, when the "Rights of Man" were debated in the public sphere, women, who were constituted as belonging outside of the public sphere and belonging to the private sphere—even if such separation did not correspond with reality—were denied the rights of citizenship both tangibly and discursively. Women were considered outside of politics and thus dependents of male, active citizens. For one discussion about how women were erased from the public sphere, see Carole Pateman, *The Sexual Contract* (Stanford: Stanford University Press, 1988).

71. Yuval-Davis, *Gender and Nation*, 2, 23.

72. John Tosh, "Hegemonic Masculinity and Gender History," in *Masculinities in Politics and War: Gendering Modern History*, ed. Stefan Dudink, Karen Hagemann, and John Tosh (Manchester: Manchester University Press, 2004), 48.

73. Simone de Beauvoir, *The Second Sex*, trans. Sheila Malovany-Chevallier and Constance Borde (New York: Vintage, 2011).

74. Many photographs exist of women playing guitar and women dressing in "male" costumes, as seen in Loren Chuse, *The Cantaoras: Music, Gender, and Identity in Flamenco Song* (New York: Routledge, 2003).

75. John F. Szwed, *Crossovers: Essays on Race, Music, and American Culture* (Philadelphia: University of Pennsylvania Press, 2005); Marshall Craig Eakin, *Becoming Brazilians: Race and National Identity in Twentieth-Century Brazil* (Cambridge: Cambridge University Press, 2017); Hermano Vianna and John Charles Chasteen, *The Mystery of Samba: Popular Music and National Identity in Brazil* (Chapel Hill: University of North Carolina Press, 1999); Adriana J. Bergero, *Intersecting Tango: Cultural Geographies of Buenos Aires, 1900–1930* (Pittsburgh: University of Pittsburgh Press, 2008); Marta Savigliano, *Tango and the Political Economy of Passion* (Boulder, CO: Westview Press, 1995). To observe the dynamics across many musical forms, see the essays in Gerhard Steingress, ed., *Songs of the Minotaur—Hybridity and Popular Music in the Era of Globalization: A Comparative Analysis of Rebetika, Tango, Rai, Flamenco, Sardana, and English Urban Folk* (Münster: LIT, 2002).

Chapter 1. Inventing an Ancient Past for a Modern Form, 1789–1875

1. José Cadalso and Juan Tamayo y Rubio, *Cartas marruecas* (Madrid: Espasa-Calpe, 1935), 79–86.

2. This brief history of the guitar is taken from Norberto Torres Cortés, "El estilo 'rasgueado' de la guitarra barroca y su influencia en la guitarra flamenca: fuentes escritas y musicales (siglo XVII)," *Revista de Investigación sobre Flamenco "La Madrugá"* (2012): 1–46; Manuel Ríos Ruiz, "Guitarra," in *Diccionario enciclopédico ilustrado del flamenco*, 2nd ed., ed. José Blas Vega and Manuel Ríos Ruiz (Madrid: Editorial Cinterco, 1990), 349–55; Thomas F. Heck et al., "Guitar,"

Grove Music Online, Oxford Music Online, https://doi.org/10.1093/gmo/9781561592630.article.43006.

3. Gerardo Arriaga, "La guitarra Renacentista," in *La guitarra española: The Spanish Guitar* (New York: New York Metropolitan Museum of Art; Madrid: Museo Municipal de Madrid, 1993), cited in Torres Cortés, "El estilo 'rasgueado,'" 3.

4. For a lengthy anthropological study of the relationship between barbers and guitars in popular Spanish culture, see Alberto del Campo and Rafael Cáceres, *Historia cultural del flamenco: El barbero y la guitarra* (Córdoba: Almuzara, 2013).

5. Torres Cortés, *Historia de la guitarra flamenca*, 13. This quote is cited as coming from Ricardo Miño, *Puerta de Triana* (Senador D-01040, Seville, 1988), which seems to be a sound recording.

6. Peter Burke is probably the most well-known scholar to assert that there had been a splitting off of popular and aristocratic culture in Europe by the eighteenth century. Peter Burke, *Popular Culture in Early Modern Europe* (Burlington, VT: Ashgate, 2010). Of course, how various forms of culture have been defined, constructed, and hierarchized has been up for debate in academic circles for decades, and the literature defining the differences between official culture, avant-garde culture, popular culture, and mass culture is too extensive to cite here. Unlike Burke, Lawrence Levine views a split between "highbrow" and "lowbrow" culture taking place in the United States during the nineteenth century. Lawrence W. Levine, *Highbrow/Lowbrow* (Cambridge, MA: Harvard University Press), 1988.

7. According to Torres Cortés, even today "the great majority of flamenco guitarists do not know how to read music." Torres Cortés, *Historia de la guitarra flamenca*, 20.

8. After 1922 the musical mythologies handed down from Manuel de Falla and Federico García Lorca cemented the status of cante jondo as the only flamenco form worthy of serious study. This has changed in the last couple of decades, but it is worth noting that some of the most important modern studies of flamenco concentrate broadly on *cante* and more specifically on cante jondo. See, for example, Ángel Álvarez Caballero, *Historia del cante flamenco* (Madrid: Alianza Editorial, 1981); Álvarez Caballero, *El cante flamenco*; García Gómez, *Cante flamenco, cante minero*; Mitchell, *Flamenco Deep Song*; Ricardo Molina and Antonio Mairena, *Mundo y formas*; Steingress, *Sociología del cante flamenco*.

9. Henry Blackburn, *Travelling in Spain in the Present Day* (London: S. Low & Marston, 1866), 208; Frances Minto Elliot, *Diary of an Idle Woman in Spain* (London: F. V. White & Company, 1884), 98; Richard Ford, *Gatherings from Spain* (London: Pallas Athene, 2000), 313; Samuel Manning, *Spanish Pictures, Drawn with Pen and Pencil* (London: Religious Tract Society, 1870), 157; Ruth Kedzie Wood, *The Tourist's Spain and Portugal* (New York: Dodd, Mead, 1913), 59.

10. The *voz afillá* takes its name from the famous nineteenth-century cantaor of the café cantante circuit, Francisco Ortega Vargas, or "Diego el Fillo." "Flamenco—Diego el Fillo," accessed October 9, 2017, http://www.andalucia.com/flamenco/musicians/diegoelfillo.htm.

11. Manuel Barrios, *Gitanos, moriscos y cante flamenco* (Seville: J. Rodríguez Castillejo, 1989); García Gómez, *Cante flamenco, cante minero*, 11–25; Mitchell, *Flamenco Deep Song*, 51–84.

12. Some of these writers boasted that Cadiz had already distinguished itself during the Roman Empire as the place with the dancers who most resembled contemporary flamenco dancers, although in a primitive form. They quoted such luminaries as Juvenal, Marcus Valerius Martial, and Pliny the Younger to provide the historical pedigree of flamenco authenticity. See, for example, Ángel Caffarena, *Geografía del cante andaluz* (Málaga: Juan Such, 1964), 19–24. For a dismantling of that myth, see Kathy Milazzo, "Dancers of Cádiz: *Puellae Gaditane* and Creations of Myth," in *Flamenco on the Global Stage: Historical, Critical and Theoretical Perspectives*, ed. K. Meira Goldberg, Ninotchka Bennahum, Michelle Heffner Hayes (Jefferson, NC: McFarland, 2015), 33–41.

13. According to one scholar, Sebastián Cerezo systematized the bolero steps in 1780. Lidia Atencia Doña, "Desarrollo histórico y evolutivo del baile flamenco: De los bailes de candil a las nuevas tendencias en el baile flamenco," *Revista de investigación sobre flamenco "La Madrugá"* (2016), 143. For more recent histories of flamenco dance, see Goldberg, Bennahum, and Hayes, *Flamenco on the Global Stage*; Hayes, *Flamenco*; José Luis Navarro and Eulalia Pablo, *El baile flamenco: Una aproximación histórica* (Córdoba: Almuzara, 2005).

14. Navarro and Pablo, *El baile flamenco*, 15.

15. For a preliminary study on sub-Saharan African influences on Spanish song and dance, see Aurelia Martín-Casares, Marga G. Barranco, "The Musical Legacy of Black Africans in Spain: A Review of Our Sources," *Anthropological Notebooks* 15, no. 2 (2009): 51–60. See also K. Meira Goldberg and Antoni Pizà, "Introduction: *Mestizajes*," in *The Global Reach of the Fandango in Music, Song and Dance: Spaniards, Indians, Africans and Gypsies*, ed. K. Meira Goldberg and Antoni Pizà (Newcastle upon Tyne: Cambridge Scholars, 2016), xiii–xxii. K. Meira Goldberg, *Sonidos Negros: On the Blackness of Flamenco* (Oxford: Oxford University Press, 2019), promises to add more depth to the scholarship on flamenco's hybrid and trans-Atlantic nature.

16. I am fully aware that I am using time frames established by European historians to discuss historical ruptures.

17. On multiple Enlightenments, see Jonathan Israel, *The Radical Enlightenment: Philosophy and the Making of Modernity (1600–1750)* (Oxford: Oxford University Press, 2002); Charles W. J. Withers, *Placing the Enlightenment: Thinking Geographically about the Age of Reason* (Chicago: University of Chicago Press, 2007).

18. Immanuel Kant, "Idea for a Universal History from a Cosmopolitan

Point of View," 1784, accessed September 23, 2017, https://www.marxists.org/reference/subject/ethics/kant/universal-history.htm.

19. For a clear distillation of this idea, see Joseph Theodoor Leerssen, *National Thought in Europe: A Cultural History* (Amsterdam: Amsterdam University Press, 2014), 93–100.

20. For recent reappraisals of the Spanish Enlightenment, see Jesús Astigarraga, *The Spanish Enlightenment Revisited* (Oxford: Voltaire Foundation, 2015); Brian R Hamnett, *The Enlightenment in Iberia and Ibero-America* (Cardiff: University of Wales Press, 2017).

21. Of course this idea of Spanish decline was more a perception than any kind of objective reality. Spain's economic and political development might not have followed the exact path as France or Britain, but neither did Germany, Italy, Greece, or any other number of European countries. The declension narrative of modern Spanish history, especially of the eighteenth and nineteenth centuries, has been challenged over the last couple of decades, especially by historians practicing in North America. See David Ringrose, *Spain, Europe, and the "Spanish Miracle," 1700–1900* (Cambridge: Cambridge University Press, 1998). For a more recent synthesis of Spanish history that puts "decline" in a much broader European perspective, see Pamela Radcliff, *Modern Spain: 1808–Present* (Hoboken, NJ: John Wiley and Sons, 2017).

22. Dorothy Noyes, "La Maja Vestida: Dress as Resistance to Enlightenment in Late-18th-Century Madrid," *Journal of American Folklore* 111, no. 440 (1998): 198–199. Approximately two hundred thousand French nationals resided in Spain in 1765. Much of this discussion of the majos comes from this piece.

23. For a more recent discussion on the discursive use of the maja for reformist purposes, see Xavier Andreu, "Figuras modernas del deseo: Las majas de Ramón de la Cruz y los orígenes del majismo," *Ayer* 78, no. 2 (2010): 25–46.

24. Noyes, "La Maja Vestida," 205, 215, n. 8.

25. The afrancesados who resisted, like those who formed and participated in the Cortes of Cadiz, received mixed responses from many quarters of Spain's populace.

26. Lajosi, "National Stereotypes and Music," 631–32.

27. Leerssen, "Nationalism," 568.

28. Don Preciso, *Colección de las mejores coplas de seguidillas, tiranas y polos que se han compuesto para cantar a la guitarra*, vol. 1 (Madrid: Repullés, 1816), 23–24. Don Preciso was the pseudonym of Juan Antonio de Iza Zamácola Ocerín. For a brief view of Don Preciso's life and works, see María Carmen García-Matos Alonso, "Un folklorista del siglo XVIII: Don Preciso," *Revista de Musicología* 4, no. 1 (1981): 295–307.

29. Don Preciso, *Colección de las mejores coplas*, 32, 32–36.

30. Steingress, *Sociología del cante flamenco*, 257–58.

31. Granted, industrialization and urbanization occurred much more slowly than in other parts of Western Europe, but places like Madrid, Barcelona,

Bilbao, and Seville were seeing their share of social dislocation from these processes.

32. Fernán Caballero was the pseudonym of Cecilia Böhl de Faber.

33. Emilio Lafuente y Alcántara, *Cancionero popular: Colección escogida de seguidillas y coplas* (Madrid: Carlos Bailly-Bailliere, 1865), vi–vii.

34. Although Pedrell's students elevated his stature in the world of musicology, some musicologists think that Pedrell's influence on Spanish composers is overrated. See, for example, Walter Aaron Clark, *Isaac Albéniz: Portrait of a Romantic* (Oxford: Oxford University Press, 2007).

35. Felipe Pedrell, *Por nuestra música* (Bellaterra, Barcelona: Universidad Autónoma de Barcelona, 1991).

36. See chapter 4 for Blas Infante's discussion and critique of Pedrell's views of flamenco.

37. The Institución Libre de Enseñanza was an independent school founded in 1876 by disaffected university professors. Following the precepts of educational theorists like John Dewey, the founders attempted to educate students free from the doctrines of church and state. Many of Spain's liberal elites were educated here until its close during the Spanish Civil War. Much of this discussion of Demófilo's life and ideas comes from Enrique Baltanás's introduction to Antonio Machado y Álvarez's *Colección de cantes flamencos, recogidos y anotados por Demófilo*, ed. Enrique R Baltanás (Seville: Signatura, 1999), 9–62, and Steingress, *Sociología del cante flamenco*, 123–37.

38. These insights on Demófilo's contributions come from Enrique Baltanás's introduction to Machado y Álvarez, *Colección de cantes flamencos*, 23–25. In the same year, Demófilo's friend and fellow *cante* aficionado, Hugo Schuchardt, published *Die cantes flamencos*, in which he argued a position diametric to Demófilo's: that cante flamenco was a form of Andalusian song that had become "Gypsified." The flamencologists of the 1950s and 1960s would latch onto Demófilo's position to claim flamenco for gitanos, whereas scholars like Steingress would build on Schuchardt's position. Steingress, *Sociología del cante flamenco*.

39. They did not always express this explicitly, but they certainly wrote enough antiflamenco tracts that demonstrated their disgust with the commercial aspects of flamenquismo.

40. This argument for hybridity is most clearly found in the works of K. Meira Goldberg, "Jaleo de Jerez and *Tumulte Noir*: Primitivist Modernism and Cakewalk in Flamenco, 1902–1917," in *Flamenco on the Global Stage: Historical, Critical and Theoretical Perspectives*, ed. K. Meira Goldberg, Ninotchka Bennahum, and Michelle Heffner Hayes (Jefferson, NC: McFarland, 2015), 143–156; Plaza Orellana, *Los bailes españoles en Europa*; Steingress, . . . *Y Carmen se fue a París*.

41. For a detailed description of who these Spanish intellectuals were and the connection between them and other European intellectuals, as well as a discussion of the wars and exile, see F. Héran, "L'invention de l'Andalousie au

XIXe, dans la littérature de voyage: Origine et function sociales de quelques images touristiques," in *Tourisme et développement regional en Andalousie*, ed. Antonio-Miguel Bernal et al. (Paris: E. de Boccard, 1979), 23–27, 26.

42. See George Henry Borrow, *The Zincali; or, An Account of the Gypsies of Spain: With an Original Collection of Their Songs and Poetry, and a Copious Dictionary of Their Language* (London: J. Murray, 1841); Richard Ford, John Murray (Firm), *A Hand-book for Travellers in Spain and Readers at Home: Describing the Country and Cities, the Natives and Their Manners, the Antiquities, Religion, Legends, Fine Arts, Literature, Sports, and Gastronomy; With Notices on Spanish History* (London: J. Murray, 1845); Ford, *Gatherings from Spain*.

43. Théophile Gautier, *A Romantic in Spain* (New York: Interlink Books, 2001), 234–235.

44. Ford and Murray, *A Hand-book for Travellers in Spain*; Gautier, *A Romantic in Spain*; Dorothy Quillinan, *Journal of a Few Months Residence in Portugal and Glimpses of the South of Spain* (London: Edward Moxon, 1847); S. Teackle Wallis, *Glimpses of Spain* (New York: Harper & Bros., 1849).

45. Unfortunately, because of the way Gypsies were viewed in nineteenth-century Europe, my language seems to imply that I do not think that gitanos were Spanish, that they were somehow a separate "race." I make no such claims. I am duplicating the language used in the nineteenth century because that is how these various people were described and understood at the time.

46. For a discussion of the cultural interchange between Spain and other western Europeans, especially the French, see Plaza Orellana, *Los bailes españoles en Europa*, 91–133; Steingress, . . . *Y Carmen se fue a París*, 51–79.

47. Although the Revolutionary Wars and subsequent monarchical restorations certainly roiled much of Europe, and the Industrial Revolution markedly transformed the European landscape, one could argue that Spain confronted even more impressive upheavals than other industrializing European nations after the Revolutionary Wars ended in 1815: five military revolts between 1814 and 1820; French military intervention to restore absolutism to Spain (1823); the diminution of Spain's empire in Spanish America (1824); three civil wars (the Carlist Wars of 1833–40, 1846–49, 1872–76); almost continuous rule by generals (1840–68); a revolution that resulted in ejecting a queen (1868), inviting a foreign monarch to rule (1870), establishing a republic that rotated through four presidents in eleven months (1873–74), and ending with a succession of military coups that would restore the monarchy (1874–75); the growth of regional nationalism in Catalonia; and, finally, a war with Cuba (1868–78).

48. I realize that many of the "entertainments" that I am about to discuss were off limits for most of the female population, that leisure was primarily a part of masculine privilege, but by the 1920s, Spanish women of the middle and working classes did attend at least some of the spectacles that had once been off limits to them. For a discussion of the relationships among modernity, modernism, and gender, see Griselda Pollock, "Modernity and the Spaces of

Femininity," in *Vision and Difference: Femininity, Feminism, and Histories of Art* (London: Routledge, 1988).

49. For a discussion of urban entertainment in Spain during this period, see José Luis Oyón, *La quiebra de la ciudad popular: Espacio urbano, inmigración y anarquismo en la Barcelona de entreguerras* (Barcelona: Ediciones del Serbal, 2008); Salaün, *El cuplé*; Carlos Serrano and Serge Salaün, *Los felices años veinte: España, crisis y modernidad* (Madrid: Marcial Pons Historia, 2006); Jorge Uría, "Lugares para el ocio. Espacio público y espacios recreativos en la Restauración española," *Historia social*, no. 41 (2001): 89–111; J. Uría, "La taberna. Un espacio multifuncional de sociabilidad popular en la Restauración española," *Hispania* 63 (2003): 571–604.

50. M. G. García, *Diccionario del teatro* (Madrid: Ediciones Akal, 1998). The cafés cantantes were modeled on the French *cafés chantantes*.

51. Flamencologists generally credit the cantaor Silverio Franconetti Aguilar (ca. 1829–89) as the creator of the commercial café cantante that specialized in flamenco performances only. Some of the following historical discussion comes from José Blas Vega, *Los cafés cantantes de Sevilla* (Madrid: Cinterco, 1987); Gómez-García Plata, "El género flamenco," in *La escena española en la encrucijada, 1890–1910*, ed. Serge Salaün, Evelyne Ricci, and Marie Salgues (Madrid: Editorial Fundamentos, 2005), 101–124.

52. For a discussion of the implications of the teatro por horas on the proliferation of zarzuela and Spanish nationalism, see Young, *Music Theater*, 21–24.

53. Mercedes Gómez-García Plata, "Culture populaire et loisir citadin: Les cafés cantantes de 1850 a 1900," in *Ocio y ocios: Du loisir aux loisirs (Espagne XVIII–XXe siécles)*, ed. Serge Salaün and Françoise Étienvre (Paris: Université du Sorbonne Nouvelle, 2006), 117.

54. This guidebook mentioned Silverio Franconetti's café cantante as one such place for Spanish dances, where many foreigners who desired "to know the customs that are fading away from modern civilization" could view the spectacle. Oddly enough, these words about modernity's effect on customs are precisely the words conservatives would use to lambaste flamenco and other modern dances and promote the return to folk dancing. Manuel Gómez Zarzuela and Vicente Gómez Zarzuela, *Guía de Sevilla, su provincia: Arzobispado, Capitanía General, Tercio Naval, Audiencia Territorial y Distrito Universitario* (Seville: La Andalucía, 1865), 83.

55. Manuel Gómez-Moreno, *Guía de Granada* (Granada: Indalecio Ventura, 1892), 469.

56. H. C. Chatfield-Taylor, *The Land of the Castanet: Spanish Sketches* (Chicago: H. S. Stone, 1896), 181–82.

57. Katharine Lee Bates, *Spanish Highways and Byways* (New York: Macmillan, 1900), 145–46.

58. Increasing numbers of guidebooks in the late nineteenth and early twentieth centuries had entertainment sections, some including descriptions of

dance shows available for tourists. For discussions of the rise of tourism in Spain and the role of guidebooks in that process, see M. Barke and J. Towner, "Exploring the History of Leisure and Tourism in Spain," in *Tourism in Spain: Critical Issues*, ed. M. Barke, J. Towner, and M. Newton (Wallingford: C. A. B. International, 1996), 3–34.

59. Karl Baedeker, *Spain and Portugal: Handbook for Travellers* (Leipzig: K. Baedeker, 1898), 389.

60. For theoretical discussions of how space and place are both produced and experienced, see Dolores Hayden, *The Power of Place: Urban Landscapes as Public History* (Cambridge, MA: MIT Press, 1997); Henri Lefebvre, *The Production of Space*, trans. Donald Nicholson-Smith (Malden, MA: Blackwell, 2009); Yi-Fu Tuan, *Space and Place: The Perspective of Experience* (Minneapolis: University of Minnesota Press, 1977). For more specific discussions of gender and space, see Pollock, "Modernity and the Spaces of Femininity," 50–90; Daphne Spain, "Gender and Urban Space," *Annual Review of Sociology* 40, no. 1 (2014): 581–98, https://doi.org/10.1146/annurev-soc-071913-043446.

61. This would change in the 1920s with the onset of ópera-flamenca, in which the artists performed in huge arenas like bullfighting rings. Originally, the term ópera flamenca was invented by an enterprising businessman named Vedrines and his brother-in-law Alberto Montserrat to avoid paying the requisite 10 percent sales tax on variety shows and cafés cantantes. Operas and orchestral entertainments were only charged 3 percent sales tax, hence the clever name change to ópera flamenca increased their take-home profits. Marta Carrasco Benítez, "Three Centuries of Flamenco," in *Flamenco on the Global Stage*, ed. K. Meira Goldberg, Ninotchka Bennahum, and Michelle Heffner Hayes (Jefferson, NC: McFarland, 2015), 25.

62. After 1856 these academies "with the objective of promoting certain dances, began to contract professional singers and gitanos to *jalear* and clap the *palmas*. This process of commercialization marks a change in the academies' didactic function to an artistic one, transforming themselves into dance salons that became a midway point between the academies and the cafés cantantes, with great organization and professionalization." Atencia Doña, "Desarrollo histórico y evolutivo del baile flamenco," 142.

63. Charles March, *Sketches and Adventures in Madeira, Portugal, and the Andalusias of Spain* (New York: Harper & Bros., 1856), 227.

64. Charles Augustus Stoddard, *Spanish Cities; with Glimpses of Gibraltar and Tangier* (New York: C. Scribner's Sons, 1892), 168–69.

65. Edmondo De Amicis, *Spain and the Spaniards*, trans. Stanley R. Yarnall (Philadelphia: H. T. Coates, 1895), 251.

66. Chatfield-Taylor, *The Land of the Castanet*, 181–82.

67. To get an idea of the kinds of entertainment one could find on the Midway Plaisance, see *The Moorish Palace and Its Startling Wonders* (Chicago: Metcalf Stationery Co., 1893); *Photographs of the World's Fair: An Elaborate Collection of*

Photographs of the Buildings, Grounds and Exhibits of the World's Columbian Exposition, with a Special Description of the Famous Midway Plaisance (Chicago: Werner, 1894); Norm Bolotin and Christine Laing, *Chicago's Grand Midway: A Walk around the World at the Columbian Exposition* (Urbana: University of Illinois Press, 2017).

68. Chatfield-Taylor, *The Land of the Castanet*, 91–93.

69. For the thoroughfares of prostitution in fin de siglo Madrid, see Javier Barreiro, "El Madrid nocturno de fines del siglo XIX, 1890," *Siglo diecinueve* 20 (2014): 113–34.

70. For a discussion of sites of prostitution in Seville, see Andrés Moreno Mengíbar, "Crisis y transformación de la prostitución en Sevilla (1885-1920), *Bulletin d'histoire contemporaine de l'Espagne* 25, special issue, "Prostitución y Sociedad en España, Siglos XIX y XX" (June 1997): 119–31. There are claims that Miguel Burrero did tolerate prostitutes soliciting in his café in Seville. See Gómez-García Plata, "Culture populaire et loisir citadin," 120–21.

71. Gómez García states that between the cardinal points of Bilbao, Cádiz, Almería, and Oviedo, there were seventy-three cafés cantantes between about 1870 and 1910. Those cardinal points do not include Barcelona, however. Blas Vega claims that there were more than eighty flamenco-themed cafés cantantes in Madrid alone between 1846 and 1936. Gómez-García Plata, "El género flamenco," 110; Blas Vega, *El flamenco en Madrid*, 20.

72. Apologies to H. L. Mencken.

73. Maite Zubiaurre, *Cultures of the Erotic in Spain, 1898-1939* (Nashville, TN: Vanderbilt University Press, 2012), 28.

Chapter 2. The Perils of Flamenco in Restoration Spain, 1875–1923

1. March, *Sketches and Adventures*, 227.
2. Ibid., 222–23.
3. A small sample of discussions about the fears and joys brought about by the rise of mass culture in industrial Paris and London include Peter Bailey, *Popular Culture and Performance in the Victorian City* (Cambridge: Cambridge University Press, 2003); Charles Rearick, *Pleasures of the Belle Epoque: Entertainment and Festivity in Turn-of-the-Century France* (New Haven, CT: Yale University Press, 1985); Vanessa R. Schwartz, *Spectacular Realities: Early Mass Culture in Fin-de-siècle Paris* (Berkeley: University of California Press, 1998); Judith R. Walkowitz, *City of Dreadful Delight: Narratives of Sexual Danger in Late-Victorian London* (Chicago: University of Chicago Press, 2011); Judith R. Walkowitz, *Nights Out: Life in Cosmopolitan London* (New Haven, CT: Yale University Press, 2012).
4. Archilés and García Carrión, "En la sombra del estado," 483–84.
5. Mary Vincent, *Spain 1833-2002: People and State* (Oxford: Oxford University Press, 2007), 120.

6. For recent historiography on caciquismo, see Javier Moreno-Luzón, "Political Clientelism, Elites, and Caciquismo in Restoration Spain (1875–1923)," *European History Quarterly* 37, no. 3 (2007): 417–41.

7. For moral panics and social purity movements in Britain, see Jeffrey Weeks, *Sex, Politics and Society: The Regulation of Sexuality since 1800*, 2nd ed. (London: Longman, 1989), 81–95. For an extensive discussion and citation of works on prostitution and its meanings in a cross-cultural context, see Timothy J. Gilfoyle, "Prostitutes in History: From Parables of Pornography to Metaphors of Modernity," *American Historical Review* 104, no. 1 (February 1999): 117–41.

8. Universal manhood suffrage existed on the books from 1890 on, but it was merely a Potemkin suffrage, whereby elections were decided in advance, and the *caciques* (party bosses), in the rural areas especially, made sure that the votes needed in Madrid were delivered by patronage, creative fraud, or threats of violence.

9. For a discussion of the constitutional protections accorded to the Church, see F. Lannon, *Privilege, Persecution, and Prophecy: The Catholic Church in Spain, 1875–1975* (Oxford: Clarendon Press, 1987), 3. Julio Cueva Merino argues that although the liberal response to the Catholic Church was pretty mild during the Restoration, the vocal anticlericalism in the public sphere alarmed and led to the mobilization of Spanish Catholics after 1901. Julio Cueva Merino, "Cultura y movilización en el movimiento católico de la Restauración (1899–1913)," in *La cultura española en la Restauración (I encuentro de historia de la Restauración)*, ed. Manuel Suárez Cortina (Santander: Sociedad Menéndez Pelayo, 1999), 183. See also Enrique Sanabria, *Republicanism and Anticlerical Nationalism in Spain* (New York: Palgrave Macmillan, 2009).

10. F. Lannon, *Privilege, Persecution, and Prophecy*, 146–47; Julio Cueva Merino, "Cultura y movilización," 183–89.

11. F. Lannon, *Privilege, Persecution, and Prophecy*, 146–47.

12. For a discussion of the Church's appropriation of the female body for the purposes of re-Christianization in the 1920s and 1930s, see Frances Lannon, "Los cuerpos de las mujeres y el cuerpo político católico: Autoridades e identidades en conflicto en España durante las décadas de 1920 y 1930," *Historia Social* 35 (1999): 65–80.

13. Mary Louise Roberts, for example, discusses France's fin-de-siècle era as a mix of "crisis and amusement" and looks at "the crucial links between the era's cultural crisis and its penchant for performance." Mary Louise Roberts, *Disruptive Acts: The New Woman in Fin-de Siècle France* (Chicago: University of Chicago Press, 2002), 2.

14. One could view this overarching concern with illicit-seeming entertainments as an example of Michel Foucault's characterization of Victorian-era sexuality. For Foucault, instead of sexual repression, what lurked beneath a veneer of Victorian-age prudery was in fact an expansive preoccupation with

and discussion of sexuality in the public sphere, so much so, that institutional forces like the Church and state worked more steadily to regulate and discipline the sexuality of "problematic" people. See Michel Foucault, T*he History of Sexuality*, vol. 1, *An Introduction* (New York: Vintage Books, 1990), esp. 18-23.

15. José Luis Ortíz Nuevo has compiled a number of articles in the Sevillan press about cafés cantantes and their deleterious effect on the public. José Luis Ortiz Nuevo, *¿Se sabe algo?*

16. *Chulos* is too supple a word to translate into English. In the late nineteenth and early twentieth centuries, a chulo was a youth of the lower classes who dressed in flashy clothing and engaged in raucous, gangster-like behaviors that challenged the authority of the dominant classes. As we shall see later in this chapter, however, aristocrats and bohemian bourgeois men appropriated chulo behavior and dress for themselves. The Spanish precursors to the chulos were Madrid's majos and majas of the eighteenth century. Later approximations of the chulo might be the 1940s Zoot Suiters in the United States or the 1950s Teddy Boys in England.

17. "De calamidades," *El Siglo futuro*, January 30, 1884, 3. Although my use of *El Siglo futuro* might seem like too sensational a source to represent mainstream Catholic opinion, its ideas are in line with other more mainstream Catholic publications like *La Unión Católica*. See below for other Catholic-leaning newspapers' and journals' views of cafés cantantes. See also, for example, "Noticias y sucesos," *ABC*, October 1, 1903, 1; Adrián de Loyarte, "La pornografía en España," *ABC*, June 3, 1911, 6.

18. "Crónica de la tarde," *La Unión Católica*, July 10, 1888, 3.

19. "El crimen de anoche," *El Siglo futuro*, May 11, 1895, 3.

20. See definition of *chulo* above. *Achulado* is merely the adjectival counterpart of *chulo*.

21. Interestingly enough, these Catholic critiques about the loss of the father's power in the household sounded very similar to critiques lodged during the same period by anticlerical critics who believed that the priest undermined the father's control over his wife and children. See Sanabria, *Republicanism and Anticlerical Nationalism*, 123-49.

22. "Dónde está el mal." *La Unión Católica*, October 1, 1898, 1.

23. "Sección de polémica," *La Lectura dominical*, September 27, 1896, 618-19.

24. Teofilo Nitram, "El fantasma," *La Lectura dominical*, December 19, 1897, 818.

25. Calls for regulation did not come solely from Catholics and conservatives, as we shall see later in this chapter.

26. For a general discussion of these social purity groups and their attempts at legislation, see Annette F. Timm and Joshua A. Sanborn, *Gender, Sex, and the Shaping of Modern Europe: A History from the French Revolution to the Present Day*, 2nd ed. (London: Bloomsbury Academic, 2016), 96-112.

27. "Los cafés cantantes," *La Unión Católica*, November 28, 1888, 1. This Orden Circular, like all others that came from the Crown, was first published in the *Gaceta* and then reprinted in newspapers.

28. "Ecos de los tribunals," *La Unión Católica*, June 13, 1889, 2.

29. There had been waves of "White Slavery" panic in Europe and North America during this period. Again, they are understood today to be indicative of society-wide anxiety over young unaccompanied women occupying city streets who were now untethered from the social controls of rural communities and who, because of their poverty, were subject to the advances of predatory men with money. See Timm and Sanborn, *Gender, Sex*, 108, and Weeks, *Sex, Politics, and Society*, 92.

30. For a discussion of the arbitrary way the Registro de Higiene was used, see Martín Turrado Vidal, *Policía y delincuencia a finales del siglo XIX* (Madrid: Ministerio del Interior; Dykinson, 2001), 243.

31. "Real Orden Plausible," *El Siglo futuro*, March 17, 1909, 2.

32. The order came out on October 19, 1913, and was published as "Policía de Espectáculos: Nuevo Reglamento," in *El Globo*, November 5, 1913, 3.

33. "Real Orden Plausible," *El Siglo futuro*, March 17, 1909, 2.

34. Ley del Descanso Dominical, March 3, 1904.

35. F. León, "Movimiento social: Ejercicios espirituales para obreros," *La Lectura dominical*, April 3, 1909, 218.

36. Jorge Uría, "La cultura popular en la Restauración: El declive de un mundo tradicional y desarrollo de una sociedad de masas," in *La cultura española en la Restauración*, ed. Manuel Suárez Cortina (Santander: Sociedad Menéndez Pelayo, 1999).

37. "Instituciones y hombres: Real Asociación de las Escuelas Dominicales," *Revista católica de cuestiones sociales* 20, no. 237 (September 1914): 189-90.

38. Ibid., 194.

39. Ibid.

40. Salaün, "La sociabilidad," 145.

41. A good example of this cross-cultural interplay and solidification of a "degenerate" landscape came from the collaboration of Belgian poet Emile Verhaeren and Spanish painter Darío de Regoyos. They traveled around Spain in 1888, commenting on and painting the bleakest parts of Spanish life. Emile Verhaeren and Darío de Regoyos, *España negra* (Madrid: Taurus, 1963).

42. For the best work bringing together the tirades against flamenco and bullfighting, see Sandra Álvarez, *Tauromachie et flamenco, polémiques et clichés: Espagne, fin XIXe-début XXe* (Paris: L'Harmattan, 2007).

43. Authenticity is a really problematic term, but some of these antiflamenquistas, including people like Demófilo, Eugenio Noel, and Benito Pérez Galdós, did write about certain cante jondo performances with admiration. It was their commercialization and the character of the followers of these performances

that really bothered them. For a discussion of this issue, see, for example, Gómez-García Plata, "El género flamenco," 101–24.

44. Eugenio Noel, *Señoritos chulos, fenómenos, gitanos y flamencos* (Córdoba: Editorial Berenice, 2014), 8.

45. See chapter 1 for a discussion of majismo. Steingress disputes this linkage between *majismo* and flamenquismo. He says that the flamenco was not a majo. Instead, "he was a new national representation, a new manifestation of the castizo." Steingress, *Sociología del cante flamenco*, 345.

46. Béla Bartók strove to create a music he deemed national by writing against the dominant idea that "genuine" Hungarian music was that which was composed by "dilettantes of the gentry class and disseminated by Gypsy musicians." Instead, he focused on the music of the peasantry as the source of true Hungarian music. See David Cooper, "Béla Bartók and the Question of Race Purity in Music," in *Musical Constructions of Nationalism: Essays on the History and Ideology of European Musical Culture, 1800–1945*, ed. Harry White and Michael Murphy (Cork: Cork University Press, 2001), 16–32.

47. *El Imparcial*, October 30, 1887, cited in Eugenio Cobo, "Antiflamenquistas antes de Noel," *La Caña: Revista de flamenco* 4 (1993): 5–13.

48. Good discussions of the antiflamenquismo writings of the above-named authors can be found in such works as Álvarez, *Tauromachie et flamenco*; Eugenio Cobo Guzmán, "El antiflamenquismo de Benito Pérez Galdós," *Revista de flamencología* 7, no. 16 (2002); Cobo, "Antiflamenquistas antes de Noel"; García Gómez, *Cante flamenco, cante minero*. More on the antiflamenquista writings of Arenal and Galdós is explored in chapter 5.

49. Sandra Álvarez, "Eugenio Noel 'l'anti-torero, aussi flamenco qu'un torero,'" in *Entre l'ancien et la lézarde (Espagne VIIIe-XXe)*, ed. Serge Salaün, 597–98.

50. Eugenio Noel, *El Flamenco: Semanario antiflamenquista*, April 12, 1914, 5.

51. To get a feeling for his ability to rant about such things, see his column in Eugenio Noel, *El Chíspero*, May 24, 1914, 14–15. Samuel Llano makes a compelling argument that Noel adapted the discourse of degeneration used by criminologists like Cesare Lombroso to define flamenquistas, and especially Gypsies, as sources of national degeneration. Samuel Llano, "Public Enemy or National Hero? The Spanish Gypsy and the Rise of *Flamenquismo*, 1898–1922," *Bulletin of Spanish Studies* 94, no. 6 (2017): 977–1004, https://doi.org/10.1080/14753820.2017.1336363.

52. Noel, *Señoritos chulos*, 24. A very detailed tirade about the *señorito chulo* can be found in the section titled "La epopeya del señorito chulo" (The epoch of the *señorito chulo*), 11–70.

53. Ibid., 52.

54. Ibid., 43.

55. Ibid., 12.

56. Ironically enough, the latifundistas gained their lands (and women) as rewards during the Reconquest of Spain. And perhaps that is Noel's point.

57. Bullfighting was often referred to as "la fiesta nacional." In this case, fiesta can have many meanings: a party, a celebration, a holiday, something that needs to be commemorated.

58. Ibid., 20–22.

59. Ibid., 156.

60. Ibid., 170–71.

61. In fact, he titled one of his book of essays *Pan y toros* (Bread and bulls). Eugenio Noel, *Pan y toros* (Valencia: F. Sempere, 1910).

62. Noel, *El Flamenco*, 14.

63. Ibid., 11–12.

64. Noel, *El Chíspero*, 8.

65. Ibid., 9.

66. The Social Question refers to the ways that all kinds of people—social reformers, politicians, religious figures, etcetera—tried to come to terms with the problems of industrialization, such as working-class unrest, extreme poverty and vast income inequality, and urban slums.

67. Santiago Castillo, *Reformas sociales: Información oral y escrita publicada de 1889 a 1893*, 5 vols., comp. Comisión de Reformas Sociales, Ministerio de Trabajo (Madrid: Centro de Publicaciones, Ministerio de Trabajo y Seguridad Social, 1985).

68. Those questions were numbers 50–53 in all cases.

69. See, for example, the report from the local commission of Alcoy in Santiago Castillo, *Reformes sociales*, vol. 4, 59.

70. "Informe del ingeniero jefe de las minas de Linares, VIII: Condición moral de los mismos," in Santiago Castillo, *Reformes sociales*, vol. 5, 165. An observer in Burgos had similar things to say about the "pernicious influence" of dances in vol. 4, 394.

71. Ibid., vol. 5, 603–4.

72. See, for example, "Guerra al funesto alcohol," *Tierra y libertad*, August 31, 1910, and "Crónica—Algo sobre flamenquismo," *Tierra y libertad*, July 6, 1916. The anarchist magazine *La Revista blanca* showcased the writings and ideas of major European cultural figures of the nineteenth and twentieth centuries. Meant to educate the working classes, it exposed readers to the writings of such diverse people as Karl Marx, Charles Darwin, and Miguel de Unamuno. For a discussion about why the anarchist press avoided talking about flamenquismo, see Carlos Serrano, "Cultura popular / Cultura obrera en España alrededor de 1900," *Historia social*, no. 4 (1989): 28.

73. Álvarez, *Tauromachie*, 208. According to Álvarez, these columns appeared between July 22, 1904, and April 7, 1905.

74. "Las corridas de toros y las tabernas," *El Socialista*, July 22, 1904, 1.

75. See, for example, "¡Abajo las corridas de toros!," *El Socialista*, October 14, 1904, 1.

76. *Vida socialista* ran from 1910 to 1914. According to the Biblioteca Nacional de España's catalog description, the magazine was "considered the first Spanish publication that combined the worker's movement with the intellectual and radical world related to the young socialists." "Vida Socialista," accessed March 16, 2018, http://hemerotecadigital.bne.es/details.vm?q=id:0004065325 &lang=en.

77. J. Alcina Navarrete, "Crónica: Espectáculo nacional," *Vida socialista*, February 11, 1912, 8. *Cupletistas* were not the same as flamenco dancers. The cuplé was another form of entertainment popular in the early twentieth century. It tended to be a bit more risqué than flamenco performances, but it incorporated certain traditional Andalusian and flamenco dances mixed in with a cabaret-like atmosphere. By this period, both the cuplé and flamenco dances could be performed in the same places. For a thorough discussion of the cuplé, see Salaün, *El cuplé*.

78. Alcina Navarrete, "Crónica: Espectáculo nacional," *Vida socialista*, February 11, 1912, 8–9.

79. Ibid., 9.

80. *Los Españoles pintados por sí mismos* (Madrid: I. Boix, 1843). This work was inspired by the French series Les français peints par eux mêmes, *Les Français peints par eux-memes: Encyclopédie morale du dix-neuvième siècle province* (Paris: Curmer, 1841). Other works that followed Los españoles included works on Spanish women, the Portuguese, Latin Americans, etcetera. Cesar Ojeda, "Los españoles pintados por sí mismos," June 18, 2012, http://www.odisea 2008.com/2012/06/los-espanoles-pintados-por-si-mismos.html.

81. *Acción socialista*, August 22, 1914, 7.

82. Thanks to Ana Moreno Garrido for this insight of "fauna" as slang.

83. Flamenco can mean many things in Spanish: a dancer, a flamingo, or a Flemish person.

84. For an analysis of the erotic cultures prevalent in Spain from the end of the nineteenth century until the end of the civil war, see Zubiaurre, *Cultures of the Erotic*.

85. P. Caballero, "Crónica Teatral," *La Lectura dominical*, November 20, 1909, 746.

86. P. Caballero, "Crónica Teatral," *La Lectura dominical*, April 23, 1910, 266.

87. Highlights of the meeting and the "memoria" published for this conference appeared in the magazine *Revista general de enseñanza y bellas artes*. Sometimes it is difficult to differentiate the author's summary of the meeting from his own feelings about pornography, but given that the numerous discussions about the ill effects of pornography during the decades prior to the civil war repeatedly employ the identical arguments, I see little harm in conflating the two.

88. "Campaña contra la pornografía," *Heraldo de Madrid*, April 21, 1911, 2.

89. Pérez Mínguez, "Intereses nacionales: purificando la raza," *Revista general de enseñanza y bellas artes*, May 1, 1911, 2. Although Spaniards cited the proliferation of pornography as the cause of France's depopulation and its consequent military unpreparedness, much of the dialogue in France blamed feminism and women's increased use of contraception for this same problem. See Karen Offen, "Depopulation, Nationalism, and Feminism in Fin-de-Siècle France," *American Historical Review* 89, no. 3 (1984): 648–76.

90. Pérez Mínguez, "Intereses nacionales," 2. This idea that cafes cantantes and other forms of musical entertainment (especially those involving dancing) act as gateways to more "pornographic" pursuits is both implicit and explicit in much of the antipornography literature of this period. See, for example, Manuel Ferrer, "Una reforma necesaria," *Revista católica de cuestiones sociales*, November 1928, 267–69.

91. Pérez Mínguez, "Intereses nacionales," 2–3.

92. The league's manifesto spoke of the "French books and newspaper publications, German postcards, Austrian films," and "Italian card games." Adolfo Buylla et al., "Liga contra la pornografía," *Boletín Oficial Eclesiástico del Obispado de Madrid-Alcalá* 26 (1911): 798.

93. Ibid. Ramiro de Maeztu had thought up the idea of forming an antipornographic league as early as 1907, but it didn't have the success of this one. Zubiaurre, *Cultures of the Erotic*, 10.

94. In fact, according to Salaün, the cuplé reinvigorated flamenco by including flamenco-like, or more specifically, Andalusian numbers, in the musical sets. Salaün makes the distinction, as do others, between flamenquista performances, which he would claim are popular songs and dances that come out of the folk tradition of Andalusia, as opposed to what many flamenco aficionados would call the "authentic" flamenco of the Gypsy, cante jondo tradition. He also argues that the middle classes' focus on the rampant sexuality of these places, besides reflecting a fear of the spread of venereal diseases among the masses, more importantly assumed that this increase in eroticism was also closely linked to the feared proletarian revolutionary ideals; thus they conflated eroticism with revolution in the masses. Salaün, *El cuplé*, 16, 39; Serge Salaün, "La sociabilidad en el teatro (1890–1915)," *Historia Social*, no. 41 (2001): 145.

Part II. Flamenco on the Regional and International Stage

1. See, for example, Celia Applegate, *A Nation of Provincials: The German Idea of Heimat* (Berkeley: University of California Press, 1990); Storm, *The Culture of Regionalism*; Augusteijn and Storm, eds., *Region and State*.

2. Storm, *The Culture of Regionalism*, 6.

3. Ibid., 10; Xosé-Manoel Núñez, "Historiographical Approaches to Subnational Identities in Europe: A Reappraisal and Some Suggestions," in *Region*

and State in Nineteenth-Century Europe: Nation-Building, Regional Identities and Separatism, ed. Joost Augusteijn and Eric Storm (New York: Palgrave Macmillan, 2014), 19.

4. Joost Augusteijn and Eric Storm, "Introduction: Region and State," in *Region and State in Nineteenth-Century Europe: Nation-Building, Regional Identities and Separatism*, ed. Joost Augusteijn and Eric Storm (New York: Palgrave Macmillan, 2014), 1-12; Núñez, "Historiographical Approaches," 19.

5. Augusteijn and Storm, "Introduction: Region and State."
6. Núñez, "Historiographical Approaches," 20.
7. Hroch, *Social Preconditions*.
8. Storm, *The Culture of Regionalism*, 10.

Chapter 3. Flamenco and Catalan Nationalism in Barcelona, 1900-1936

A version of this chapter was first published as an article in *Hispania*. I would like to thank the Consejo Superior de Investigaciones Científicas for allowing me to reprint a revised version here. Sandie Holguin, "'Vergüenza y ludibrio de las ciudades modernas': Los nacionalistas ante el flamenco en Barcelona, 1900-1936," *Hispania* 73, no. 244 (2013): 439-68.

1. Guillermo López, *Barcelona sucia* (Barcelona: Registro de Hygiene, ca. 1900), 55. Paco Villar attributes this quote to articles published in *La Publicidad* on October 26 and September 9, 1901. Paco Villar, *Historia y leyenda del Barrio Chino, 1900-1992* (Barcelona: La Campana, 1996), 42.

2. For the popularity of the café cantante in Catalonia, see Eugenio Cobo, "Los escritores catalanes del siglo XIX ante el flamenco," *Candil* 129 (2001): 3935-51. For the sardana and cants corals, see Stanley Brandes, "The Sardana: Catalan Dance and Catalan National Identity," *Journal of American Folklore* 103, no. 407 (January-March 1990): 24-41; Joan-Lluís Marfany, *La cultura del catalanisme: El nacionalisme català en els seus inicis* (Barcelona: Editorial Empúries, 1995).

3. I am not saying that immigration was a problem, but certainly Catalan industrialists and Catalan nationalists perceived it as such.

4. Modernisme, not to be confused with Modernism, was the local Catalan equivalent of French art nouveau, the British Arts and Crafts Movement, the German Jugendstil, and the Austrian Secession movements.

5. See, for example, Chatfield-Taylor, *The Land of the Castanet*; Edward Hutton, *The Cities of Spain* (New York: Macmillan, 1906); Charles Augustus Stoddard, *Spanish Cities: With Glimpses of Gibraltar and Tangier* (New York: C. Scribner's Sons, 1892).

6. The statistic of 859 people per hectare is for the year 1859. Montserrat Miller, *Feeding Barcelona, 1714-1975: Public Market Halls, Social Networks, and Consumer Culture* (Baton Rouge: Louisiana State University Press, 2015), 67.

7. Villar, *Historia y leyenda*, 18. The journalist Francisco Madrid gave the district the name "Barrio Chino," and it stuck: "Because District Five, like New York, like Buenos Aires, like Moscow, all have their own 'Chinatown.'" Francisco Madrid, "Los bajos fondos de Barcelona," *El Escándalo*, October 22, 1925, 4.

8. Because the names of the streets were written in Castilian and not Catalan for the majority of years between the nineteenth century and 1939, with the brief exception of the years right before the civil war, I have decided to keep the toponyms in Castilian.

9. For works on Cerdà's ideas for the Eixample, see Institut Cerdà, *Cerdà, urbs i territori: Planning Beyond the Urban; A Catalogue of the Exhibition Mostra Cerdà, urbs i territori*, held September 1994 through January 1995, Barcelona (Madrid: Electa; Fundació Catalana per a la Recerca, 1996); Ildefonso Cerdá, *Cerdá: The Five Bases of the General Theory of Urbanization*, ed. Arturo Soria y Puig (Madrid: Electa, 1999).

10. Pere Gabriel, "La Barcelona obrera y proletaria," in *Barcelona, 1888–1929: Modernidad, ambición y conflictos de una ciudad soñada*, ed. Alejandro Sánchez Suárez (Madrid: Alianza Editorial, 1994), 96.

11. C. Ealham, *Class, Culture, and Conflict in Barcelona, 1898–1937* (London: Routledge, 2005), 5.

12. López, *Barcelona sucia*, 17.

13. For two classic works detailing the tumultuous years of Barcelona during the Restoration period, see J. Romero Maura, *La Rosa de Fuego: El obrerismo barcelonés de 1899 a 1909* (Madrid: Alianza, 1989) and Joan Connelly Ullman, *La semana trágica* (Barcelona: Ediciones Ariel, 1972).

14. Villar, *Historia y leyenda*, 23–25.

15. Francisco Hidalgo Gómez, *Carmen Amaya: Cuando duermo sueño que estoy bailando* (Barcelona: Libros PM, 1995), 27.

16. Ibid., 23.

17. Luis Cabañas Guevara, *Biografía del Paralelo, 1894–1934: Recuerdos de la vida teatral, mundana y pintoresco del barrio más jaranero y bellicioso de Barcelona* (Barcelona: Ediciones Memphis, 1945), 7.

18. Pere Gabriel, "La Barcelona obrera y proletaria," in *Barcelona, 1888–1929: Modernidad, ambición y conflictos de una ciudad soñada*, ed. Alejandro Sánchez Suárez (Madrid: Alianza Editorial, 1994), 100.

19. Cabañas Guevara disagreed with this characterization, saying that Montmartre was a moribund place, whereas the Paralelo teemed with life. The Montmartre had a distinctly artistic and bohemian character, the Paralelo an industrial and working-class one. Cabañas Guevara, *Biografía del Paralelo teatral*, 89–91.

20. Oyón, *La quiebra de la ciudad popular*, 339.

21. Gabriel, "La Barcelona obrera y proletaria," 100–101.

22. Hidalgo Gómez, *Carmen Amaya*, 63.

23. Francisco Madrid, *Sangre en Atarazanas*, 7th ed. (Barcelona: n.p., 1926), 67; Villar, *Historia y leyenda*, 128.

24. I am not going to enter the debate on the "authenticity" of any particular music. Aficionados of the day, however, constantly referred to the authenticity or lack of authenticity of a particular place. See, for example, Sebastià Gasch, *Barcelona de nit* (Barcelona: Editorial Selecta, 1957), 69–70; Francisco Hidalgo Gómez, *Como en pocos lugares: Noticias del flamenco en Barcelona* (Barcelona: Carena, 2000); Villar, *Historia y leyenda*, 98.

25. For a particularly good discussion of the cultural geography of the Barrio Chino, see C. Ealham, "An Imagined Geography: Ideology, Urban Space, and Protest in the Creation of Barcelona's 'Chinatown,' c. 1835–1936," *International Review of Social History* 50, no. 3 (2005): 373–97.

26. For a detailed description of the most famous trangressive club in the Barrio Chino, see Paco Villar, *La Criolla: La puerta dorada del Barrio Chino* (Barcelona: Comanegra: Ajuntament de Barcelona, 2017).

27. Adolfo Bueso, *Recuerdos de un cenetista*, 2 vols. (Barcelona: Ariel, 1978), 80–81.

28. Casas del Pueblo were clubs where working-class people could congregate to socialize and learn. The clubs were often equipped with libraries and they often invited speakers to educate their members. *Hurdismo* relates to the mountain territory known as Las Hurdes in Caceres. By the late nineteenth century it was already known to be one of the most destitute places in Spain, marked by a starving population with numerous birth defects and diseases. This region gained even greater notoriety after Luis Buñuel filmed *Las Hurdes: Land without Bread* (1933). Francisco Madrid, "Los bajos fondos de Barcelona," *El Escándalo*, October 22, 1925, 4–5.

29. Villar, *Historia y leyenda*, 42.

30. J. Roca y Roca, "La semana en Barcelona," *La Vanguardia*, July 16, 1899. Cited in Marfany, *La cultura del catalanisme*, 85.

31. Clinton D. Young, "Theatrical Reform and the Emergence of Mass Culture in Spain," *Sport in Society* 11, no. 6 (2008): 630–42. See also Salaün, *El cuplé*. For a discussion of the zarzuela, the cuplé, and other forms of musical entertainment in early twentieth-century Spain, see Serrano and Salaün, *Los felices años veinte*.

32. Josep María Torras i Bages, *La tradició catalana* (Barcelona: Ediciones 62, 1981), 81.

33. Santiago Rusiñol, *Obres Completes* (Barcelona: Biblioteca Perenne, 1947), 485–86, cited in Cobo, "Los escritores catalanes," 3937.

34. See chapter 5 for Rusiñol's involvement in the Concurso de Cante Jondo.

35. For the classic work on the "invention of tradition," see Hobsbawm and Ranger, *The Invention of Tradition*.

36. Catalan nationalists also attacked zarzuelas and the *género chico* for their popularity in Catalonia, but the criticism of that genre seems to be linked much

more to Castilianization and the loss of the Catalan language and is not nearly as tied to vice as is flamenco. The criticism lodged against the zarzuela is less rabid than that against flamenco and the cafés cantantes. Marfany argues—rightly, I think—that the popularity of the género chico and cafés cantantes in Catalonia occurred precisely because Barcelona was the most industrialized area in Spain. Barcelona had the best economic resources to bring in commercial entertainment and the infrastructure to support it. J. L. Marfany, "'Al damunt dels nostres cants...': Nacionalisme, modernisme i cant coral a la Barcelona del final de segle," *Recerques*, no. 19 (1987): 85.

37. Torras i Bages, *La tradició catalana*, 81.

38. Ibid., 83.

39. Josep Armengou, *Nacionalisme català: Idees i pensaments de Mn. Josep Armengou* (n.p.: n.p., 1980), 131. These immigrant women he is referring to were Andalusians and Murcians, as he elaborates on 135-36.

40. López, *Barcelona sucia*, 54, 61-62. See chapter 2 for Noel's comparison.

41. Much of my discussion of the sardanas and orfeóns comes from the works of Joan-Lluis Marfany. He convincingly writes about the sardana as an invented tradition and of the orfeóns as a conduit for creating Catalan national identity. He briefly mentions the antiflamenquismo element of these musical forms, but he does not concentrate on this particular argument. Similarly, Antonio Cobo mentions the rejection of flamenco by Catalan cultural nationalists, but he does not spend much time analyzing why the rejection takes place. Marfany, *La cultura del catalanisme*; Cobo, "Los escritores catalanes"; Marfany, "Al damunt dels nostres cants...," 85. For more general discussions of Catalan nationalism, see Teresa Abelló i Güell et al., *L'època dels nous moviments socials: 1900-1930* (Barcelona: Fundació Enciclopèdia Catalana, 1995); Ramon Amigó i Anglès, Pere Anguera i Nolla and Borja de Riquer i Permanyer, *La consolidació del món burgès: 1860-1900* (Barcelona: Fundació Enciclopèdia Catalana, 1996); Albert Balcells, Geoffrey J. Walker, *Catalan Nationalism: Past and Present* (New York: St. Martin's Press, 1996); Borja de Riquer i Permanyer, *Història, política, societat i cultura dels Països Catalans* (Barcelona: Enciclopèdia Catalana, 1995); Borja de Riquer i Permanyer et al., *Història de la Catalunya contemporània* (Barcelona: Pòrtic, 1999); Josep Maria Fradera, *Cultura nacional en una sociedad dividida: Cataluña, 1838-1868*, trans. Carles Mercadal Vidal (Madrid: Marcial Pons, 2003).

42. For a brief history of Spanish and Catalan folklorists' and musicologists' work in the late nineteenth and early twentieth centuries, especially the work of Felip Pedrell and the research of the Arxiu d'Etnografia i Folklor de Catalunya, see Martí, "Folk Music Studies."

43. I am using the terms *orfeóns* and *cants corals* almost interchangeably. Orfeóns tended to be the places for choirs, and cants corals tends to refer to the kinds of songs—that is, songs sung in a chorus.

44. Marfany, *La cultura del catalanisme*, 307.

45. Borja de Riquer i Permanyer et al., *Història de la Catalunya contemporània*, 146.
46. Balcells, *Catalan Nationalism*, 26; Borja de Riquer et al., *Història de la Catalunya contemporània*, 146; Gabriel, "La Barcelona obrera y proletaria," 92.
47. Marfany, *La cultura del catalanisme*, 308-10. See also Gabriel, "La Barcelona obrera y proletaria," 91-92.
48. Anthony Smith, "The Origins of Nations," in *Becoming National: A Reader*, ed. G. Eley and R. G. Suny (Oxford: Oxford University Press, 1996), 120.
49. Santiago Rusiñol, "Cançons del poble," cited in Eugenio Cobo, "Los escritores catalanes," 3937.
50. Xosé Aviñoa, "El teatre líric català antecedents, desenvolupament i epígons (1894-1908): L'aportació musical, plàstica i literària," *Anales de literatura española* 15 (2002): 223-29.
51. Jascinto E. Tort y Daniel, "Algunas consideracions sobre la música popular," *Butlletí del Centre Excursionista de Catalunya* (July-September 1881): 155, cited in Marfany, "Al damunt dels nostres cants . . . ," 101.
52. Luis G. Urbina, "Estampas de viaje: Ciudades de España," *Cosmopolis*, May 1919, 175. In a more humorous vein, Catalan nationalists were trying to create Catalan cuplés to compete with the popular Spanish ones on the Barcelona stage. Scriptwriter Rossend Llurba advocated for a Catalan cuplé and music hall to combat the idea that Catalans were "a little too austere and given to transcendentalism." Anna Carbonell, "El cuplet català," in *Història, política, societat i cultura dels Països Catalans*, ed. Borja de Riquer i Permanyer (Barcelona: Enciclopèdia Catalana, 1995), 360.
53. Thanks to Clinton Young for the observation that Bretón was from Salamanca.
54. Marfany, *La cultura del catalanisme*, 325.
55. Joan Maragall, "La sardana," *Visions i Cants*, 66, and "Rotos y descosidos, *El diluvio*, II, 52 (June 1, 1907), both cited in ibid., 322.
56. Marfany, *La cultura del catalanisme*, 313; Pere Gabriel, "Sociabilitat de les classes treballadores a la Barcelona d'entreguerres, 1918-1936," in *Vida obrera en la Barcelona de entreguerras, 1918-1936*, ed. José Oyón (Barcelona: Centre de Cultura Contemporània de Barcelona, 1998), 103-4.
57. Bon Jan, "Purificació," *La Renaixensa*, May 14, 1899, cited in Marfany, "Al damunt dels nostres cants . . . ," 32.
58. Hidalgo Gómez, *Como en pocos lugares*.
59. Lluís Millet, "Per què," *Revista músical catalana* 1, no. 1 (January 1904): 1-2.
60. Lluís Millet, "La Sardana," *Revista músical catalana*, no. 25 (September 1905): 181-82. Many thanks to Montserrat Miller for help with that pesky translation.
61. *Ritme*, no. 1 (May 2, 1923): 3.

62. Claudi Fuster i Sobrepere, *Catàleg de la premsa musical barcelonina des dels seus orígens fins el final de la Guerra Civil (1817-1939)* (Barcelona: Arxiu Municipal, 2002) There were six journals named *La sardana*, of varying duration, between 1821 and 1926. Jacinto Torres Mulas, *Las publicaciones periódicas musicales en España (1812-1990): Estudio crítico-bibliográfico; repertorio general* (Madrid: Instituto de Bibliografía Musical, 1991), 733-36. Original titles of the journals listed in the text: *La aurora: Organo de la Asociación de los Coros de Clavé; Catalunya nova; Resorgimento portaveu de la "Unión de Sociedades Corales y Orfeones de Clavé"; Butlletí de l'orfeó de Sants; Orfeó levant; Revista catalana de música; La sardana.*

63. Table reconstructed from Torres Mulas, *Las publicaciones periódicas musicales en España*, 836. Unfortunately, I have not been able to get circulation statistics for these journals.

64. Pére Gabriel argues that Barcelona veered off the path of Castilianization because of the influx of foreigners during and after World War I. Their migration created a cosmopolitan city. Additionally, the repression of Catalan nationalism under Primo bred a resistant Catalan culture that also helped to weaken Castilian culture, especially in the Paralelo. I would make the finer distinction that cosmopolitanism weakened *both* Catalan and Castilian national identity, that one of the signal traits of modernity is the triumph of cosmopolitan identities over more national or regional ones. Gabriel, "La Barcelona obrera y proletaria," 101.

65. Mica Nava, *Visceral Cosmopolitanism: Gender, Culture and the Normalisation of Difference* (New York: Berg, 2007), 5. For more on cosmopolitanism in London, see Walkowitz, *Nights Out.*

66. For a discussion of Primo de Rivera's "authoritarian nationalist project" and his turn toward Andalusia as a symbol of "joyful Spain," see Alejandro Quiroga, *Making Spaniards: Primo de Rivera and the Nationalization of the Masses, 1923-30* (New York: Palgrave Macmillan, 2014), esp. 172-73.

67. In fact, one could draw humorous parallels between the staging of "Little Andalusia" in 1920s and 1930s Barcelona with Luis García Berlanga's 1953 film, *Bienvenido, Mister Marshall.*

68. Bueso, *Recuerdos de un cenetista*, 74.

69. One of the first and most famous of these chroniclers of Barcelona, Alfred de Musset, had never even been to Barcelona. That did not prevent him from writing "Avez-vous vu dans Barcelone une andalouse au teint bruni?" (from the poem "L'Andalouse," 1830). Several Catalan critics found de Musset's words annoying, at the very least. One ventured to say, "Musset's Andalusian Barcelonan has done more damage than a hailstorm." Andreu Avelí Artís, "La llegenda de Barcelona," *L'opinió*, September 22, 1933, 1, 4.

70. Ibid., 4.

71. Paul Morand, "Catalan Night," in *Fancy Goods: Open All Night*, trans. Ezra Pound (New York: New Directions, 1984), 89-90. Originally published as *Ouvert la Nuit* (1922).

72. J. Aiguader i Miró, "La perversitat del districte cinquè," *Mirador*, May 23, 1929, 3.

73. Bueso, *Recuerdos de un cenetista*, 76–77.

74. This was the era of Opera Flamenca, when flamenco began to move away from the cafés cantantes and into bigger arenas such as theaters and bullrings. Contemporary critics (of the 1920s and 1930s) as well as many flamencologists today view the professionalization and "massification" of Opera Flamenca as indicators of flamenco's decline. See, for example, José Blas Vega, "Recorrido por la Barcelona de los cafés cantantes y colmaos flamencos," *La Caña: Revista de flamenco* 25 (1999): 5–20. Gómez García Plata does not view flamenco's flight into mass culture as necessarily a bad thing, since it was the commercialization of the genre that made it possible for it to remain widely popular, even today. La Villa Rosa also seems to have become even more commercialized after Borrull's death in 1926. Gómez-García Plata, "El género flamenco," 121.

75. Josep M. Planes i Martí, *Nits de Barcelona perfils* (Barcelona: Proa, 2001), 69. The essay from which this is taken was originally published in *Mirador*, March 28, 1929, 2. This sentiment is repeated in "Las informaciones de actualidad: Un rincón de Andalucía en Barcelona," *El Escándalo*, March 4, 1926, 4–5.

76. For more discussion of Juana "la Macarrona," see chapter 5.

77. Planes i Martí, *Nits de Barcelona perfils*, 70.

78. For discussions of how tourism is staged, see, for example, Dean MacCannell, *The Tourist: A New Theory of the Leisure Class* (New York: Schocken Books, 1976). Gasch tells people who want an authentic flamenco experience to bypass the Villa Rosa because it is really a cabaret organized for tourists and turns everything into a kitschy españolada. Gasch, *Barcelona de nit*, 70. *Españolada* is the general term used to describe entertainments that deal in overwrought stereotypes of Spaniards and Spanish national character, which were most often based on some kind of Andalusian identity.

79. Bueso, *Recuerdos de un cenetista*, 77–79. These kinds of "performances" could also be seen in La Bodega Andaluza and Un Rincón de Andalucía.

80. The Pueblo Español was "115 interconnected examples of Spanish vernacular and monumental architecture." Jordana Mendelson, *Documenting Spain: Artists, Exhibition Culture, and the Modern Nation, 1929–1939* (University Park: Penn State University Press, 2005), 4. It still stands today at the former site of the 1929 Exposition.

81. For discussions of how plans changed for the Pueblo Español and how competing discourses of Spanish and Catalan nationalisms were hashed out, see Robert A. Davidson, *Jazz Age Barcelona* (Toronto: University of Toronto Press, 2009), and Mendelson, *Documenting Spain*, 1–38.

82. "El Pueblo Español," *Diario Oficial de la Exposición Internacional, Barcelona 1928*, May 24, 1929.

83. Mendelson, *Documenting Spain*, 17.

84. Planes i Martí, *Nits de Barcelona*, 141.

85. Mario Bois, *Carmen Amaya o la danza del fuego* (Madrid: Espasa Calpe, 1994), 38. For a more recent discussion of Carmen Amaya's life and a gorgeous catalog of flamenco images from the World's Fair, see Montse Madridejos Mora, *Carmen Amaya* (Barcelona: Edicions Bellaterra, 2013); Montse Madridejos Mora and E. Martín Corrales, *El flamenco en la Barcelona de la Exposición Internacional 1929–1930* (Barcelona: Bellaterra, 2012).

86. Gasch, *Barcelona de nit*, 70.

87. Planes i Martí, *Nits de Barcelona*, 141.

88. "Relativo a la Semana Andaluza," Exposition 1929, Fiestas-Actos Varios 47167, Arxiu Municipal de Barcelona. The idea of the Organizing Commission of Andalusia Week in the Exposition of Barcelona and the Catalan Week of the Exposition of Seville was to have a cultural exchange between both regions and take advantage of the popularity of both expositions.

89. For more discussion of Carmen Amaya, see Bois, *Carmen Amaya*.

90. Hidalgo Gómez, *Como en pocos lugares*, 208. For a more specific discussion of the various people who performed in flamenco theaters and benefit concerts in Barcelona during the war, see Eloy Martín Corrales, "Flamenco en la Barcelona revolucionaria: Julio de 1936–mayo de 1937," *Candil* 129 (2001): 3983–97.

91. Hidalgo Gómez, *Como en pocos lugares*, 212. This process is explored in part III.

Chapter 4. The Marriage of Flamenco, Politics, and National Liberation, 1914–1936

1. Isidro de las Cagigas, "Apuntaciones para un estudio del regionalismo andaluz," part 2, *Bética*, October 5, 1914.

2. It was published in three parts, issues 16–18, on September 20, October 5, and October 20, 1914.

3. This portrayal of Andalusia as a beautiful woman is not so far off the mark. Foreigners who wrote travel narratives about Andalusia almost always portrayed Andalusian women as dark-haired beauties. One decade after this speech, dictator Miguel Primo de Rivera's propaganda expanded this stereotype of Andalusian women to encompass all of Spain. As Alejandro Quiroga writes, "*Primoriverrista* propaganda represented Spain as a joyful and beautiful Andalusian young lady." Quiroga, *Making Spaniards*, 172.

4. For an example of an Andalusian regional nationalist who categorically rejected these stereotypes, see the essay by José María Izquierdo in Manuel Ruiz Lagos, *Ensayistas del mediodía (Mentalidades e ideologías autóctonas andaluzas en el periodo de entreguerras)* (Seville: Biblioteca de la Cultura Andaluza, 1985), 153. For a general discussion of Andalusian regional nationalism in this period, see Universo andalucista, "Mario Méndez Bejarano," accessed January 2, 2017, http://universoandalucista.blogspot.com/2011/02/mario-mendez-bejarano .html; Eric Calderwood, "'In Andalucía, There are No Foreigners': Andalucismo

from Transperipheral Critique to Colonial Apology," *Journal of Spanish Cultural Studies* 15, no. 4 (2014): 399–417; José Manuel Cuenca Toribio, "La primera etapa del andalucismo," in *Espacio, tiempo, y forma: Historia contemporánea* (Madrid: UNED, Facultad de Historia y Geografía, 1993), 377–92; Matthew Machin-Autenrieth, *Flamenco, Regionalism and Musical Heritage in Southern Spain* (London: Routledge, 2017); M. T. Newton, "Andalusia: The Long Road to Autonomy," *Journal of Area Studies* (Series 1) 3, no. 6 (1982): 27–32.

5. I obviously do not believe in essences as analytical categories. I am trying to use the language and ideas of the day to flesh out the author's meanings.

6. Excerpt from Mario Méndez Bejarano, in Ruiz Lagos, *Ensayistas del mediodía*, 47.

7. This idea falls right in line with how Eric Storm characterizes the development of regionalist cultures between 1880 and 1945. Regionalist cultures remained "organically connected to the broader fatherland" and they really represented "a new phase in the nation-building process as most 'new' regional identities supplemented the existing national identities by vastly broadening the national heritage and by providing it with local roots." Storm, *The Culture of Regionalism*, 10.

8. Cuenca Toribio, "La primera etapa del andalucismo," 377.

9. Much of what is discussed here about Andalusian regional nationalism comes from Juan Antonio Lacomba's introduction to Blas Infante, *El ideal andaluz* (Madrid: Tucar Ediciones, 1976), 21–34.

10. For conditions of rural laborers in southern Spain, see Adrian Shubert, *A Social History of Modern Spain* (London: Routledge, 1996), chap. 2. For the intellectual roots of Spanish anarchism, see Antonio Elorza, *Anarquismo y utopia: Bakunin y la revolución social en España (1868–1936)* (Madrid: Ediciones Cinca, 2013); George Richard Esenwein, *Anarchist Ideology and the Working-Class Movement in Spain, 1868–1898* (Berkeley: University of California Press, 1989).

11. Richard Alan Nelson, "George, Henry (1839–1897)," in *Encyclopedia of Business Ethics and Society*, ed. Robert R. W. Kolb (Thousand Oaks, CA: Sage, 2008), 992–93.

12. Ruiz Lagos, *Ensayistas del mediodía*, 47.

13. Ibid., 48–49.

14. Ibid., 68. See chapter 5 for my discussion of the Concurso de Cante Jondo.

15. For more information about Cagigas's life and his vision for Andalusia, see Manuel-Enrique Gutiérrez Camacho, *Vida y obra de Isidro de las Cagigas* (Seville: Fundación Blas Infante, 2007).

16. Isidro de las Cagigas, "Apuntaciones para un estudio del regionalismo andaluz," *Bética*, September 20, 1914.

17. Isidro de las Cagigas, "Apuntaciones para un estudio del regionalismo andaluz," part 2, *Bética*, October 5, 1914, 1–4. This idea that Spaniards/Andalusians achieved their "racial strength" through an admixture of many races

instead of through some kind of racial purity gained currency in the late nineteenth century. Joshua Goode explores this phenomenon in his important work *Impurity of Blood*.

18. Isidro de las Cagigas, "Apuntaciones para un estudio del regionalismo andaluz," conclusion, *Bética*, October 20, 1914.

19. *Boletín Oficial de las Cortes Generales, Congreso de los Diputados, VII Legislatura*, no. 448, Serie D: General, 29 November 2002, p. 12, http://www.congreso.es/public_oficiales/L7/CONG/BOCG/D/D_448.PDF.

20. José del Castillo Díaz composed the music for the anthem.

21. Infante, *El ideal andaluz*.

22. Ibid., 48.

23. Ibid., 62.

24. Ibid., 62, 65. Dr. Olóriz y Aguilera's ideas about racial fusion can be found throughout Goode, *Impurity of Blood*.

25. Infante, *El ideal andaluz*, 102.

26. Ibid., 69–102.

27. Ibid., 74–76.

28. All of these ideas can be found throughout ibid.

29. Blas Infante, *Orígenes de lo flamenco y secreto del cante jondo (1929–1933)* (Seville: Junta de Andalucía, Consejería de Cultura, 1980); Blas Infante Pérez, *La verdad sobre el complot de Tablada y el estado libre de Andalucía* (Seville: Junta Liberalista de Sevilla, 1979).

30. Infante Pérez, *La verdad sobre el complot*, 44.

31. Ibid., 63–65.

32. Interestingly enough, there is little discussion of the Jewish expulsion here and he does not seem to credit them in the development of flamenco music. Contrast that with Cagigas, who believed that Andalusia held a great debt to the cultural influences of the Jews—so much so, that he wanted to repatriate Sephardic Jews back to Spain.

33. Infante Pérez, *La verdad sobre el complot*, 77.

34. Infante, *Orígenes de lo flamenco*, 14.

35. Ibid., 18.

36. Ibid., 22. Infante differs from someone like Adorno, however, in that he does not disparage popular music the way Adorno does.

37. Ibid.

38. Ibid., 27–35.

39. Ibid., 35.

40. Ibid., 39.

41. Infante explores many versions of this thesis in this work, but covering them all would lead to a kind of mind-numbing repetition. Some included Flemish people and gitanos who traveled into North Africa and then into Spain, or into Bohemia and then into Spain. Or, one of my favorites: the gitanos imitated the dress of Charles I's courtiers—again associated with Flanders—and their

clothing became known as flamenco clothing. My version is a distillation of these various theories. The numerous permutations of the Flanders theory can be found in ibid., 39-75.

42. Ibid., 47, 49.

43. Even in English, I have been astounded by the number of people who have come up to me to say some variant of, "Oh, have you seen any flamingo dances lately?"

44. Infante, *Orígenes de lo flamenco*, 56.

45. Ibid., 61.

46. Ibid., 68.

47. Ibid., 72. He also castigates the musicologist and zarzuela composer Francisco Asenjo Barbieri for trying to argue a variant of Pedrell's thesis. See p. 75.

48. Ibid., 73-74.

49. Ibid., 75.

50. Ibid., 76.

51. Infante Pérez, *La verdad sobre el complot*, 65.

52. Infante, *Orígenes de lo flamenco*, 88-89.

53. Ibid., 91-92.

54. For a brief description of Wagner's contributions to modern opera, see Barry Millington, "(Wilhelm) Richard Wagner," in *The New Grove Dictionary of Opera*, vol. 4, ed. Stanley Sadie (London: Macmillan, 1992), 1054-84.

55. Infante, *Orígenes de lo flamenco*, 100.

56. For a brief description of Krausism and its effect on intellectuals in the nineteenth and twentieth centuries, see Sandie Holguín, *Creating Spaniards: Culture and National Identity in Republican Spain* (Madison: University of Wisconsin Press, 2002), 20-23. For a discussion of Krausism's effects on flamenco, especially in Demófilo's work, see Washabaugh, *Flamenco Music* (London: Routledge, 2016), 55-62.

57. Infante, *Orígenes de lo flamenco*, 108. This discussion of the various palos for cante and baile that belong to the flamenco genre extends for some twenty to twenty-five pages.

58. Ibid., 125. Although Gerhard Steingress's histories and analyses of flamenco are some of the finest around, his distinction between Andalusian and flamenco ones is equally obtuse: according to him flamenco was Andalusian music that had been "Gypsified." Steingress, *Sociología del cante flamenco*, 129-30.

59. Infante, *Orígenes de lo flamenco*, 128-29.

60. Ibid., 139.

61. Ibid., 145-46.

62. Ibid., 146-50.

63. Ibid., 150.

64. Ibid., 157.

65. Ibid., 162-67.
66. The *felamengu*/flamenco connection has been debunked by most contemporary scholars of flamenco.
67. Infante, *Orígenes de lo flamenco*, 166-67.
68. Mitchell, *Flamenco Deep Song*, 53.
69. Infante, *Orígenes de lo flamenco*, 152-53.

Chapter 5. Spain on Display Abroad and at Home, 1867–1922

1. Julien Tiersot, *Musiques pittoresques: Promenades musicales à l'Exposition de 1889* (Paris: Librairie Fischbacher, 1889), 71.
2. For a good discussion of the debates surrounding the españolada overkill at the numerous Parisian Expositions between 1855 and 1900, see Luis Sazatornil Ruiz and Ana Belén Lasheras Peña, "París y la españolada: Casticismo y estereotipos nacionales en las Exposiciones Universales (1855-1900)," *Mélanges de la Casa de Velázquez* 35, no. 2 (2005): 265-90.
3. See, for example, Fauser, *Musical Encounters*; Bjarne Stoklund, "The Role of the International Exhibit in the Construction of National Cultures," *Ethnologie Europaea* 24, no. 1 (1994): 35-44; Mauricio Tenorio-Trillo, *Mexico at the World's Fairs: Crafting a Modern Nation* (Berkeley: University of California Press, 1996).
4. Most International Expositions had a government-sponsored guide to the nation's exhibits at the fair. These guides generally excluded entertainment. See, for example, Comité Ejecutivo de España en la Exposición Universal de París, *Catálogo de la sección española en la Exposición Universal de París de 1889* (Paris: Chaix, 1889); Comisión General de España, *Catálogo de la Exposición Universal de Chicago de 1893* (Madrid: Ricardo Rojas, 1893).
5. See, for example, Pougin's account of how the Gitanos de Granada came to perform in 1889. Arthur Pougin, *Le théâtre à l'Exposition universelle de 1889: Notes et descriptions, histoire et souvenirs* (Paris: Librairie Fischbacher, 1890), 104-5.
6. The relationship between tourism and flamenco in nontraditional areas is covered in chapter 7.
7. My choice of exhibition locations was limited by geographical and linguistic concerns as well as by the paucity of source material about Spanish entertainment available for these fairs. While it would make sense to discuss the World's Fairs held on Spanish soil, the 1888 and 1929 Expositions in Barcelona have already been dissected in chapter 3.
8. Paul Greenhalgh, *Ephemeral Vistas: The Expositions Universelles, Great Exhibitions, and World's Fairs, 1851–1939* (Manchester: Manchester University Press, 1988), 3-6.
9. Paul Greenhalgh notes, "In 1851 the only real elements identifiable specifically as mass entertainment, apart from refreshment facilities, were concerts

given by orchestras and brass bands. By 1890 the situation had dramatically changed." Ibid., 41-42. The bulk of the following account of the history of entertainment at the fairs comes from ibid., 41-47.

10. European nations rejected spaces for pavilions in the park outside the Exhibition Hall; therefore, Parisian organizers invited non-European nations to construct buildings "in their indigenous architectural styles." Volker Barth, "Paris 1867," in *Encyclopedia of World's Fairs and Expositions*, ed. John J. E. Findling and Kimberly K. D. Pelle (Jefferson, NC: McFarland, 2008), 42.

11. Ibid.

12. Greenhalgh, *Ephemeral Vistas*, 42.

13. R. Reid Badger, "Chicago 1893," in *Encyclopedia of World's Fairs and Expositions*, ed. John J. E. Findling and Kimberly K. D. Pelle (Jefferson, NC: McFarland, 2008), 119-20.

14. "Conservative estimates in 1908 suggested every million visits to the Franco-British Exhibition generated three million pounds business for the hotels, transport systems, restaurants and post-offices of London." Greenhalgh, *Ephemeral Vistas*, 48.

15. "More of the Great Show at Paris," *Harper's New Monthly Magazine*, November 1, 1867, 787.

16. Carlos Frontaura y Vázquez, *Viaje cómico a la Exposición de Paris* (Madrid: Administración de El Cascabel, 1867), 192.

17. Ventura Ruiz Aguilera, "Revista de la semana," *El Museo Universal* 48 (1866): 378, cited in Sazatornil Ruiz and Lasheras Peña, "París y la españolada," 279.

18. Frontaura y Vázquez, *Viaje cómico*, 250.

19. Ibid., 199-201.

20. Descriptions of the façade can be found in World Fair, Exposition Universelle, *Guide de visiteur a l'Exposition Universelle de 1878: Itinéraire en huit et en quatre jours objets remarquables a visiter* (Paris: Chaix, 1878); Ángel Fernández de los Ríos, *La Exposición Universal de 1878: Guía-itinerario para los que la visiten, descripción razonada rara los que no hayan de verla, recuerdo para los que la hayan visto* (Madrid: English y Gras, 1878); Paris Glücq, *L'album de l'Exposition* (Paris: [Glücq], 1878); Josep Yxart and Rosa Cabré, *La descoberta de la gran ciutat, París, 1878* (Tarragona: Institut d'Estudis Tarraconenses Ramon Berenguer IV, 1995).

21. Yxart and Cabré, *La descoberta de la gran ciutat*, 34.

22. Clovis Lamarre and L. Louis-Lande, *L'Espagne et l'Exposition de 1878* (Paris: Librairie Ch. Delagrave, 1878), 206.

23. *Pandereta* literally means "tambourine," but it is shorthand for the image of Spain created by and for tourists. It is closely related to the term *españolada*. In other words, *pandereta* refers to the tired clichés used to represent Spain.

24. For a discussion of this little-known failed exhibition in London, see Kirsty Hooper, "A Tale of Two Empires? The Earl's Court Spanish Exhibition

(1889)," *Modern Languages Open* (2014), https://doi.org/10.3828/mlo.voi1.5. A list of entertainments at this exhibition can be found in Spanish Exhibition, *The Spanish Exhibition, 1889: Official Daily Programme of Music and Entertainments* (London: Waterlow & Sons, 1889).

25. M. Montejo, "Letter to Don Segismundo Moret," April 30, 1888, Ministerio de Asuntos Exteriores, Sección Exposiciones y Concursos, H3213. This archive no longer exists as such. Archival material from the MAE was transferred to the Archivo General de la Administración in Alcalá de Henares. I have not been able to discover how the material has been organized in its new resting place.

26. *Pro Forma Prospectus, 1889, The Spanish Exhibition in London*, Exposiciones y Concursos, H3213 (1888): Ministerio de Asuntos Exteriores, Sección Exposiciones y Concursos, H3213. This archive no longer exists as such. Information has been transferred to the AGA, but I do not know how it has been classified now.

27. Hooper concludes, "The Earl's Court Spanish Exhibition of 1889 was a financial, political, and commercial failure for its stakeholders, both Spanish and British." Hooper, "A Tale of Two Empires?" This online source is not paginated. This quotation is from the conclusion.

28. One could argue that Paris's 1937 Exposition made Spain even more famous, given the displays created by Pablo Picasso, Joan Miro, and Josep Renau to attract sympathy for Republican Spain during the civil war, but entertainment, although evident in displays of folk dancing, was less important than the graphic arts on display. For a discussion of the Spanish Pavilion in 1937, see Catherine Blanton Freedberg, *The Spanish Pavilion at the Paris World's Fair* (New York: Garland, 1986); Mendelson, *Documenting Spain*, chap. 5.

29. Fauser, *Musical Encounters*, 6–7, 15.

30. Ch. G., "La Musique à l'Exposition,' *L'Art musical* 28 (1889): 75, cited in ibid., 7.

31. The illustrations by Drum focus on the fiery female dancers and present an odd picture of a female matador, although there is no evidence that there were any female matadors at the exposition. In another cartoon he denigrates the male dancer as having little grace and shows him posing in what one might consider a feminine posture. Bac compares the female dancers to the Javanese dancers . . . and to snakes.

32. Ibid., 16. Fauser makes the argument that "the French presentation and reception of music at and around the Exposition Universelle mirrored, focused, and amplified cultural concerns in France in the late 1880s and contributed to the shaping of the performance of, and critical debate about, music in the subsequent decade" (12). Given that the 1889 Exposition commemorated the one-hundred-year anniversary of the French Revolution, the Spanish monarchy declined to fund or publicly endorse Spanish participation in the fair, lest the Spanish government appear to endorse revolution or a Republic. Still, there was enough pressure from various Spanish chambers of commerce across the

nation to maintain a presence at the exposition. In the end, a conglomeration of businesses, regional industries, and private citizens funded a pavilion and a variety of exhibits. This explains why Spain still played such a prominent role in this exposition. Ana Belén Lasheras Peña, "España en París la imagen nacional en las Exposiciones Universales, 1855-1900" (PhD diss., Universidad de Cambria, 2010), 301-6.

33. The Programs of Major Foreign Concerts at the Trocadéro can be found in Fauser, *Musical Encounters*, 321-330; for Spain, see 326-28.

34. Ibid., 256, 264.

35. I was able to discover the full names of the following people from the Flamencas por Derecho website (flamencasporderecho.com): José Arce Durán (El Chivo) and his three daughters, Soledad Arce, Matilde Arce, and Viva Arce; and Antonio de la Rosa Pichiri (El Pichiri). Juana Vargas (Juana la Macarrona) was already famous by the time of the exposition.

36. These names come from Arthur Pougin's account. Pougin, *Le théâtre*, 105-6.

37. Tiersot, *Musiques pittoresques*, 72-73; Pougin, *Le théâtre*, 108.

38. F. G., "Au pays des gitanas," *Le Gaulois*, July 14, 1889, 3.

39. Pougin, *Le théâtre*, 105-6.

40. Paul Margueritte, "Gitanas et druses," in *L'Exposition de Paris (1889), publiée avec la collaboration d'écrivains spéciaux: Édition enrichie de vues, de scènes, de reproductions d'objets d'art, de machines*, ed. Exposition Universelle de 1889 (Paris: La Librairie illustrée, 1889), 7.

41. Ibid. The term *almées* became a French synonym for belly dancers.

42. For an example of this process, see Mrinalini Sinha, *Colonial Masculinity: The "Manly Englishman" and the "Effeminate Bengali" in the Late Nineteenth Century* (Manchester: Manchester University Press, 1995).

43. G. Lenôtre, "Courrier de l'Exposition," *Le monde illustré*, August 31, 1889, 131.

44. "Au pays des gitanas," *Le gaulois*, July 14, 1889, 3.

45. "L'Exposition: Chronique du Champ de Mars," *Le petit journal*, July 14, 1889, 2.

46. El Chivo and his daughters were actually from Seville. All had a history of traveling in the professional flamenco circuit. El Chivo had been dancing professionally since the 1870s. See Ángeles Cruzado, "Soledad Arce, la estrella de las Gitanas de la Exposición (I) | Flamencas por derecho," accessed October 15, 2017, www.flamencasporderecho.com/soledad-arce-i/.

47. See, for example, Margueritte, "Gitanas et druses," 7. Fauser notes that there were numerous performers from the Middle East and the Sudan, almost all of them lumped together as Arab. Performers included Egyptians, Sudanese, Algerians, and Moroccans. She also argues that French organizers, spectators, and critics spent much of the 1889 Exposition trying to define that which was authentic. Fauser, *Musical Encounters*, 231-35, 12-13.

48. Ibid., 165-95.

49. Ibid., 236-37.

50. F. G. from *Le gaulois* remarked on how the Gypsies arrived "in a straight line" from Granada, the women incarnating a modern version of Victor Hugo's Gypsy, Esmeralda, performing as they do in "all the cities of Spain." "Au pays des gitanas," *Le gaulois*, July 14, 1889, 3.

51. She remarked that "Spain does not distinguish itself with its industry." Emilia Pardo Bazán, "Cartas sobre la Exposición," *La España moderna* 1, no. 8 (August 1889): 146. Similar complaints about the flamenquismo of the performance and its spectators can also be found in IOB, "Crónicas de la Exposición de París," *La ilustración española y americana*, July 15, 1889, 19-22.

52. Pardo Bazán, "Cartas sobre la Exposición," October 1889, 94.

53. See Ríos Ruiz, vol. 2, 216.

54. Emilia Pardo Bazán, "Cartas sobre la Exposición," *La España moderna* 1, no. 10 (Oct. 1889): 94-98.

55. Benito Pérez Galdós, *Las cartas desconocidas de Galdós en "La Prensa" de Buenos Aires*, ed. and trans. William Hutchinson (Madrid: Ediciones Cultura Hispánica, 1973), 364.

56. Ibid., 366.

57. Fyodor Dostoevsky, *Notes from the Underground*, trans. Constance Garnett (New York: Dover, 1992), 60-68.

58. José de Castro y Serrano, "Paris en '89: La España flamenca," *La ilustración española y americana*, October 30, 1889, 246-47. This piece was later reprinted by the *antiflamenquista* extraordinaire Eugenio Noel in his short-lived newspaper, *El chíspero*. Eugenio Noel, *El chíspero*, May 24, 1914, 2-4.

59. Castro y Serrano, "Paris en '89, 246.

60. See chapter 4 for a discussion of Andalusian regionalism and Islamic culture and history.

61. Ibid.

62. "Airs of Other Days: Early Spanish Music and Instruments to Be Reproduced," *Chicago Daily Tribune*, April 2, 1893, 39.

63. Arie Sneeuw found one reference in *La Época*, June 4, 1893. Sneeuw, *Flamenco en el Madrid*, 55-56. My research through archives and newspapers found nothing that confirmed that this group ever performed there.

64. *The Moorish Palace and Its Startling Wonders*.

65. Some of the following account comes from Sazatornil Ruiz, Belén Lasheras Peña, "París y la españolada: Casticismo y estereotipos nacionales en las exposiciones universales (1855-1900)," *Mélanges de la Casa de Velázquez* 35 (2005): 279-81, but I came to some of the conclusions independently through other sources.

66. Announcement of his award can be found in *La ilustración española y americana*, no. 23 (June 22, 1900): cover and p. 359.

67. Official descriptions can be found in French and English. See, respectively, *Guide illustré du Bon marché: L'Exposition et Paris au vingtième siècle* (Paris:

P. Brodard, 1900), 120 and *Harper's Guide to Paris and the Exposition of 1900* (London: Harper & Brothers, 1900), 184.

68. Alfonso de Mar, "Paris y la Exposición: Impresiones a vuela pluma," *Hispania* 29 (1900): 137–138, cited in Sazatornil Ruiz and Belén Lasheras Peña, "París y la españolada," 282.

69. Emilia Pardo Bazán, *Cuarenta días en la Exposición* (Madrid: Administración, 1908), 181.

70. Juan Valero de Tornos, *España en París en la Exposición Universal de 1900: Estudio de costumbres sobre Exposiciones Universales* (Madrid: P. Núñez, 1900), 59–60.

71. Ibid., 21.

72. Pardo Bazán, *Cuarenta días en la Exposición*, 48; Valero de Tornos, *España en París*, 63.

73. César Silió Cortés, Angel Guerra, *Otro desastre más (España en París)* (Valladolid: Imp. Castellana, 1900).

74. Ibid., 28, 45.

75. Bartók, however, tried to cleanse any "Gypsiness" from his conception of Hungarian music. Cooper, "Béla Bartók," 16–32.

76. For a look at the importance of flamenco to the European avant-garde, see the catalog that accompanied an exhibit on flamenco and art at the Reina Sofía Museum: Patricia Molins and Pedro G. Romero, eds., *The Spanish Night: Flamenco, Avant-garde and Popular Culture, 1865–1936* (Madrid: Museo Nacional Reina Sofia, 2008).

77. In an interview he did in December 1913, Debussy recalled the spell he fell under when he first heard La Macarrona and Soledad. Claude Debussy, François Lesure, and Richard Langham Smith, *Debussy on Music: The Critical Writings of the Great French Composer Claude Debussy* (Ithaca, NY: Cornell University Press, 1988), 300.

78. Falla said that one could hear in Debussy the germ of music produced by Andalusian guitars and remarked that "Spanish musicians have neglected, including disdained, these effects, considering them as something barbarous." Federico Sopeña, *Manuel de Falla: Escritos sobre música y músicos, Debussy, Wágner, el cante jondo* (Buenos Aires: Espasa-Calpe, 1950), 55. Falla had already begun to incorporate gitano music in *La vida breve* (1905), and it was this composition that caused Debussy to take Falla seriously as a composer. Thanks to Clinton Young for this observation. Much of the discussion of Falla's work with French and Russian composers and their influence on his music can be found in Hess, *Manuel de Falla*.

79. I will continue to use the word "Orient" in this discussion, with all of its Orientalist baggage, because it was the term employed uncritically by all these theorists of cante jondo and flamenco.

80. Jorge de Persia, *I Concurso de Cante Jondo: Edición conmemorativa, 1922–1992: Una reflexión crítica* (Granada: Archivo Manuel de Falla, 1992); Mitchell, *Flamenco Deep Song*, chap. 11.

81. Llano, "Public Enemy or National Hero?
82. Sopeña, *Manuel de Falla*, 140. The ILE was a renowned school founded in 1876 that was meant to be independent from the church and state. It educated generations of Spain's intellectual and artistic elites. For a discussion of the role of the ILE in employing various forms of culture in the service of national regeneration, see Holguín, *Creating Spaniards*.
83. Federico García Lorca, "El cante jondo (primitivo canto andaluz)," 19 February 1922, was reprinted in installments over the end of February and the beginning of March in *El noticiero granadino*. The facsimile of these articles can be found in De Persia, *I Concurso de cante jondo*.
84. Ibid.
85. Ibid. For Falla's "new modality," see Sopeña, *Manuel de Falla*, 125.
86. Sopeña, *Manuel de Falla*, 130–31.
87. Ibid., 49–53, 132–37. García Lorca's "El cante jondo" in De Persia, *I Concurso de cante jondo*.
88. García Lorca, "El cante jondo."
89. For a discussion of the numerous polemics surrounding the contest, see De Persia, *I Concurso de cante jondo*, 28–35.
90. "Professional" was defined as "all those who sing publicly, contracted or paid by entertainment businesses or by individuals." Sopeña, *Manuel de Falla*, 141–45.
91. The spectators and participants on the sidelines read like a Who's Who of Spanish culture and the European avant-garde: the composers and musicologists Manuel de Falla, Adolfo Salazar, Roberto Gerhard, Ángel Barrios, Miguel Salvador, Lamote de Grignon, Conrado del Campo, Enrique Fernández Arbós, Bartolomé Pérez Casas, Joaquín Turina, Federico Mompou, Óscar Esplá, Felipe Pedrell, Andrés Segovia, Igor Stravinsky, and Maurice Ravel; politicians and literati Antonio Gallego Burín, Alfonso Reyes (from Mexico), Hermenegildo Giner de los Ríos, Fernando de los Ríos, Miguel Cerón, José María Rodríguez Acosta, Ignacio Sánchez Mejías, Federico García Lorca, Juan Ramón Jiménez, Ramón Pérez de Ayala, Salvador Rueda, Ramón Gómez de la Serna, Juan de la Encina, Edgar Neville, and Antonio and Manuel Machado; and painters Manuel Ángeles Ortiz, Santiago Rusiñol, and Ignacio Zuloaga. Actual performers were the guitarists Amalio Cuenca, Manuel Jofré ("El Niño de Baza"), and Andrés Segovia, and singers Antonio Chacón, Manuel Torres, Pastora Pavón, "El Centeno," Juana "La Macarrona," Diego Bermúdez, Antonio del Pozo, and Manolo "Caracol." Ramón María Serrera Contreras, "Falla, Lorca y Fernando de los Ríos: Tres personajes claves en el concurso de cante jondo de Granada de 1922" (Real Academia Sevillana de Buenas Letra, 2010), 373–74.
92. See "Moon Phases 1922," accessed April 17, 2017, https://www.calendar-12.com/moon_calendar/1922/july.
93. Timothy Mitchell recounts that story, which he takes from Blas Vega and José Carlos de Luna. None of the research I have conducted on the Great

Exhibition, including keyword newspaper searches, mentions any such person as an entertainer. Mitchell, *Flamenco Deep Song*, 170.
94. Ríos Ruiz, *El gran libro del flamenco*, vol. 2, 65.
95. Mitchell, *Flamenco Deep Song*, chap. 11.
96. Gómez-García Plata, "El género flamenco, 121.

Part III. Flamenco and the Franco Regime

1. José Gamboa cites performer Juanito Valero as an example of somebody who met this ill fate. Gamboa, *Una historia del flamenco*, 278.
2. Information about what happened to flamenco performers during and immediately after the war can be found in ibid., 258-78, and Eloy Martín Corrales, "Flamenco en la Barcelona revolucionaria," 3983-97.

Chapter 6. Rebuilding the Fractured Nation, 1939–1953

1. Regional nationalism was one of the major issues fought over during the Spanish Civil War. Basque and Catalan nationalists wanted autonomy within the Spanish state, and the Catalans achieved it during the Second Republic. The Nationalists rejected regional autonomy and spent the years of the Franco regime suppressing any signs of regional nationalism.
2. For a small sampling of the literature on fascism, culture, and identity outside Spain, see R. Ben-Ghiat, "Italian Fascism and the Aesthetics of the 'Third Way,'" *Journal of Contemporary History* 31, no. 2 (1996): 293-316; Victoria De Grazia, *The Culture of Consent: Mass Organization of Leisure in Fascist Italy* (Cambridge: Cambridge University Press, 2002); Roberto Illiano and Massimiliano Sala, "Italian Music and Racial Discourses during the Fascist Period," in *Western Music and Race*, ed. Julie Brown (Cambridge: Cambridge University Press, 2007), 182-200; Michael H. Kater, "Forbidden Fruit? Jazz in the Third Reich," *American Historical Review* 94, no. 1 (1989): 11-43; George Mosse, "Fascist Aesthetics and Society: Some Considerations," *Journal of Contemporary History* 31, no. 1 (1996): 245-52.
3. The army was the third pillar, but I will not discuss it in this chapter. During the early years of the Franco regime, there emerged an *antipandereta*, *antiespañolada*, discourse, which also explains some of the official attitudes against flamenco. See Zira Box Varela, "Anverso y reverso de la nación: El discurso de la antiespañolada durante los primeros años 40," *Hispania* 75, no. 249 (January-April 2015): 237-66.
4. This expression has been attributed to Oscar Wilde, George Bernard Shaw, and even Robert Frost, but there is no evidence that any of these men actually said these words.
5. For discussions of the Coros y Danzas, see Estrella Casero García, *La*

España que bailó con Franco (Madrid: Editorial Nuevas Estructuras, 2000); Luis Otero, *La Sección Femenina* (Madrid: EDAF, 1999).

6. Benedict XV, *Sacra Propediem*, January 6, 1921, accessed November 1, 2013, http://www.vatican.va/holy_father/benedict_xv/encyclicals/documents/hf_ben-xv_enc_06011921_sacra-propediem_en.html.

7. Conferencia Episcopal Española, "Metropolitanos españoles: Pastoral colectiva sobre la inmodestia de las costumbres públicas, 30 abril 1926," in *Documentos colectivos del episcopado español: 1870-1974*, ed. Jesús Iribarren (Madrid: La Ed. Católica, 1974), 119.

8. Ibid., 121-23. For discussions of the Church's anxieties about modernity in the 1920s and 1930s and how they project that anxiety onto women's bodies, see J. J. Díaz Freire, "La reforma de la vida cotidiana y el cuerpo femenino durante la dictadura de Primo de Rivera," in *El rumor de lo cotidiano: estudios sobre el País Vasco contemporáneo*, ed. Luis Castells (Bilbao: Universidad del País Vasco, 1999), 225-58; Frances Lannon, "Los cuerpos de las mujeres y el cuerpo político católico: Autoridades e identidades en conflicto en España durante las décadas de 1920 y 1930," *Historia social*, no. 35 (1999): 65-80.

9. Díaz Freire, "La reforma de la vida cotidiana," 232-34.

10. *Reseña de la primera Asamblea Contra la Pública Inmoralidad/organizada con carácter nacional por la Liga de Madrid, de acuerdo con la Barcelona y Valencia* (Madrid: Tipografía Católica de Alberto Fontana, 1927) 5, 16. Thanks to Enrique Sanabria for finding this source and providing the requisite information for me. For a preview of what people were supposed to expect from the conference, see Juan de Hinojosa, "Ante un congreso," *Revista católica de cuestiones sociales*, September 1927, 150-54.

11. Manuel Ferrer, "Una reforma necesaria," *Revista católica de cuestiones sociales*, November 1928, 268. As mentioned above, the 1913 law enabled young women in that age bracket to work in these places as long as they had parental permission.

12. "Campaña contra la inmoralidad," *ABC* (Seville), September 22, 1933, 27.

13. For their attempts at campaigns during the Second Republic, see "Campaña contra la inmoralidad (1933-1935)," AC, Section 56-1-6, Junta Técnica Nacional de la Acción Católica. There is evidence that local campaigns for austerity and modesty were held in Seville and Córdoba in 1937. See *ABC* (Seville), July 22, 1937, 14; September 1, 1937, 18; September 9, 1937, 21.

14. For example, José Ortega y Gasset, in his idolatry of Friedrich Nietzsche, had a particular disdain for the "mass man" and his culture. See José Ortega y Gasset, *The Revolt of the Masses*, trans. Kenneth Moore (Notre Dame, IN: University of Notre Dame Press, 1985).

15. Letter from the president of the CEOM to the Secretario del Secretariado Central de Espectáculos de la Junta Nacional de Acción Católica, Madrid, February 20, 1950, AC, 3.101, Espectáculos, Oficina Nacional Permanente de

Espectáculos, archivador 100/serie 1/carpeta 1. *Filmor* and *Ecclesia* had already been publishing during the Republic, but they obviously carried more institutional weight after 1939. CONCAPA also published a weekly newspaper, *Hogar*, which included ratings and reviews of films and plays.

16. Aurora Morcillo has written a great deal about the shaping of gender roles, but especially women's in both the early and late Franco regime. She coined the phrase "True Catholic Womanhood" to describe the ideological precepts by which girls and women should operate under National Catholicism. For the early years of the regime, see Aurora G. Morcillo, *True Catholic Womanhood: Gender Ideology in Franco's Spain* (DeKalb: Northern Illinois University Press, 2000).

17. *ABC* (Seville), July 2, 1939, 5.

18. "Algunos temas a tratar sobre los distintos puntos de la Campaña," Campaña de Austeridad y Modestia, 1939, AC.

19. "Slogans of the Campaña de Austeridad y Modestia, 1939," Campaña de Austeridad y Modestia, 1939, AC.

20. "Encuestas a las Uniones Diocesanas sobre la Campaña de Austeridad y Modestia," in ibid. My tabulations of these results came from looking at twenty-nine of these surveys.

21. Flores del Romeral, *Contra el cine inmoral: La J. F. de A .C. Española—Lo extranjerizante* (Zaragoza: Octavio y Peláez, 1939), 13.

22. See the previous chapter on the place of the cante jondo for the Spanish avant-garde.

23. Flores del Romeral, *Contra el cine inmoral*, 14.

24. Ibid., 16.

25. For Nazis and jazz, see, for example, Kater, "Forbidden Fruit?," 11–43. On racialized language describing flamenco performers, see the previous chapter. On the way that flamenco assimilated aspects of the cakewalk and jazz performed by African Americans, see Goldberg, "Jaleo de Jerez and *Tumulte Noir*," 143–56.

26. Carlos Salicrú Puigvert, *¿Es lícito bailar? Cuestiones candentes acerca de la moralidad pública*, 2nd ed. (Barcelona: La Hormiga de Oro, 1947); Rufino Villalobos Bote and Sebastián Jiménez, *¿Es pecado bailar? ¿No es pecado bailar? Respuesta serena y objetiva a estas apasionantes preguntas de la juventud de hoy* (Badajoz: Secretariado de Propaganda de la Juventud Masculina de Acción Católica, 1948). These arguments about the sinfulness of dancing do not end in the 1940s. One can still find tracts with similar arguments in the 1960s. See Jeremias de las Santas Espinas, *Juventud en llamas: El baile moderno* (Bilbao: Redención, 1965); Vicente Hernández García, *El baile: Moral y pastoral* (Madrid: Studium, 1961).

27. F. A. Vuillermet, Miguel Barquero, *Los Católicos y los bailes modernos*, trans. Miguel Barquero (Barcelona: Eugenio Subirana, 1927).

28. Villalobos Bote and Jiménez, ¿Es pecado bailar?, 27.

29. Salicrú Puigvert, ¿Es lícito bailar?; Villalobos Bote and Jiménez, ¿Es pecado bailar?, 52–53.

30. Villalobos Bote and Jiménez, ¿Es pecado bailar?, 56. The one notable exception to this idea that regional dances were suitable came from Cardinal Segura, the archbishop of Seville, who banned any kind of dancing in his diocese. Ramón Garriga, *El Cardenal Segura y el Nacional-Catolicismo* (Barcelona: Editorial Planeta), 286–87. See his pastoral letter condemning most forms of dance: "Carta pastoral sobre los bailes, la moral católica y la ascética cristiana," *Boletín Oficial Eclesiástico del Arzobispado de Sevilla* 87 (1946): 182–214.

31. These fears were made explicit, too, in the May 1941 Campaign of Austerity and Modesty. Slogans such as "May the jota and innocent dances return. We do not want to turn celebrations into orgies" were de rigueur. Organizers also warned against the "voluptuous feelings" that dance could arouse, especially the modern ones "derived or related to tango and other common American dances." "Asociación de las Jóvenes de Acción Católica: Conclusiones de la Semana de Austeridad y Modestia," Campaña de Austeridad y Modestia, 1941, AC.

32. Puigvert, ¿Es lícito bailar?, 12.

33. Villalobos Bote and Jiménez, ¿Es pecado bailar?, 56; Salicrú Puigvert, ¿Es lícito bailar?, 26.

34. Villalobos Bote and Jiménez, ¿Es pecado bailar?, 61, 63. Their quote is a bit misleading. Pereda argues that in this republic of dance, when the man has the right to wander from woman to woman asking for dance partners, women have the duty to refuse for modesty's sake. He also says that the public plays the role of scandal enforcer instead of husbands or fathers. See "Esbozos: Fisiología del baile," accessed May 10, 2017, https://es.wikisource.org/wiki/Esbozos:_Fisiolog%C3%ADa_del_baile.

35. Villalobos Bote and Jiménez, ¿Es pecado bailar?, 199.

36. Again, this fight against foreignness and modernity was not limited to the Catholic Church and its conservative allies (as discussed in chapters 2 and 3); neither was it limited to Spain. For example, Henry Ford feared that "Negro jazz" and the Jews who funded and promoted jazz music were overrunning the United States and ruining American values. In response, he began a reeducation project in folk dancing and music which, as one author argues, provided the foundation for folk dancing being taught across the country's schools. Emery C. Warnock, "The Anti-Semitic Origins of Henry Ford's Arts Education Patronage," *Journal of Historical Research in Music Education* 30, no. 2 (April 2009): 79–102.

37. José Antonio Primo de Rivera, "Ideas of the Falange," in *Modern Spain: A Documentary History*, ed. John Cowans (Philadelphia: University of Pennsylvania Press, 2003), 167.

38. It is customary to refer to José Antonio and Pilar Primo de Rivera by

their first names, perhaps to distinguish them from their father, the dictator Miguel Primo de Rivera.

39. See Morcillo, *True Catholic Womanhood*; Kathleen, Richmond, *Women and Spanish Fascism: The Women's Section of the Falange, 1934–1959* (London: Routledge, 2003).

40. For a discussion of the role of music, dance, and folklore during the Franco regime, see Martí, "Folk Music Studies," 107–40; Carmen Ortíz, "The Uses of Folklore in the Franco Regime," *Journal of American Folklore* 112, no. 446 (1999): 479–96; Casero García, *La España*.

41. Casero García, *La España*, 23.

42. José Primo de Rivera, "Estatutos de la Sección Femenina," December 1934, accessed November 21, 2018, https://www.scribd.com/doc/83507351/Estatutos-de-la-Seccion-Femenina-1934.

43. Pilar Primo de Rivera, "Discurso de Pilar Primo de Rivera en la III Consejo Nacional de la Sección Femenina de F.E.T. y de las J.O.N.S.," Zamora, 1939, in Pilar Primo de Rivera, *Discursos, circulares, escritos* (Madrid: Sección Femenina de F.E.T. y de las J.O.N.S., 1942), 20.

44. Pilar Primo de Rivera, "La música como unidad," in ibid., 131.

45. Pilar Primo de Rivera, "Discurso de Pilar Primo de Rivera," in ibid., 21. Strangely enough, Pilar did not allow people to sing and dance songs from outside the region where they grew up. Casero García, *La España*, 46.

46. José Antonio Primo de Rivera, "Patria: La gaita y la lira," *Falange española*, January 11, 1934.

47. Beatriz Martínez del Fresno, "Women, Land, and Nation: The Dances of the Falange's Women's Section in the Political Map of Franco's Spain," in *Music and Francoism* (Turnhout: Brepols, 2013), 116.

48. Ibid., 120.

49. Ortíz, "The Uses of Folklore," 488.

50. Of course, much of this research was specious and ill-informed. In fact, the SF knew little about traditional songs and dances of regional Spain. They had to reconstruct many of the dances from the memories of village elders, for many of the Spanish musicologists ended up in exile after the war. The Coros y Danzas also changed some of the clothing of the "authentic" village dances and, in the early years, eliminated men from the dances to protect the women's modesty. See Casero García, *La España*, 63–97.

51. Their roles are discussed briefly in ibid., 47, 54.

52. For the eighteenth and nineteenth centuries, see chapters 1 and 2; for the twentieth century, see chapter 5. For the Misiones Pedagógicas, see Holguín, *Creating Spaniards*.

53. "Las mujeres de la Falange rendirán en Medina del Campo su homenaje al Caudillo y al ejército de España," *Fotos, Revista Nacionalsindicalista*, May 20, 1939, in Luis Otero, *La Sección Femenina*, 26–27.

54. The first series of competitions began on February 27, 1942, and ended

on July 3, 1942. Three Catalan groups won the first national competition. Casero García, *La España*, 48.

55. Pilar Primo de Rivera, *Recuerdos de una vida* (Madrid: Dyrsa, 1983), 249; Casero García, *La España*, 48. No actual date is given for when the sixty thousand people participated.

56. "Primer concurso nacional de Coros y Danzas de la Falange Femenina," *ABC*, June 19, 1942, 12. See also "Concurso Nacional de Cantos y Danzas," *Vértice*, August 1942, n.p.

57. In addition to the examples provided in this chapter, one can look at the collection of NO-DO films put out by the Spanish government to see performances interspersed among other newsworthy items. One film that featured many performances of the Coros y Danzas can be found in A. Macasolí, director, "Danzas españolas," 1955, *NO-DO documentales*, IMAGN544, Filmoteca Española. See also Saturnino Rodríguez Martínez, *El NO-DO: Catecismo social de una época* (Madrid: Editorial Complutense, 1999).

58. Nieves de Hoyos Sancho, "Cantos y bailes españoles," *Vértice*, November 1943, 63.

59. This quotation makes much more sense in Spanish than in English because *historia* means both story and history: "Como lo que ellas hacen no son 'historias,' sino Historia, no les asusta el estudio de las más remotas antigüedades." "El concurso nacional de Coros y Danzas de la Falange Femenina," *ABC*, December 16, 1948.

60. Casero García, *La España*, 49.

61. There and the International Folkloric Festival in Langollen, UK, where three other groups from the Coros y Danzas—from Córdoba, Segovia, and El Ferrol—placed second and third. Luis Suárez Fernández, *Crónica de la Sección Femenina y su tiempo* (Madrid: Asociación "Nueva Andadura," 1993), 217.

62. Primo de Rivera, *Recuerdos de una vida*, 199–200.

63. Ramiro de Maeztu articulated and developed the ideas of Hispanidad most clearly in *Defensa de la Hispanidad*. Ramiro de Maeztu, *Defensa de la hispanidad* (Valladolid: Aldus, 1938).

64. Pilar Primo de Rivera, "Farewell Speech to the First Coros y Danzas Group to Go to Latin America (Given in Cadiz), 1948, Archivo Documental de 'Nueva Andadura.' Cultura. Coros y Danzas, Viajes al Extranjero, 74:1, Cádiz, 1948, RAE.

65. Primo de Rivera, *Recuerdos de una vida*, 201.

66. "El Mundo a través de nuestros corresponsales: ABC en Buenos Aires," *ABC*, May 12, 1948, 13.

67. José María Doussinague, *Carta a Pilar Primo de Rivera, por el Excmo. Sr. D. José Ma. Doussinague con motivo de la visita a tierras de América de los Coros y Danzas de la Sección Femenina* (n.p.: n.p., 1950), 9.

68. Pilar Primo de Rivera, "La música como unidad," in Pilar Primo de Rivera, *Discursos, circulares, escritos*, 131. Dating this article is difficult because

although the publication date on this collection of writings is 1942, the Coros y Danzas had not toured Latin America yet. There is nothing in this piece that tells us to whom she is speaking or where she is speaking, but she uses the informal "you" as if talking directly to Spaniards and Latin Americans. On a lighter but still telling note, Pilar recounted how when the Coros y Danzas landed in Peru, lines of people waited to greet them. A person asked the dancers where they were from, and a dancer said, "From Extremadura." The person replied, "The land of chorizos," and the girl, "without missing a beat, responded, smiling, 'and the Conquistadors!'" Primo de Rivera, *Recuerdos de una vida*, 203.

69. Suárez Fernández, *Crónica de la Sección Femenina*, 217.

70. Casero García, *La España*, 79.

71. The primary source accounts with the most information about the Coros y Danzas are *Bailando hasta el cruz del sur* by Rafael García Serrano, written contemporaneously at the height of the Coros y Danzas fame; Pilar's memoirs, *Recuerdos de una vida*; and Luis Fernández Suárez, *Crónica de la Sección Femenina y su tiempo*. The latter two accounts were written after the end of the Franco regime, and so we have to assume that they are trying to fashion their place in the Franco regime in the most positive light. Contemporary accounts of the Coros y Danzas in the newspaper *ABC* corroborate some of these narratives. Rafael García Serrano, *Bailando hasta la Cruz del Sur* (Madrid: Gráficas, 1953); Primo de Rivera, *Recuerdos de una vida*; Suárez Fernández, *Crónica de la Sección Femenina*.

72. Primo de Rivera, *Recuerdos de una vida*, 202.

73. Ibid. In a letter published in the Falange newspaper *Arriba*, Pilar thanks the Coros y Danzas for their work: "Because of your marvelous grace so many Spaniards absent from the far-away Patria have felt nostalgia for it." *Arriba*, August 8, 1948, cited in Suárez Fernández, *Crónica de la Sección Femenina*, 218. For repression under the Franco regime, see Paul Preston, *The Spanish Holocaust* (London: HarperCollins, 2008).

74. This was part of a speech that Pilar asked Rafael García Serrano to make during the Festival of Music and Dance in Granada, 1952. Cited in Suárez Fernández, *Crónica de la Sección Femenina*, 23.

75. Ibid., 226.

76. Ibid., 232.

77. Michael Richards, *After the Civil War: Making Memory and Re-making Spain since 1936* (Cambridge: Cambridge University Press, 2013).

78. Doussinague, *Carta a Pilar Primo de Rivera*, 14.

79. "Demonstration at Theatre," *Manchester Guardian*, February 20, 1952, 7.

80. John Martin, "Spanish Dancers Give Varied Show: 100 Youths Brought Here for Cancer Benefit Program Entertain at Carnegie," *New York Times*, June 5, 1953, 17.

81. Casero García, *La España*, 52.

82. Primo de Rivera, *Recuerdos de una vida*, 202.

83. When applying for entrance into the United States—that is, before the Base Treaties of 1953 forged an official alliance between the United States and Spain—the Coros y Danzas represented themselves as merely a school of Spanish Dance. Casero García, *La España*, 52.

84. "Script: Spanish Festival Dancers," Aug. 24, 1950, Archivo Documental de "Nueva Andadura." Cultura. Música—Coros y Danzas, 1942-1958, Carpeta 46A, 9-1, RAH.

85. "Dances of Spain," *Times of London*, February 20, 1952, 2.

86. John Martin, "Spanish Dancers Give Varied Show."

87. W. A., "Spanish Group Scores in Program at Shrine," *Los Angeles Times*, June 26, 1953, B7.

88. Given how the wording in these articles are remarkably similar, emphasizing the diversity of Spanish dance, the amateur makeup of the group, and the need to save traditional Spanish song and dance, I have to surmise that the SF, at the very least, handed these newspaper columnists press kits with the germane talking points. See, for example, "La Epoca visita a las componentes de la Embajada artística española," *La época*, April 15, 1948; "Un espectáculo de arte ofreció el conjunto folklórico español," *La nación*, April 16, 1948; "Fue celebrado en el Colón el Cuadro Coros y Danzas de España," *La prensa*, April 16, 1948; "Un folklore puro y limpio espeja el ritmo el color de los coros y danzas populares de España," *Los principios*, May 27, 1948; Dolores de Pedrozo y Sturdza, "Folk Dancing in Spain Today," *Ballet* 12 (1952): 18-22; Faubion Bowers, "The Preservation of the Dance in Spain," *Dance Magazine* 31, no. 4 (April 1952): 18-21; P. Révoil, "Les Choeurs et Danses de la Phalange ont sauve de l'oubli les vieux chants et les danses espagnoles," 1952, Archivo Documental de "Nueva Andadura." Cultura. Musica-Coros y Danzas, 1942-1958, Carpeta 46a, Item #112, RAH.

89. Révoil, "Les Choeurs et Danses."

90. De Pedrozo y Sturdza, "Folk Dancing in Spain Today."

91. Joaquín Juste, Letter from Joaquín Juste to María Victoria Eiroa, (1955). *ABC*, October 3, 2007, called her the cofounder of the SF. AGA (03) 051.023, legajo 60. TOP 23/27.704-28.302 GR 7, No. 1, April 4, 1955.

92. Antonio-Prometeo Moya and Pilar Primo de Rivera, *Últimas conversaciones con Pilar Primo* (Madrid: Caballo de Troya, 2006), 323.

93. Suárez Fernández, *Crónica de la Sección Femenina*, 229.

94. Ibid. Much has been written about the role of cultural exchanges in softening Cold War politics. For a small sampling of such works, especially from the point of view of the United States, see Clare Croft, *Dancers as Diplomats: American Choreography in Cultural Exchange* (Oxford: Oxford University Press, 2015); Walter L. Hixson, *Parting the Curtain: Propaganda, Culture, and the Cold War* (New York: St. Martin's Press, 1996); Naima Prevots, *Dance for Export: Cultural Diplomacy and the Cold War* (Hanover, NH: Wesleyan University Press,

1998); Yale Richmond, *Cultural Exchange and the Cold War: Raising the Iron Curtain* (University Park: Penn State University Press, 2004).

95. Suárez Fernández, *Crónica de la Sección Femenina*, 217.

96. Ibid., 233.

97. Jorge Rock, "Sol de España a través de la niebla londinense: Comentarios de la actuación de los Coros y Danzas de España en Londres," 1952, Archivo Documental de "Nueva Andadura." Cultura. Musica-Coros y Danzas, 1942–1958, Carpeta 46a, Item #19, RAH.

98. See, for example, "Script—Spanish Festival Dancers. Thursday, Aug. 24, 1950," Archivo Documental de "Nueva Andadura." Cultura. Musica-Coros y Danzas, 1942–1958, Carpeta 46a, 9–1, RAH. Elsa Brunelleschi, a dance teacher who studied Spanish dance in Barcelona before working as a teacher at the London Ballet, enjoyed the dances but criticized the program. See Elsa Brunelleschi, "Songs and Dances of Spain: 1," *Ballet* 12 (1952): 26–30.

99. There is one undated program whose production value puts it in the 1950s. A search on WorldCat reveals that this program is found in three libraries in Southern California only, which leads me to believe that it was produced for the limited tour in Southern California in 1950. The second program comes from 1953, and the third from 1965.

100. Falange Española Tradicionalista y de las Juntas Ofensivas Nacional-Sindicalistas, Sección Femenina, *Canciones y danzas de españa* (Madrid: Sección Femenina de Falange Española Tradicionalista y de las J.O.N.S., 1953), introduction.

101. Ibid.

102. Sección Femenina de F.E.T. y de las J.O.N.S., *Songs and Dances of Spain* (Madrid: Vicente Rico, S.A., 1965).

103. Manuel and Antonio Machado, both poets, were the sons of Demófilo, the author of *Colección de cantes flamencos*, covered in chapter 1.

104. Sección Femenina, *Songs and Dances of Spain*.

105. Ibid.

106. Ibid.

Chapter 7. Tourism and the Return of Flamenco, 1953–1975

1. Carlos González Cuesta, "Estudio sobre la propaganda turística y su cuantía de Carlos González Cuesta," 1953, AGA, sección cultura, 49.04, caja 18520.

2. Ibid.

3. In addition to international pressures on the Franco regime, the regime itself practiced economic autarky. For a discussion of autarky as a conscious policy of retribution in the Franco regime, see Michael Richards, *A Time of Silence:*

Civil War and the Culture of Repression in Franco's Spain, 1936–1945 (Cambridge: Cambridge University Press, 1998), and Antonio Cazorla Sánchez, *Fear and Progress: Ordinary Lives in Franco's Spain, 1939–1975* (Chichester: Wiley-Blackwell, 2010).

4. The Franco regime began nurturing its tourism industry with the National Tourism Plan of 1952. For a discussion of the interplay between Francoist political aspirations for Spain and international tourism and travel, see Sasha D. Pack, *Tourism and Dictatorship: Europe's Peaceful Invasion of Franco's Spain* (New York: Palgrave Macmillan, 2006). For an exploration of Spain's cultivation of U.S. tourists through advertising campaigns and Hollywood films, see Neal M. Rosendorf, *Franco Sells Spain to America: Hollywood, Tourism and Public Relations as Postwar Spanish Soft Power* (London: Palgrave Macmillan, 2014).

5. Pack, *Tourism and Dictatorship*, 148–52.

6. Much of the information on the development of tourism in the pre-Franco years comes from Barke and Towner, "Exploring the History of Leisure," 3–34; Ana Moreno Garrido, *Historia del turismo en España en el siglo XX* (Madrid: Síntesis, 2007); Pack, *Tourism and Dictatorship*; Rafael Esteve Secall, Rafael Fuentes García, *Economía, historia e instituciones del turismo en España* (Madrid: Ediciones Pirámide, 2000); Storm, "Una España más española. La influencia del turismo en la imagen nacional," in *Ser españoles: Imaginarios nacionalistas en el siglo XX*, ed. Javier Moreno Luzón and Xosé Manoel Núñez Seixas (Barcelona: RBA, 2013), 530–60.

7. This portion of text from the Royal Decree is cited in Moreno Garrido, *Historia del turismo*, 75.

8. Francisco Javier Sánchez Cantón, *Spain (Divulgation and Propaganda)* (Madrid: Gráficas Reunidas, 1926), 78–79. Of the guidebooks put out by the Patronato Nacional del Turismo, I could not find any that made any mention of flamenco entertainment, not even in the guides for Córdoba or Seville.

9. Jorge Villaverde, a scholar who is currently working on this Sunny Spain Exhibition, was kind enough to share his research with me. The summary of that exhibition comes from his forthcoming dissertation, "Sunny Spain at London, 1914: Creación, negociación y difusión de un imaginario español" (Universitario Europeo de Florencia); Ana Moreno Garrido and Jorge Villaverde, "De un sol a otro: Turismo e imagen exterior española (1914-1984)," *Ayer* (forthcoming).

10. Cited in Moreno Garrido and Villaverde, "De un sol a otro."

11. For the tourism projects of the PNT, see Moreno Garrido, *Historia del turismo*, chap. 6.

12. For nineteenth-century seaside tourism, see John K. Walton and Jenny Smith, "The First Century of Beach Tourism in Spain: San Sebastián and the Playas del Norte from the 1830s to the 1930s," in *Tourism in Spain: Critical Issues*, ed. M. Barke and J. Towner (Wallingford: CAB International), 35–61.

13. *Spain: Make It San Sebastian*, pamphlet/brochure, 1936, Thomas Cook Archives.

14. The Nationalists also took advantage of their military victories by conducting packaged tours for foreigners of battlegrounds they had already conquered. These tours were known as the Rutas de Guerra and were renamed the Rutas Nacionales after the war ended. See Sandie Holguín, "'National Spain Invites You': Battlefield Tourism during the Spanish Civil War," *American Historical Review* 110, no. 5 (2005): 1399–426. See also Moreno Garrido, *Historia del turismo*, chap. 7.

15. For a detailed discussion of the Franco regime's use of soft power to legitimize the Francoist state and to usher in hordes of American tourists, see Rosendorf, *Franco Sells Spain to America*.

16. Pack, *Tourism and Dictatorship*, 45–51; Rosendorf, *Franco Sells Spain to America*, 22.

17. Moreno Garrido, *Historia del turismo*, 192–94.

18. Pack, *Tourism and Dictatorship*, 68.

19. See ibid., chap. 2; Rosendorf, *Franco Sells Spain to America*, chap. 1.

20. Ernesto Bacharach Natan, *Estudio sobre la propaganda turística y su cuantía*, 1953, AGA, sección cultura, 49.04, caja/legajo 18519.

21. Neal Rosendorf's work covers the extensive advertisement campaigns that the Franco regime employed to garner tourists. Rosendorf, *Franco Sells Spain to America*.

22. Some version of this strategy can be found in reports written by Luis Fernández Fuster and Antonio Ranz Olmo, Justo Ros Emperador, Ernesto Bacharach Natan, and Carlos González Cuesta, all titled "Estudio sobre la propaganda turística y su cuantía," 1953. AGA, sección cultura, 49.04, caja 22, legajos 18518, 18519, 18520.

23. Dirección Nacional de Turismo, *Espagne*, 1954, AGA, sección cultura, (3)49.04, caja/legajo 22/20032, top. 22/69.04-74.03.

24. Dirección General del Turismo, *España*, 1957, AGA, sección cultura, (3) 49.04, caja 20032, top. 22/69.704-74.703.

25. Rafael Calleja, *Apología turística de España: Cuatrocientas treinta y nueve foto-grafías de paisajes, monumentos y aspectos típicos españoles* (Madrid: Dirección General del Turismo, 1943), title page, 45.

26. Rafael Calleja and José Manuel Pita Andrade, *Nueva apología turística de España* (Madrid: Dirección General del Turismo, 1957), 11.

27. Ibid.

28. Ibid., 13.

29. Ibid., 30.

30. Ibid., n.p.

31. The Concurso Nacional de Cante Jondo en Córdoba was the first of such contests in Córdoba. It became a triannual affair and was renamed the Concurso Nacional de Flamenco en Córdoba in 1962. After that, the name became Concurso Nacional de Flamenco de Córdoba. Ateneo de Córdoba, "Concurso Nacional de Arte Flamenco de Córdoba—Ateneo de Córdoba," accessed

October 21, 2017, http://ateneodecordoba.com/index.php/Concurso_Nacional _de_Arte_Flamenco_de_Córdoba.

32. Brief information about Cortijo El Guajiro can be found in "El Patio Sevillano's History," accessed June 24, 2018, http://www.elpatiosevillano .com/historia.php?l=en. See also José Blas Vega and Manuel Ríos Ruiz, *Diccionario enciclopédico ilustrado del flamenco*, vol. 1 (Madrid: Editorial Cinterco, 1990), 346.

33. Moreno Garrido, *Historia del turismo*, 209.

34. For more discussion of the "deregionalization of flamenco," see Washabaugh, *Flamenco*," 162–63.

35. Ibid., 210. You can see some of these posters on the Turespaña website: https://turismo.janium.net/janium-bin/referencista.pl?Id=20180628014136, accessed June 27, 2018.

36. *Summer Holidays in Spain and Portugal, Balearic Islands, Malta, Gibraltar and Cyprus*, pamphlet/brochure, 1950, Thomas Cook Archives.

37. *Summer Holidays in Spain, Portugal, Balearic Islands, Malta, Gibraltar and Cyprus*, pamphlet/brochure, 1951, Thomas Cook Archives.

38. *Winter Sunshine, 1952–53*, pamphlet/brochure, and *Summer Holidays in Spain and Portugal, Balearic Islands, Malta, Gibraltar and Cyprus*, pamphlet/brochure, 1953, Thomas Cook Archives.

39. "Fly with Us to Spain" in the Thomas Cook brochure *Holidays in Spain and Portugal, Balearic Isles, Andorra, Madeira, Malta, Gibraltar, Cyprus*, 1954, Thomas Cook Archives.

40. See Pack, *Tourism and Dictatorship*, 83–103, for a detailed description of the economic changes in the Spanish tourist industry.

41. Moreno Garrido, *Historia del turismo*, 242; Pack, *Tourism and Dictatorship*, 110.

42. Pack, *Tourism and Dictatorship*, 105–27, 153–55.

43. DGT, "Ruta de Santiago: Estudio Turístico Preliminar," n.d. [1962], AGA, 3:49.05/22599, cited in ibid., 158.

44. Pack, *Tourism and Dictatorship*, 149.

45. "In Spain they say, 'aquí está su casa,' and 'San Sebastian: Gateway to Romantic Spain,'" *Holidaymaking*, 1957, magazine, Thomas Cook Archives.

46. "Big, Gay, San Sebastian—But See How Inexpensive!," *Holidaymaking*, 1959, magazine, Thomas Cook Archives.

47. *Holidaymaking*, 1963, magazine, Thomas Cook Archives.

48. *Holidays in Spain and Portugal, the Balearic Isles, Madeira, Canary Islands, Malta, Gibraltar, Libya, Tunisia and Morocco*, 1963, brochure, Thomas Cook Archives.

49. *Holiday in Spain*, presented by ATESA, photography and narration by Gerald Hooper (1950s), film 16, tape 11, Thomas Cook Archives.

50. *Costa Brava*, A British Films Ltd. Production, produced by John Rowdon for British Transport Films (1950s), Tape 3, Film Can 4, Thomas Cook Archives.

51. *Majorca—Stay in the Sun*, presented by Thomas Cook, a British Films Ltd. Production, produced by John Rowdon for British Transport Films (1958), tape 16, film can 25, Thomas Cook Archives.

52. *Magic of Majorca*, an Inforum Production, produced and directed by Lionel Griffith, narration by David Hamilton (1960s), film 21, tape 14, Thomas Cook Archives.

53. Evidence for Spain's presence and the various Spanish performances can be found in "Zambra Scores in Paris," *Spanish Newsletter*, July 1, 1962, 8; August Cockx and J. Lemmens, *Les Expositions Universelles et Internationales en Belgique de 1885 à 1958* (Brussels: Editorial-Office, 1958); *Exposition Universelle et Internationale de Bruxelles, 1958: Guide Official* (Tournai, Belgium: Desclée & Cie, 1958); *Exposition Universelle et Internationale de Bruxelles 1958: Les arts* (Brussels: Comisarie Général de Gouvernement, 1958); G. Jacquemyns and Eliane Jacquemyns, *L'exposition de 1958: Son succès auprés des Belges* (Brussels: Institut Universitaire d'Information Sociale et Économique, 1959). Nieves de Hoyos Sancho's *Traditions and Local Customs of Spain* (Madrid: Inter-Ministerial Organizing Committee for the Spanish Pavillion, 1958 Brussels Universal and International Exhibition, 1958) may have been handed out to the visitors to the Spanish Pavilion, although my evidence for this claim is indirect.

54. According to surveys handed out to visitors at the fair, the most-visited pavilions were the United States at 92.6 percent, the USSR at 92.4 percent, and France at 86.5 percent. By comparison, only 51 percent of the visitors entered the Spanish pavilion. Jacquemyns and Jacquemyns, *L'exposition de 1958*, 45.

55. The regime's year-long celebration, "25 Years of Peace," commemorated the end of the civil war and the beginning of Franco's reign. The celebrations emphasized the peace and unity brought on by Franco and the Nationalist forces that had saved Spain from the ravages of the Left and regional nationalists. For a discussion of the relationship between cultural diplomacy and traditional state diplomacy, see Akira Iriye, *Cultural Internationalism and World Order* (Baltimore: Johns Hopkins University Press, 1997).

56. Comisaría General para la Feria Mundial de Nueva York, *New Official Guide: Pavilion of Spain* (New York: Office of the Commissioner of the Pavilion of Spain for the New York World's Fair 1964-65, 1965), 11.

57. Statistics calculated from data provided by Instituto de Estudios Turísticos in Moreno Garrido, *Historia del turismo*, 240.

58. Rosendorf, *Franco Sells Spain to America*, 155.

59. Ibid., 155, 184. For insight into the New York World's Fair Commission's negotiations with the Franco regime, see Bruce Nicholson, *Hi, Ho, Come to the Fair: Tales of the New York World's Fair of 1964-1965* (Huntington Beach, CA: Pelagian Press, 1989).

60. For a wider discussion of the displays and entertainments at the New York World's Fair, see Antonio Alcoba López, *El pabellón que hizo patria: 40 años después (Historia de la joya de la Feria Mundial de Nueva York, 1964-1965, en textos e*

imágenes) (Madrid: Facultad de Ciencias de la Información, Universidad Complutense, Servicio de Publicaciones, 2004); Rosendorf, *Franco Sells Spain to America*, chap. 6.

61. Comisaría General, *New Official Guide*, 136.

62. As the Spanish saw it, "the discovery of America was a Spanish glory" conveniently ignored by all the Italian Americans who also paraded down Fifth Avenue for the Columbus Day Parade. J. Ramírez de Lucas, "'La Semana de España' en Nueva York," *Blanco y negro*, October 24, 1964.

63. "Spanish 4-Master Is Welcomed Here," *New York Times*, May 9, 1965, 88; "St. Patrick's Patio Is Scene of Dancing by Spanish Groups," *New York Times*, May 9, 1965, 42.

64. "Dancers and Art Scheduled with Philharmonic Concerts," *New York Times*, May 25, 1965, 46.

65. "Sal de España en Nueva York," *Blanco y negro*, October 3, 1964.

66. Enrique Meneses, "Éxito español en la feria mundial," *Blanco y negro*, May 2, 1964.

67. Enrique Meneses, "Visite con Blanco y Negro la Feria de Nueva York," *Blanco y negro*, May 16, 1964, 53–56.

68. Gades had already acted and danced in a Spanish film, *Los tarantos*, a year earlier with Carmen Amaya. For Durán, see "Zambra Scores in Paris," *Spanish Newsletter*, July 1, 1962, 8. For Vargas, see the programs *Pavilion of Spain, New York World's Fair, 1965* and *Flamenco by Manuela Vargas from Sevilla*, 1965, both at the New York Public Library for the Performing Arts.

69. F. Estrada Saladich, *La Feria Mundial de New York* (Barcelona: Revista El Mueble, 1965), 329.

70. Paul Dammar et al., *Antonio Gades* (New York: Pavilion of Spain, New York World's Fair, 1964); José María Cruz Novillo, Francisco Gómez, and Francisco Ontañón, *Zambra, Tablao Flamenco* (Madrid: Orbe, 1964); *Manuela Vargas, Flamenco Dancer, Theatre of Spanish Pavilion, World's Fair, New York, 1965*; *Pavilion of Spain, New York World's Fair, 1965, Flamenco by Manuela Vargas from Sevilla*, 1965.

71. Dammar et al., *Antonio Gades*.

72. See chap. 5.

73. Cruz Novillo, Gómez, and Ontañón, *Zambra*.

74. Ibid.

75. Ibid.

76. Information about the original name comes from building permits requested by Antolín Fernán Alonso Casares (the owner of Tablao Zambra) in September and November 1954 for the address Calle Ruiz de Alarcón, 7. Archivo de Secretaría, sección Obras-Industrias, expediente 37-234-35 and expediente 39-491-11-0, Archivo de Villa, Madrid.

77. Cruz Novillo, Gómez, and Ontañón, *Zambra*.

78. Allen Hughes was the exception to this rule. He called the Coros y Danzas "a delightful assortment of folk dances and music" but dubbed flamenco

dances as "somewhat slow and somewhat too general for American consumption." Allen Hughes, "Ethnic Dances Abound for Visitors to Fair," *New York Times*, June 15, 1965, 33.

79. Nelson Lansdale, "'Everything Here Is Chaos': A Preliminary Report on Dance at the 1964 New York World's Fair," *Dance Magazine*, June 1964, 22-23.

80. Charles Boultenhouse, "Flamenco Dancing in the Pavilion of Spain: New York World's Fair, 1964," *Ballet Review*, 1965, 13-18.

81. "'Isn't Life That Way Here?,'" *Newsweek*, July 20, 1964, 74. Note the similarity between this review in 1964 and the one by the writer for the *New York Times* in 2017. See coda.

82. Charles Boultenhouse, "Flamenco Dancing in the Pavilion of Spain: New York World's Fair, 1964," *Ballet Review*, 1965, 15.

83. "Isn't Life That Way Here?," 75.

84. "Dance: Back to the Singing Cafés," *Time*, June 18, 1965, 73.

85. "'Isn't Life That Way Here?,'" 74-75.

86. Boultenhouse, "Flamenco Dancing in the Pavilion of Spain," 15.

87. "'Isn't Life That Way Here?,'" 75. See chapter 5 for the feminization of El Pichiri.

88. "The Jewel of the Fair," *Life Magazine*, August 7, 1964, 80-84. The pavilion was dismantled and moved to St. Louis in 1969. In 1976 it was sold and remodeled to become the Breckenridge Inn. In 1979 the Marriott Hotel chain bought the inn and integrated the pavilion into the hotel's lobby. In 2007 the Hilton chain bought the hotel, remodeled again, and left little of the architecture of the original pavilion. "Pavilion of Spain," *New York World's Fair, 1964/1965*, accessed October 23, 2017, http://www.nywf64.com/spain10.shtml.

89. All these advertisements can be found in *Harper's Bazaar*, January 1965.

90. Comisaría General, *New Official Guide*.

91. There were exceptions, of course. About fifty veterans of the Abraham Lincoln Brigade, who had fought in the Spanish Civil War on the side of the Republicans, protested at least once in front of the Spanish Pavilion. Alcoba López, *El pabellón que hizo patria*, 37-38.

92. "Spanish Pavilion Closes," *Spanish Newsletter*, October 31, 1965, 7.

93. "Tourism Booms," *Spanish Newsletter*, Oct. 31, 1965, 8, cited in Rosendorf, *Franco Sells Spain to America*, 186.

94. This information comes from a script written by José Luis Fernández Hua for broadcast on Radio y Televisión Española in 1963. AGA, sección cultura, (3) 49.05, caja 25347.

95. *Exposición Nacional de Recursos Turísticos: Expotur, Madrid-1963; (Palacio de exposiciones del Instituto Nacional de Industria, 20 junio-20 julio)* (Madrid: Subsecretaría de Turismo, 1963). I am making the claim that the contents of the tourism exhibit in New York and those of the Expotur were the same because the descriptions of the two are almost identical.

96. AGA, sección cultura, (3) 49.06, caja 30041; (3) 49.05, caja 25437.

97. See "Una Exposición De Turismo," NO-DO Imágenes, directed by Sánchez and Melcón (1963); "Noticias Breves: Semana dominicano-española en Santo Domingo. Inauguración de la 'EXPOTUR,'" NO-DO (January 27, 1969); "Informaciones y reportajes: La 'Expotur' en Colombia. El Presidente Pastrana Borrero, inaugura la exposición," NO-DO (February 15, 1971), all in Filmoteca Española Archive.

98. "La Mostra Del Turismo Spagnolo Inaugurata al Palazzo Reale de Milano," *L'Osservatore Romano*, November 12, 1965; Jaime Alba, "Asunto: Exposición conozca España en Rio," October 18, 1965, AMAE, Madrid, Sección Exposiciones, Signatura R7949, Expediente 79. The contents of this archive were moved to the AGA, so I do not know how they were reclassified.

99. Antonio Diolano, "Contra todo pronóstico (y a pesar de los 'esfuerzos' italianos) 200,000 personas visitaron la 'Expotur' en cinco días," *La Prensa*, January 31, 1964, clipping found in AGA, sección cultura, (3) 49.05, caja 25347.

100. The series comprised at least five films, eleven minutes each, and all directed by Joaquín Bernaldo de Quirós, all called *El pueblo baila*. Filmoteca Española Archive, Madrid.

101. That asymmetry changed after the New York World's Fair.

Coda

1. See Turespaña official websites, accessed April 26, 2018, http://www.spain.info and https://www.spainin10sec.com (the latter link has become inaccessible since this chapter was written). For further information about this campaign, see "Spanish Tourist Office Launches 'Spain in 10 Seconds' across 15 Countries," *Travel Daily*, April 18, 2018, https://www.traveldailymedia.com/spain-in-10-seconds/.

2. Lucas Peterson, "Vibrant and Seductive Seville, Easy on the Wallet," *New York Times*, June 7, 2017.

3. See introduction to chapter 4.

4. Machin-Autenrieth, *Flamenco*; Washabaugh, *Flamenco Music*; Francisco Aix Gracia, *Flamenco y poder: Un estudio desde la sociología del arte* (Madrid: Fundación SGAE, 2014).

5. Ángel Álvarez Caballero, "Del Nacionalflamenquismo al renacimiento," in *Los intelectuales ante el flamenco*, Cuadernos Hispanoamericanos Complementarios 9–10, ed. Ángel Álvarez Caballero (Madrid: Instituto de Cooperación Iberoamericana, 1992), 109–19.

6. He is sometimes included among the Generation of '27 to which García Lorca belonged, but sheepishly so because he threw in his lot with the Nationalists. Neville would later write the essay on Antonio Gades for the 1964 World's Fair. See chapter 7.

7. See chapter 6.

8. Edgar Neville, "Duende y Misterio del Flamenco," clip by FcoJavierNerja,

uploaded December 5, 2017, accessed February 13, 2018, https://www.youtube.com/watch?v=YF9QWXamhjE.

9. Andrés Raya, "1958: Año en que se publicó la "Antología del Cante Flamenco," *Flamenco en mi memoria* (blog), August 2, 2015, https://memoriaflamenca.blogspot.com/2015/08/1958-ano-en-que-se-publico-la-antologia.html; Ángel Álvarez Caballero, *La discoteca ideal de flamenco* (Barcelona: Planeta, 1995), 25–26.

10. Anselmo González Climent, *Flamencología* (Córdoba: Ayuntamiento de Córdoba, 1989). See chapter 1 for more information on Démofilo.

11. For the 1922 Concurso de Cante Jondo, see chapter 5.

12. "Cátedra de Flamencología y Estudios Folklóricos Andaluces," in *Diccionario enciclopédico ilustrado del flamenco*, vol. 1, ed. José Blas Vega and Manuel Ríos Ruiz (Madrid: Editorial Cinterco, 1988), 170–72.

13. Ricardo Molina and Antonio Mairena, *Mundo y formas del cante flamenco* (Madrid: Revista de Occidente, 1963). See the introduction to this book.

14. For a detailed analysis of this series, see Washabaugh, *Flamenco*, 139–79, from which much of my analysis comes.

15. Ibid., 161.

16. Ibid., 170–73.

17. Ibid., 157.

18. "Rumba catalana," accessed February 15, 2018, https://flamenco.one/en/glossary/rumba-catalana/.

19. "Morente Cotelo, Enrique," in *Diccionario enciclopédico ilustrado del flamenco*, vol. 2, ed. José Blas Vega and Manuel Ríos Ruiz (Madrid: Editorial Cinterco, 1988), 516–18.

20. "Entrevista, Enrique Morente," Flamenco-World.com, accessed February 15, 2018, https://web.archive.org/web/20070511042637/http://flamenco-world.com/artists/morente/morente09062006.htm.

21. "Spanish Constitution," accessed November 21, 2018, http://www.parliament.am/library/sahmanadrutyunner/ispania.pdf. As of this writing, Catalans held a referendum—illegal by constitutional standards—on Catalan independence from Spain. Those Catalan politicians who pushed for the vote are now either under arrest or in exile. The Spanish government has stripped some of the Catalans' power, although new elections were held for the regional government in December. Catalonia's status is currently in a foggy limbo.

22. For use of this term, see Yuko Aoyama, "Artists, Tourists, and the State: Cultural Tourism and the Flamenco Industry in Andalusia, Spain," *International Journal of Urban and Regional Research* 33, no. 1 (2009): 80–104.

23. See the introduction to part II for a discussion of the various caveats about the terms "regionalist" and "nationalist."

24. Parlamento de Andalucía, "Estatuto de Autonomía Para Andalucía," accessed May 1, 2018, http://www.juntadeandalucia.es/export/drupaljda/estatuto81.pdf.

25. Washabaugh, *Flamenco Music and National Identity in Spain*, 84.

26. Matthew Machin-Autenrieth, "Flamenco? Algo Nuestro? (Something of Ours?): Music, Regionalism and Political Geography in Andalusia, Spain," *Ethnomusicology Forum* 24, no. 1 (2015): 12–13.

27. To see how UNESCO defines an Intangible Cultural Heritage of Humanity, see "Text of the Convention for the Safeguarding of the Intangible Cultural Heritage," accessed March 6, 2018, https://ich.unesco.org/en/convention#art2.

28. Ibid.

29. Machin-Autenrieth, "Flamenco?," 13.

30. Ibid. Aix Gracia, *Flamenco y poder*, 318–33.

31. I have taken the term "nested identities" from S. Balfour, A Quiroga, *The Reinvention of Spain* (New York: Oxford University Press, 2007), to talk about the simultaneous identities that people (or institutions) can hold. Thus, one can be a Sevillian, Andalusian, and Spaniard at the same time, without necessarily feeling any conflict between these individual identities.

32. Gómez-García Plata, "El género flamenco," 121.

33. Aoyama defines world music as "music that evokes certain international localities." Aoyama, "Artists," 81, 86.

34. For a thorough statistical analysis of these various interlocking interests as of 2009, see ibid.

35. "Bienvenido al Centro Andaluz de Documentación del Flamenco," Junta de Andalucía, accessed March 6, 2018, www.centroandaluzdeflamenco.es.

36. "España es cultura," *España Global*, accessed March 8, 2018, www.marcaespana.es.

37. Marisol Paul, "Baile flamenco para reforzar la Marca España," in *La economía del turismo, motor con Marca España: Todo nuevo bajo el sol* (Madrid: LID, 2014), 165.

38. The Japanese are the outlier here. In 2016 Japanese were 0.8 percent of tourists to Andalusia and 0.3 percent of those in Spain. Statistics come from Consejería de Turismo y Deporte, "Balance del Año Turístico en Andalucia," 2016, http://www.juntadeandalucia.es/turismoydeporte/publicaciones/estadisticas/bata_2016.pdf.

39. Ibid.

40. Isabel Ferrer, "Ocho capitales europeas saturadas de turistas se unen frente a Airbnb," *El país*, January 29, 2018, https://elpais.com/economia/2018/01/28/actualidad/1517154558_107147.html; Fernando Bernal, "¿Hasta cuándo podremos vivir en el centro de las ciudades? Así nos afecta la turistificación," *El País*, March 22, 2018, https://elpais.com/elpais/2018/03/21/tentaciones/1521621650_321611.html.

41. InterMedia News, "Las Mujeres No Olvidamos. Sevilla, 1936-2013," uploaded May 25, 2013, accessed March 15, 2018, https://www.youtube.com/watch?feature=player_embedded&v=syd8mVCyZJs.

42. Raúl Limón, "La Virgen de la Macarena y la memoria de Queipo de Llano," *El País*, July 27, 2017, https://elpais.com/cultura/2017/07/25/actualidad/1500981143_596376.html. In more recent months, there seems to have been some movement toward accommodation between those who want to have Queipo's remains removed and Queipo's family, who had previously resisted such demands. Javier Martín Arroyo and Eva Sáiz, "La Basílica de la Macarena acepta retirar los restos de Queipo de Llano," *El País*, July 18, 2018, https://elpais.com/politica/2018/07/16/actualidad/1531763422_811016.html.

43. "Las Mujeres No Olvidamos."

44. See the YouTube clip, especially 2:40–3:30. For a contemporary news account of that day's events, see "Homenaje a mujeres represaliadas ante la tumba de Queipo de Llano," *El Diario*, May 25, 2013, https://www.eldiario.es/andalucia/Homenaje-mujeres-represaliadas-Quiepo-Llanos_0_136136480.html.

45. Unless otherwise indicated, quotes come from the group's website, accessed March 16, 2018, http://flo6x8.com/. For more information on their practices, see this newscast: Georges Walker, "Flamenco contra los abusos de los bancos," uploaded December 29, 2010, accessed March 16, 2018, https://www.youtube.com/watch?v=Cqvcke8Xe9I.

46. Most of their filmed performances can be viewed at their website, http://flo6x8.com/.

47. Carlos del Chacal, "Rumba banquero santander (bueno para el provincial)," uploaded January 29, 2011, accessed March 17, 2018, https://www.youtube.com/watch?v=JscJOG1rIEQ.

48. "Bankia, pulmones y branquías," June 2012, accessed March 17, 2018, http://www.flo6x8.com/content/flo6x8-bankia-pulmones-y-branquias-junio-2012. Before heading the bank, Rodrigo Rato was managing director of the IMF. He would later be arrested in April 2015 for fraud, embezzlement, and money laundering, and his name was also found in the Panama Papers. He was convicted of these crimes in 2017. See Carlos Segovia, "Rodrigo Rato dejó a deber dinero incluso a la Hacienda de Panamá," *El Mundo*, April 18, 2016, http://www.elmundo.es/espana/2016/04/18/5714087ee2704ed7068b4632.html; Sam Jones, "Former IMF Chief Gets Four Years in Jail for Embezzlement in Spain," *The Guardian*, February 23, 2017, https://www.theguardian.com/world/2017/feb/23/former-imf-chief-gets-four-years-jail-after-corruption-trial-in-spain.

49. Flo6x8, "FLO6x8 en el Parlamento-Acortando distancias," uploaded June 26, 2014, accessed March 17, 2018, https://www.youtube.com/watch?v=KxHBWmVRB8A. The Troika refers to the Central Bank of Europe, the IMF, and the European Commission.

50. See chapter 4.

Bibliography

Archives and Libraries

Archivo de Acción Católica, Madrid, Spain (AC)
Archivo de la Comunidad de Madrid (ACM)
Archivo General de la Administración, Alcalá de Henares, Spain (AGA)
Archivo del Ministerio de Asuntos Exteriores, Madrid (AMAE). Now defunct. Archives moved to AGA.
Archivo Municipal de Sevilla, Seville, Spain.
Archivo Nacional de la "Nueva Andadura," Real Academia de la Historia, Madrid (RAH)
Archivo de Villa, Madrid
Arxiu Municipal de Barcelona, Barcelona, Spain
Biblioteca de Catalunya, Barcelona
Biblioteca Nacional de España, Madrid
Centro Andaluz de Documentación del Flamenco, Jerez de la Frontera, Spain
Centro de Documentación Turística de España, Instituto de Turismo de España, Madrid
Filmoteca Española, Madrid

New York Public Library for the Performing Arts, Performing Arts Research Collections, New York City, USA
Newberry Library, Chicago, USA
Thomas Cook Archives, Peterborough, United Kingdom
University of Chicago Library, Special Collections Research Center, World's Columbian Exposition, Chicago
University of Illinois, Chicago. Special Collections and University Archives Department, Century of Progress Collection, Chicago

Newspapers and Magazines

ABC (1942, 1948, 2007)
ABC (Seville) (1933, 1939)
Acción socialista (1914)
Ballet (1952)
Ballet Review (1965)
Bética (1914)
Blanco y negro (1964)
Boletín oficial de las Cortes Generales (2002)
Boletín oficial eclesiástico del Arzobispado de Sevilla (1946)
Boletín oficial eclesiástico del Obispado de Madrid-Alcalá (1911)
Chicago Daily Tribune (1893)
El Chíspero (1914)
Cosmópolis (1919)
Dance Magazine (1952, 1965)
El Diario (2013)
El Escándalo (1925, 1926)
La España moderna (1889)
El Flamenco: Semanario antiflamenquista (1914)
Le Gaulois (1889)
El Globo (1913)
Falange española (1934)
The Guardian (2017)
Harper's Bazaar (1965)
Harper's New Monthly Magazine (1867)
Heraldo de Madrid (1911)
La Ilustración española y americana (1889, 1900)
La Lectura dominical (1896, 1897, 1909, 1910)
Life Magazine (1964)
Los Angeles Times (1953)
Manchester Guardian (1952)
Mirador (1929)
Le Monde illustré (1889)

El Mundo (2016)
Newsweek (1964)
New York Times (1953, 1965, 2017)
L'Opinió (1933)
L'Osservatore Romano (1965)
El País (2003, 2017, 2018)
Le Petit journal (1889)
Revista católica de cuestiones sociales (1914, 1927, 1928)
Revista general de enseñanzas y bellas artes (1911)
Revista musical catalana (1904, 1905)
Ritme (1923)
El Siglo futuro (1884, 1895, 1909)
El Socialista (1904)
Spanish Newsletter (1962, 1965)
Tierra y libertad (1910, 1916)
Time (1965)
Times of London (1952)
La Unión Católica (1888, 1889, 1898)
Vértice (1942, 1943)
Vida socialista (1912)

Primary Sources

Armengou, Josep. *Nacionalisme català: Idees i pensaments de Mn. Josep Armengou.* N.p.: n.p., 1980.
Baedeker, Karl. *Spain and Portugal: Handbook for Travellers.* Leipsig: K. Baedeker, 1898.
Bates, Katharine Lee. *Spanish Highways and Byways.* New York: Macmillan, 1900.
Benedict XV. *Sacra Propediem.* Jan. 6, 1921. Accessed November 1, 2013. http://www.vatican.va/holy_father/benedict_xv/encyclicals/documents/hf_ben-xv_enc_06011921_sacra-propediem_en.html.
Blackburn, Henry. *Travelling in Spain in the Present Day.* London: S. Low & Marston, 1866.
Borrow, George Henry. *The Zincali; or, An Account of the Gypsies of Spain: With an Original Collection of Their Songs and Poetry, and a Copious Dictionary of Their Language.* London: J. Murray, 1841.
Bueso, Adolfo. *Recuerdos de un cenetista.* 2 vols. Barcelona: Ariel, 1978.
Cabañas Guevara, Luis. *Biografía del Paralelo, 1894-1934: Recuerdos de la vida teatral, mundana y pintoresco del barrio más jaranero y bellicioso de Barcelona.* Barcelona: Ediciones Memphis, 1945.
Cadalso, José and Juan Tamayo y Rubio. *Cartas marruecas.* Madrid: Espasa-Calpe, 1935.

Caffarena, Ángel. *Geografía del cante andaluz*. Málaga: Juan Such, 1964.
Calleja, Rafael. *Apología turística de España: Cuatrocientas treinta y nueve fotografías de paisajes, monumentos y aspectos típicos españoles*. Madrid: Dirección General del Turismo, 1943.
Calleja, Rafael, and José Manuel Pita Andrade. *Nueva apología turística de España*. Madrid: Dirección General del Turismo, 1957.
Cerdà, Ildefonso. *Cerdà: The Five Bases of the General Theory of Urbanization*. Edited by Arturo Soria y Puig. Madrid: Electa, 1999.
Chatfield-Taylor, H. C. *The Land of the Castanet: Spanish Sketches*. Chicago: H. S. Stone, 1896.
Comisaría General para la Feria Mundial de Nueva York. *New Official Guide: Pavilion of Spain*. New York: Office of the Commissioner of the Pavilion of Spain for the New York World's Fair 1964–65, 1965.
Comisión General de España. *Catálogo de la Exposición Universal de Chicago de 1893*. Madrid: Ricardo Rojas, 1893.
Comité Ejecutivo de España en la Exposición Universal de París, 1889. *Catálogo de la sección española en la Exposición Universal de París de 1889*. París: Chaix, 1889.
Conferencia Episcopal Española, "Metropolitanos españoles: Pastoral colectiva sobre la inmodestia de las costumbres públicas, 30 April 1926." In *Documentos colectivos del episcopado español: 1870–1974*, edited by Jesús Iribarren, 117–23. Madrid: La Ed. Católica, 1974.
Consejería de Turismo y Deporte. "Balance del Año Turístico en Andalucia." 2016. http://www.juntadeandalucia.es/turismoydeporte/publicaciones/estadisticas/bata_2016.pdf.
Cruz Novillo, José María, Francisco Gómez, and Francisco Ontañón. *Zambra, Tablao Flamenco*. Madrid: Orbe, 1964.
Dammar, Paul, Edgar Neville, Alfredo Mañas, and José Manuel Caballero Bonald. *Antonio Gades*. New York: Pavilion of Spain, New York World's Fair, 1964.
De Amicis, Edmondo. *Spain and the Spaniards*. Translated by Stanley R. Yarnall. 2 vols. Philadelphia: H. T. Coates, 1895.
De Beauvoir, Simone. *The Second Sex*. Translated by Sheila Malovany-Chevallier and Constance Borde. New York: Vintage, 2011.
Debussy, Claude, François Lesure, and Richard Langham Smith. *Debussy on Music: The Critical Writings of the Great French Composer Claude Debussy*. Ithaca, NY: Cornell University Press, 1988.
Don Preciso. *Colección de las mejores coplas de seguidillas, tiranas y polos que se han compuesto para cantar a la guitarra*. 2 vols. Madrid: Repullés, 1816.
Dostoevsky, Fyodor. *Notes from the Underground*. Translated by Constance Garnett. New York: Dover, 1992.
Doussinague, José María. *Carta a Pilar Primo de Rivera, por el Excmo. Sr. D. José Ma. Doussinague con motivo de la visita a tierras de América de los Coros y Danzas de la Sección Femenina*. N.p.: n.p., 1950.

Bibliography

Elliot, Frances Minto. *Diary of an Idle Woman in Spain*. London: F. V. White, 1884.
Ellis, Havelock. *The Soul of Spain*. Boston: Houghton Mifflin, 1914.
España Global. "España es cultura." Accessed March 8, 2018. www.marca españa.es.
Los españoles pintados por sí mismos. Madrid: I. Boix, 1843.
Estrada Saladich, F. *La Feria Mundial de New York*. Barcelona: Revista El Mueble, 1965.
Exposición Nacional de recursos turísticos: Expotur, Madrid-1963; Palacio de exposiciones del Instituto Nacional de Industria, 20 junio–20 julio. Madrid: Subsecretaría de Turismo, 1963.
Exposition Universelle et Internationale de Bruxelles 1958: Les arts. Brussels: Comisarie Général de Gouvernement, 1958.
Exposition Universelle et Internationale de Bruxelles, 1958: Guide Official. Tournai, Belgium: Desclée & Cie, 1958.
Falange Española Tradicionalista y de las Juntas Ofensivas Nacional-Sindicalistas. Sección Femenina. *Canciones y danzas de españa*. Madrid: Sección Femenina de Falange Española Tradicionalista y de las J.O.N.S., 1953.
Fernández de los Ríos, Ángel. *La Exposición Universal de 1878: Guía-itinerario para los que la visiten, descripción razonada rara los que no hayan de verla, recuerdo para los que la hayan visto*. Madrid: English y Gras, 1878.
Flamenco Cleaning Services. "Welcome to Flamenco Cleaning Services." Accessed October 29, 2017. http://www.flamencocleaningservices.com/.
"Flamenco contra los abusos de los bancos." Accessed March 16, 2018. https://www.youtube.com/watch?v=Cqvcke8Xe9I.
"Flamenco—Diego el Fillo." Accessed October 9, 1917. http://www.andalucia.com/flamenco/musicians/diegoelfillo.htm.
"Flamenco-History." Accessed October 4, 2017. http://www.andalucia.com/flamenco/history.htm.
Flamenco One. "Rumba Catalana." Accessed February 15, 2018. https://flamenco.one/en/glossary/rumba-catalana/.
Flamenco-World.com. "Entrevista Enrique Morente." Accessed February 18, 2018. https://web.archive.org/web/20070511042637/http:/flamenco-world.com/artists/morente/morente09062006.htm.
Flo6×8. Accessed November 23, 2018. www.flo6×8.com.
Flores del Romeral. *Contra el cine inmoral: La J. F. de A. C. Española—Lo extranjerizante*. Zaragoza: Octavio y Peláez, 1939.
Ford, Richard. *Gatherings from Spain*. Edited by Ian Robertson. London: Pallas Athene, 2000.
Ford, Richard, and John Murray (Firm). *A Hand-book for Travellers in Spain and Readers at Home: Describing the Country and Cities, the Natives and Their Manners, the Antiquities, Religion, Legends, Fine Arts, Literature, Sports, and Gastronomy; With Notices on Spanish History*. London: J. Murray, 1845.

Les Français peints par eux-memes: Encyclopédie morale du dix-neuvième siècle province. Paris: Curmer, 1841.
Frommer's Spain. "Things to Do in Spain." Accessed April 26, 2018. https://www.frommers.com/destinations/spain.
Frontaura y Vázquez, Carlos. *Viaje cómico a la Exposición de Paris.* Madrid: Administración de El Cascabel, 1867.
García Berlanga, Luis, dir. *Bienvenido Mr. Marshall.* 1953.
García Lorca, Federico. "El cante jondo (primitivo canto andaluz)." In Jorge de Persia, *I Concurso de cante jondo: Edición conmemorativa 1922–1992; Una reflexión crítica.* Granada: Archivo Manuel de Falla, 1992.
García Serrano, Rafael. *Bailando hasta la Cruz del Sur.* Madrid: Gráficas, 1953.
Gasch, Sebastià. *Barcelona de nit.* Barcelona: Editorial Selecta, 1957.
Gautier, Théophile. *A Romantic in Spain.* New York: Interlink Books, 2001.
Glücq, Paris. *L'Album de l'exposition, 1878.* Paris: [Glücq], 1878.
Goldberg, K. Meira. *Sonidos Negros: On the Blackness of Flamenco.* Oxford: Oxford University Press, 2019.
Gómez-Moreno, Manuel. *Guía de Granada.* Granada: Indalecio Ventura, 1892.
Gómez Zarzuela, Manuel, and Vicente Gómez Zarzuela. *Guía de Sevilla, su provincia: Arzobispado, capitanía general, tercio naval, audiencia territorial y distrito universitario.* Seville: La Andalucía, 1865.
Guide illustré du bon marché: L'Exposition et Paris au vingtième siècle. Paris: P. Brodard, 1900.
Harper's Guide to Paris and the Exposition of 1900. London: Harper & Brothers, 1900.
Harper's New Monthly Magazine. "More of the Great Show at Paris." November 1, 1867.
Hernández García, Vicente. *El baile: Moral y pastoral.* Madrid: Studium, 1961.
Hoyos Sancho, Nieves de. *Traditions and Local Customs of Spain.* Madrid: Inter-Ministerial Organizing Committee for the Spanish Pavilion, 1958 Brussels Universal and International Exhibition, 1958.
Hutton, Edward. *The Cities of Spain.* New York: Macmillan, 1906.
Infante, Blas. *El ideal andaluz.* Madrid: Tucar Ediciones, 1976.
Infante, Blas. *Orígenes de lo flamenco y secreto del cante jondo (1929–1933).* Ediciones de la Consejería de Cultura de la Junta de Andalucía. Seville: Junta de Andalucía, Consejería de Cultura, 1980.
Infante Pérez, Blas. *La verdad sobre el complot de Tablada y el estado libre de Andalucía.* Seville: Junta Liberalista de Sevilla, 1979.
Jacquemyns, G., and Eliane Jacquemyns. *L'exposition de 1958: Son succès auprés des Belges.* Brussels: Institut Universitaire d'Information Sociale et Économique, 1959.
Jeremias de las Santas Espinas. *Juventud en llamas: El baile moderno.* Bilbao: Redención, 1965.

Junta de Andalucía, Consejería de Cultura. Centro Andaluz de Documentación del Flamenco. "Bienvenido al Centro Andaluz de Documentación del Flamenco." Accessed March 6, 2018. centroandaluzdeflamenco.es.

Kant, Immanuel. "Idea for a Universal History from a Cosmopolitan Point of View." Accessed September 23, 2017. https://www.marxists.org/reference/subject/ethics/kant/universal-history.htm.

Lafuente y Alcántara, Emilio. *Cancionero popular: Colección escogida de seguidillas y coplas.* Madrid: Carlos Bailly-Bailliere, 1865.

Lamarre, Clovis, and L. Louis-Lande. *L'Espagne et l'Exposition de 1878.* Paris: Libraire Ch. Delagrave, 1878.

Lonely Planet, Spain. Accessed November 23, 2018. https://www.lonelyplanet.com/spain.

López, Guillermo. *Barcelona sucia.* Barcelona: Registro de Hygiene. ca. 1900.

Macasolí, A., dir. *Danzas españolas.* 1955.

Machado y Álvarez, Antonio. *Colección de cantes flamencos, recogidos y anotados por Demófilo.* Edited by Enrique R. Baltanás. Seville: Signatura, 1999.

Madrid, Francisco. *Sangre en Atarazanas.* 7th ed. Barcelona: n.p., 1926.

Maeztu, Ramiro de, and Isidro Gomá y Tomás. *Defensa de la hispanidad.* Valladolid: Aldus, 1938.

Manning, Samuel. *Spanish Pictures, Drawn with Pen and Pencil.* London: Religious Tract Society, 1870.

Manuela Vargas, Flamenco Dancer, Theatre of Spanish Pavilion, World's Fair, New York, 1965.

March, Charles. *Sketches and Adventures in Madeira, Portugal, and the Andalusias of Spain.* New York: Harper & Bros., 1856.

Margueritte, Paul. "Gitanas et druses." In *L'Exposition de Paris (1889), publiée avec la collaboration d'écrivains spéciaux: Édition enrichie de vues, de scènes, de reproductions d'objets d'art, de machines,* edited by Exposition Universelle de 1889, 7. Paris: La Librairie Illustrée, 1889.

The Moorish Palace and Its Startling Wonders. Chicago: Metcalf Stationery, 1893.

Morand, Paul. "Catalan Night." In *Fancy Goods: Open All Night,* 65–95. Translated by Ezra Pound. New York: New Directions, 1984.

Moya, Antonio-Prometeo, and Pilar Primo de Rivera. *Últimas conversaciones con Pilar Primo.* Madrid: Caballo de Troya, 2006.

"Las Mujeres no Olvidamos. Sevilla, 1936–2012." Accessed March 15, 2018. https://www.youtube.com/watch?feature=player_embedded&v=syd8mVCyZJs.

Neville, Edgar. "Duende y misterio del flamenco (clip)." Accessed February 13, 2018. https://www.youtube.com/watch?v=YF9QWXamhjE.

Noel, Eugenio. *Pan y toros.* Valencia: F. Sempere, 1910.

Noel, Eugenio. *Señoritos chulos, fenómenos, gitanos y flamencos.* Córdoba: Editorial Berenice, 2014.

Nordau, Max Simon. *Degeneration*. New York: D. Appleton, 1905.
Ortega y Gasset, José. *The Revolt of the Masses*. Translated by Kenneth Moore. Notre Dame, IN: University of Notre Dame Press, 1985.
Pardo Bazán, Emilia. *Cuarenta días en la Exposición*. Madrid: Administración, 1908.
Parlamento de Andalucía. "Estatuto de Autonomía Para Andalucía." Accessed May 1, 2018. http://www.juntadeandalucia.es/export/drupaljda/estatuto 81.pdf.
Pavilion of Spain, New York World's Fair, 1965, Flamenco by Manuela Vargas from Sevilla. 1965.
Pedrell, Felipe. *Por nuestra música*. Bellaterra, Barcelona: Universidad Autónoma de Barcelona, 1991.
Pérez Galdós, Benito. *Las cartas desconocidas de Galdós en "La Prensa" de Buenos Aires*. Edited and translated by William Hutchinson. Madrid: Ediciones Cultura Hispánica, 1973.
Photographs of the World's Fair: An Elaborate Collection of Photographs of the Buildings, Grounds and Exhibits of the World's Columbian Exposition, with a Special Description of the Famous Midway Plaisance. Chicago: Werner, 1894.
Planes i Martí, Josep M. *Nits de Barcelona perfils*. Barcelona: Proa, 2001.
Pougin, Arthur. *Le théâtre à l'Exposition Universelle de 1889: Notes et descriptions, histoire et souvenirs*. Paris: Librairie Fischbacher, 1890.
Preston, Paul. *The Spanish Holocaust*. London: HarperCollins, 2008.
Primo de Rivera, José Antonio. "Estatutos de la Sección Femenina." December 1934. Accessed November 21, 2018. https://www.scribd.com/doc/83507351/Estatutos-de-la-Seccion-Femenina-1934.
Primo de Rivera, José Antonio. "Ideas of the Falange." In *Modern Spain: A Documentary History*, edited by John Cowans, 167–70. Philadelphia: University of Pennsylvania Press, 2003.
Primo de Rivera, José Antonio. "Patria: La gaita y la lira." *Falange Española*, January 11, 1934.
Primo de Rivera, Pilar. *Discursos, circulares, escritos*. Madrid: Sección Femenina de F.E.T. y de las J.O.N.S., 1950.
Primo de Rivera, Pilar. *Recuerdos de una vida*. Colección biografía y memorias. Madrid: Dyrsa, 1983.
"El Pueblo Español." *Diario Oficial de la Exposición Internacional, Barcelona 1928*. May 24, 1929.
Quillinan, Dorothy. *Journal of a Few Months Residence in Portugal and Glimpses of the South of Spain*. London: Edward Moxon, 1847.
Reseña de la Primera Asamblea Contra la Pública Inmoralidad/organizada con carácter nacional por la Liga de Madrid, de acuerdo con la Barcelona y Valencia. Madrid: Tipografía Católica de Alberto Fontana, 1927.
"Rumba Banquero Santander (Bueno para el provincial)." Accessed March 17, 2018. https://www.youtube.com/watch?v=JscJOG1rIEQ.

Salicrú Puigvert, Carlos. *¿Es lícito bailar? Cuestiones candentes acerca de la moralidad pública*. 2nd ed. Barcelona: La Hormiga de Oro, 1947.
Sánchez Cantón, Francisco Javier. *Spain (Divulgation and Propaganda)*. Madrid: Gráficas Reunidas, 1926.
Santiago Castillo, Alonso, ed. *Reformas sociales: Información oral y escrita publicada de 1889 a 1893*. Compiled by Comisión de Reformas Sociales, Ministerio de Trabajo. 5 vols. Madrid: Centro de Publicaciones, Ministerio de Trabajo y Seguridad Social, 1985.
Sección Femenina de F.E.T. y de las J.O.N.S. *Songs and Dances of Spain*. Madrid: Vicente Rico, S.A., 1965.
Silió Cortés, César, and Angel Guerra. *Otro desastre más (España en París)*. Valladolid: Imp. Castellana, 1900.
Spain's Official Tourism Portal. Accessed April 26, 2018. www.spain.info.
"Spanish Constitution." Accessed November 21, 2018. http://www.parliament.am/library/sahmanadrutyunner/ispania.pdf.
Spanish Exhibition. *The Spanish Exhibition, 1889: Official Daily Programme of Music and Entertainments*. London: Waterlow & Sons, 1889.
Stoddard, Charles Augustus. *Spanish Cities: With Glimpses of Gibraltar and Tangier*. New York: C. Scribner's Sons, 1892.
Suárez Fernández, Luis. *Crónica de la Sección Femenina y su tiempo*. Madrid: Asociación "Nueva Andadura," 1993.
Tiersot, Julien. *Musiques pittoresques: Promenades musicales à l'Exposition de 1889*. Paris: Librairie Fischbacher, 1889.
Torras i Bages, Josep María. *La tradició catalana*. Barcelona: Edicions 62, 1981.
UNESCO. *Intangible Cultural Heritage*. Accessed March 6, 2018. https://ich.unesco.org.
Valero de Tornos, Juan. *España en París en la Exposición Universal de 1900: Estudio de costumbres sobre Exposiciones Universales*. Madrid: P. Núñez, 1900.
Verhaeren, Emile, and Darío Regoyos. *España negra*. Madrid: Taurus, 1963.
Villalobos Bote, Rufino, and Sebastián Jiménez. *¿Es pecado bailar? ¿No es pecado bailar? Respuesta serena y objetiva a estas apasionantes preguntas de la juventud de hoy*. Badajoz: Secretariado de Propaganda de la Juventud Masculina de Acción Católica, 1948.
Vuillermet, F. A., and Miguel Barquero. *Los Católicos y los bailes modernos*. Translated by Miguel Barquero. Barcelona: Eugenio Subirana, 1927.
Wallis, S. Teackle. *Glimpses of Spain; or, Notes of an Unfinished Tour in 1847*. New York: Harper & Bros., 1849.
Wood, Ruth Kedzie. *The Tourist's Spain and Portugal*. New York: Dodd, Mead, 1913.
World Fair and Exposition Universelle. *Guide de visiteur a l'Exposition Universelle de 1878: Itinéraire en huit et en quatre jours objets remarquables a visiter*. Paris: Chaix, 1878.
Yxart, Josep, and Rosa Cabré. *La descoberta de la gran ciutat, París, 1878*. Tarragona: Institut d'Estudis Tarraconenses Ramon Berenguer IV, 1995.

Secondary Sources

Abelló i Güell, Teresa, Jordi Casassas i Ymbert, and Borja de Riquer i Permanyer. *L'època dels nous moviments socials: 1900-1930*. Barcelona: Fundació Enciclopèdia Catalana, 1995.
Aix Gracia, Francisco. *Flamenco y poder: Un estudio desde la sociología del arte*. Madrid: Fundación SGAE, 2014.
Alcoba López, Antonio. *El pabellón que hizo patria: 40 años después (Historia de la joya de la Feria Mundial de Nueva York, 1964-1965, en textos e imágenes)*. Madrid: Facultad de Ciencias de la Información, Universidad Complutense, Servicio de Publicaciones, 2004.
Álvarez, Sandra. "Eugenio Noel 'l'anti-torero, aussi flamenco qu'un torero.'" In *Entre l'ancien et la lézarde (Espagne VIIIe-XXe)*, edited by Serge Salaün, 597-620. Accessed September 21, 2016. http://crec-paris3.fr/wp-content/up loads/2011/07/ancien-et-nouveau-20-Alvarez.pdf.
Álvarez, Sandra. *Tauromachie et flamenco, polémiques et clichés: Espagne, fin XIXe-début XXe*. Recherches et documents—Espagne. Paris: L'Harmattan, 2007.
Álvarez Caballero, Ángel. *El cante flamenco*. Madrid: Alianza, 1998.
Álvarez Caballero, Ángel. "Del Nacionalflamenquismo al renacimiento." In *Los intelectuales ante el flamenco*, edited by Ángel Álvarez Caballero, 109-19. Cuadernos Hispanoamericanos Complementarios 9-10. Madrid: Instituto de Cooperación Iberoamericana, 1992.
Álvarez Caballero, Ángel. *La discoteca ideal de flamenco*. Barcelona: Planeta, 1995.
Álvarez Caballero, Ángel. *Gitanos, payos y flamencos*. Madrid: Editorial Cinterco, 1988.
Álvarez Caballero, Ángel. *Historia del cante flamenco*. Madrid: Alianza Editorial, 1981.
Álvarez Junco, José. "España: El peso del estereotipo." *Claves de razón práctica* 48 (1994): 3-12.
Álvarez Junco, José. *Mater Dolorosa: La idea de España en el siglo XIX*. Madrid: Taurus, 2001.
Amigó i Anglès, Ramon, Pere Anguera i Nolla, and Borja de Riquer i Permanyer. *La consolidació del món burgès: 1860-1900*. Barcelona: Fundació Enciclopèdia Catalana, 1996.
Anderson, Benedict R. *Imagined Communities: Reflections on the Origin and Spread of Nationalism*. New York: Verso, 1991.
Andreu, Xavier. "Figuras modernas del deseo: Las majas de Ramón de la Cruz y los orígenes del majismo." *Ayer* 78, no. 2 (2010): 25-46.
Andreu Miralles, Xavier. *El descubrimiento de España: Mito romántico e identidad nacional*. Barcelona: Taurus, 2016.
Aoyama, Yuko. "Artists, Tourists, and the State: Cultural Tourism and the Flamenco Industry in Andalusia, Spain." *International Journal of Urban and*

Regional Research 33, no. 1 (2009): 80–104. https://doi.org/10.1111/j.1468-2427.2009.00846.x.

Applegate, Celia. *Bach in Berlin: Nation and Culture in Mendelssohn's Revival of the "St. Matthew Passion."* Ithaca, NY: Cornell University Press, 2014.

Applegate, Celia. *A Nation of Provincials: The German Idea of Heimat.* Berkeley: University of California Press, 1990.

Applegate, Celia, and Pamela Maxine Potter. *Music and German National Identity.* Chicago: University of Chicago Press, 2002.

Archilés, Ferrán, and Marta García Carrión. "En la sombra del estado: Esfera pública nacional y homogenización cultural en la España de la Restauración." *Historia contemporánea* 45 (2012): 483–518.

Archilés, Ferrán, and Manuel Martí. "Un país tan extraño como cualquier otro: La construcción de la identidad nacional española contemporánea." In *El siglo XX: Historiografía e historia*, edited by María Cruz Romeo and Ismael Saz, 245–78. Valencia: Universitat de València, 2002.

Arriaga, Gerardo. "La guitarra Renacentista." In *La guitarra española: The Spanish Guitar*, 63–65. New York: New York Metropolitan Museum of Art; Madrid: Museo Municipal de Madrid, 1993.

Astigarraga, Jesús. *The Spanish Enlightenment Revisited.* Oxford: Voltaire Foundation, 2015.

Atencia Doña, Lidia. "Desarrollo histórico y evolutivo del baile flamenco: De los bailes de candil a las nuevas tendencias en el baile flamenco." *Revista de investigación sobre flamenco "La Madrugá,"* no. 12 (2016): 139–53.

Ateneo de Córdoba. "Concurso Nacional de Arte Flamenco de Córdoba—Ateneo de Córdoba." Accessed October 21, 2017. http://ateneodecordoba.com/index.php/Concurso_Nacional_de_Arte_Flamenco_de_Córdoba.

Augusteijn, Joost, and Eric Storm. "Introduction: Region and State." In *Region and State in Nineteenth-Century Europe: Nation-Building, Regional Identities and Separatism*, edited by Joost Augusteijn and Eric Storm, 1–12. New York: Palgrave Macmillan, 2012.

Augusteijn, Joost, and Eric Storm, eds. *Region and State in Nineteenth-Century Europe: Nation-Building, Regional Identities and Separatism.* New York: Palgrave Macmillan, 2012.

Aviñoa, Xosé. "El teatre líric català antecedents, desenvolupament i epígons (1894–1908): L'aportació musical, plàstica i literària." *Anales de literatura española* 15 (2002): 223–29.

Badger, R. Reid. "Chicago 1893." In *Encyclopedia of World's Fairs and Expositions*, edited by John E. Findling and Kimberly D. Pelle, 116–25. Jefferson, NC: McFarland, 2008.

Bailey, Peter. *Popular Culture and Performance in the Victorian City.* Cambridge: Cambridge University Press, 2003.

Balcells, Albert, and Geoffrey J. Walker. *Catalan Nationalism: Past and Present.* New York: St. Martin's Press, 1996.

Balfour, S., and A. Quiroga. *The Reinvention of Spain*. New York: Oxford University Press, 2007.

Barke, M., and J. Towner. "Exploring the History of Leisure and Tourism in Spain." In *Tourism in Spain: Critical Issues*, edited by M. Barke, J. Towner, and M. Newton, 3–34. Wallingford: C. A. B. International, 1996.

Barreiro, Javier. "El Madrid nocturno de fines del siglo XIX, 1890." *Siglo diecinueve* 20 (2014): 113–34.

Barrios, Manuel. *Gitanos, moriscos y cante flamenco*. Seville: J. Rodríguez Castillejo, 1989.

Barth, Volker. "Paris 1867." In *Encyclopedia of World's Fairs and Expositions*, edited by John E. Findling and Kimberly D. Pelle, 37–44. Jefferson, NC: McFarland, 2008.

Ben-Ghiat, R. "Italian Fascism and the Aesthetics of the 'Third Way.'" *Journal of Contemporary History* 31, no. 2 (1996): 293–316.

Bennahum, Ninotchka. *Antonia Mercé, "La Argentina": Flamenco and the Spanish Avant garde*. Hanover, NH: University Press of New England, 2000.

Bergero, Adriana J. *Intersecting Tango: Cultural Geographies of Buenos Aires, 1900–1930*. Pittsburgh: University of Pittsburgh Press, 2008.

Beyen, Marnix, and Maarten Van Ginderachter. "General Introduction: Writing the Mass into a Mass Phenomenon." In *Nationhood from Below*, edited by Marnix Beyen and Maarten Van Ginderachter, 3–22. Basingstoke: Palgrave Macmillan, 2012.

Billig, Michael. *Banal Nationalism*. London: Sage, 1995.

Blas Vega, José. *Los cafés cantantes de Sevilla*. Madrid: Cinterco, 1987.

Blas Vega, José. *El flamenco en Madrid*. Córdoba: Almuzara, 2006.

Blas Vega, José. "Recorrido por la Barcelona de los cafés cantantes y colmaos flamencos." *La Caña: Revista de flamenco* 25 (1999): 5–20.

Blas Vega, José, and Manuel Ríos Ruiz. *Diccionario enciclopédico ilustrado del flamenco*. 2 vols. Madrid: Editorial Cinterco, 1990.

Boggs, Bruce A. "Riffing in Spanish: Flamencos and Flamenquismo in the Popular Theater." Unfinished manuscript.

Bohlman, Philip Vilas. *The Music of European Nationalism: Cultural Identity and Modern History*. ABC-CLIO World Music Series. Santa Barbara, CA: ABC-CLIO, 2004.

Bois, Mario. *Carmen Amaya o la danza del fuego*. Madrid: Espasa Calpe, 1994.

Bolotin, Norm, and Christine Laing. *Chicago's Grand Midway: A Walk around the World at the Columbian Exposition*. Urbana: University of Illinois Press, 2017.

Box Varela, Zira. "Anverso y reverso de la nación: El discurso de la antiespañolada durante los primeros años 40." *Hispania* 75, no. 249 (January–April, 2015): 237–66. https://doi.org/10.3989/hispania.2015.009.

Brandes, Stanley. "The Sardana: Catalan Dance and Catalan National Identity." *Journal of American Folklore* 103, no. 407 (January–March 1990): 24–41.

Bibliography

Breuilly, John. *Nationalism and the State*. Chicago: University of Chicago Press, 1994.
Burke, Peter. *Popular Culture in Early Modern Europe*. Burlington, VT: Ashgate, 2010.
Calderwood, Eric. "'In Andalucía, There Are No Foreigners': Andalucismo from Transperipheral Critique to Colonial Apology." *Journal of Spanish Cultural Studies* 15, no. 4 (2014): 399–417. https://doi.org/10.1080/14636204.2014.991488.
Campo, Alberto del, and Rafael Cáceres. *Historia cultural del flamenco: El barbero y la guitarra*. Córdoba: Almuzara, 2013.
Capel Martínez, Rosa María. "Life and Work in the Tobacco Factories: Female Industrial Workers in the Twentieth Century." In *Constructing Spanish Womanhood: Female Identity in Modern Spain*, edited by Victoria Lorée Enders and Pamela Beth Radcliff, 131–50. Albany: State University of New York Press, 1999.
Carbonell, Anna. "El cuplet català." In *Història, política, societat i cultura dels Països Catalans*, edited by Borja de Riquer i Permanyer, 360–61. Barcelona: Enciclopèdia Catalana, 1995.
Carrasco Benítez, Marta. "Three Centuries of Flamenco." In *Flamenco on the Global Stage: Historical, Critical and Theoretical Perspectives*, edited by K. Meira Goldberg, Ninotchka Bennahum, and Michelle Heffner Hayes, 23–32. Jefferson, NC: McFarland, 2015.
Casero García, Estrella. *La España que bailó con Franco*. Madrid: Editorial Nuevas Estructuras, 2000.
Cazorla Sánchez, Antonio. *Fear and Progress: Ordinary Lives in Franco's Spain, 1939–1975*. Chichester: Wiley-Blackwell, 2010.
Chamberlin, J. Edward, and Sander L. Gilman, eds. *Degeneration: The Dark Side of Progress*. New York: Columbia University Press, 1985.
Charnon-Deutsch, Lou. *The Spanish Gypsy: The History of a European Obsession*. University Park: Penn State Press, 2004.
Chinoy, Clara. "The First Academy of Flamenco Dance: Frasquillo and the 'Broken Dance' of the Gitanos." In *Flamenco on the Global Stage: Historical, Critical and Theoretical Perspectives*, edited by K. Meira Goldberg, Ninotchka Bennahum, and Michelle Heffner Hayes, 143–56. Jefferson, NC: McFarland, 2015.
Chuse, Loren. *The Cantaoras: Music, Gender, and Identity in Flamenco Song*. New York; London: Routledge, 2003.
Clark, Walter Aaron. *Isaac Albéniz: Portrait of a Romantic*. Oxford: Oxford University Press, 2007.
Cobo, Eugenio. "Antiflamenquistas antes de Noel." *La Caña: Revista de flamenco* 4 (1993): 5–13.
Cobo, Eugenio. "Los escritores catalanes del siglo XIX ante el flamenco." *Candil* 129 (2001): 3935–51.

Cobo Guzmán, Eugenio. "El antiflamenquismo de Benito Pérez Galdós." *Revista de flamencología* 7, no. 16 (2002): 37–44.
Cockx, August, and J. Lemmens. *Les Expositions Universelles et Internationales en Belgique de 1885 à 1958*. Brussels: Editorial-Office, 1958.
Connell, J., and C. Gibson. *Sound Tracks: Popular Music, Identity and Place. Critical Geographies*. London: Routledge, 2002.
Cooper, David. "Béla Bartók and the Question of Race Purity in Music." In *Musical Constructions of Nationalism: Essays on the History and Ideology of European Musical Culture, 1800–1945*, edited by Harry White and Michael Murphy, 16–32. Cork: Cork University Press, 2001.
Croft, Clare. *Dancers as Diplomats: American Choreography in Cultural Exchange*. Oxford: Oxford University Press, 2015.
Cruces Roldán, Cristina. *El flamenco y la música andalusí: Argumentos para un encuentro*. Barcelona: Ediciones Carena, 2003.
Cruces Roldán, Cristina. *Más allá de la música: Antropología y flamenco; Sociabilidad, transmisión y patrimonio*. Seville: Signatura Ediciones de Andalucía, 2002.
Cruzado, Ángeles. "Soledad Arce, la estrella de las Gitanas de la Exposición (I) | Flamencas por derecho." April 11, 2016. Accessed October 15, 2017. http://www.flamencasporderecho.com/soledad-arce-i/.
Cuenca Toribio, José Manuel. "La primera etapa del andalucismo." In *Espacio, tiempo, y forma: Historia contemporánea*, 372–92. Madrid: UNED: Facultad de Historia y Geografía, 1993.
Cueva Merino, Julio. "Cultura y movilización en el movimiento católico de la Restauración (1899–1913)." In *La cultura española en la Restauración (I encuentro de historia de la Restauración)*, edited by Manuel Suárez Cortina, 169–92. Santander: Sociedad Menéndez Pelayo, 1999.
Curtis, Benjamin W. *Music Makes the Nation: Nationalist Composers and Nation Building in Nineteenth-Century Europe*. Amherst, NY: Cambria Press, 2008.
Dahlhaus, Carl. "Nationalism and Music." In *Between Romanticism and Modernism: Four Studies in the Music of the Later Nineteenth Century*, 79–101. Translated by Mary Whittall. Berkeley: University of California Press, 1980.
Davidson, Robert A. *Jazz Age Barcelona*. Toronto: University of Toronto Press, 2009.
De Grazia, Victoria. *The Culture of Consent: Mass Organization of Leisure in Fascist Italy*. Cambridge: Cambridge University Press, 2002.
Díaz Freire, J. J. "La reforma de la vida cotidiana y el cuerpo femenino durante la dictadura de Primo de Rivera." In *El rumor de lo cotidiano: Estudios sobre el País Vasco contemporáneo*, edited by Luis Castells, 225–58. Bilbao: Universidad del País Vasco, 1999.
Duara, Prasenjit. *Rescuing History from the Nation: Questioning Narratives of Modern China*. Chicago: University of Chicago Press, 1995.
Eakin, Marshall Craig. *Becoming Brazilians: Race and National Identity in Twentieth-Century Brazil*. Cambridge: Cambridge University Press, 2017.

Ealham, C. *Class, Culture, and Conflict in Barcelona, 1898-1937.* London: Routledge, 2005.
Ealham, C. "An Imagined Geography: Ideology, Urban Space, and Protest in the Creation of Barcelona's 'Chinatown,' c. 1835-1936." *International Review of Social History* 50, no. 3 (2005): 373-97.
Elorza, Antonio. *Anarquismo y utopia: Bakunin y la revolución social en España (1868-1936).* Madrid: Ediciones Cinca, 2013.
Esenwein, George Richard. *Anarchist Ideology and the Working-Class Movement in Spain, 1868-1898.* Berkeley: University of California Press, 1989.
Esteve Secall, Rafael, and Rafael Fuentes. *Economía, historia e instituciones del turismo en España.* Madrid: Ediciones Pirámide, 2000.
Fauser, Annegret. *Musical Encounters at the 1889 Paris World's Fair.* Eastman Studies in Music. Rochester: University of Rochester Press, 2005.
Foucault, Michel. *The History of Sexuality.* Vol. 1, *An Introduction.* New York: Vintage Books, 1990.
Fradera, Josep Maria. *Cultura nacional en una sociedad dividida: Cataluña, 1838-1868.* Translated by Carles Mercadal Vidal. Madrid: Marcial Pons, 2003.
Freedberg, Catherine Blanton. *The Spanish Pavilion at the Paris World's Fair.* 2 vols. New York: Garland, 1986.
Frolova-Walker, Marina. *Russian Music and Nationalism: From Glinka to Stalin.* New Haven, CT: Yale University Press, 2007.
Fuster i Sobrepere, Claudi. *Catàleg de la premsa musical barcelonina des dels seus orígens fins el final de la Guerra Civil (1817-1939).* Barcelona: Arxiu Municipal, 2002.
Gabriel, Pere. "La Barcelona obrera y proletaria." In *Barcelona, 1888-1929: Modernidad, ambición y conflictos de una ciudad soñada,* edited by Alejandro Sánchez Suárez, 88-107. Madrid: Alianza Editorial, 1994.
Gabriel, Pere. "Sociabilitat de les classes treballadores a la Barcelona d'entreguerres, 1918-1936." In *Vida obrera en la Barcelona de entreguerras, 1918-1936,* edited by José Luis Oyón, 99-126. Barcelona: Centre de Cultura Contemporània de Barcelona, 1998.
Gamboa, José Manuel. *Una historia del flamenco.* Pozuelo de Alarcón, Madrid: Espasa Calpe, 2005.
García, M. G. *Diccionario del teatro.* Madrid: Ediciones Akal, 1998.
García Gómez, Génesis. *Cante flamenco, cante minero: Una interpretación sociocultural.* Barcelona: Editorial Anthropos, 1993.
García Gómez, Génesis. "Volksgeist y género español." In *Flamenco y nacionalismo: Aportaciones para una sociología política del flamenco,* edited by Gerhard Steingress and Enrique Baltanás, 193-206. Seville: Fundación el Monte, 1998.
García-Matos Alonso, María Carmen. "Un folklorista del siglo XVIII: Don Preciso." *Revista de Musicología* 4, no. 2 (1981): 295-307.
Garriga, Ramón. *El Cardenal Segura y el Nacional-Catolicismo.* Barcelona: Editorial Planeta, 1977.

Gellner, Ernest. *Nations and Nationalism*. Ithaca, NY: Cornell University Press, 1983.
Gilfoyle, Timothy J. "Prostitutes in History: From Parables of Pornography to Metaphors of Modernity." *American Historical Review* 104, no. 1 (February 1999): 117–41.
Goldberg, K. Meira. "Jaleo de Jerez and *Tumulte Noir*: Primitivist Modernism and Cakewalk in Flamenco, 1902–1917." In *Flamenco on the Global Stage: Historical, Critical and Theoretical Perspectives*, edited by K. Meira Goldberg, Ninotchka Bennahum, and Michelle Heffner Hayes, 143–56. Jefferson, NC: McFarland, 2015.
Goldberg, K. Meira. *Sonidos Negros: On the Blackness of Flamenco (Currents in Latin American and Iberian Music)*. Oxford: Oxford University Press, 2018.
Goldberg, K. Meira, Ninotchka Bennahum, and Michelle Heffner Hayes. *Flamenco on the Global Stage: Historical, Critical and Theoretical Perspectives*. Jefferson, NC: McFarland, 2015.
Goldberg, K. Meira, and Antoni Pizà. "Introduction: *Mestizajes*." In *The Global Reach of the Fandango in Music, Song and Dance: Spaniards, Indians, Africans and Gypsies*, edited by K. Meira Goldberg and Antoni Pizà, xiii–xxii. Newcastle upon Tyne: Cambridge Scholars, 2016.
Gómez Amat, Carlos, Joaquín Turina Gómez, and Alicia de Larrocha. *La Orquesta Sinfónica de Madrid: Noventa años de historia*. Madrid: Alianza Editorial, 1994.
Gómez-García Plata, Mercedes. "Culture populaire et loisir citadin: Les cafés cantantes de 1850 a 1900." In *Ocio y ocios: Du loisir aux loisirs (Espagne XVIII–XXe siécles)*, edited by Serge Salaün and Francoise Étienvre, 110–26. Paris: Université du Sorbonne Nouvelle, 2010. http://crec-paris3.fr/wp-content/uploads/2011/07/07-gomezm.pdf.
Gómez-García Plata, Mercedes. "El género flamenco: Estampa finisecular de la España de pandereta." In *La escena española en la encrucijada, 1890–1910*, edited by Serge Salaün, Evelyne Ricci, and Marie Salgues, 101–24. Madrid: Editorial Fundamentos, 2005.
González Climent, Anselmo. *Flamencología*. Córdoba: Ayuntamiento de Córdoba, 1989.
Goode, Joshua. *Impurity of Blood: Defining Race in Spain, 1870–1930*. Baton Rouge: Louisiana State University Press, 2009.
Grande, Félix. *Memoria del flamenco*. Madrid: Espasa-Calpe, 1979.
Greenhalgh, Paul. *Ephemeral Vistas: The Expositions Universelles, Great Exhibitions, and World's Fairs, 1851–1939*. Manchester: Manchester University Press, 1988.
Gutiérrez Camacho, Manuel-Enrique. *Vida y obra de Isidro de las Cagigas*. Seville: Fundación Blas Infante, 2007.
Hamnett, Brian R. *The Enlightenment in Iberia and Ibero-America*. Cardiff: University of Wales Press, 2017.

Hayden, Dolores. *The Power of Place: Urban Landscapes as Public History*. Cambridge, MA: MIT Press, 1997.
Hayes, Michelle Heffner. *Flamenco: Conflicting Histories of the Dance*. Jefferson, NC: McFarland, 2009.
Heck, Thomas F., et al. "Guitar." 2001. https://doi.org/10.1093/gmo/9781561592630.article.43006.
Héran, F. "L'invention de l'Andalousie au XIXe, dans la littérature de voyage: Origine et fonction sociales du quelques images touristiques." In *Tourisme et développement regional en Andalousie*, edited by Antonio-Miguel Bernal et al., 21–40. Paris: E. de Boccard, 1979.
Hess, Carol A. *Manuel de Falla and Modernism in Spain: 1898–1936*. Chicago: University of Chicago Press, 2001.
Hidalgo Gómez, Francisco. *Carmen Amaya: Cuando duermo sueño que estoy bailando*. Barcelona: Libros PM, 1995.
Hidalgo Gómez, Francisco. *Como en pocos lugares: Noticias del flamenco en Barcelona*. Barcelona: Carena, 2000.
Hixson, Walter L. *Parting the Curtain: Propaganda, Culture, and the Cold War*. New York: St. Martin's Press, 1996.
Hobsbawm, E. J., and T. O. Ranger. *The Invention of Tradition*. Cambridge: Cambridge University Press, 1992.
Holguín, Sandie. *Creating Spaniards: Culture and National Identity in Republican Spain*. Madison: University of Wisconsin Press, 2002.
Holguín, Sandie. "National Spain Invites You: Battlefield Tourism during the Spanish Civil War." *American Historical Review* 110, no. 5 (2005): 1399–426.
Hooper, Kirsty. "A Tale of Two Empires? The Earl's Court Spanish Exhibition (1889)." *Modern Languages Open* (2014). https://doi.org/10.3828/mlo.v0i1.5.
Hroch, Miroslav. *Social Preconditions of National Revival in Europe: A Comparative Analysis of the Social Composition of Patriotic Groups among the Smaller European Nations*. New York: Cambridge University Press, 1984.
Illiano, Roberto, and Massimiliano Sala. "Italian Music and Racial Discourses during the Fascist Period." In *Western Music and Race*, edited by Julie Brown, 182–200. Cambridge: Cambridge University Press, 2007.
Institut Cerdà. *Cerdà, urbs i territori: Planning beyond the Urban; A Catalogue of the Exhibition. Mostra Cerdà, urbs i territori, held September 1994 through January 1995, Barcelona*. Madrid: Electa; Fundació Catalana per a la Recerca, 1996.
Iriye, Akira. *Cultural Internationalism and World Order*. Baltimore: Johns Hopkins University Press, 1997.
Israel, Jonathan. *The Radical Enlightenment: Philosophy and the Making of Modernity (1600–1750)*. Oxford: Oxford University Press, 2002.
Jackson, Jeffrey H. "Making Jazz French: The Reception of Jazz Music in Paris, 1927–1934." *French Historical Studies* 25, no. 1 (2002): 149–70.
Jackson, Jeffrey H., and Stanley C. Pelkey. *Music and History: Bridging the Disciplines*. Jackson: University Press of Mississippi, 2005.

Johnson, James H. *Listening in Paris: A Cultural History*. Berkeley: University of California Press, 1996.
Kaplan, Temma. "Female Consciousness and Collective Action: The Case of Barcelona, 1910-1918." *Signs: Journal of Women in Culture and Society* 7, no. 3 (1982): 545-66.
Karthas, Ilyana. *When Ballet Became French: Modern Ballet and the Cultural Politics of France, 1909-1939*. Montreal: McGill-Queen's University Press, 2015.
Kater, Michael H. "Forbidden Fruit? Jazz in the Third Reich." *American Historical Review* 94, no. 1 (1989): 11-43. https://doi.org/10.2307/1862076.
Lajosi, Krisztina. "National Stereotypes and Music." *Nations and Nationalism* 20, no. 4 (2014): 628-45. https://doi.org/10.1111/nana.12086.
Lannon, F. *Privilege, Persecution, and Prophecy: The Catholic Church in Spain, 1875-1975*. Oxford: Clarendon Press, 1987.
Lannon, Frances. "Los cuerpos de las mujeres y el cuerpo político católico: Autoridades e identidades en conflicto en España durante las décadas de 1920 y 1930." *Historia social*, no. 35 (1999): 65-80. http://www.jstor.org/stable/40340713.
Lasheras Peña, Ana Belén. "España en París: La imagen nacional en las Exposiciones Universales, 1855-1900." PhD diss., Universidad de Cantabria, 2010.
Leblon, Bernard. *Gypsies and Flamenco: The Emergence of the Art of Flamenco in Andalusia*. Hatfield: University of Hertfordshire Press, 2003.
Leerssen, Joep. "Nationalism and the Cultivation of Culture." *Nations and Nationalism* 12, no. 4 (2006): 559-78.
Leerssen, Joseph Theodoor. *National Thought in Europe: A Cultural History*. Amsterdam: Amsterdam University Press, 2014.
Lefebvre, Henri. *The Production of Space*. Translated by Donald Nicholson-Smith. Malden, MA: Blackwell, 2009.
Levine, Lawrence W. *Highbrow/Lowbrow*. Cambridge, MA: Harvard University Press, 1988.
Llano, Samuel. "Public Enemy or National Hero? The Spanish Gypsy and the Rise of *Flamenquismo*, 1898-1922." *Bulletin of Spanish Studies* 94, no. 6 (2017): 977-1004. https://doi.org/10.1080/14753820.2017.1336363.
Llano, Samuel. *Whose Spain? Negotiating "Spanish Music" in Paris, 1908-1929*. Oxford: Oxford University Press, 2012.
MacCannell, Dean. *The Tourist: A New Theory of the Leisure Class*. New York: Schocken Books, 1976.
Machin-Autenrieth, Matthew. "Flamenco? Algo Nuestro? (Something of Ours?): Music, Regionalism and Political Geography in Andalusia, Spain." *Ethnomusicology Forum* 24, no. 1 (2015): 4-27.
Machin-Autenrieth, Matthew. *Flamenco, Regionalism and Musical Heritage in Southern Spain*. London: Routledge, 2017.
Madridejos Mora, Montse. *Carmen Amaya*. Barcelona: Edicions Bellaterra, 2013.

Madridejos Mora, Montse, and E. Martín Corrales. *El flamenco en la Barcelona de la Exposición Internacional 1929-1930*. Barcelona: Bellaterra, 2012.

Marco, Tomás. *Spanish Music in the Twentieth Century*. Cambridge, MA: Harvard University Press, 1993.

Marfany, J. L. "'Al damunt dels nostres cants...': Nacionalisme, modernisme i cant coral a la Barcelona del final de segle." *Recerques*, no. 19 (1987): 85-113.

Marfany, Joan-Lluís. *La cultura del catalanisme: El nacionalisme català en els seus inicis*. Barcelona: Editorial Empúries, 1995.

Martí, Josep. "Folk Music Studies and Ethnomusicology in Spain." *Yearbook for Traditional Music* 29 (1997): 107-40.

Martín-Casares, Aurelia, and Marga G. Barranco. "The Musical Legacy of Black Africans in Spain: A Review of Our Sources." *Anthropological Notebooks* 15, no. 2 (2009): 51-60.

Martín Corrales, Eloy. "Flamenco en la Barcelona revolucionaria: Julio de 1936-Mayo de 1937." *Candil* 129 (2001): 3983-97.

Martínez del Fresno, Beatriz. "Women, Land, and Nation: The Dances of the Falange's Women's Section in the Political Map of Franco's Spain." In *Music and Francoism*, edited by Gemma Pérez Zalduondo and Germán Gan Quesada, 357-406. Turnhout: Brepols, 2013.

Mendelson, Jordana. *Documenting Spain: Artists, Exhibition Culture, and the Modern Nation, 1929-1939*. University Park: Penn State University Press, 2005.

Milazzo, Kathy. "Dancers of Cádiz: *Puellae Gaditane* and Creations of Myth." In *Flamenco on the Global Stage: Historical, Critical and Theoretical Perspectives*, edited by K. Meira Goldberg, Ninotchka Bennahum, and Michelle Heffner Hayes, 33-41. Jefferson, NC: McFarland, 2015.

Miller, Montserrat. *Feeding Barcelona, 1714-1975: Public Market Halls, Social Networks, and Consumer Culture*. Baton Rouge: Louisiana State University Press, 2015.

Millington, Barry. "(Wilhelm) Richard Wagner." In *The New Grove Dictionary of Opera*, vol. 4, edited by Stanley Sadie, 1054-84. London: Macmillan, 1992.

Mitchell, Timothy. *Flamenco Deep Song*. New Haven, CT: Yale University Press, 1994.

Molina, Margot. "La reina de la bata de cola." *El País*, April 6, 2003. https://elpais.com/diario/2003/04/06/andalucia/1049581344_850215.html.

Molina, Ricardo, and Antonio Mairena. *Mundo y formas del cante flamenco*. Madrid: Revista de Occidente, 1963.

Molins, Patricia, and Pedro G. Romero, eds. *The Spanish Night: Flamenco, Avant-garde and Popular Culture, 1865-1936*. Madrid: Museo Nacional Reina Sofia, 2008.

Morcillo, Aurora G. *True Catholic Womanhood: Gender Ideology in Franco's Spain*. DeKalb: Northern Illinois University Press, 2000.

Moreno Garrido, Ana. *Historia del turismo en España en el siglo XX*. Madrid: Síntesis, 2007.

Moreno Garrido, Ana, and Jorge Villaverde. "De un sol a otro: Turismo e imagen exterior española (1914-1984)." *Ayer*. Forthcoming.

Moreno-Luzón, Javier. "Political Clientelism, Elites, and Caciquismo in Restoration Spain (1875-1923)." *European History Quarterly* 37, no. 3 (2007): 417-41.

Moreno Luzón, Javier, Ferran Archilés i Cardona, Fernando Molina Aparicio, and Sebastian Balfour. *Construir España: Nacionalismo español y procesos de nacionalización*. Madrid: Centro de Estudios Políticos y Constitucionales, 2007.

Moreno Luzón, Javier, and Xosé M. Núñez Seixas, eds. *Los colores de la patria: Símbolos nacionales en la España contemporánea*. Madrid: Tecnos, 2017.

Moreno Luzón, Javier, and Xosé M. Núñez Seixas, eds. *Metaphors of Spain: Representations of Spanish National Identity in the Twentieth Century*. New York: Berghahn, 2017.

Moreno Mengíbar, Andrés. "Crisis y transformación de la prostitución en Sevilla (1885-1920)." *Bulletin d'histoire contemporaine de l'Espagne* 25. Special issue, *Prostitución y sociedad en España, siglos XIX y XX* (June 1997): 119-31.

Mosse, George L. "Fascist Aesthetics and Society: Some Considerations." *Journal of Contemporary History* 31, no. 2 (1996): 245-52.

Nava, Mica. *Visceral Cosmopolitanism: Gender, Culture and the Normalisation of Difference*. Oxford: Berg, 2007.

Navarro, José Luis, and Eulalia Pablo. *El baile flamenco: Una aproximación histórica*. Córdoba: Almuzara, 2005.

Nelson, Richard Alan. "George, Henry (1839-1897)." In *Encyclopedia of Business Ethics and Society*, edited by Robert W. Kolb, 992-93. Thousand Oaks, CA: Sage, 2008.

Newton, M. T. "Andalusia: The Long Road to Autonomy." *Journal of Area Studies (Series 1)* 3, no. 6 (1982): 27-32. https://doi.org/10.1080/02613530.1982.9673577.

Nicholson, Bruce. *Hi, Ho, Come to the Fair: Tales of the New York World's Fair of 1964-1965*. Huntington Beach, CA: Pelagian Press, 1989.

Noyes, Dorothy. "La Maja Vestida: Dress as Resistance to Enlightenment in Late-18th-Century Madrid." *Journal of American Folklore* 111, no. 440 (1998): 197-217.

Núñez, Xosé-Manoel. "Historiographical Approaches to Sub-national Identities in Europe: A Reappraisal and Some Suggestions." In *Region and State in Nineteenth-Century Europe: Nation-Building, Regional Identities and Separatism*, edited by Joost Augusteijn and Eric Storm, 13-35. New York: Palgrave Macmillan, 2014.

Núñez, Xosé-Manoel. "The Region as *Essence* of the Fatherland: Regionalist Variants of Spanish Nationalism (1840-1936)." *European History Quarterly* 31, no. 4 (2001): 483-518.

O'Connor, D. J. "Representations of Women Workers: Tobacco Strikers in the 1890s." In *Constructing Spanish Womanhood: Female Identity in Modern Spain*,

edited by Victoria Lorée Enders and Pamela Beth Radcliff, 131–72. Albany: State University of New York Press, 1999.
Offen, Karen. "Depopulation, Nationalism, and Feminism in Fin-de-Siècle France." *American Historical Review* 89, no. 3 (1984): 648–76.
Ojeda, Cesar. "Los españoles pintados por sí mismos." June 18, 2012. http://www.odisea2008.com/2012/06/los-espanoles-pintados-por-si-mismos.html.
Ordóñez Eslava, Pedro. "Qualities of Flamenco in the Francoism: Between the Renaissance and the Conscience of Protest." In *Music and Francoism*, edited by Gemma Pérez Zalduondo and Germán Gan Quesada, 265–83. Turnhout: Brepols, 2013.
Ortíz, Carmen. "The Uses of Folklore in the Franco Regime." *Journal of American Folklore* 112, no. 446 (1999): 479–96.
Ortiz Nuevo, José Luis. *¿Se sabe algo? Viaje al conocimiento del arte flamenco según los testimonios de la prensa sevillana del XIX, desde comienzos del siglo hasta el año en que murió Silverio Franconetti (1812–1889)*. Seville: Ediciones El Carro de la Nieve, 1991.
Otero, Luis. *La Sección Femenina*. Madrid: EDAF, 1999.
Oyón, José Luis. *La quiebra de la ciudad popular: Espacio urbano, inmigración y anarquismo en la Barcelona de entreguerras*. Barcelona: Ediciones del Serbal, 2008.
Pack, Sasha D. *Tourism and Dictatorship: Europe's Peaceful Invasion of Franco's Spain*. New York: Palgrave Macmillan, 2006.
Palma, Luis, María Luisa Palma, José Luis Martin, and Isidoro Cascajo. "Live Flamenco in Spain: A Dynamic Analysis of Supply, with Managerial Implications." *International Journal of Arts Management* 19, no. 3 (2017): 58–70.
Parakilas, James. "How Spain Got a Soul." In *The Exotic in Western Music*, edited by Jonathan Bellman, 137–93. Boston: Northeastern University Press, 1998.
Pardo Ballester, Trinidad. *Flamenco: Orientalismo, exoticismo y la identidad nacional española*. Granada: Universidad de Granada, 2017.
Pateman, Carole. *The Sexual Contract*. Stanford: Stanford University Press, 1988.
Paul, Marisol. "Baile flamenco para reforzar la Marca España." In *La economía del turismo, motor con Marca España: Todo nuevo bajo el sol*, 163–68. Madrid: LID, 2014.
Persia, Jorge de. *I Concurso de Cante Jondo: Edición conmemorativa, 1922–1992; Una reflexión crítica*. Granada: Archivo Manuel de Falla, 1992.
Pick, Daniel. *Faces of Degeneration: A European Disorder, c. 1848–c. 1918*. Cambridge: Cambridge University Press, 1989.
Pineda Novo, Daniel. "El flamenco, tradición y vanguardia." *Revista de flamencología* 5, no. 9 (1999): 81–84.
Plaza Orellana, Rocío. *Los bailes españoles en Europa: El espectáculo de los bailes de España en el siglo XIX*. Colección de flamenco Amuzara. Serie baile. Córdoba: Almuzara, 2013.

Plaza Orellana, Rocío. *El flamenco y los románticos: Un viaje entre el mito y la realidad*. Seville: Bienal de Arte Flamenco, 1999.
Pohren, D. E. *The Art of Flamenco*. Morón de la Frontera: Society of Spanish Studies, 1967.
Pollock, Griselda. "Modernity and the Spaces of Femininity." In *Vision and Difference: Femininity, Feminism, and Histories of Art*, 50–90. London: Routledge, 1988.
Prevots, Naima. *Dance for Export: Cultural Diplomacy and the Cold War*. Hanover: Wesleyan University Press, 1998.
Quiroga, Alejandro. *Making Spaniards: Primo de Rivera and the Nationalization of the Masses, 1923–30*. New York: Palgrave Macmillan, 2007.
Quiroga, Alejandro. "The Three Spheres: A Theoretical Model of Mass Nationalisation; The Case of Spain." *Nations and Nationalism* 20, no. 4 (2014): 683–700. https://doi.org/10.1111/nana.12073.
Radcliff, Pamela Beth. *Modern Spain: 1808 to the Present*. Hoboken, NJ: John Wiley and Sons, 2017.
Raya, Andrés. "1958: Año en que se publicó la "Antología del Cante Flamenco." *Flamenco en mi memoria* (blog), August 2, 2015. https://memoriaflamenca.blogspot.com/2015/08/1958-ano-en-que-se-publico-la-antologia.html.
Rearick, Charles. *Pleasures of the Belle Epoque: Entertainment and Festivity in Turn-of-the-Century France*. New Haven, CT: Yale University Press, 1985.
Richards, Michael. *After the Civil War: Making Memory and Re-making Spain since 1936*. Cambridge: Cambridge University Press, 2013.
Richards, Michael. *A Time of Silence: Civil War and the Culture of Repression in Franco's Spain, 1936–1945*. Cambridge: Cambridge University Press, 1998.
Richmond, Kathleen. *Women and Spanish Fascism: The Women's Section of the Falange, 1934–1959*. London: Routledge, 2003.
Richmond, Yale. *Cultural Exchange and the Cold War: Raising the Iron Curtain*. University Park: Penn State University Press, 2004.
Ringrose, David R. *Spain, Europe and the "Spanish Miracle," 1700–1900*. Cambridge: Cambridge University Press, 1998.
Ríos Ruiz, Manuel. "Guitarra." In *Diccionario enciclopédico ilustrado del flamenco*, edited by José Blas Vega and Manuel Ríos Ruiz, 349–55. 2nd ed. 2 vols. Madrid: Editorial Cinterco, 1990.
Ríos Ruiz, Manuel. *El gran libro del flamenco*. 2 vols. Madrid: Calambur, 2002.
Riquer i Permanyer, Borja de. "La débil nacionalización española del siglo XIX." *Historia social* 20 (1994): 97–114.
Riquer i Permanyer, Borja de. *Història, política, societat i cultura dels Països Catalans*. Barcelona: Enciclopèdia Catalana, 1995.
Riquer i Permanyer, Borja de, Josep M. Roig i Rosich, Manel Risques, and Àngel Duarte. *Història de la Catalunya contemporània*. Barcelona: Pòrtic, 1999.
Roberts, Mary Louise. *Disruptive Acts: The New Woman in Fin-de Siècle France*. Chicago: University of Chicago Press, 2002.

Rodríguez Martínez, Saturnino. *El NO-DO: Catecismo social de una época*. Madrid: Editorial Complutense, 1999.
Romero Maura, J. *La Rosa de Fuego: El obrerismo barcelonés de 1899 a 1909*. Madrid: Alianza, 1989.
Rosendorf, Neal M. *Franco Sells Spain to America: Hollywood, Tourism and Public Relations as Postwar Spanish Soft Power*. London: Palgrave Macmillan, 2014.
Roshwald, Aviel. *The Endurance of Nationalism: Ancient Roots and Modern Dilemmas*. Cambridge: Cambridge University Press, 2006.
Ruiz Lagos, Manuel, ed. *Ensayistas del mediodía (Mentalidades e ideologías autóctonas andaluzas en el periodo de entreguerras)*. Seville: Biblioteca de la Cultura Andaluza, 1985.
Said, Edward W. *Orientalism*. New York: Vintage Books, 2003.
Salaün, Serge. *El cuplé (1900–1936)*. Madrid: Espasa Calpe, 1990.
Salaün, Serge. "La sociabilidad en el teatro (1890–1915)." *Historia social*, no. 41 (2001): 127–46. http://www.jstor.org/stable/40340789.
Sanabria, Enrique. *Republicanism and Anticlerical Nationalism in Spain*. New York: Palgrave Macmillan, 2009.
Savigliano, Marta. *Tango and the Political Economy of Passion*. Boulder, CO: Westview Press, 1995.
Sayers, William. "Spanish *Flamenco*: Origin, Loan Translation, and In- and Out-Group Evolution (Romani, Caló, Castilian)." *Romance Notes* 48, no. 1 (2007): 13–22.
Sazatornil Ruiz, Luis, and Ana Belén Lasheras Peña. "París y la españolada: Casticismo y estereotipos nacionales en las Exposiciones Universales (1855–1900)." *Mélanges de la Casa de Velázquez* 35, no. 2 (2005): 265–90.
Schwartz, Vanessa R. *Spectacular Realities: Early Mass Culture in Fin-de-siècle Paris*. Berkeley: University of California Press, 1998.
Serrano, Carlos. "Cultura popular / Cultura obrera en España alrededor de 1900." *Historia social*, no. 4 (1989): 21–31. http://www.jstor.org/stable/40340197.
Serrano, Carlos, and Serge Salaün. *Los felices años veinte: España, crisis y modernidad*. Madrid: Marcial Pons Historia, 2006.
Serrera Contreras, Ramón María. "Falla, Lorca y Fernando de los Ríos: Tres personajes claves en el concurso de cante jondo de Granada de 1922." Real Academia Sevillana de Buenas Letras, 2010. http://dialnet.unirioja.es/servlet/oaiart?codigo=3691110.
Shubert, Adrian. *Death and Money in the Afternoon: A History of the Spanish Bullfight*. New York: Oxford University Press, 1999.
Shubert, Adrian. *A Social History of Modern Spain*. London: Routledge, 1996.
Sinha, Mrinalini. *Colonial Masculinity: The "Manly Englishman" and the "Effeminate Bengali" in the Late Nineteenth Century*. Manchester: Manchester University Press, 1995.
Smith, Anthony D. *The Ethnic Origins of Nations*. Oxford: Blackwell, 1987.

Smith, Anthony. "The Origins of Nations." In *Becoming National: A Reader*, edited by G. Eley and R. G. Suny. Oxford: Oxford University Press, 1996.
Sneeuw, Arie C. *Flamenco en el Madrid del XIX*. Córdoba: Virgilio Márquez, 1989.
Sopeña, Federico, ed. *Manuel de Falla: Escritos sobre música y músicos, Debussy, Wágner, el cante jondo*. Buenos Aires: Espasa-Calpe, 1950.
Sopeña Ibáñez, Federico. *Historia de la música española contemporánea*. Madrid: Ediciones Rialp, 1958.
Spain, Daphne. "Gender and Urban Space." *Annual Review of Sociology* 40, no. 1 (2014): 581–98. https://doi.org/10.1146/annurev-soc-071913-043446.
Steingress, Gerhard. *Flamenco postmoderno: Entre tradición y heterodoxia; Un diagnóstico sociomusicológico (escritos 1989–2006)*. Seville: Signatura, 2007.
Steingress, Gerhard. *Sociología del cante flamenco*. 2nd ed. Seville: Signatura, 2006.
Steingress, Gerhard, ed. *Songs of the Minotaur—Hybridity and Popular Music in the Era of Globalization: A Comparative Analysis of Rebetika, Tango, Rai, Flamenco, Sardana, and English Urban Folk*. Münster: LIT, 2002.
Steingress, Gerhard. . . . *Y Carmen se fue a París: Un estudio sobre la construcción artística del género flamenco (1833–1865)*. Colección de Flamenco. Serie Ensayo. Córdoba: Editorial Almuzara, 2006.
Steingress, Gerhard, and Enrique Jesús Rodríguez Baltanás, eds. *Flamenco y nacionalismo: Aportaciones para una sociología política del flamenco; Actas del I y II Seminario Teórico sobre arte, mentalidad e identidad colectiva, Sevilla, junio de 1995 y 1997*. Seville: Fundación Machado, 1998.
Stoklund, Bjarne. "The Role of the International Exhibit in the Construction of National Cultures." *Ethnologie Europaea* 24, no. 1 (1994): 35–54.
Storm, Eric. *The Culture of Regionalism: Art, Architecture and International Exhibitions in France, Germany and Spain, 1890–1939*. Manchester: Manchester University Press, 2010.
Storm, Eric. "Una España más española: La influencia del turismo en la imagen nacional." In *Ser españoles: Imaginarios nacionalistas en el siglo XX*, edited by Javier Moreno Luzón and Xosé M. Núñez Seixas, 530–60. Barcelona: RBA, 2013.
Szwed, John F. *Crossovers: Essays on Race, Music, and American Culture*. Philadelphia: University of Pennsylvania Press, 2005.
Tenorio-Trillo, Mauricio. *Mexico at the World's Fairs: Crafting a Modern Nation*. Berkeley: University of California Press, 1996.
Timm, Annette F., and Joshua A. Sanborn. *Gender, Sex, and the Shaping of Modern Europe: A History from the French Revolution to the Present Day*. 2nd. ed. London: Bloomsbury Academic, 2016.
Torrecilla, Jesús. *España exótica: La formación de la imagen española moderna*. Boulder, CO: Society of Spanish and Spanish-American Studies, 2004.
Torres Cortés, Norberto. "El estilo 'rasgueado' de la guitarra barroca y su influencia en la guitarra flamenca: Fuentes escritas y musicales (siglo XVII)." *Revista de investigación sobre flamenco "La Madrugá"* 6 (2012): 1–46.

Torres Cortés, Norberto. *Historia de la guitarra flamenca: El surco, el ritmo y el compás*. Córdoba: Almuzara, 2005.

Torres Mulas, Jacinto. *Las publicaciones periódicas musicales en España (1812–1990): Estudio crítico-bibliográfico; repertorio general*. Madrid: Instituto de Bibliografía Musical, 1991.

Tosh, John. "Hegemonic Masculinity and Gender History." In *Masculinities in Politics and War: Gendering Modern History*, edited by Stefan Dudink, Karen Hagemann, and John Tosh, 41–58. Manchester: Manchester University Press, 2004.

Tuan, Yi-fu. *Space and Place: The Perspective of Experience*. Minneapolis: University of Minnesota Press, 1977.

Turrado Vidal, Martín. *Policía y delincuencia a finales del siglo XIX*. Madrid: Ministerio del Interior; Dykinson, 2001.

Ullman, Joan Connelly. *La semana trágica*. Barcelona: Ediciones Ariel, 1972.

Universo andalucista. "Mario Méndez Bejarano." Accessed January 2, 2017. http://universoandalucista.blogspot.com/2011/02/mario-mendez-bejarano.html.

Uría, Jorge. "La cultura popular en la Restauración: El declive de un mundo tradicional y desarrollo de una sociedad de masas." In *La cultura española en la Restauración*, edited by Manuel Suárez Cortina, 103–44. Santander: Sociedad Menéndez Pelayo, 1999.

Uría, Jorge. "Lugares para el ocio: Espacio público y espacios recreativos en la Restauración española." *Historia social*, no. 41 (2001): 89–111. http://www.jstor.org/stable/40340787.

Uría, Jorge. "La taberna: Un espacio multifuncional de sociabilidad popular en la Restauración española." *Hispania* 63, no. 214 (2003): 571–604.

Van Ginderachter, Maarten, and Marnix Beyen, eds. *Nationhood from Below: Europe in the Long Nineteenth Century*. Basingstoke: Palgrave Macmillan, 2012.

Vázquez, Oscar E. *The End Again: Degeneration and Visual Culture in Modern Spain*. University Park: Penn State University Press, 2017.

Vianna, Hermano, and John Charles Chasteen. *The Mystery of Samba: Popular Music and National Identity in Brazil*. Chapel Hill: University of North Carolina Press, 1999.

Villar, Paco. *La Criolla: La puerta dorada del Barrio Chino*. Barcelona: Comanegra; Ajuntament de Barcelona, 2017.

Villar, Paco. *Historia y leyenda del Barrio Chino, 1900–1992*. Barcelona: La Campana, 1996.

Villaverde, Jorge. "Sunny Spain at London, 1914: Creación, negociación y difusión de un imaginario español." Dissertation in progress, Insituto Universitario Europeo de Florencia.

Vincent, Mary. *Spain 1833–2002: People and State*. Oxford: Oxford University Press, 2007.

Walkowitz, Judith R. *City of Dreadful Delight: Narratives of Sexual Danger in Late-Victorian London*. Chicago: University of Chicago Press, 2011.

Walkowitz, Judith R. *Nights Out: Life in Cosmopolitan London*. New Haven, CT: Yale University Press, 2012.

Walton, John K., and Jenny Smith. "The First Century of Beach Tourism in Spain: San Sebastián and the Playas del Norte from the 1830s to the 1930s." In *Tourism in Spain: Critical Issues*, edited by M. Barke and J. Towner, 35-61. Wallingford: CAB International, 1996.

Warnock, Emery C. "The Anti-Semitic Origins of Henry Ford's Arts Education Patronage." *Journal of Historical Research in Music* 30, no. 2 (2009): 79-102.

Washabaugh, William. *Flamenco Music and National Identity in Spain*. London: Routledge, 2016.

Washabaugh, William. *Flamenco: Passion, Politics and Popular Culture*. Oxford: Berg, 1996.

Weber, William. *Music and the Middle Class: The Social Structure of Concert Life in London, Paris and Vienna between 1830 and 1848*. London: Routledge, 2017.

Weeks, Jeffrey. *Sex, Politics and Society: The Regulation of Sexuality since 1800*. 2nd ed. London: Longman, 1989.

White, Harry, and Michael Murphy, eds. *Musical Constructions of Nationalism: Essays on the History and Ideology of European Musical Culture, 1800-1945*. Cork: Cork University Press, 2001.

Withers, Charles W. J. *Placing the Enlightenment: Thinking Geographically about the Age of Reason*. Chicago: University of Chicago Press, 2007.

Young, Clinton D. *Music Theater and Popular Nationalism in Spain, 1880-1930*. Baton Rouge: Louisiana State University Press, 2016.

Young, Clinton D. "Theatrical Reform and the Emergence of Mass Culture in Spain." *Sport in Society* 11, no. 6 (2008): 630-42.

Yuval-Davis, Nira. *Gender and Nation*. London: Sage, 1997.

Zatañía, Estela. *Flamencos de Gañanía: Una mirada al flamenco en los cortijos históricos del bajo Gaudalquivir*. Seville: Ediciones Giralda, 2008.

Zubiaurre, Maite. *Cultures of the Erotic in Spain, 1898-1939*. Nashville, TN: Vanderbilt University Press, 2012.

Index

Page numbers in italics indicate illustrations.

Acción Católica, 65; austerity and modesty campaigns of, 180, 182-84, 186
Adorno, Theodor, 134, 296n36
advertising, 18, 235; flamenco dancing and, 156, 209, 219; tourism and, 14, 209, 212, 219, 222, 235, 314n4
afrancesados: rejection of, 35-39, 274n25. See also *ilustrados*
Al andalus, 10, 124, 127, 129, 135, 168, 201, 259
Alas, Leopoldo. See Clarín
Albaicín, 51
Albéniz, Isaac, 166
Alcina Navarrete, José, 82-83
alegrías, 155, 202
Alfonso XIII, 119, 181, 207
Alhambra, 150, 163, 164, 171, 245
almées, 158, 301n41. See also belly dancers

Almela Meliá, Juan, 82
Álvarez Agulo, Tomás, 82
Amaya, Carmen, 119, 120, 174, 244, *245*
Amicis, Edmondo de, 51
anarchism, 116-25
anarchists: *antiflamenquismo* and, 79, 81, 284n72; Restoration system and, 62-65; violence and 63-64, 102
Andalusia: as representation of Spain, 40, 57, 76, 123, 190, 199, 204, 229, 238; as savior of Spain, 122-24, 126-29; importance for flamenco's development, 42-44. See also national identity
Andalusian Autonomy Statute: 1981, 129-30, 249, 250; 2007, 251; desire for, 132
Andalusian Institute of Flamenco (Instituto Andaluz del Flamenco), 251
Anderson, Benedict, 13

Anselm Clavé, Josep, 109
anticlericalism, 65, 280n9, 281n21
antiflamenquismo: Catholic Church and, 65-73; conservatives and, 65-73; progressive regenerationists and, 73-79; reasons for, 59-60; working classes and, 79-88
antiflamenquistas, 59, 74, 108
Anti-pornography League. *See* Liga Contra la Pornografía
Antonio (Antonio Ruiz Soler), 245
Aoyama, Yuko, 249, 252, 322n33
Archilés, Ferrán, 60
Arce, Matilda. *See* Matilda
Arce, Soledad. *See* Soledad
Arce, Viva. *See* Viva
Arce Durán, José. *See* El Chivo
Armengou, Josep, 107, 290n39
Asamblea Contra la Pública Inmoralidad (Assembly Against Public Immorality), 181
Asamblea Federalista de Antequera (1883), 125
Asociación de Padres de Familia, 65
Asociación de Señoras, 89
ATESA, 224-25
austerity and modesty campaigns, 180, 183-84, 186. *See also* Acción Católica
autonomy: Andalusian, 124, 125, 126, 129-30, 132, 143, 249, 250, 251; Catalan, 64, 95, 102, 107, 123, 143; political, 94-95, 124, 128, 249, 305n1; regional, 23, 95, 123, 126, 305n1
avant-garde, 23, 145-46, 166-67, 170, 172, 272n6, 303n76, 304n91
Avelí Artís, Andreu, 115
Azorín (José Martínez Ruiz), 75

Bac, F., 152, 159
bailoara(s), 66, 84, 85, 88, 120, 160, 214, 243, 245, 252, 259
baile flamenco, 49, 50, 120, 207; cross-cultural influences on, 33-34, 42-44; history of, 32-34, 42-44
bajos fondos, 104-5, 115-16, 119. *See also* Barrio Chino
bandits: as part of *flamenquismo*, 76-77; as stereotype of Spain, 15, 84, 122, 128, 149, 150, 206, 240
"Bankia, pulmones y branquías," 256
Barcelona, 12, 27, 44, 45, 53, 57, 65, 78, 97, 98, 108-9, 111, 113, 122, 181, 244, 247, 248, 255, 289-90n36; 1929 Barcelona International Exposition and, 118-20; *bajos fondos* and, 104-5, 115-16, 119; Barrio Chino and, 92, 104-6, 112, 115, 116, 117, 288n7; *cafés cantantes* and, 97, 105-7; Catalan identity and, 108-9, 113, 292n64; entertainment zones and, 102-5; foreign influx to, 115-18; history of, 99-102; interwar period, 114-15; migration to, 101; during Spanish Civil War, 120, 174
Barrera, Manuel de la, 50
Barrera, Miguel de la, 50
Barrio Chino, 92, 104-6, 112, 115, 116, 117, 288n7
Bartók, Béla, 17, 166, 283n6, 303n75
Beauvoir, Simone de, 21
belly dancers, 21, 52, 148, 152, 157, 158, 160, 301n41. *See also* almées
Beltrán Gómez, Manuela, 254
Bergson, Henri, 130
Bermúdez, Diego. *See* El Tío Tenazas
Bética, 122, 128
Beyen, Marnix, 15
Bizet, Georges, 43
Bizet, René, 115
Black Legend, 15, 119, 193, 269n51
Böhl de Faber, Cecilia. *See* Fernán Caballero
bolero, 33, 44, 50, 230, 259
Borrow, George, 43
Borrull, Miguel, 116-18, 119, 120, 293n74
Boultenhouse, Charles, 233, 234
Bueso, A., 115, 117
bulerías, 78, 256
bullfighter(s), 77, 105, 116, 136, 138, 149, 151, 153, 163, 165
bullfighting, 7, 8, 36, 71, 74, 80, 81-82, 127, 128, 164, 243; linked with flamenco, 12, 16, 59 74, 75, 76, 78, 83, 149, 160; as modern, 12, 45; as national scourge, 59, 68, 75, 76, 78, 83, 149, 160; as national stereotype, 9, 16, 119, 122, 144, 160, 206,

Index

208, 217, 220, 243; as symbol of national identity, 8, 75, 149, 150, 160, 217, 249, 284n57; tourists and, 213, 214, 216
bullfights. *See* bullfighting
bullrings, 88, 132, 164; entertainment and, 68, 71, 81; as sites for flamenco performances, 173, 278n61, 293n74
Burrero, Miguel, 52, 279n70
Buylla, Adolfo A., 90, 91

cabarets, 10, 12, 47, 57, 66, 89, 91, 103, 104–5, 114, 115, 181, 285n77, 293n78
cachucha, 44
caciquismo, 61, 63, 125, 132
Cadalso, José, 27, 28, 35, 43, 50
Café Burrero, 52, 53, 164
Cairo Street. *See* Rue de Cairo
Carco, Francis, 115
Café Burrero, 52, 53, 53, 164
cafés cantantes, 11, 43, 44, 46–47, 50, 60, 74, 103, 132, 155, 167, 174, 215, 259, 277n50, 279n71; Catalan nationalism and, 97–99, 107–8, 110–12, 289–90n36; Catholic opposition to, 66–73; criminality and, 67; flamenco in, 10, 41, 46–47, 52, 58, 106, 173; inauthenticity and, 172, 251–52; locations of, 53–56, 100, 104; pornography and, 88–91; prostitution and, 57, 181; regulation of, 69–72, sexuality and, 58–59, 108, 234; tourism and, 48, 118; vice and, 67–73, 82–84, 90, 97–98; working-class elites' opposition to, 66–73
Café Silverio, 47, 160
Cagigas, Isidro de las, 122–23, 127–29, 130, 242
Calleja, Rafael, 214–15
Cánovas del Castillo, Antonio, 61–62, 64
cantaor(es)/a(s), 10, 47, 66, 165, 170, 171, 240, 248, 259, 261
cante flamenco, 34, 47, 120, 139, 140, 169, 207, 253, 297n57; ancient past of, 127, 139, 247; authenticity and, 42, 170, 246, 248; history of, 32, 39–42; 50, 247, 275n38
cante jondo: as art, 132, 166–72, 191, 214–15, 231–32; as authentic, 106, 127, 286n94; ancient past of, 133, 169, 201, 231, 303n6; as protest, 256; as source of shame, 75, 78, 82, 160; Blas Infante and, 134, 138, 139, 142; Federico García Lorca and, 139, 168–69, 170, 184, 231–32, 272n8; history of, 32; Manuel de Falla and, 139, 168, 170, 184, 191, 272n8
Cante Jondo Contest: Córdoba (1956), 215, 246; Granada (1922), 127, 146, 215. *See also* Concurso de Cante Jondo
cants corals, 98, 108–11, 113, 259, 290n43
Carco, Francis, 115
Carmen: as stereotype of Spain, 119, 153
cartas marruecas, 27–28
Castanets, 4, 28, 84, 153, 155, 161; as symbol of Andalusia, 16, 201; as symbol of Spain, 3, 29, 30, 75, 149, 206, 213, 217
Castellón Campos, Agustín. *See* Sabicas
Castro y Serrano, José de, 161–62
Catalan nationalists, 22, 61, 64, 95, 114, 120, 125, 133, 143, 305n1; *antiflamenquismo* and, 97–99, 101–2, 105–7; cultural identity and, 108–13, 115, 118, 289–90n36, 291n52
Catholic Church, 23, 35, 244; *antiflamenquismo* and, 22, 59; *cafés cantantes* and, 66–73; Coros y Danzas and, 203, 228; dance and, 179–87; female bodies and, 182, 184, 280n12; female sexuality and, 185–86, 280–81n14; during Franco regime, 174, 178; during Restoration, 61, 63, 65–66
Centro Andaluz de Flamenco, 252
Cerdà, Ildefons, 101
Chacón, Antonio, 171, 301n91
Charnon-Deutsch, Lou, 19
Chatfield-Taylor, H. C., 47, 52–53
chulos, 67, 76–78, 149, 260, 281n16; and *señorito chulo*, 76–78
cigarreras, 4
Clarín (Leopoldo Alas), 75
colonial gaze, 243
colonial voice, 47, 242
colonialism, 133, 159, 194, 215, 233, 243
Combarieu, Jules, 137
Comisión de Reformas Sociales, 80
Comisión Episcopal de Ortodoxia y Moralidad (CEOM), 183

commercial entertainment, 45, 46–47, 54, 78, 98, 111, 146, 225
Commission des Auditions Musicales, 154
Connell, John, 17
conservatives, 63, 73, 78, 79, 105, 179, 181, 183, 277n54
Conservatives (political party), 61
Concurso de Cante Jondo: Córdoba (1956), 246, 315n31; Granada (1922), 146, 168–69, 171, 190, 215, 231, 246. *See also* Cante Jondo Contest
Concurso Nacional de Arte Flamenco, 246, 315n31
Confederación Católica Nacional de Padres de Familia (CONCAPA), 183, 306–7n15
coplas, 40, 77, 139, 140, 260; *copla andaluza*, 139; *copla flamenca*, 138; *copla gitana*, 139
Córdoba, 27, 51, 126, 204, 215, 224, 246, 315n31
Coros y Danzas de España, 179, 187–203, 205, 214, 226, 230, 232, 245, 246, 247, 260; 188–90, 194; American reactions to at NY World's Fair, 233–34; authenticity and, 190, 191, 309n50; as cultural ambassadors, 192–99, 229; didacticism and, 199–203; geography and, 200; Latin American tour and, 192–96; as means of Spanish unification, national reconciliation and, 192, 195–96; neocolonialism and, 192–94, 310–11n68; NO-DO and, 240, 310n57; protests against, 196–98; as representation of Spanish diversity, 191, 213, 229; Spanish Pavilion and, 227–29
Corrales González, Matilde. *See* Matilde Corral
Cortijo El Guajiro, 215, *216*, *217*
cosmopolitanism, 8, 114, 292n64; as problem of modernity, 9, 183; Spanish nationalism as a reaction against, 34, 181, 183
Costa, Joaquín, 75
Costa Blanca, 215, 221, 222
Costa Brava, 215, 221, 222, 225
Costa Brava (film), 225
Costa del Sol, 222
costumbrista, 40, 52

Cuba, 61, 64, 68; influences on flamenco music, 12, 33, 248
Cuenca Toribio, José Manuel, 124
cultural anxieties, 20, 50, 60, 62–65, 66, 88, 98, 101, 106, 107–8
culture: folk, 108, 201; mass, 8, 9, 44, 138, 183, 232, popular, 31, 138, 207; as resistance to foreign cultures, 39–40
cuplé, 57, 91, 184, 285n77, 286n94, 291n52
cupletistas, 82, 285n77
Curtis, Benjamin, 17

Dahlhaus, Carl, 17
dance, Andalusian, 42, 44, 162, 190, 191, 200–201, 207, 214, 215, 230, 232, 285n77, 286n94; as ancient, 32, 162, 200–201, 202
dance, biblical, 185–86
dance, modern: as immoral, 184–87
dance academies, 11, 44, 46, 47, 50, 58, 182, 278n62
dance halls, 66, 72, 103, 104, 114, 181, 183, 186
Davillier, Charles, 6, 31, 43
Debussy, Claude: Gypsies of Granada and, 166–67, 170, 231; influence on Spanish avant-garde, 167–68, 170, 231
degeneration, 9, 73, 107, 168, 185, 265n20, 283n51
Demófilo, 41, 138, 139, 275n38. *See also* Machado y Álvarez, Antonio
Desmore, Frances, 168
Dirección Nacional de Turismo (DGT), 209, 214, 221
Domènech i Montaner, Lluís, 109
Don Preciso (Juan Antonio de Iza Zamácola Ocerín), 39
Doré, Gustave, 6, 7, 31, 32, 43
Drum (caricaturist), 152, 153, 300n31
Duende y misterio de flamenco, 230, 244, 246, 247
Durán, Rosa, 226, 230, 234

Eiroa, María Victoria, 198
Eixample, 101
El amor brujo, 167
El Caracol (Manuel Ortega), 171, 304n91
El Chivo (José Arce Durán), 155

Index

El Desastre. *See* Spanish-American War
El Farruco (Antonio Montoya Flores), 215
El ideal andaluz, 130
El Imparcial (café cantante, Madrid), 160
Ellis, Havelock, 3
El Niño de Utrera (Juan Mendoza Domínguez), 120, 174
El Pichiri (Antonio de la Rosa Pichiri), 155, 158
El Siglo futuro, 67, 281n17
El Solitario. *See* Estébanez Calderón, Serafín
Elssler, Fanny, 44
El sombrero de tres picos, 167
El Tío Tenazas (Diego Bermúdez), 171
Enlightenment, 28, 271n70; reforms and, 35; Spanish reaction against, 34
españolada, 119, 144, 169, 170, 204, 214, 217, 260, 293n78, 298n2
Estébanez Calderón, Serafín, 135
Estrada Saladich, F., 230
Excursionist Movement, 108, 206
exoticism, 145, 151, 153, 159, 199, 238
exotic Other: Andalusia/Spain as, 19, 148, 240; flamenco performers as, 155, 157, 232, 240
Expotur, 205, 226, 238-39
expulsion, 10, 32, 124, 129; of Jews, 129, 131, 296n32; of Muslims, 129, 131, 133, 140-41

Falange Española (Spanish Falange), 23, 95, 174, 178, 183, 187, 193, 194, 197, 244
Falla, Manuel de, 17, 135, 138, 151, 154, 159, 232; *cante jondo* and, 127, 132, 139, 167-68, 169, 170, 172, 184, 191, 201, 231, 272n8; Concurso de Cante Jondo and, 127, 168-69; Debussey and, 166-70, 231, 303n8
Fandango, 33, 43, 54, 149, 155, 202, 225
fascism, 178, 188, 238
fascists, 23, 178, 197, 210, 238, 255; culture and, 178, 189, 193. *See also* Falange Española
Fauser, Annegret, 151, 154, 159
federalism, 23, 124, 125
federal republicanism, 125
felamengu, 10, 141, 298n66

Ferdinand and Isabel (Catholic monarchs), 63, 131, 140, 163, 178
Fernán Caballero, *pseud.* (Cecilia Böhl de Faber), 40
Fernanda de Utrera (Fernanda Jiménez Peña), 245
Fernández Diaz, Antonio. *See* Fosforito
Fernández Porras, María. *See* Imperio de Granada
flamenco: advertising and, 209, 212, 213, 218-20, 223-24, 234-37; ancient roots of, 232-33; Andalusian regionalism and 130, 247; Andalusia's importance to development of, 42-44; aristocrats and, 36, 46, 74, 77, 281n16; authenticity, 104, 191, 232, 282n43, 289n24; commercial sites of, 54-57, 162; cross-class appeal and, 92; cultural hybridity and, 166-67; as degeneration, 77, 282n41; as flamingo, 136, 297n43; as flemish, 135, 136-37, 161, 296n1; foreigners and, 113-19, 154, 174; *gitanos*/Gypsies and, 10, 11, 19-20, 21, 28, 32, 33, 41, 48, 50, 135, 136, 141, 160, 162, 198, 199, 206, 225, 232, 248, 264n7, 275n38, 278n62, 286n94; guitar and, 21, 31-32; in historiography, 8-10; Intangible Cultural Heritage of Humanity, 6, 251, 322n7; Jews and, 295n32; as libertarian, 137-38; as modern, 9, 11-12, 29; as national heritage, 251; national identity and, 92, 179, 240, 251; origins of, 132, 133-42, 232; professionalization and, 53, 172, 252; Romanticism and, 43-44; Spanish decline and, 28-29, 66; as target for people's anxieties, 50, 66, 91; tourists and, 47-53, 206-10; after transition to democracy, 248-53; vice and, 57, 66, 68, 77-78, 80, 112, 162, 239
flamenco art-complex, 249, 252, 253
Flamenco Dance Museum, 252
flamenco dancers: feminization of males and, 158; and sexualization of females, 21, 48, 84, 150, 153, 157-60, 234; stereotypes of, 15, 86, 122, 145, 162, 164, 209, 212, 217, 219, 222, 223, 224, 225, 236, 237, 239, 244; and symbols of degeneration,

flamenco dancers (*continued*)
  77; symbols of national identity and, 15, 47, 75, 145, 162, 209, 219, 228, 239, 244
flamencomania, 9
flamenquismo, 74, 81, 92, 123; 283n72; *majismo* and, 74, 283n45
flamenquistas, 74
Flo6×8, 255–57
folk dances. *See* Coros y Danzas de España
folklore, 85, 168, 169, 205; Andalusian, 120, 198, 232, 244; competitions, 194; and creation of national unity, 190–92, 197, 198, 200; as opposition to flamenco, 199; regional, 94; societies, 41; Spanish, 145, 198, 221; tourism and, 205, 213, 214
folklorists, 8, 17, 38–39, 41, 108, 132, 134, 136, 138, 191, 198, 290n42
Ford, Henry, 308n36
Ford, Richard, 43
Fortuny, Mariano, 52
Fosforito (Antonio Fernández Díaz), 215
Foucault, Michel, 280–81n14
Fraga, Manuel, 221
Franconetti Águilar, Silverio, 46, 160, 277n51
Franco regime: flamenco and, 23, 175, 174, 179, 190, 191, 205, 215, 227, 228, 231, 239, 240, 244, 247, 265n21; folklore and, 9, 120, 187, 189, 228, 309n40; tourism and, 175, 205, 206, 210–16, 221–26, 227, 231, 240
French Revolution, 17, 29, 60, 276n47, 300n32; nationalism and, 34, 110
Frontaura, Carlos, 149–50

Gabriel, Pere, 103–4, 292n64
Gades, Antonio, 229, 230–31, 234, 318n68
García, Germán R., 72
García Berlanga, Luis, 16, 292n67
García Carrión, Marta, 60
García de Sáez, Miguel, 227
García Lorca, Federico: *cante jondo* and, 127, 132, 139, 168–70, 172, 272n8; co-optation by Franco regime and, 231–32
García Matos, Manuel, 190
García Palacios, Ángeles, 254
García Rodríguez, Rafael. *See* Rafael El Negro

Gasch, Sebastià, 119, 293n78
Gautier, Theophile, 43
Gellner, Ernest, 13
Gender, 13, 18–20, 77, 88, 107, 243
gender roles, 8, 9, 21, 180; flamenco dancers and, 151–53
Generation of '98, 75
George, Henry, 125
Gibson, Chris, 17
Gilbert, Marie Dolores Eliza Rosanna. *See* Montes, Lola
gitanos: aristocratic alliance with, 28, 33; Coros y Danzas and, 20; flamenco and, 11, 19–20, 28, 32, 33, 41, 135, 141, 160, 162, 206, 248, 275n38, 278n62; locations of, 47, 51, 52–53; race and, 19, 41, 159, 168, 276n45; as representative of Andalusia, 136, 139, 247; Spanish national identity and, 12, 136; stereotypes of, 19–20, 30, 31–32, 52, 76, 118, 162, 204, 206; as unrepresentative of Andalusia, 136, 139, 247. *See also* Gypsies
Glinka, Mikhail, 170
Gómez de la Serna, Ramón, 171, 304n91
Gómez-García Plata, Mercedes, 11, 251, 293n74
González Climent, Anselmo, 246
González Cuesta, Carlos, 204, 213, 240
Goode, Joshua, 18, 295–96n17
Goya, Francisco, 35, 36, 245, 246
Granada: as a center for flamenco, 27, 51, 52, 168, 204, 206, 224, 245
Granados, Enrique, 166
Grand Teâtre de l'Exposition, 155, 156, 162
Gual, Adriá, 110
guidebooks, 47–48, 207, 277n54, 277–78n58, 314n8
Guimerá, Ángel, 110
guitar: barbers and, 30; classical, 29, 30, 31, 230; *estilo rasgueado* and, 30, 31; flamenco and, 21, 31–32; history of, 29–32; lower classes and, 30–31; as national stereotype, 150, 164, 165, 199, 201, 213
Guy-Stéphan, Marie, 44
Gypsies: aristocratic alliance with, 74; dancers and, 44, 158, 160, 202, 221; flamenco and, 10, 20, 21, 48, 50, 136, 198,

Index

199, 225, 232, 264n7, 286n94; locations of, 53, 54; race and, 18–20, 161; Spanish national identity and, 15, 20, 50, 154, 170, 198, 199, 243; stereotypes of, 43, 51–52, 53, *88*, 144, 150, 160, 164, 199, 243, 302n50. See also *gitanos*
Gypsies of Granada, 144, 155–62, 166, 170
Gypsy handkerchief dance, 43

Herder, Johann Gottfried, 17, 38, 39, 41
Hernández, Miguel, 248
Hernández Sempelayo, María Josefa, 193
Hidalgo Gómez, Francisco, 100, 120
Hobsbawm, Eric, 13
Holiday in Spain, 224
Hoyos, Cristina, 252
Hoyos Sancho, Nieves de, 191
Hroch, Miroslav, 95

Iberia Airlines, 212, 213; advertisements for, 216–21, 235
ilustrados, 35, 36, 74, 260
Imperio de Granada (María Fernández Porras), 120
Infante, Blas, 162, 168; Andalusian nationalist and, 22, 123, 126, 127, 128; criticism of Spanish musicologists and, 134–36, "father of Andalusian nationalism," 250; flamenco as social critique and, 134, 257; origins of flamenco and, 133–42; regionalism and, 123, 124, 129–32
Institució Catalana de Música, 109
Institución Libre de Enseñanza, 41, 169, 275n37, 304n82
Institute for Catalan Studies, 108
Instituto Andaluz del Flamenco. See Andalusian Institute of Flamenco
International Expositions, 18, 23, 93, 104, 145, 165, 248; Barcelona 1888, 102, 104; Barcelona 1929, 99, 118–20; Brussels 1958, 226; Chicago 1893, 52, 163; entertainment at, 145, 146–49, 229–36; history of, 146–48; London 1851, 146, 171; national identity and, 144–45; New York 1964–65, 201, 226–38, 240; Paris 1867, 148; Paris 1878, 148; Paris 1889, 144, 147, 150–53, 155–56, 170, 300n32;

Paris 1900, 163–66, 170, 231; Paris 1937, 300n28; Seville, Ibero-American 1929, 119; Spanish entertainment at, 148–66
Iza Zamácola Ocerín, Juan Antonio de. *See* Don Preciso

Javanese dancers (International Exposition, Paris 1889), 151–52, 158, 159, 300n31
jaleo, 10, 260
jazz, 22, 91, 103, 104, 114, 173, 248; rise of mass culture and, 12, 16; as sign of degeneration, 185, 186, 308n36
Jerez de la Frontera, 27, 88, 246, 247
Jiménez, Juan Ramón, 171, 304n91
Jiménez Peña, Fernanda. *See* Fernanda de Utrera
Jocs Florals. *See* Juegos Florales
jota, 12, 154, 155, 186, 202, 207, 214, 308n31
Juana "La Macarrona" (Juana Vargas), 116, 155, 160, 166, 171, *172*
Juegos Florales, 122, 126, 127, 128. *See also* Jocs Florals
juerga, 28, 33, 43, 44, 46, 50, 51, 75, 169, 260
Junta de Andalucía, 10, 250–52

Kant, Immanuel, 34
Krausism, 139

La Criolla, 105, 115
"La fauna nacional," 84
Lafuente Alcántara, Emilio, 40
La Golondrina, 171
Lajosi, Krisztina, 17
Landsdale, Nelson, 233
La Niña de los Peines (Pastora Pavón), 116, 171
La Unión Católica, 70, 281n17
La verdad sobre el complot de Tablada y el Estado libre de Andalucía, 132, 142
Leerssen, Joep, 14, 38
Les Apaches, 166–67
Ley del descanso dominical, 71–72, 81
liberalism, 61
libertarian, 123, 133, 138, 142
Liga Contra la Pornografía, 89–91
Llano, Samuel, 168, 283n51
Lomax, Alan, 168

López, Guillermo, 99, 101, 107–8
López, Pilar, 230, 245
Los españoles pintados por sí mismos, 83–84

Machado, Antonio, 41, 171, 304n91, 313n103
Machado, Manuel, 41, 171, 202, 304n91, 313n103
Machado y Álvarez, Antonio, 41. *See also* Demófilo
Machado y Núñez, Antonio, 41
Macmaster, Neil, 270n67
Madrid: *cafés cantantes* and, 45, 46, 48, 53–55, 57, 67, 164, 222, 224, 232, 244, 248; as center for flamenco performances, 27, 160, 174, 222, 224, 226, 232, 244, 248
Madrid, Francisco, 105, 288n7
Magic of Majorca, 225
Mairena, Antonio, 245, 246–47
majismo, 36, 74, 260, 283n45
Majorca, 225
Majorca—Stay in the Sun, 225
majos/majas, 35–36, 35, 74–75, 77, 260, 281n16, 283n45
Manchin-Autentrit, Matthew, 251
Mar, Alfonso de, 164
Marca España, 252
March, Charles, 50, 58–59
Marfany, Joan-Luís, 109, 289–90n36
Margueritte, Paul, 157–58
María Luz, 245
Martinetes, 169
Martínez del Fresno, Beatriz, 189
Martínez Ruiz, José. *See* Azorín
Martínez Sierra, María, 167
Martínez Vilches, Juan. *See* Pericón de Cádiz
Matilda (Matilda Arce), 155
Matilde Corral (Matilde Corrales González), 215, 217
Maura, Antonio, 81
Méndez Bejarano, Mario, 126–27, 128
Mendoza Domínguez, Juan. *See* El Niño de Utrera
Menéndez y Pidal, Ramón, 190
Menenes, Enrique, 229
Mérimée, Prosper, 43
Mestres, Apel·les, 110

Michelet, Henri, 137
Michelin Man, 48–49
Middle Eastern dancers, 21, 158, 159
Midway Plaisance, 52, 147–48, 163
Millet, Lluís, 112
Ministry of Information and Tourism (MIT), 205–6, 211, 222, 226, 231–32, 238
Mitchell, Timothy, 171, 304n93
modernisme, 99, 109, 110, 287n4
modernity, 7, 99, 114, 146, 150, 165, 190, 225, 242, 276n48, 292n64; anxiety about, 9, 29, 98, 179, 180, 182, 191, 192, 240, 277n54, 306n8, 308n36
modesty (female), Catholic Church and, 71, 73, 180–83, 185–87, 308n31n34; Coros y Danzas and, 203
Molina, Ricardo, 246–47
Montes, Lola, (Marie Dolores Eliza Rosanna Gilbert), 44
Montoya Flores, Antonio. *See* El Farruco
Moral Panics, 62, 179–82, 280n7
Morand, Paul, 115–16
Morente, Enrique, 248
Moret, Segismundo, 69, 80, 150
Múñoz Diaz. *See* Eugenio Noel

nacional-flamenquismo, 243, 244–45, 246, 251
National Catholicisim, 174, 178, 188, 244, 249, 307n16
national identity: as Andalusian, 57, 88, 128, 201, 207, 228, 248; Catalan and, 98, 109, 111, 113, 115, 290n41; as feedback loop, 23, 170, 216; flamenco and, 9, 21, 22, 23, 46, 48, 92, 93, 179, 230, 244, 248, 249, 251; gender and, 20; international expositions and, 144–45; music and, 16–18, 41, 98; Spain and, 8, 12, 74, 93, 123, 143, 145, 146, 170, 177, 178, 179, 205, 227, 228; theories of, 8–16, 94, 107
nationalism: Andalusian, 23, 122–26; banal, 7; Catalan, 98, 107–13; gender and, 20; regional, 93, 94, 98, 123; theories of, 8–16, 94
Nationalists (Spanish Civil War), 130, 148, 177–78, 180, 182, 195, 202, 209, 231, 248, 255, 315n14

Index

National Plan for Tourism, 211
Nava, Mica, 114
Navarro, José Luis, 33
newspapers: Catholic, 67–70, 183; foreign, 151, 197–98, 212, 234–35, 238, 239; regionalist, 128; socialist, 81–83, 85–87; Spanish, 191, 199, 228
NO-DO (*Noticieros y Documentales*), 239–40, 310n57
Noel, Eugenio (Eugenio Múñoz Díaz), 75–79, 82, 108, 168, 172, 282n43, 284n56
Noyes, Dorothy, 35
Núñez de Arce, Gaspar, 74
Núñez Meléndez, José. *See* Pepe el de la Matrona
Núñez Seixas, Xosé Manoel, 94

ólé (dance), 43–58
Olóriz y Aguilera, Federico, 130, 296n24
ópera flamenca, 174, 278n61, 293n74
Orfeó Català, 109, 110
orfeóns, 98, 108–11, 112–13, 120, 260
Orient, 129, 162, 167–68, 214, 303n79
Oriental: Andalusia as, 43, 133, 162, 168, 228, 231–33; *cante jondo* as, 169–70; flamenco as, 161, 206, 232–33; Spain as, 163, 206–7, 214, 228, 243
Orientalism, 19, 44, 148, 150, 158, 159, 164, 201, 231–33, 234, 242; Andalusian identity and, 43, 44, 231–33; Spanish national identity and, 21, 44, 231–33
Orígenes de lo flamenco y secreto del cante jondo, 132–33
Ortega, Manuel. *See* El Caracol
Ortega y Gasset, José, 84, 306n14
Ortíz, Carmen, 189

Pablo, Eulalia, 33
Pack, Sasha, 221
Paco de Lucía (Francisco Gustavo Sánchez Gómez), 248
Palau de la Música Catalana, 109–20
palos, 12, 78, 138, 139, 155, 169, 245, 246, 248, 255, 260, 297n57
palmas, 10, 33, 230, 260, 278n62
pandereta, 150, 204–7, 221, 226, 240, 299n23
Paralelo, 99, 103–4
Pardo Bazán, Emilia, 75, 160, 161, 164, 165, 168, 170
Pastora Imperio (Pastora Rojas Monje), 167
patriarchal authority, 67–68, 181, 184, 281n21; breakdown of, 108, 186
Patronato Nacional de Turismo (PNT), 208–9
Pavón, Pastora. *See* La Niña de los Peines
payos, 11, 12, 266n31
"Peace through Understanding," 226
Pedrell, Felipe, 171, 275n34; criticism of, 132, 135–37; flamenco and, 41, 136; musical nationalism and, 40
Pepe el de la Matrona (José Núñez Melendez), 246
Pérez Blanco, Trinidad. *See* Trini España
Pérez Galdós, Benito, 75, 160–61, 168, 170, 282n43
Perico el del Lunar (Pedro del Valle Pichardo), 246
Pericón de Cádiz (Juan Martínez Vilches), 246
petenera, 141, 191
petimetre, 35, 37, 74
Pi i Margall, Francisco, 125
Pitarra, Serafí, 110
pitos, 10, 260
Planes i Martí, Josep, 119
polos, 39, 169
Pope Benedict XV, 180
Pope Pius X, 180
pornography, 73, 88, 116, 181, 286n89; antipornography campaigns, 71, 88–91, 182, 285n87; *cafés cantantes* as, 88–91, 186, 286n90; *flamenquismo* and, 74
Primo de Rivera, José Antonio, 187, 188, 189, 308n38
Primo de Rivera, Miguel, 61, 64, 114, 126, 179, 294n3
Primo de Rivera, Pilar, 187–88, 190, 192–93, 194, 195, 198, 308n38, 310–11n68
Primo de Rivera regime, 173
prostitution, 54, 57, 62, 70, 72, 80, 90, 102, 104, 105, 112, 116, 181, 182
Proudhon, Pierre-Joseph, 125
Pueblo Español, 118–19, 293n80

Queipo de Llano, Gonzalo, 254–55
Quiroga, Alejandro, 13, 292n66, 294n3

race, 8, 9, 11, 18–20, 41, 52, 91, 129, 131, 136, 151, 169, 184, 186, 191, 231, 232, 276n45, 295n17
racial fusion, 18, 129, 130, 295–96n17
Rafael El Negro (Rafael García Rodríguez), 215, 217
Ranger, Terrence, 13
Raval (el), 99–103, 117, 247
Ravel, Maurice, 166, 304n91
Reconquest, 126, 129, 131, 133, 135, 284n56
Reconquista. *See* Reconquest
regenerationism, 64
regenerationists, 63, 79, 131; flamenco and, 73, 78, 83, 105; *flamenquismo* and, 92, 123
regionalism: Andalusian, 122–23, 162, 247; cultural, 295n7; political, 94–95, 124, 125
Reglamento de Policía de Espectáculos, 71, 182
Republicans, 62, 63, 125, 182, 190, 205; during Spanish Civil War, 148, 195, 209, 210
Restoration: politics of, 60–65; social dislocation and, 62–65
Restoration system, 60–65
Revolution of 1868, 60, 98
Rey, Fernando, 245
Ribera y Tarragó, Julián, 134–35
Richards, Michael, 196
Ridruejo, Eulalia, 193
Rimsky-Korsakov, Nikolai, 17
Rito y geografía del cante, 247
Rodríguez Marín, Federico, 136
Rojas Monje, Pastora. *See* Pastora Imperio
Romanticism, 32, 43, 144
Rosa Pichiri, Antonio de la. *See* El Pichiri
Ronda española, 194, 196
Royal Commission of Tourism and Artistic Culture, 207
Rue de Cairo (International Exposition, Paris, 1889), 151, 157, 164
Ruiz Soler, Antonio. *See* Antonio
rumba catalana, 12, 120, 248

"Rumba Rave 'Banquero,'" 256
Rusiñol, Santiago de, 106–7, 110, 171, 404n91

Sabicas (Agustín Castellón Campos), 120, 174
Sacra Propedium (1921), 180
Sacromonte, 47, 51, 52, 104, 158, 164
Said, Edward, 19
Salicrú Puigvert, Carlos, 185–86
Salillas y Panzano, Rafael, 19
Sánchez Cantón, F., 207
Sánchez Gómez, Francisco Gustavo. *See* Paco de Lucía
sardana, 98, 108, 109, 110–13, 120, 128, 189, 195, 202, 203, 207, 214, 248, 260, 290n41; as remedy against decadence, 112–13
Schuchardt, Hugo, 41, 132, 275n25
Sección Femenina, 23, 178, 187–205, 260; Coros y Danzas and, 179, 187, 190–205, 227, 240
Second Republic, 119, 126, 168, 173, 179, 182, 190, 254, 305n1
Segovia, Andrés, 171, 304n91
seguidillas, 33, 35, 39, 40, 154
señoritos, 133, 261; *flamenquismo* and, 74, 76–77, 136; and *juergas*, 33, 46
Servicio Nacional de Turismo, 209
Seville: as center for flamenco, 27, 44, 45, 47, 48, 50, 51, 52, 53–54, 56, 78, 104, 150, 158, 160, 164, 174, 204, 206, 215, 224, 242, 244, 247, 253–54
sevillanas, 128, 154
siguiriya, 169, 171, 259
socialists, 62, 64, 79, 81, 88, 182
Social Question, 79–81, 284n66
Sokol, Harry, 197
soleares, 79, 169, 171, 191, 201, 245, 259
Soledad (Soledad Arce), 155, 157, 166, 303n77
"Spain is different" campaign, 20, 62–63, 206, 213
Spanish-American War, 98, 105, 164, 165
Spanish Civil War, 98, 171–74, 209, 231, 232, 248
Spanish Exhibition at London's Earl Court (1889), 150–51, 300n27

Index

Storm, Eric, 94, 295n7
Stravinsky, Igor, 166, 167, 171, 304n91
Suárez Fernández, Luis, 195-96, 198-99, 311n71
Sunny Spain Exhibit (1914), 207-8

tablaos, 10, 119, 168, 169, 174, 191, 215, 226, 232, 239, 240, 247, 252, 261
Tablao Zambra, 226, 230, 231-32, 234
tango (Argentina), 22, 91, 103, 104, 180, 186, 308n31
tangos (Spain), 155, 181
taverns, 10, 41, 45, 46, 47, 50, 58, 59, 66, 67, 68, 70-72, 78, 79, 81-82, 102, 106-7, 108, 169, 172, 173
Teatre Líric Català, 110
teatro ínfimo, 57
teatro por horas, 46, 277n52
theaters, 4, 45, 68, 147, 153, 186; flamenco in, 33, 78, 140, 252, 293n74
Thomas Cook Tours, 48, 208-9, 216-17, 221, 222-25
tipos populares, 83-88
Tito (illustrator), 85, 86, 87, 88
Torres y Bages, Josep, 106-7
Tort y Daniel, Jascinto, 110
Tosh, John, 20
tourism, 9, 14, 22, 23, 46, 47, 48, 50-54, 126, 148, 175, 179, 201, 203, 206-26; cultural, 208; Franco regime and, 203, 210-26; mass, 204-5
tourist boom, 16, 200, 203, 210-26
tourist industry, 23, 44, 166, 205, 206-7, 208, 209, 211, 221, 225-26, 244, 246, 248, 253, 314n4
travel narratives, 4, 43, 47, 54, 88, 268n50, 294n3
Trini España (Trinidad Pérez Blanco), 215
Turespaña, 249, 250
Turina, Joaquín, 166, 171, 304n91
turno pacífico, 61
"25 Years of Peace," 227, 317n55

Unamuno, Miguel de, 75, 284n72

UNESCO, 188; Intangible Cultural Heritage of Humanity list and, 6, 251, 322n27
unity in diversity, 95, 178, 189, 198, 200, 203, 228, 240
urbanization, 8, 11, 12, 39, 45, 46, 61, 62, 66, 101-2, 274n31
Uría, Jorge, 72

Vajda, Ladislow, 196
Valera, Juan, 3
Valero de Tornos, Juan, 164-65
Valle Pichardo, Pedro del. *See* Perico el del Lunar
Vargas, Juana. *See* Juana "La Macarrona"
Vargas, Manuela, 215, 230, 234, 238
Vega Inclán, Benigno de la, 207, 208
Villalobos Bote, Rufino, 185, 186
Villa Rosa (La), 116-18, 119, 293n78
Viñas, Ricardo, 166
violence: in *cafés cantantes*, 69; *flamenquismo* and, 74; interclass, 64; military, 64; nationalist, 178; revolutionary, 64, 102; working class, 75, 99, 102, 253
Viva (Viva Arce), 155
voz afillá, 32, 261, 273n10
Vuillermet, 185

Wagner, Richard
Wallis, S. Teackle, 3-6
Washabaugh, William, 9, 11, 247
"We Women Do Not Forget," 254-55
women: regulation of sexuality, 70-73, 182
World's Fairs. *See* International Expositions

xenophobia, 184-85

Young, Clinton, 18, 291n53
Yuval-Davis, Nira, 20
Yxart, Josep, 150

zarzuela, 18, 45, 57, 103, 105-6, 107, 110, 114, 148, 160, 261, 289-90n36
zortzico, 154
Zuluoga, Ignacio, 171